On Loss and Losing

On Loss and Losing

Beyond the Medical Model of Personal Distress

Melvyn L. Fein

Routledge
Taylor & Francis Group
LONDON AND NEW YORK

First published 2012 by Transaction Publishers

2 Park Square, Milton Park, Abingdon, Oxfordshire OX14 4RN
711 Third Avenue, New York, NY 10017

Routledge is an imprint of the Taylor & Francis Group, an informa business

First issued in paperback 2017

Copyright © 2012 Taylor & Francis

All rights reserved. No part of this book may be reprinted or reproduced or utilised in any form or by any electronic, mechanical, or other means, now known or hereafter invented, including photocopying and recording, or in any information storage or retrieval system, without permission in writing from the publishers.

Notice:
Product or corporate names may be trademarks or registered trademarks, and are used only for identification and explanation without intent to infringe.

Library of Congress Catalog Number: 2011010280

Library of Congress Cataloging-in-Publication Data

Fein, Melvyn L.
　On loss and losing: beyond the medical model of personal distress/ Melvyn L. Fein.
　　p. cm.
　ISBN 978-1-4128-4250-1
　1. Suffering—Social aspects.　2. Social psychology.　3. Social medicine. I. Title.
　BF789.S8F45 2011
　155.9'3—dc22

2011010280

ISBN 13: 978-1-4128-4250-1 (hbk)
ISBN 13: 978-1-138-51272-6 (pbk)

For Vassili Economopoulos;
A real mensch who will long be missed

Contents

Preface		ix
1.	Call Me Crazy!	
	The Legend of the Neurotic Wolf; Social Killers; A Trip to the Hospital; A Historic Error	1
2.	Witches, Mad Doctors, and Pseudo-Sociologists	
	The Bad Old Days; The Coming of Wisdom; The Arrival of Compassion; Psychotherapy and Deinstitutionalization; "Medical" Sociology; Moral Arbiters; Sociological Lapses	25
3.	On Losing	
	Sore Losers; Loss; Losing; The Loss/Losing Nexus; The Social/Suffering Connection; Loss/Losing and the DSM Disorders; A Caveat	59
4.	Resocialization	
	A Sovereign Remedy; The Repetition Compulsion; Denial; Protest; Sadness; Renegotiation	99
5.	Roles	
	The Division of Labor; Traits versus Roles; Role Scripts; Role Partners; Dysfunctional Roles; Gender Roles	135
6.	Ranks	
	King of the Mountain; Roles and Functions; Leaders and Tyrants; Caste and Class; Situational Stupidity; Bureaucracies	173

7. Relationships
   Intimacy; Relationship Negotiations; Sex; Choosing
   a Partner; Courtship; Divorce; The Children of Divorce   211

8. Beliefs
   Cognitive Communities; Irrationality; Faith; Lies;
   Pseudoscience   247

9. Morality
   Moral Communities; Moral Logic; Hardball without
   an Umpire; For the Greater Good?; Idealism; Values;
   Character   275

10. Beyond the Utopias
    A Distinction with a Difference; Accepting Limits;
    Amelioration; Cyclic Therapy   307

Bibliography   333

Index   355

Preface

One of my surprises in sharing this text with readers has been the nonchalance with which they have accepted its central thesis. Whether college students, sociologists, social workers, psychologists, neurophysiologists, or even physicians, most are more critical of the standard medical model of personal distress than I would have supposed. Few, it seems, relish having to declare themselves defective in order to address issues of individual suffering. Furthermore, they are insulted when told they must become pill poppers in order to feel better.

Why then is the medical model so dominant? If so many people are uncomfortable with it, why do the media and schools offer it as *the* rational approach to personal problems? Indeed, how can this be so with the ascendancy of medicine itself so recent? After all, it is only a century since doctors obtained their current prestige and a bare half-century since psychiatry moved out of the mental asylum. Why then does it seem there is no viable alternative to "mental illness" explanations?

The reason may be due to the imperfect and piecemeal nature of proposed substitutes. What frequently come to mind are the musings of social dropouts who achieve bliss by chanting in unison or adopting mysticism. Rather than investigate personal discomforts with dispassion, these folks generally seek refuge in a flight from reality. The scientific credentials of medicine, in contrast, have become so deeply ingrained that challenging them feels like rejecting science per se. What's more, for most of us, science is rock-solid and completely objective.

Even the scientific critics of the medical model seem eccentric. Most notable among these has been Dr. Thomas Szasz. Several decades ago he made a splash by insisting that mental illness was a "myth." The trouble is that it is not. There are very real diseases of the brain that deserve to be treated with the best modern medicine can offer. Failing to distinguish between these and what Szasz called "problems in living" was a romantic error; one as quixotic as those of religious cultists. Sadly, this has surrounded critics of the medical model with an aura of softheadedness.

Thus, what is needed is a legitimate alternative to medicalism. People rightly demand a believable account of personal suffering. Quite understandably, few responsible observers would consider abandoning medical solutions without identifying a workable replacement. Mind you, partial answers have been available for some time. One of these is provided by family therapy. Concerned with interpersonal dynamics as opposed to physiological failings, this modality has sought to improve relationships rather than "cure" individuals. The problem is that its "therapists" have addressed only a small slice of what goes wrong. What is needed is something more comprehensive. In what follows, a social theory grounded in the normal human reactions to loss and losing is offered as such an option.

Another reason the medical model has become so dominant is that it has been institutionalized. Though of recent vintage, its organizational ascendancy is deeply entrenched. Within short order, millions of people have developed the mind-set and personal interest in perpetuating it. On a structural level, thousands of jobs depend on its continuation. With most service providers either paid by insurance carriers or government agencies, they must furnish a recognized diagnosis or forego reimbursement. Even psychologists have been cowed into honoring psychiatric categories. Despite their qualms, a don't-rock-the-boat mentality has come to prevail.

Meanwhile, on a cultural level, constant repetition has convinced most people that depression and anxiety are diseases. These beliefs have become part of the conventional wisdom not because they were carefully vetted, but because they seem modern and enlightened. The result is that critics of the medical model have come to seem like peevish outsiders. Deprived of a legitimate soapbox, they are condemned to wander in the wilderness unheard. Prestige is instead bestowed upon that which derives from the establishment. In such an environment, effective treatment is not what matters; only what seems effective.

Over a quarter of a century ago, I began to think of myself as a clinical sociologist. The idea was exhilarating. Here was a novel way of looking at personal problems that suggested potentially significant advances. Ironically, Harry Stack Sullivan and John Bowlby, both psychiatrists, must be credited with introducing me to the power of personal relationships. This led to speculation that if knowledge of such arrangements were supplemented by sociological insights, the result would be productive.

In what follows, I attempt to make the case for a sociological interpretation of personal distress. Mind you, some personal suffering derives from biological sources. Genuine mental illnesses can spill over to cause social dysfunctions, while social dysfunctions can precipitate physiological disorders. Moreover, it can be difficult to tell where one begins and the other ends. Nevertheless, it is important to recognize the separate social etiology of much human suffering. Loss and losing cause distress independent of medically based mental conditions.

Our journey will begin with a fable designed to distinguish social problems from medical ones. We human beings must first be understood as social animals. Were we not, we would never have achieved the enormous successes that distinguish us from other species. With this, however, has come a host of vulnerabilities. The mechanisms that enable us to work together also introduced numerous individual difficulties. The problem is that we do not necessarily associate these with their true sources.

It also develops that we human beings hate mysteries. When something does not seem to make sense, we seek answers. With respect to personal problems emanating from social sources, there appear to be two possibilities; one religious, the other scientific. Most religious explanations point to spiritual causes. Either people defy divine ordinances or are visited by evil apparitions. Consequently, theologians have postulated relief as coming from exorcism and similar mechanisms, including burning witches. Scientific theories, on the other hand, have concentrated on medical explanations. They have offered "cures" to physiological disorders. In recent times, the latter option has been thought both more effective and humane. In reality, it is often neither.

A clue to a third option came from Drs. Sullivan and Bowlby. Sullivan emphasized the importance of strong interpersonal relationships for optimum individual functioning, whereas Bowlby stressed the need for reliable interpersonal attachments. From the latter, it followed that personal "losses" created considerable distress—including deep depressions. Left out of this equation, however, were instances of "losing." The difference between losses and losing is essentially that with loss one has an attachment that is subsequently severed, whereas with losing one fights for a satisfying relationship that never comes to fruition. Moreover, there are three principal types of structural losing, namely, dysfunctional social roles, dysfunctional social statuses, and dysfunctional interpersonal bonds. Also implicated are culturally based instances of losing that follow from irrational social beliefs and dysfunctional moral commitments.

If this is true, if instances of losing satisfying roles, ranks, and relationships or of being betrayed by unfounded beliefs and impracticable social standards is destabilizing, the resulting personal distress does not need to be cured as would a disease. What is required is "resocialization." Just as losses must be mourned before a person can move on to establish substitute attachments, so instances of losing must be grieved so that a person can adopt strategies better suited to winning. Instead of feeling compelled to repeat unsuccessful behavioral patterns, these must be relinquished by navigating denial, protest, sadness, and renegotiation phases. Each of these needs to be completed before personal distress can be overcome.

Resocialization does not occur without first relinquishing efforts to reverse historic defeats, but it cannot be concluded without discovering how to achieve authentic victories. This means that the anxieties and sadness at the heart of the mourning process need to be endured so that a person can acquire the emotional and relationship skills to prevail. With respect to dysfunctional roles, it must be understood that divisions of labor are part of being social. Nonetheless, not all roles are created equal. Some are more satisfying than others. The trick is to know how to negotiate specific roles with role partners so that these allow for personal satisfactions. How a person thinks, feels, and acts may all need to be reorganized to facilitate success.

With respect to dysfunctional social statuses, it must be realized that we human beings are hierarchical animals. We are all motivated to fight for greater power than our peers. Of course, we cannot all become "king of the mountain." Still, most of us can avoid falling to the lowest depths. We can learn to utilize our abilities so that we do reasonably well in the tests of strength that confer status. Success in these will influence our social class positions and organizational accomplishments.

As to dysfunctional personal relationships, it must be understood that nowadays intimate relationships are voluntary. Whether we achieve, or maintain, loving relationships depends on an ability and dedication to doing so. Enduring relationships, as opposed to fleeting sexual encounters, are constructed between moral equals. People must develop the personal maturity to choose a suitable partner, to work in tandem to navigate the dangerous shoals of courtship, and to become expert in the dual concern negotiations of ongoing commitments. A failure to do so can result in the familiar pitfalls of divorce.

When it comes to belief systems, we humans are often betrayed by our social orientations. We suffer bouts of losing because we believe things that are profoundly untrue. The reason we do is that we belong to cognitive communities. Much of what we know is learned from others. This propensity enables us to comprehend much more than we could were we left to our own devices, but it also exposes us to being deceived. Whether intentionally or not, those upon whom we depend may lead us astray. They can lie to us or merely cajole us into participating in the faiths to which they are committed. Either way, we can make bad choices.

Finally, our moral commitments can be defective. Instead of protecting us from the inevitable conflicts inherent in being social, they sometimes precipitate inadvertent injustices. Because morality does not consist of an inviolable compendium of categorical imperatives, the ways that it is created and enforced have unintended side effects. Even our ideals can lead us astray. They often prompt us to quest after the impossible, with the consequence that we disregard the possible.

In the end, by eschewing the temptations of the medical model, we can improve our personal and collective circumstances. We will never obtain perfection, but in recognizing the social and individual limitations of the human condition, most of us can do better than hitherto. Modern medicine is one of the marvels of human civilization, but as with all human institutions it has constraints. Those of us who aspire to improvements must acknowledge these while we seek to ameliorate our situations. We can do better if we are honest, courageous, and prepared to accept what is feasible. This is difficult, but doable.

Should this occur, both our mind-sets and social associations may have to be reorganized. No doubt, this would entail substantial resistance. Nonetheless, it too is possible. Our current social and intellectual arrangements may seem preordained, but they are not. They have a long history, nevertheless a correspondingly lengthy future awaits them.

1

Call Me Crazy!

> *[The] diagnostic criteria and the DSM-IV Classification of mental disorders reflect a consensus of current formulations of evolving knowledge in our field. (From the DSM-IV)*

The Legend of the Neurotic Wolf

Once upon a time, in a National Park far, far away, but not very long ago, there lived an ordinary wolf. He was no bigger than most wolves; nor was he smarter than his peers. Neither was he exceptionally attractive nor remarkably ugly. Timber (let us for convenience call him that, even though this was not his given name) was a regular, everyday canine. Mind you, as a wolf, he was not very introspective and therefore did not realize how ordinary he was. In fact, he did not even think of himself as a wolf. Just as did most of his comrades, he merely went about his daily rounds with scarcely a thought or care (or so it seemed).

As an average wolf, Timber belonged to a run of the mill pack. In their native territory of "Jellystone," he and his pack-mates wandered about unfettered, each day engrossed in wolf-type activities. They tracked down deer, elk, and buffalo; they raised their young; they bayed at the moon. Like most other wolves, they also defended their terrain against intruders. Should foreign wolves appear unannounced, they would be unceremoniously driven off. The pack likewise kept clear of human beings, especially those toting guns or cameras. These were given a wide berth when spotted from afar, essentially because they were a threat. All in all, had members of the band been able to answer the question "Are you happy?" they would have done so in the affirmative. As I say, they were ordinary wolves; hence, it would not have occurred to them that there might be another way to live.

Then one day into this bucolic lifestyle wandered a guileless stranger. A young man with the best of intentions (William by name), he was studying to be an ethologist (i.e., an animal behaviorist) at a local university. Himself an ordinary person, his goal was to track the pack and record its doings. As a scientist in training, he genuinely wanted to understand what was going on so as to share his findings with his colleagues. This, needless to say, was a strenuous assignment that required time and patience. Following the troop from a respectful distance, William spent countless hours, during several seasons, observing their behaviors through a powerful set of binoculars, and then meticulously entering his reflections in the notebooks he always kept at his side. Eventually a pattern emerged. Not all the wolves conducted themselves in the same manner. One, above the others, caught his attention. This was none other than Timber. For some reason, he seemed the odd wolf out.

Unlike the other wolves, Timber did not look happy. More often alone than the rest, at times he appeared to be sulking. Sometimes he even seemed anxious. William noticed that Timber often walked with his head down and his tail between his legs. Instead of frolicking with his pack-mates, when in their company, his distress increased. Almost every time he advanced toward them, they responded by snapping their teeth at him, in which case he fell to the ground and rolled over on his back. One of his colleagues seemed particularly antagonistic. A large male, with an aristocratic bearing, "Hero" (so dubbed by William) snarled whenever Timber came within range. Lifting his top lip up and back, he growled in a manner so threatening that Timber regularly retreated in haste. At such moments, William could make out the sadness in Timber's eyes and the trembling in his limbs.

These clashes were even worse when food was at stake. When, for instance, the pack had taken down a deer, Timber would hover in the background waiting for the others to consume their fill. Should hunger motivate him to approach the carcass too hastily, Hero would spring to the offensive and drive him off. To this Timber reacted by hurriedly, albeit meekly, withdrawing. The same sort of thing occurred when Timber attempted to play with the pack's pups. Should Hero fail to notice, he might get away with a few moments of messing about, but the mood was instantly broken once he was caught. He would then pathetically return to his isolation without so much as protesting the unfairness of his situation.

William was appalled by this pattern. His heart went out to an underdog who did not have the self-confidence to assert his rights. For some reason lacking in self-esteem, Timber's misery apparently made him a target for the others. But what could be the cause? What would induce an apparently normal animal to abandon his own interests and recoil into unhappy semi-isolation? The only thing that made sense was that Timber was suffering from a "mental disorder." Although not visibly ill, he was evidently in the grip of a functional disease that interfered with his ability to behave appropriately. Something in his brain was not working as it should and therefore preventing him from living up to his potential. Unquestionably the victim of either a depressive or anxiety disorder (or both), a chemical imbalance hindering the operation of his neural synapses was probably at fault. Perhaps this was genetic. Perhaps it resulted from a biological trauma. Either way, something clearly had to be done. Just as William would have felt obligated to take a family pet to a veterinarian to treat a tumor, he felt responsible for curing Timber. Although he realized scientists are supposed to remain neutral, long months of intimate association had aroused his compassion.

But how to help, that became the operative question. Clearly Timber could not be referred for psychotherapy. Hopelessly unreflective, much less able to speak, he could not participate in a talk therapy. No, the clinical couch was out, even if it might theoretically uncover the repressed memories of a harrowing childhood. The only bona fide possibility was chemotherapy. A pill that would alter the seratonin levels in his brain might do the trick. By facilitating the electrical connections that underlay his personality, it would adjust his character in a positive direction. His mood would brighten, and he would quickly become more assertive. Instead of deferring to his comrades, he would stand his ground, thereby regaining their respect. Within short order, normal functioning would be restored and Timber would become an ordinary wolf in every respect.

To this end, William worked his way into closer proximity with the pack. Eventually he was able to provide meat for the group and to smuggle Prozac into the pieces that went to Timber. These capsules did their magic and Timber's depression lifted. Within days, his eyes glowed, and his fur took on a healthy sheen. No longer handicapped by the combination of disorders that made him an outcast, he was welcomed back into the fold. Now viewed approvingly even by Hero, his self-image took a quantum leap skyward. At long last content with himself, William was proud of performing this magic.

The moral of this story is clearly that even neurotic wolves deserve medical attention. Because they too are biological creatures, they too are subject to brain malfunctions that can be corrected by the humane application of medications. In the end, an enlightened and systematic brain science can be harnessed to rescuing millions of wild creatures from the grip of mental illness.

Animal activists might like this account to end right here, but, sad to relate, it is a myth. I made it up. Ethologists have not taken to interpreting wolf behavior in this manner; nor have they recommended a medical approach to improving their quality of life. Few, if any, describe their subjects as afflicted by depressive and/or anxiety disorders. Indeed, they adopt an entirely different explanation for what occurred between Timber and his pack-mates. Instead of regarding him as "neurotic," they look at the larger social pattern in which he is embedded. Their approach becomes apparent if for "Timber" we substitute the term "gamma." The third letter in the Greek alphabet, it is a shorthand means of identifying a social animal's relative rank. Likewise, if for "Hero," we adopt the appellation "alpha," we instantly recognize him as the pack leader. In other words, the best explanation of what was going has to do with the nature of the pack hierarchy, not the putative mental illness of one of its members.

Most animal observers comprehend the relationship between Timber and Hero as one of dominance and submission. They realize that wolf packs do not consist of bands of equals. Some members are, in Orwell's memorable phrase, "more equal than others." They also know that those at the top of the heap live better than those at the bottom. They eat more, procreate more frequently, and beat up on their inferiors more regularly. Indeed, much of what occurs between members of the pack reflects mechanisms for affirming comparative status. Who is the boss is so important that the alpha animal does not allow his subordinates to forget his status. Nor are his underlings remiss in signaling that they understand their place. They recognize that were they to omit displays of weakness, they would make themselves vulnerable to efforts at enforcement. Past experience having taught them that these are apt to be painful, they head them off by ostentatiously deferring to the more powerful animal. This essentially is what Timber was doing by rolling over on his back whenever Hero growled. It is also why he tucked his tail between his legs or hovered on the margins of the pack at feeding time.

Although it is difficult to know what is on a wolf's mind, dominant animals give the impression of feeling good about themselves. Their body language expresses not only self-confidence, but self-satisfaction.

Conversely, subordinate animals look sad and frightened. They are constantly glancing over their shoulders to determine who might be preparing to snap at them. Some studies of baboons have suggested that this insecurity produces stomach ulcers. In any case, subservient animals are visibly harried. Less well groomed, often thinner, and uncomfortable in playing with their peers, they appear to lead lives of "quiet desperation." Maybe it is anthropomorphic to suggest that they are "unhappy," but it certainly comes across that way. Just as it is almost impossible to gaze into the eyes of a dog that has been beaten and not see the distress, so most of us would perceive the misery in the eyes of an omega wolf. If this is so, then some forms of personal distress are side effects of hierarchical position. Not victims of a chemical imbalance, those in its grip are reacting to a normal aspect of how their species organizes itself. In other words, they are not suffering from a mental disorder, but from the bad fortune of being social "losers."

Again, if this were so, the cure William sought would not have worked. Even if the production of neurotransmitters in Timber's brain were altered by the introduction of Prozac, this, by itself, would not have altered his rank. Assuming that the chemical brightened his mood and filled him with self-confidence, consider its impact on his relations with the others. For the sake of brevity, let us contemplate the link between Timber and Hero. Suppose a supercharged Timber approached his nemesis with a newfound swagger. How would Hero have reacted? The answer is that he would not have been amused. Rightly interpreting this as a challenge, he would have responded accordingly. Furthermore, given his physical strength and long practice in asserting himself, there is a good chance he would have won the ensuing fracas. This would have required Timber to flee and re-acknowledge his inferiority. Were the molecules of serotonin traveling between his synapses to interfere with this display, Hero would have attacked again, and unless submission was forthcoming, Hero might continue until Timber was dead. Far from medicine bringing pleasure, unless Timber was able to best Hero in a test of strength, he would continue to suffer.

Among wolves confusing social subordination with mental disorder is absurd. It is a mistake of such proportions that professional ethologists never make it. Indeed, it is so inappropriate that even laypersons would consider it a joke. They too understand that social organization can profoundly influence individual behaviors. Why then are parallel circumstances difficult to accept among human beings? Why do so many well-educated people endorse medical explanations for a plethora of personal problems? Few would dispute that ours too is a social species. Why then deny that the way that we maintain communal stability can have personally painful consequences? As we shall soon see, there are powerful reasons for believing that "loss and losing" have just such an impact.

Social Killers

Sometimes we describe a person in an awkward position as having been dropped "naked into the world." The image elicited is of someone standing alone in their birthday suit, perhaps shivering in the midst of a field replete with numerous unfriendly beasts. There also exists a venerable literary conceit that contrasts the physical weakness of the human body with the comparative prowess of our animal rivals. Unaccompanied by friends, and clothed only in skin, we dread the prospect of having to fend off a lion jogging in our direction. We know that our teeth are no match for his nor our fingernails a defense against his claws. In a one-on-one showdown, we would come up short; hence we shrink from the ordeal. Nor do we match up with the protective inventories of prey species. A zebra only yards away may look like a bountiful source of meat, but should we begin moving toward it, it would outrun us with ease. Even within touching distance, it might kick back with lethal hooves. How then have our kind been able to survive, much less prevail? Obviously, so feeble that no other creature has reason for alarm, we are nevertheless still here. It would seem that we should have driven into extinction, yet we have become the planet's dominant species. What accounts for this miracle?

Despite our apparent frailty, we are accomplished killers. As intelligent tool-users, we can multiply our personal strength exponentially. Far from being unaided predators, we challenge other creatures by skillfully wielding weapons that allow us to best them—with ease. We do not use teeth and claws, but guns and knives. We do not pursue prey in our bare feet, but climb on horseback or atop a speeding Jeep. Our killing mechanisms are endless. They include spears and swords, bolos and boomerangs, traps and nets, antibiotics and antiseptics (for small critters), clubs and arrows, fire and slings, and harpoons and bombs (for large critters). Nor have we neglected the means for approaching potential victims. These include boats, helicopters, and camouflage suits; not to mention long-distance weapons. All this, and we have yet to mention our most lethal advantage. We are, in the final analysis, social killers. Just as wolves take down large herbivores in packs, so we hunt big game in teams. Even before the emergence of Cro-Magnons, when confronted with a dangerous adversary, we ganged up on it. We coordinated our efforts—often attacking from several directions at once. Spear points embedded in mastodon bones provide evidence that we resorted to this strategy for some time. It has, in fact, been suggested that our massive brains arose precisely to keep track of the relationships needed for the hunt.

Yet herein lies a serious difficulty. The problem is how to maintain social solidarity in large groups. Anthropological data indicate that the size of human bands progressed steadily after our ancestors split off from chimpanzee-like apes. Eventually, the upper limit was reached at about 150 within the nomadic bands that preceded the agricultural revolution. Nevertheless, as Thomas Hobbes pointed out centuries ago, in addition to being lethal, individual humans can be remarkably selfish. People may not pursue their self-interests all the time, but they often do—with vigor. In order to beat out rivals, they even resort to unfair tactics, sometimes escalating these to the point of homicide. Hobbes posited a state of nature in which a "war of all against all" was the norm. Individuals would be so intent on depriving the weak of their treasure that life would be "nasty, brutish, and short" for all—including the strong.

From where Hobbes stood during the English Civil War, the only imaginable salvation was for the strongest individual to prevent bloodshed. Hobbes assumed this must be monarch. Aided by a compact based on enlightened self-interest, the king would be a veritable giant who could intimidate others into behaving. A hundred years later, Jean-Jacques Rousseau, after closely observing the shenanigans of the French royal court, concluded that aristocrats caused more trouble than they thwarted. In their selfishness, they regularly created property and honors over which to compete. This spread a poison through the system that encouraged conflicts, which frequently turned sadistic. In Rousseau's opinion, civilization was the culprit. Contrary to Hobbes, he believed government did not forestall violence, but bred it. The only valid answer was to raise children so that they did not squander the generosity embedded in their biological heritage. If they could be taught to retain a sense of self, they would actualize what Lincoln later called "the better angels" of our natures.

The dispute between Rousseau and Hobbes is still with us—today clothed as political clashes between liberals and conservatives. Whatever the changes since their day, there can be no doubt people are still potentially dangerous creatures. Despite enormous differences in size and talent, every individual remains capable of killing every other individual. The old possess the ability to murder the young, and vice versa; men can slay women, and vice versa; the healthy can eliminate the handicapped, and vice versa. Methods for achieving mayhem are readily at hand; limited only by the imaginations of would-be assassins. Besides such obvious weapons as guns and knives, people can suffocate their bedmates with pillows or strangle the unwary by sneaking up and choking them with garrotes. They can poison the food of complete strangers or lie in wait with automobiles to run over unsuspecting pedestrians. They can even drop bricks from highway overpasses or fly jetliners into office towers. Recent events have made it plain that it is impractical to anticipate all the possibilities; they are too numerous.

What then can guarantee our safety? Modern societies have grown so large, and our dependence on strangers is so pervasive that we cannot retreat into separate, hermetically sealed caves. Nor can we reflexively depend on the enlightened policies of a federal government. Although a centrally directed war on terrorists may sometimes be necessary, of itself it cannot provide the day-to-day protections ordinary life requires. Nor has altruism become so prevalent that people can always rely on the good intentions of others. Both Hobbes and Rousseau made worthy suggestions, but these were never sufficient. Were we to follow either of their recommendations, we would, within a short period, be entangled in debilitating webs of conflict. For better or worse, neither the government, nor the innate goodness of individuals, is adequate to provide the glue necessary to keep mass societies functioning smoothly.

Yet given the opportunities for turmoil, things run relatively smoothly. Though people every day experience occasions during which they could kill one another, most of the time they do not. What accounts for this? It cannot be that they are continuously afraid of being caught by Big Brother. They know the police are not around in the middle of the night, yet they stop for red lights nonetheless. Nor are people universally loving. The fact is that most are neutral regarding most others most of the time. As complete strangers, they normally treat one another as inanimate objects.

It turns out that mechanisms for maintaining social order are both complicated and abundant. There is no single reason why people get along with one another. Nor do these operate with machine-like efficiency. Although they allow us to work safely with others, well-known glitches periodically place us in jeopardy. After all, people do sometimes kill and cheat others. They even go to war with one another. What is more, these protective mechanisms have side effects that cause their own difficulties. Even when a society as a whole benefits, some individuals do not. They pay a price so that others can enjoy contentment and security.

Among the familiar, but incompletely appreciated, instruments that structure social relationships is hierarchy. People everywhere organize themselves into ranks that determine how they will behave toward one another. Some are placed "above" and others "below," largely on the basis of relative power. Social class is probably the most pervasive stratification device, but others, including bureaucracy, are almost important. As a rule, these inhibit conflict by specifying such things as how scarce resources are distributed. But hierarchies do much more than this; they specify who shall lead and who follow. As significantly, they shape the lifestyles individuals adopt. Their effect on personal satisfaction is therefore colossal—much greater, and subtler, than is normally realized.

Also essential in structuring how individuals interact are the social roles they occupy. Over and above their relative dominance, people are not interchangeable in terms of the tasks they perform. As Emile Durkheim insisted, there exists a social division of labor that specifies the chores in which people engage. Who will be the butcher, the baker, or the candlestick maker? Who the mommy, the daddy, or the baby bear? Or who is the man, the woman, the hero, or the scapegoat? All of these assignments are of enormous import to those who play them, as well as to their role partners. Each of us, in fact, depends on numerous role performances for food, information, and protection. Our roles are therefore a crucial means of guiding interpersonal dealings. As a result, should they fail in their missions, they can be exceedingly troublesome.

Similar considerations apply to our personal relationships. If role assignments dictate that individuals are not interchangeable, this is *a fortiori* true of interpersonal attachments. Arbitrarily swapping bed partners will not satisfy people in love with specific others. Nor would a mother be content to have just any maternity ward baby pressed into her arms. Lovers want to embrace their own loved ones and mothers their own babies. There is no mystery in this. A group of human beings is not a shoal of fish. Each member of the former recognizes particular others, having connections with some, but not others. Moreover, when their relationships go wrong, the outcomes can be painful. People literally lose their will to live or their zest for living. Here too the bonds that join people together can function as a source of misery.

Somewhat different in the manner they hold societies together, and therefore the channels through which they cause personal injury, are shared beliefs. People are not only smart; they communicate their intelligence within cognitive communities. Groups of people know more than any individual because the experiences and talents of its members are broader than any one person. Individuals learn vital lessons from their forbearers, from their more adventurous peers, and even from their offspring. They also learn from impersonal vehicles such as books and movies. When these lessons are accurate, they open a myriad of doors. Not only do they unlock a wealth of possibilities, they allow individuals to coordinate activities by seeing things from compatible perspectives. When, however, errors are substituted for facts, or lies for honest judgments, people can be led astray. They then stumble into dangerous morasses rather than profitable enterprises. Instead of helping to build a glorious German nation, they bestow their allegiance on a blood-splattered Nazi dictatorship. Or, on a more personal level, they operate on the belief that they are stupid because an envious parent once told them so.

Another cultural pitfall akin to erroneous beliefs is flawed moral rules. Just as people share understandings about how the world is put together, so they share prescriptions regarding how it "should" be put together. Because conflicts can be pervasive, if people are to live in harmony, communal rules are required to tamp down excesses. Besides governmentally enforced laws, a large array of informal norms supplies the requisite controls. Among these, moral imperatives are the most potent. They forbid the dangerous behaviors and impose beneficial ones. But because moral codes are human creations, they too can be corrupt. This was the case when the Nazis decreed that Jews, Slavs, and Gypsies be exterminated. Today it seems hard to credit, but most Germans were convinced that this was proper. Indeed, they believed it imperative for justice to prevail. This, of course, had the effect of visiting misery on many innocent victims. Nor should it be forgotten that this ethical consensus was forged in vicious street fights between storm troopers and communist gangs. Ironically, even when morality brings peace, the negotiations through which it is fashioned can be harmful.

In short, if wolves create pain through the means by which they maintain the pack integrity, people create more damage through the mechanisms used to maintain theirs. With larger, more complex societies, they have more options for hurting one another. Most of these, to be sure, operate unconsciously. People may not intend to inflict injure, but do so with pitiless regularity. This is one of the worst side effects of social organization. Furthermore, because these devices are nearly invisible, they are difficult to correct. Just as Hero was unaware of what he was doing to Timber, and Timber was unaware of what he was doing to himself, so individual human beings participate in brutal activities without recognizing these. Worse still, the mechanisms that hold societies together induce blindness. Unhappily, there is reason to believe they must—that is, if they are to have salutary effects. It is difficult to image a paradox more profound, but if intelligent, social, tool-using killers such as ourselves are to maintain our effectiveness, then we must, to some extent, gouge out our own eyes. Ironically, we surround ourselves with mysteries—only some of which are soluble—so as to preserve our socially maintained place at the apex of the animal kingdom.

It is also essential to recognize that one of the things most of our bonds have in common is that they entail a measure of "losing." People get hurt, in part, because they are forced to endure losses they cannot avert. Thus, in hierarchies, there are both winners and losers. Ranking systems in which everyone wins are a contradiction in terms. Nor are there social divisions of labor in which everyone gets to do what he or she wants. Because not all jobs are equally satisfying, some get stuck with unpleasant ones. Similarly, personal relationships do not always work. Love may be an ideal aspired to by virtually everyone, but love can be lost, and when it is, the pain may be unendurable. It should also be evident that people are not always in touch with reality. They are frequently frustrated because they are persuaded that something is true when it is not. Sometimes they are even betrayed by the promises of perverted moralities. In fact, the rules people impose on themselves ensure that some will bear distasteful burdens. All in all, the processes that enable people to live together in harmony also make it certain that most will experience personal defeats. And defeat, lest it escape our notice, hurts.

A Trip to the Hospital

If you will bear with me, I propose to demonstrate what can go wrong by sharing several personal experiences.[1] Mystery and loss are an inescapable aspect of growing up—including for me. The many things I failed to understand, the setbacks I sustained, and the misery I sometimes felt, occasionally, left me wondering if I were crazy. Mine was not a happy childhood. My father was a bully, and my mother was emotionally withdrawn. Although they were habitually in conflict, one of the few things upon which they agreed was that I was an inept loser who could not be trusted to make simple decisions. Even when I earned money from odd jobs, I was not allowed to spend it on the grounds that my choices would be foolish. Nevertheless I had dreams. Eventually, I would grow up to take charge of my own destiny. One day I would be a great man. In the meantime, I had to settle for a vivid fantasy life. Most days on my walk to high school, I imagined becoming a super-scientist who would discover the secrets of the universe. Alternatively, I fanaticized about being a super-politician who would give speeches so inspirational that immense crowds would cheer me on. Later in the day, upon returning home, I, in fact, hid in a corner pouring over a book of maps, making believe that I was a conquering general more triumphant than Napoleon.

The crunch came years later when I moved out on my own. Unlike my dreams, adulthood did not bring automatic mastery. All too often I did not know what to do. Nor did most things turn out as I hoped. This was true with regard to school. Physics, I discovered, was not going to be my career. No Einstein, the requisite math gave me fits. Chemistry was little better, but later when I abandoned it and landed in philosophy, it felt too empty to constitute a career. This left me unprepared for a real job. As a result, when I wound up on the streets of New York, I had no idea where to seek employment. My love life was similarly inept. I had always been afraid of girls, but now my anxieties grew worse. No one seemed prepared to love me. Still I persevered and found myself in a live-in relationship. Yet it soon blew up. The woman with whom I became involved had serious emotional problems, hence when our disagreements intensified, she took her revenge through sexual cheating. It was at this point that I sought psychotherapy.

Freud, when asked to explain the criteria for mental health, responded that they were an ability to work and an ability to love.

I apparently had neither. Nor had I an ability to play. Whatever I touched turned to dross. Nothing seemed fun or worth doing. Nonetheless seeking professional help was a huge undertaking. My father regularly warned me that I was crazy; hence, enlisting a therapist would only confirm his diagnosis. According to him, I was a dreamer who lacked common sense. Chronically out of touch with reality, my opinions were unworthy of respect. As bad, I could not prove him wrong. However much I disliked my situation, I could not extricate myself from it. Instead I now proposed to trust a perfect stranger; one paid to be helpful. How humiliating! Worse still, what if this person took advantage of my confusion? How would I know the difference between help and manipulation?

At the outset, therapy was not what I expected. There were no sudden revelations. There was no an instant lifting of my discontent. If anything, I felt more anxious than ever. My therapist, though I came to depend on her, did not explain what was happening. She simply guided me along. Nevertheless I noticed improvements. I seemed more in touch with what had happened to me, although I remained confused about my life course and inept in personal relationships. Perhaps I was mentally defective after all. Perhaps I was crazy. Even after returning to school and obtaining a doctorate in sociology, this question lingered like an itch that would not be scratched. Ultimately, I got a job in a psychiatric hospital hoping to find out. For the next decade, I functioned as an employment counselor attached to various mental health facilities. To my relief, I found I was not insane. Whatever my troubles, they were different from those of the schizophrenics and manic-depressives with whom I interacted. They had brain disorders; I did not.

My initiation into these differences came swiftly. On my first day, a hospital patient stuck her head around the corner of my office and brightly proclaimed that I was her new counselor. After plopping down opposite me and indulging in a bit of small talk, she soon changed the subject. A scowl descended across her visage as she explained she was the victim of a serious predicament. The staff at her group home had unfairly decided to kick her out. Could I be of help? The following week, there was to be a meeting concerning her status. Would I serve as her advocate? Possessing no information beyond that which she imparted, I nonetheless agreed, but indicated that I would first read her chart and talk to her therapist. This, she decided, was quite all right. Since justice was on her side, the facts would bear her out. After she departed, I ruminated on what had happened, and although unsure of the truth, was impressed by the openness and passion to which I had been exposed.

Upon subsequently receiving an official invitation to the conference, I arrived expecting a reasoned investigation into my client's situation. But this was not what transpired. With the patient herself present, the group home counselors began by indicating that the decision to eject her had already been made. Taken aback by this preemption, I questioned their reasons. The response came not from the group home staff, but from the hospital therapist. She abruptly informed me that I did not know what I was talking about. Then, when I did not respond with deference, she turned her attention to the client. After a series of contradictory questions directed at this flustered young woman—much as if delivered by a prosecuting attorney—the girl cracked. Instead of the articulate responses with which she began, her eyes and words indicated that she was now hallucinating. At this the therapist looked toward me in triumph. While she said nothing, her features conspired to send the message: "Do you see how crazy this girl is?"

At the moment, I was scandalized. How dare a professional induce hallucinations in a patient in order to make a point with me? Yet while I was not to change my mind about the impropriety of this strategy, I soon discovered this client was more damaged than I first realized. In the beginning, she seemed normal, and rather like the socially oppressed persons my sociological training prepared me to encounter. Further events, however, demonstrated serious problems with reality. Mere months later, with spring beginning to melt the snows of winter, she was living in her own apartment. Despite her freedom, however, she decided the walls were getting uncomfortably close. Cramped by her own clothing, she sought relief by removing every stitch. When this proved inadequate, she ventured outside to parade down the center of Main Street. Soon the police arrived to escort her to the psychiatric hospital where within another few months she was again assigned to me.

As before, things began well. At first, she appealed for help in overcoming her difficulties. She acknowledged that she had done wrong, but insisted that she would make every effort to learn why she had "messed up." Nevertheless, in our subsequent conversations, although she expressed a desire to cooperate, she never made progress. There were also those odd moments when no one seemed to be at home. During these, her responses became so disjointed that they made no sense. Then one day, I received a call from a hospital therapist telling me to cease counseling her. Refusing to tell me why, this specialist maintained that it would be "unprofessional" to do otherwise. Several more months went by, punctuated by additional mystifying incidents, before I discovered the client had been going around the hospital telling everyone (but me) that I had impregnated her. Related with the utmost sincerity, her message was accepted at face value. Only later evidence that she was not pregnant saved me from dismissal.

By now it dawned on me that people with schizophrenic disorders were sometimes convinced of things that were not factual. They really could be deluded, hear voices, or adopt a fractured logic. In stark contrast, however odd I sometimes felt, none of these "symptoms" visited me. Confused, yes; anxious, sometimes; uncertain of my directions, most definitely. Yet an inability to distinguish fantasies from actualities was not my problem. Nor was I incapable of controlling my impulses. I did not, as one client did, rob a bank because he believed a chimpanzee instructed him to do so. (This patient was later caught delivering his loot by pushing it through the bars of his partner's cage.) No, my challenges were of a different order.

This was made more unambiguous when I counseled a client suffering from catatonic schizophrenia. He—let us call him Tom—was hospitalized in his late teens. Until then a promising student, one day he stopped talking or moving. About a year of aggressive pharmacology went by before he was again to interact with others. Still, most people continued to find him unintelligible. It was at this juncture that I was asked to try my hand. Straining with every fiber of my being to understand him, we soon made a connection. Even so, most of what he told me had to be deciphered, much as one would an oddly constructed puzzle. Fortunately, when I shared with him what I thought he said, more often than not he confirmed my conjectures.

From this I learned that shortly before his difficulties arose his father, a minister, had deserted his mother. Tom blamed himself for this breakup. As the oldest son, he believed it was his responsibility both to protect his mother and to honor his father. Nevertheless, in his anger, he had done neither well. Separate contacts soon convinced me that Tom's mother was a possessive woman and his father a self-righteous manipulator, yet Tom was conscious of none of this. It took years of conversations before he acknowledged that they might have been responsible for some of what had happened. According to the pop-Freudian model, this awareness should have dispelled his symptoms. It did not. While Tom made progress during the ten years I knew him, he remained oddly stiff and almost impossible for strangers to decode. Most people liked him—he was very sweet tempered—but no one considered him "normal." This, of course, was not their reaction to me. Not everyone liked me, and some thought me peculiar, but no one placed me in the same category.

I also came to recognize that clients who appeared normal might have mental issues more acute than mine. This was so for one woman diagnosed as manic-depressive. Warm, well groomed, and easy to talk to, she could have passed for anyone's favorite maiden aunt. All the same, getting to know her was a journey through Alice's looking glass. My introduction to her delusions came one day when she explained how the people on the television soap operas were sending her coded messages. The characters appeared to be conversing with each other, but were really warning her of impending tragedies. At first incredulous that she meant what she was saying, it swiftly became apparent she did. Furthermore, nothing could dissuade her. Not sweet reason; not further evidence. The contrast with me was clear. While I too had occasional episodes of paranoia, these were relatively minor and never induced me to entertain fantasies with her level of conviction. Nor, despite my periodic anger, had I killed my infant child and fried it up on a stove, as had another of my clients. Nor was I so obsessive-compulsive that I spent hours attempting to straighten my cafeteria chair, as did yet another hospital patient. No, my difficulties were different in kind.

Although, in some ways, remaining in the dark about why life dealt me so many setbacks, working at a psychiatric facility satisfied me that mental illness was not one of these. Years of therapy enabled me to engage in effective work, if not untroubled intimacy, but techniques that succeeded with me did not help the truly "crazy." They were too far removed from reality, and too fragile, to benefit from introspection. The term "crazy" was, to be sure, pejorative, and therefore unfair, but these people were odd. Something was wrong with their brains that was not with my own. My discontent came from a different source; one that required a different treatment.

A Historic Error

We human beings hate mysteries. In an episode of *Star Trek: The Next Generation*, the Starship Enterprise stumbles upon a planet whose inhabitants so crave privacy that they threaten to destroy the ship and its entire crew. The solution reached is to erase any memories of the encounter from all aboard. For a while, this tactic works, but when anomalies appear, the captain and his team delve into their provenance. Following a series of faint leads—such as plants that demonstrate more growth than they should—they determine the truth. At this point, the aliens again threaten to destroy the vessel. To this the captain responds by observing that you cannot present human beings with a mystery and not expect them to attempt to solve it. The only way to allay their curiosity is not to arouse it in the first place. He was right. We *Homo sapiens* may not always come to the correct conclusion, but unless we devise a "reasonable" one, we experience a discomfort that allows us no rest. This has apparently happened with respect to the irregularities identified as "mental illness." The incongruous behaviors and feelings linked under this rubric have been sufficiently irritating to demand an explanation—and therefore have obtained more than a few.

Regrettably, with respect to many of these anomalies, the answers adopted have been wrong. Specifically, personal problems of the sort I endured do not fit comfortably into the same category as mental diseases. Shoehorned into this model because no satisfactory alternative seemed available, they have been grossly misunderstood. Personal and mental problems have been with us for a long time—certainly for as long as our species has wandered the planet—so long that when first recognized, few explanations presented themselves. Although those that did would today seem inadequate, they were the only games in town.

In general, two classes of answer surged to the fore. One might be designated the *invisible* solutions and the other, conversely, the *visible*. The first sort included all things spiritual. From this perspective, the world was perceived to be in the clutches of imperceptible forces that must be controlled lest they wreck havoc. The souls of dead ancestors, the essences of trees and streams, and the dreams of a Great Creator were all credited with organizing inexplicable events. When the rains did not fall, when the hunting was bad, when a child died of an unknown malady, or when a wife cheated on her husband, the winds and the heavens were anthropomorphized to provide a plausible motive. It was then possible to appease this agent by providing evidences of respect. If approached using the right formula, a hostile spirit might relent and supply the appropriate relief. These recipes might be verbal; they might be expressed in terms of a ceremonial dance. Sometimes they entailed a material or emotional sacrifice. But whatever their form, the invisible force was expected to abstain from further damage, and, in the best cases, to furnish protection.

The visible answers, in contrast, included the precursors of our modern scientific ones. They were more tangible than Gods and nymphs, but nevertheless frequently imperceptible to mere mortals. One of the long-lasting Greek contributions to human knowledge was the conviction that the world was constructed of four elements, namely earth, air, fire, and water. Varying combinations of these explained why ordinary materials possessed so many different qualities. Unlike alternative metaphysical accounts, such as Plato's "essences," these elements could be validated experimentally. These experiments were not of the controlled sort we now require, but were attempts to put speculations to the test. In contemporary philosophical parlance, their hypotheses were verifiable in principle, or more properly, disconfirmable. They could be proved or disproved through observation.

When the ancients turned to mysteries of the human condition, they naturally made use of familiar options. Why people got sick was of obvious interest. Something needed to be done because more than physical or mental discomfort was at stake. Life itself could be on the line. For those who believed in invisible, that is, in spiritual explanations, an accepted cause might be a curse from an enemy. In this case, the agent of distress might be a ghost who had been persuaded to do the bidding of a witch. Other maladies could occur because a God had been insulted and was taking revenge. In still other cases, a malicious force, such as an incubus, attached itself to an unwitting victim in the middle of the night. Unless it was driven off, the target would helplessly succumb to despair.

In contrast, among the visible causes of disease were those said to correspond to the four elements. The human body supposedly responded to a balance of four humors. These were phlegm, blood, yellow bile, and black bile. When they operated in harmony, so did the various organs, but when not, they did not. Blood, for instance, might be in over supply, in which case, health could be restored by bloodletting. Sometimes it was the organs themselves that went haywire. Thus, when the uterus pulled loose from its moorings and meandered around the thorax, it caused hysteria. This explained why only women became hysterical and suggested that smelling salts might chase the offending part back into its rightful position.

In time, as the visible explanations became more sophisticated, the invisible ones were derided as superstitious. They became synonymous with ignorance and were shunned by educated people. This also applied to theories of mental health. Individuals who continued to place their faith in religious assumptions, such as demonic possession, were ridiculed for refusing to accept the advances of modern science. Ultimately, the study of the brain, a very tangible organ, supplanted earlier visions about a netherworld of evil spirits.

Once this scenario was accepted, it followed that medicine was the appropriate discipline for treating human suffering. If the choice was between the scientific and the superstitious, and medicine represented science, then virtually all forms of distress could be interpreted as versions of mental illness. That this was a false choice was not perceived. Nor was it appreciated that it assimilated mysterious forms of misery to the less mysterious. Indeed, what appeared to be the only reasonable course was a "moralized" conjecture. The disease model was not only correct; it was virtuous. Merely questioning it implied that a person did not care about the suffering of others. This further enshrined medicine as *the* rational option. Since only it was true and humane, why would any sensible person deny that afflictions such as depression were other than diseases?

Yet neither of these suppositions is correct. Medicine is not uniquely moral nor unerringly scientific. As we shall see in the next chapter, doctors, just as religious leaders before them, have a history of inflicting pain. They too are human beings who do foolish things for self-aggrandizement. Nor is science automatically free of error. Merely because people seek the truth does not ensure they will find it. In fact, maintaining that only medicine can elucidate personal distress has perpetuated a grave historical error. It has ignored an alterative paradigm because it was not as tangible as physical bodies covered in pustules.

Contrary to the classical division between science and superstition, personal suffering, most notably anxiety and depression, can be understood as having social causes. Societies, although they are not as substantial as human bodies, are real. They consist, for the most part, of interpersonal relationships that cannot be touched, but are quite factual. Emile Durkheim, one of the founders of sociology, went to great lengths to establish these as "social facts." Thus, he insisted that suicide rates, while not subject to physical manipulation, are not imaginary. Nor are the enduring emotional bonds between individuals. Marriage, for instance, is a genuine phenomenon even though it cannot be verified merely by glancing at a couple. Why then can't similar circumstances explain personal misery? Even in the case of schizophrenia, which probably has biological roots affliction, why should its triggers be solely physical? That they *must* have certainly not been established.

But if personal distress can have social sources, why has this not been recognized? The ancient Greek foray into distinguishing religion from science occurred over two millennia ago. Hasn't there been sufficient time for people to recognize a distinction other than between the visible and the invisible? The answer lies in our reactions to loss and losing. Conflicts inherent in the human condition generate impulses to cover up the pain of defeat. People do not perceive the social causes of their suffering because their social natures direct them away from recognizing them. The paradox of being social is that the last thing people are prepared to understand are the implications of being social. Although they may be amused by mistaken attributions of a gamma wolf's chemical brain imbalance, they find no incongruity in doing the same for people.

This difficulty was recognized at the dawn of "sociology." August Comte, the author of the term, believed human knowledge passed through three discernable eras. The first was the religious, the second the metaphysical, and the third the scientific. Each built on the advances of the preceding and hence could appear only in the order they did. Within the sciences, there was another predetermined sequence. This was between the physical and the social sciences. The latter came last because they required a reflexivity their predecessors did not. Put another way, people required a higher degree of sophistication to free themselves of the biases that interfered with accurately accessing their situation. If they had trouble measuring gas pressure or slicing into a cadaver to examine the position of the uterus, they had far more difficulty in scrutinizing factors impacting their self-interests. The ultimate irony was that Comte, when his dreams of scientific glory faded, created a religion of science with himself as high priest. Evidently recognizing the difficulties in being objective about social matters did not protect him from sliding into subjectivism. The same applies to contemporary medical theorists. They declare that they are seeking to purify our insights into psychiatric matters, but their discomfort with the breadth of the human predicament prompts them to narrow their purview.

The current state of affairs can be gauged by observing the disagreement between two prominent psychiatrists. Allan Hobson, a professor of psychiatry at Harvard Medical School and the director of Neurophysiology at the Massachusetts Mental Health Center, stands in one corner. The coauthor of *Out of Its Mind: Psychiatry in Crisis*, he champions the further medicalization of personal distress. A staunch believer in brain science, he is appalled by the depths to which contemporary psychiatry has fallen. Lamenting that where once his fellow head doctors were among the best and brightest, the psychiatric ranks are now filled with medical school graduates from the bottom of their classes. He attributes this to what has become a boring job in which doctors see patients for an average of twenty minutes and then write prescriptions for psychotropic medications. In order to avert this, Hobson recommends that psychiatrists become full-fledged brain doctors. Instead of confining themselves to tweaking the dosages of patients they scarcely know, they should take advantage of recent advances in neurology to apply brain physiology to particularized complaints. The alternative is to continue the scholasticism of a discipline that recognizes over eighteen hundred diagnostic categories and promotes the "idea that rote diagnosis and pill-pushing are acceptable." According to Hobson, neither "mindless" pharmacology nor "brainless" psychodynamics should dominate.

And yet he is perfectly happy to blur the line between genuine mental illness and personal distress. Thus he blandly states that the main concerns of psychiatry are anxiety disorders, depression, and schizophrenia. That the first two are different in kind from the third does not occur to him. Indeed, in his review of the former, he begins by stating "the depressive disorders tied to irrational sadness have a lot in common with the anxiety disorders tied to irrational fear. Both are *mysterious* emotional problems. Both involve stress. Both work through many of the same brains structures, processes and pathways" (italics added). While he observes that depression and anxiety are related to normal and useful, emotional processes, he also maintains that "if gloom has no obvious cause or goes on and on for a clearly abnormal length of time, it crosses into the realm of mental illness." Although he acknowledges that "at the lower end of the disease spectrum it is hard to tell what are exaggerated but still normal responses and what are mild cases of mental illness," he has no doubt that most cases that come to medical attention are genuine diseases. Moreover he states the same about anxieties and phobias. They are similarly difficult to distinguish from normal fears, but likewise merit psychiatric attention.[2]

What is peculiar about this stance is that Hobson admits, "we aren't sure just what causes panic attacks, they appear clearly related to conditioning—only in this case the conditioning stimuli are not obvious external ones like snakes or the sounds of battle, but instead are internal stimuli . . . or relatively gentle external stimuli—especially ones associated with prior attacks." To this he adds: This "classification is odd, being based on the excess worry and anxiety remaining after all other causes are accounted for." In other words, anxiety disorders are a residual category. They are what you have when you do not understand what you have. Hobson then goes on to explain that "people suffering from long-term grief, major depression, or mania typically recover on their own . . . , [but] we aren't sure how that works." He even confesses that psychotropic drug effectiveness is partly due to the supportive nature of the therapeutic relationship, nevertheless he consigns this assistance to a secondary position despite the lacunae in the physiological data. For him, this is not a problem because he is firmly convinced that whatever our current medical limitations, one day they will be surmounted and physiology will be supreme.

On the other hand, Hobson also writes that, "any ill that is *mysterious* stands a better chance of being poorly dealt with than one that is understood" (italics added). One might imagine that this would give him pause regarding the sources of depression and anxiety, but he cites this caveat in connection with schizophrenia. It, he declares, is "in a good spot to be handled badly, because it is *the most mysterious* of mental ills" (italic again added). Yet, if anything, less is known about the biology of depression and anxiety. Nowadays virtually everyone agrees that the major psychoses exhibit a genetic component, while the same is not true about what used to be called "neuroses." Emotional dysfunctions are alleged to be physiological precisely because they remain mysterious. Those seeking concrete answers have literally hypostasized their causes.

Arrayed against Hobson is Elio Frattaroli. A psychiatrist in private practice and the associate director of the Psychoanalytic Center of Philadelphia's psychotherapeutic training program, in his book *Healing the Soul in the Age of the Brain*, he objects to this false concreteness. An advocate of what have become "old-fashioned" psychodynamic techniques, he balks at a medical model that denies the existence of something analogous to a soul and treats symptoms rather than people. In his words, what is needed is "a science that acknowledges the existence of an inner self, one that views the person not merely as a 'pack of neurons,' but as a human being, a science that views anxiety not merely as a chemical imbalance, but as *a wake-up call for the soul.*" Despite more than a nod to the Freudian unconscious, Frattaroli can be considered a defender of the spiritual faction. Insisting on a distinction between the mind and body that Hobson would find nonsensical, he believes in an inner-observer that cannot be refuted. Although he refuses to pin this down, it clearly corresponds with the "mysterious" inner-spirit of yore. Furthermore, Frattaroli is adamant that unless this is respected, life has no meaning.

Notwithstanding the millennia that have gone by since religion and science locked horns, their respective approaches to personal distress show no signs of vanishing. Nor are they likely to as long as the mystery underlying individual distress persists. Because uncertainties demand answers, partisans on both sides will remain disgruntled unless they can be convinced that there are alternative reasons why people become desolate. In the chapters that follow, an effort will be made to demonstrate these. Such causes can be found in the nature of social relations and more specifically in the normal responses to the losses intrinsic to social experience. While mental illnesses exist, and neurological processes underlie emotional and thought patterns, a large class of personal reactions cannot be explained without recourse to interpersonal processes. These may not be as material neurons, but are every bit as real.

If this is true, the implications are profound. It would mean that religious rituals and psychopharmacology are of less benefit than their advocates assert. More importantly, it would indicate that many forms of human unhappiness can neither be cured nor exorcized. Produced neither by biological malfunctions, nor spiritual meddling, they are only accessible to the mechanisms that modify social relations. But because these are circumscribed, absolute happiness are not feasible. Since the human condition is social, loss—and pain—can never be completely eradicated. Like it or not, feeding a gamma wolf with Prozac will not relieve its distress. Then again, neither would a religious conversion. Sad to say, gamma wolves are condemned to periods of distress—and so are people. Thankfully, we are human beings—who being potentially more introspective—can do more to protect ourselves than wolves. We can engage in resocialization.

Notes

1. Before I continue, I must apologize for this excursion into egoism. Sigmund Freud in his masterwork on dream analysis introduced many examples that he failed to identify as from his own life. Although they were the source of his information, he concealed their provenance on the assumption that honesty would undermine his credibility. He wanted, instead, to project a façade of scientific objectivity. While I too seek to be taken seriously, I believe that social science should be reflexive. The only authentic way to judge evidence derived from human experience is to be given insight into the character of that experience.
2. An amusing illustration of the confusion surrounding the conjunction between anxiety and depression was found in Zoloft commercials. Exactly the same disembodied heads and schematic neurons were utilized to promote a neurotransmitter theory of both conditions. While the ads began by affirming that their cause in not known, they concluded with the tag line "When you know more about what's wrong, you can make it right."

2

Witches, Mad Doctors, and Pseudo-Sociologists

> *Nya, nya, nya, nya, nya!*
> *Nya, nya, nya, nya, nya! (A children's refrain)*

The Bad Old Days

Kids can be cruel. When they encounter a playmate significantly different from themselves, they gang up to torment this luckless innocent. He or she is surrounded by a gaggle of chanting, finger-pointing bullies intent of driving the deviant to distraction. According to medical advocates, this is how the mentally ill have traditionally been treated. Because they were regarded as dangerous outcasts, people with spiritualist inclinations castigated, rather than helped them.

In the 1950s, socially inept teenagers went through a period of being described as "spastic." Later dubbed "nerds," these victims were mercilessly teased for a purported lack of sophistication. Instead of sympathizing, their peers compared them with the physically disabled, implying that they too were biologically defective. Aside from what this revealed about a lack of compassion for sufferers of cerebral palsy and epilepsy, it bespoke insensitivity to the socially mysterious. Afraid of sliding into clumsiness themselves, the accusers adopted an out-of-hand rejection of what seemed gauche. The penalties then imposed were none other than the ones they expected to be visited on themselves. This sort of mindless rejection was also embodied in ancient superstitions; hence it is regarded as one of the chief reasons why medical experts should treat mental illness. It is also why it is thought essential that doctors minister to extravagant modes of personal distress.

Once upon a time, London consigned its madmen to incarceration in Bedlam. Nowadays synonymous with mental disorder, this institution's inmates were beaten and chained with an indifference that was standard during the early modern period. What made the place significant, however, was that its patients' bizarre behavior was visible to ordinary citizens. Much as in a petting zoo, their ravings were observable for a fee. In order to support the place, the better classes of society were allowed to wander its halls to gape at its screaming and posturing prisoners. Bereft of reason, the latter were dealt with like animals because they were considered little better.

Michel Foucault assures us that in medieval Europe, the insane were prevented from offending ordinary citizens by being set adrift in "ships of fools." Although much of what has been written about these vessels is probably apocryphal, the attitude they represent signifies an impatience with the abnormal. Because people did not know what to do with madness, they decided that out-of-sight was better than torture. After all, the mental specialists who then plied their trade recommended such interventions as long-term confinement and exorcism. With outlandish conduct believed to result from demonic intervention, it was judged imperative to drive the devil out of his henchmen—whether or not they voluntarily consorted with him. If this entailed the use of chains and whips, God's work still needed to be done.

In their more virulent forms, these attacks took the form of witch hunts. The Germans writers Johann Sprenger and Heinrich Kraemer codified this inclination as an ideology that for a time was akin to a mass religious movement. Their *Malleus Maleficarum* (The Witch's Hammer) described the causes, consequences, and appropriate cures for associating with the netherworld. Upon their advice, dissenters, schismatics, and the mentally ill, if they could not be restored to the fold, were set to the torch. Burning at the stake was the fate of thousands of hapless old crones. Accused of vices such as infidelity, ambition, and lust, they were portrayed as having engaged in sexual orgies with evil spirits. In fact, many of those charged were cantankerous widows so hard to get along with that their death served as a focal point for relieving community tensions. Often themselves conspiring in these events by admitting to having trafficked with incubi or succubae, before they were dispatched, they might be stripped and have their pubic hair shaved because, as was widely known, the devil rejoiced in hiding out in the genital region. All the while, respected churchmen gave these doings their blessings, either by adjudicating these matters or by supervising the executions.

Witches, Mad Doctors, and Pseudo-Sociologists

In the American colonies, one of the last spasms of this lunacy occurred in Salem Massachusetts. Initiated on the testimony of several teenage girls, the town's magistrates condemned more than two dozen persons to death. Often convicted on "spectral" evidence, that is, on visions the accusers claimed to experience, the hysteria did not abate until after the spouses of prominent figures were also accused. While the cause of this terror is under dispute—some point to a clash between local clerics and others to fears of an Indian uprising—for many months religious convictions became the vehicle for ridding the community of persons regarded as "different" and therefore dangerous.

By the mid-nineteenth century, in economically advanced countries such as the United States, spiritually based persecutions were out of fashion. Fewer parents justified disciplining their children by a need to "beat the devil out of them," nor were better-educated persons willing to accept the manacles and lashes with which crazy persons were previously restrained. One of the reformers, Dorothea Dix, traveled around the northern states to document the horrors to which the insane were subjected. Many, she testified, were confined in the basements of their relatives. Others were incarcerated in jails alongside violent felons. Considered the dregs of society, few members of the community cared about their fate. Dix herself was scandalized. With passion, and unflagging energy, she successfully petitioned state legislatures to open mental hospitals dedicated to the humane treatment of these unfortunates. Initially labeled "asylums," these were to be places of respite and recuperation. Optimistic that madness was an illness like any other, these now "patients" were expected to recover and return to the community.

By the early twentieth century, conventional wisdom has coalesced around the value of competent medical interventions. The commonplace attitude was exemplified in the popular play *Arsenic and Old Lace*. Although a comedy, replete with a comic mental asylum, none of the characters—save two crazy maiden aunts—were in any doubt that the uncle, who regularly charged up a stairway blaring a bugle in the belief that this was San Juan Hill and that he was Teddy Roosevelt, needed to be hospitalized. To deprive him of this remedy was considered inhumane. This then became the chief indictment against spiritual interventions. Now believed grounded in fictions, these were blamed for denying unfortunates genuine relief. Not even the great commercial success of another movie, *The Exorcist*, altered this conclusion. A rotating adolescent head and green vomit made excellent entertainment, but such images no longer persuaded even faithful churchgoers that religion possessed a suitable means of addressing teenage rebelliousness. So general had become the conviction that personal distress was medical that when individuals who encountered marital problems betook themselves to pastoral counselors, they were more apt to receive psychiatrically informed advice than scriptural guidance.

The Coming of Wisdom

Knowledge, as opposed to unadulterated faith, is said to have flowered in ancient Greece. Individuals in distress began to seek advice from scientifically oriented physicians, rather than spiritual leaders. Instead of consulting the bones of dead chickens or imploring revered clerics to enunciate magical words, they demanded treatment derived from an understanding of how the body worked. Mistakes were, to be sure, made. The uterus was not, as supposed, a little animal that scurried around the female body causing trouble, nor did an excess of black bile produce melancholia. Nevertheless, observations, rather than unsubstantiated faith, came to be considered the portal to high-quality intercessions. In time, this would blossom into rational Western-style medicine ultimately responsible for saving millions of lives.

Still it would take millennia before this wisdom reached a critical mass. Medicine might celebrate empiricism, but for most of its history, its insights were faulty. While the pivotal virtue of science is that it builds on concrete observations, serious errors accumulated along the way. During the Middle Ages, for instance, it was the doctors who insisted on bleeding patients, including the mentally ill. It was not until the mid-nineteenth century that the germ theory of disease replaced the four humors. There was also a general belief that a well-regulated digestive system, and, more particularly, a regularity of the bowels, was essential for personal contentment. This conviction exhibited itself in an obsession with enemas. Today it seems amazing, but for centuries physicians supervised injecting exotic substances, including smoke, up the anuses of their patients.

Nor did such blunders suddenly terminate with the advent of modern times. One of the great advances of the early nineteenth century was phrenology. Today considered a superstition, examining the bumps on a person's head to determine his personality was then hailed a medical miracle. The assumption was that if some areas of the brain were larger than others, this indicated that the faculty supported by that part of the organ must be overdeveloped. Although we now recognize this is not true, the perspective concentrated attention on the brain as the seat of behavior. Likewise when the Viennese semi-charlatan Friedrich Mesmer captivated France with his theories of animal magnetism, he laid the foundation for later investigations into hypnotism and neuro-electricity. In the meantime, he managed to bamboozle a multitude of gullible aristocrats into parting with large sums of money. Even venerable hypotheses about hysteria received a quasi-scientific updating. Since anatomists had recently established that the uterus was incapable of significant movement, it was conjectured that gases emanating from the organ must be responsible for the condition. Designated "the vapors," well into the Civil War era, up-to-the-minute young Southern belles attributed their fainting spells to these mysterious fumes.

Toward the end of the nineteenth century, medicalized theories about mental conditions cranked into high gear. One of the more trendy diagnoses was "neurasthenia." Characterized by a lethargy attributed to overworking the nervous system, one of the recommended treatments, aside from restful trips to Europe, was a therapeutic jolt of electricity. Indeed, for a while, doctor-administered electrical shocks became the salubrious cure for a host of ills. The term "neurosis" also became widespread during this period. In this case, various anxieties were thought to result from an inflammation of the nerves. Although no such irritations were detected, because a physiological substrate for emotional maladies was deemed indispensable, one was surmised.

Since this was the Victorian age, it was assumed that sexuality was at the root of countless miseries. To be licentious was imagined to disturb delicate chemical balances and therefore to impair health. Worst of all, of course, was masturbation. This precursor to adult wantonness was forbidden to the young. As every well-informed physician knew, playing with one's sexual parts led to blindness and mental retardation. More treacherous than syphilis, this shameless lack of self-control betokened a character so dissolute that unless the act was immediately terminated, all hope was lost.

Sexuality also played a featured role in the concurrent theories of Sigmund Freud. A physician by training, and a biological researcher in his formative years, he is usually credited with "psychologizing" psychotherapy. Famed for dream analysis and the "talking cure" for of hysteria and melancholia, he nevertheless pioneered a series of concepts grounded in a mythological physiology. Foremost in this theoretical arsenal was the "libido." Supposedly a sexual energy that governed individual motivation, this fluid-like substance was hypothesized to concentrate in different parts of the body, for example, the mouth, the anus, and the genitals, thereby accounting for childhood sexuality. Although no such life force was ever detected, it long remained decisive in explaining why patients became fixated at particular developmental stages. While Freud himself did not compound the error by reifying this substance, one of his disciples, Wilhelm Reich, did. He transmuted libido into "orgone" and constructed orgone boxes designed to accumulate its power.

Freud also introduced an ethereal tripartite mental machinery. Although in his earlier years he investigated neurons, even inventing a new means of staining them, he began to speak of the "ego," the "id," and the "superego." While he knew this architecture did not correspond to an observable physiology, he treated these as if they were homunculi. The id, for instance, was depicted as the unconscious wellspring of instinctual impulses. Always imprecise in its dimensions, it was nevertheless believed to be a powerful driver of human action.

Until almost the 1960s, Freudianism was the last word in scientific psychiatry. Its mythology was the holy grail to psychoanalysts, who at the time were the most prestigious of all mental health workers. But then fashions changed. A new breed of psychiatrist demanded a more empirical orientation. This began to take shape with the emergence of the American Psychiatric Association's (APA) *Diagnostic and Statistical Manuals*. Designed to systematize and, therefore, stabilize the diagnosis of patient complaints, these began as slim neo-Kraepelinian volumes, but graduated into mini-telephone books. Entire series of mental disorders that had not previously existed came to be precisely delineated. In fact, what most characterized these handbooks was their perpetual mutation. The DSM-III (Diagnostic and Statistical Manual of Mental Disorders) was the watershed in this regard. It consciously sought to separate psychiatry from its Freudian roots and substitute a sequence of "disorders" based on observed symptoms, rather than hypothetical etiologies. The problem with these "syndromes," however, was that often the only thing that held them together was their appearance on the same page. Thought of as "diseases," even though this word was scrupulously eschewed, the exercise of producing them piggybacked on previous attitudes toward mental illness.

Whereas the DSM's instituted the practice of reasoning in terms of "functional disorders," the mantra among practicing physicians was that "mental illnesses were diseases like any other." A palpable exaggeration, conditions such as "conduct disorders," were anything but similar to the measles. Yet this disparity was assiduously overlooked. Though anxieties, depressions, and adjustment disorders might exhibit no identifiable physiological indicators, they were treated as if they did. Psychiatrists began to talk about "chemical imbalances" despite the fact that in diagnosing their patients they never consulted blood tests to determine their presence. A great deal had been learned about neurotransmitters and the genetic preconditions of schizophrenia and manic depression, yet these advances produced an enormous leap of faith. Absolutely certain the biological causes of the "neurotic" conditions would soon yield to science, practitioners acted as if they already had. Fortified in these attitudes by the revolutionary achievements of freshly discovered psychotropic medications, they demanded, and to a large extent, received, the deference accorded their more physiologically oriented brethren.

What must be insisted upon, however, is that this was not science. It was no more grounded in solid data than were phrenology or neurasthenia. Far from representing a wisdom different in kind than that proclaimed by the spiritualists, it derived its explanatory power from the unseen, and perhaps, unseeable. Whatever the advances in understanding the psychoses, these did not automatically explain the origins of personal distress. Serotonin and dopamine were undoubtedly potent chemical agents, and the influence of the limbic system is decisive in appreciating the mechanisms of human emotions, but neither preempted a comprehension of "personality disorders." While the DSMs segregated these onto what was identified as a nonmedical axis, the practical effect was to subsume them under the same rubric as other mental states. Psychologists complained about this medical imperialism, but possessing neither the prestige, nor the political influence, of their competitors, they had little choice but to accept a newfound status as medical handmaidens.

The Arrival of Compassion

As much a myth as the scientific accuracy of medicine is its superior humanity. Doctors are prone to reminding laypersons that the Hippocratic oath pledges them to do no harm and, therefore, that unlike spiritualists, they are constitutionally incapable of participating in persecutions such as witch hunts. What they neglect is their own history of inflicting pain. Lest it go unremembered, the full title of Bedlam was St. Mary of Bethlehem Hospital. The institution was, in fact, under the supervision of physicians. Although the church ran medieval hospitals, doctors were every bit as culpable as priests for shackling and mocking the era's madmen. Psychiatry, like other disciplines, has been fond of constructing hagiographies for its predecessors and cautionary tales regarding rivals. Eager to establish the legitimacy of its authority, it sponsors histories that paint a glowing a portrait of its contributions. This puffery alleges that one of the crucial moments in the march to medical enlightenment was the courageous act of Philippe Pinel in striking the chains off mental patients during the French Revolution. This is represented as an unprecedented act of compassion, yet what goes unreported is that he did so as the chief physician at Bicetre and the Salpetriere. His was not an insurrection against spiritualists, but a protest against other "mad doctors." It was they who endorsed fetters and whips to control those in their care.

Nowadays, we tend to think of doctors as employing the least painful interventions possible, but historically the situation has been quite otherwise. Taking your medicine was long synonymous with swallowing something that tasted awful. Indeed, it was assumed that unless it was unpleasant, it could not be effective. Moreover, until recently, going to the doctor was more likely to result in death than a cure. To illustrate, George Washington was apparently bled to death after contracting no more than a cold, while Samuel Pepys was reluctant to be operated upon for urinary stones lest he not emerge from the procedure. Even Kings were not exempt from the excruciating ministrations of court physicians. Thus when Charles II of England developed the seizures that were later to take his life, he was subjected to purges, cauterizations, and blistering. Red-hot irons were placed on his skull and naked feet, and his urine was scalded through the lavish use of cantharides. Cupping, emetics, and a total of fifty-five drugs were administered within a period of five days. Not surprisingly, the king's tongue and mouth became inflamed partly from the medications and partly from where his teeth were forced apart during his convulsions.

When the problem was specifically mental, the treatment was no better. Thus George III, the "tyrant" of the American Revolution, received a comeuppance to satisfy the most vengeful American patriot. When he began to suffer the symptoms of what has since been diagnosed as porphyry, he was placed under the care of a distinguished mad doctor. As correctly rendered in the movie *The Madness of King George*, he was against his will "encased in a machine that left him no liberty of motion." His physician, on the assumption that the monarch's strange outbursts were within his conscious control, sought to dominate his patient with a withering gaze. Frequently beaten and starved, George was also subjected to menacing language. And of course, he was blistered, bled, and dosed with emetics. And yet this was the most progressive treatment of its day. Some members of the court were appalled by these events, but they did not object too strenuously because this was the norm. No one expected mad doctors to be paragons of compassion.

Across the Atlantic, conditions were little better. Republican virtue did not extend to crazy persons. Here Dr. Benjamin Rush, the honored friend of John Adams, and the designated father of American Psychiatry, although frequently described as bringing scientific kindness to his patients, did so in a manner we today might find odd. The inventor of various devices for swirling the mentally ill around to induce a therapeutic dizziness, he believed in awakening people from their delusions via shocks and subterfuges. In one case, he proudly wrote about pulling a chair out from under a client who believed he was made of glass and then showing him shards of a broken goblet. In another case, he allowed a patient to urinate upon another who believed himself a flower. The second was told that they had been "watered." According to Rush, such "mortification" possessed curative powers.

Before proceeding to additional examples of psychiatric benevolence, it may be salutary to point out that nonmedical practitioners were simultaneously experimenting with more kindly interventions. Whereas Pinel is usually credited with promoting the "moral" treatment of the insane, more influential was Samuel Tuke. A Quaker layman, he founded the York Retreat as a model of enlightened therapy. From its beginnings, the seriously disturbed were never bound or flogged, but instead taken on peripatetic talks through the gardens. Tuke called this antecedent of Freud's techniques a "moral treatment" and claimed it worked miracles. Patients apparently did flourish when dealt with respectfully, so much so that reformers from all over Europe made the pilgrimage to his institution to study his methods. For a while, kindness became all the rage. Indeed, Tuke, more than Pinel, was the inspiration for the "asylum" movement so favored by Dorothea Dix. Moreover, testimony from the beginnings of these institutions suggests that they were at first gentle and caring. It was not until their successes prompted physicians to initiate a successful campaign to become their superintendents that they descended into the callous snake pits of living memory. Ironically, it was the association of these superintendents that ultimately formed the basis of the APA.

Among the remedies favored by the budding psychiatric hospitals were the straitjacket and a variety of water therapies that dunked, sprayed, scalded, and sometimes nearly drowned their beneficiaries. When electricity became fashionable, many individuals were hooked up to batteries and shocked back to their senses. Some doctors resorted to clitoridectomies in order to reduce the sexual passions of female patients who were assumed to be suffering from a surfeit of libido. Eventually with the advent of the twentieth century, these torments became more refined. Electricity having become more reliable, convulsive treatments delivered dramatic currents it was hoped might shake schizophrenics back to sanity. That these pulses were frequently so strong they broke bones was not considered a decisive handicap. Nor was the fact that these shocks frequently disorganized the memory so seriously the victims had difficulty in managing life tasks. Moreover, if electricity did not work, insulin might. When it was serendipitously discovered that an insulin-induced coma cleared the mental state of some psychotics, even the life-threatening aspects of this procedure were taken in stride.

Still, far and away the most heinous of these drastic physiological cures were lobotomies. Psychosurgery to sever the neural connections between parts of the brain was introduced by Dr. Egas Moniz on the presumption that this prevented disruptive electrical signals from instigating psychiatric symptoms. Having noticed that this procedure had a calming effect on his patients, Moniz advocated it as an all-purpose cure. In his original formula, for which he was subsequently awarded a Nobel Prize, the good doctor drilled two holes in the top of the skull into which he inserted a scalpel with which to cut the cerebral tissue. This practice was, unfortunately, both expensive and dangerous. It, therefore, required American ingenuity to transform it into a miracle cure.

But Dr. Walter Freeman was quite up to the task. Subsequently lionized in *Life* magazine for his groundbreaking innovations, Freeman was the father of the prefrontal lobotomy. A wonderful propagandist, but a cavalier surgeon, he literally traveled from hospital to hospital to promote his wares. The administrators of these institutions would line up their most troublesome inmates and on an assembly line schedule file them into his operating room. There the good doctor performed his trans-orbital technique by inserting an ice pick over the eyeball, piercing the orbit, and then wiggling this instrument back and forth—very like a windshield wiper—through the gray matter. The result of this not particularly delicate routine was to convert previously obstreperous individuals into vegetables. Nonetheless, they were mental patients, so few laypersons were outraged. Repeatedly assured this was in the best interests of the seriously impaired, they had little interest in examining these matters for themselves.

Happily the worst of these horrors are behind us. Lobotomies are no longer performed and elector-convulsive therapy has been tamed. Nevertheless, problems still abound in the prescription of psychoactive drugs. Some of these preparations are so potent that they cause irreversible brain damage. Tardive dyskinesia, in which overmedication produces uncontrollable movements of the tongue, is assiduously guarded against, but a blankness of effect due medication is quite common. The general rule is that once a prescription demonstrates adverse consequences, a substitute is placed in its stead. For many, this means that the nonmedical aspects of their complaints are never addressed. As long as they can cope, and make few complaints, their treatment is deemed a success—this even though it never leads a full life.

Psychotherapy and Deinstitutionalization

During the heyday of the Freudianism, it was assumed that when one entered psychotherapy, one would participate in a growth experience. The psychiatrist would ask probing questions about the patient's relationships with his or her parents, and in the end insights would emerge that would restructure the client's personal space. He or she would become more mature and lingering bugaboos from early childhood be forever banished. Potential analysands still imagine that this is what is in store for them when they make an appointment with an HMO's behavioral unit, but they are apt to be disappointed. The economics of mental health have become such that traditional long-term analyses are by and large a thing of the past. Brief therapy and drug maintenance are the mainstays of the moment. If a patient is believed to need a talk therapy, it will not be for the five of six times a week Freud recommended, nor will it last for the years once customary. Because all that is expected is for the patient to learn how to cope, once this is achieved, victory is declared. For others not considered suitable candidates for the emotional turmoil of the traditional methods, a prescription for an antidepressant or an antianxiety pill will have to do. Just as Prof. Hobson complains, the psychiatrists who administer these concoctions spend no more than twenty minutes with a person and may never see him or her again, except if an adverse reaction demands closer supervision.

Once, not very long ago, the medical community made a distinction between *covering* and *uncovering* therapies. The latter were devoted to plumbing the depths of a client's psyche so as to assist him or her in remembering, but more importantly, reexperiencing the traumatic experiences that interfered with personal development. Because this was a delicate project, replete with terrors and confusions, it was thought essential to invest time and expertise in establishing a solid personal relationship between the helper and helpee. Only this could provide the courage and guidance to navigate the emotional minefield that stretched out before the client. Brief therapies, however, can afford to be less personal. They depend on teaching the client how to utilize his or her defenses to suppress that which might be overwhelming. Because a capacity to avoid panic may be all that is needed to function, this is all that is supplied. The same logic, of course, applies to medications. If a chemical agent can smother fears sufficiently for someone to keep going, that may be all either party expects.

Eviscerated further by the directions taken by modern psychiatry have been the services offered to the truly mentally ill. Because the line dividing them from those suffering from personal distress has been blurred, they are frequently treated as if they were in better shape than they are. Shortly after the advent of psychotropic medications, some experts began to assert that these could serve as a substitute for hospitalization. By this time, the asylums were being derided as warehouses that exacerbated the troubles of the mentally ill. If, in their place, medication could control the major symptoms of insanity, these unfortunates could safely be released into the community, then maintained in a fairly normal state by receiving the requisite prescriptions from community mental health centers.

As humane as this sounded, it swiftly became evident that these predictions were wildly optimistic. First, the medications did not work as well as expected. The hallucinations and delusions of the mentally ill might not be as florid as previously, but these individuals were far from normal. Most could not really participate in the occupations and relationships typical of most others. Not as disruptive as formerly, they nonetheless remained unusual. Worse than this, because the hospitals no longer supervised their medications, they were less inclined to take them. Since attendance at community mental health centers was voluntary, a large proportion failed to show up. Discontented with the side effects of their prescriptions, many concluded that they would be better off drug-free. When their symptoms subsequently returned, a further feature of the recent reforms entered the scene.

With the mentally ill having been depicted as suffering from a disease like any other, and as possessing the same essential humanity as those in personal distress, it seemed to follow that they were entitled to conventional legal protections. No longer would it be acceptable to shuttle them off involuntarily to what reputed to be a medical facility. Everyone now understood that mental hospitals were like prisons, and it was therefore unconscionable to incarcerate someone without due process because he or she behaved strangely. The inevitable conclusion was that without genuine consent, the insane could not be confined, that is, unless a judge concluded they were a present danger to themselves or others. Since most of these persons were not, they were released on their own recognizance.

It was at this point that the nation discovered itself in the grip of an unanticipated problem. Quite suddenly, battalions of displaced persons began to show up living under bridges or camped out in cardboard boxes. In seeking out subway tunnels or sidewalk heating grates to escape the winter winds, many of these shabby-looking souls took to defecating in public or engaging in intrusive panhandling. Almost as suddenly, a new breed of political advocates began to agitate for government-sponsored housing to rescue these victims of the capitalist system. "Homelessness" had been discovered as a social calamity. The airwaves were now filled with passionate spokespersons eager to explain how a lack of affordable housing consigned millions of ordinary Americans to a life of discomfort and uncertainty. Even families with small children were not exempt. All that had to happen was for the breadwinner to lose his or her job, and the whole lot would be out on the street. Unmentioned by smooth-talking media philanthropists was the phenomenon of "deinstitutionalization." Apparently unaware that hundreds of thousands of mental patients had recently been liberated into the community, they were equally innocent of knowledge that many of these were unable to adjust to their newfangled freedom and consequently found their way onto the streets.

With several decades of experience behind us, it is now possible to declare with considerable confidence that roughly one-third of the homeless are mentally ill, one-third chemically dependent, and one-third the victims of economic catastrophes. Nevertheless, it is the mentally ill and the chemically dependent who are most troublesome. They are the ones living in the cardboard boxes, the ones working as squeegee-men, and ones who refuse to move into decent housing even when this is available. Moreover, the mentally ill are often not fully aware of their limitations. They have been told to make decisions about their own lives, but they do not have the perspicuity to do so wisely. Neither do they have the capacity to live in family situations, nor the inclination to conform to community standards. Unless compelled to go for treatment, many will not. In this case, regarding them as if they were almost normal condemns them to greater misery than they would otherwise experience, even in mental institutions. It also forces ordinary people to put up with behaviors they would never tolerate from more competent peers. In the end, overestimating the powers of medicine and underestimating the impairments of mental illness place unnecessary burdens on those who are both ill and well. Perhaps it is not too far wrong to assert that a misplaced faith in the capacities of medical science precipitated "reforms" that were not reforms. Sorrowfully, because their sponsors have been unwilling to admit their mistakes, they have relegated untold numbers of blameless bystanders to preventable hassles.

"Medical" Sociology

Medicine, by its very nature, is biologically oriented. It almost always assigns the cause of patient complaints to physiological conditions. Disease is typically considered a matter of the body machinery failing to function as it should. The paradigmatic instance is a communicable disease produced by a microscopic organism. Hordes of bacteria, brigades of viruses, or armies of tiny worms invade the body and prevent it from performing its regular tasks. Breathing becomes impaired, digestive processes trigger unexpected pain, or bleeding pustules break out on the skin. If these eruptions do not kill the patient, they make his or her life miserable. Another common manifestation of disease is the nutritional disorder. A person fails to ingest the proper vitamins and develops beriberi or perhaps after nibbling on paint chips falls acquires lead poisoning. Then there are the genetic conditions. Sometimes the biological blueprints from which our bodies spring provide faulty directions. Individuals are born with a hole between the chambers of the heart or with lungs clogged by cystic fibrosis. In these circumstances, they may not have the energy to pursue ordinary social enterprises. And finally, there are occasions when physical organs go haywire for both known and unknown reasons. People develop an aggressive cancer that blocks their bowels, or an incipient diabetes robs them of the insulin they need to digest sugar, or hypothyroidism slows their metabolism and makes them feel sluggish. These ills might be due to infections, genetic anomalies, or injuries sustained in utero. Sometimes people even have difficulty breathing because someone has shot them in the chest. Flat-out physical damage obstructs mundane functions. Finally, with regard to true mental illnesses, there are actual brain dysfunctions. Some people are doomed to a surplus (or surfeit) of neurotransmitters as a result of a genetic defect or chemical dependency.

Nonetheless most physicians are aware that the majority of mental diagnoses are not associated with identifiable physiological conditions, hence their talk of "functional" disorders. A functional disorder is one in which something is wrong with how a person operates, but where nothing physiological is ostensibly broken. In this case, the temptation to make the invisible visible by providing it with a concrete name can be irresistible. Why does fire burn? Puzzled medieval scientists were hesitant to acknowledge that they did not know. As a result, they confidently announced that fire was caused when phlogiston was released into the atmosphere. Did they have independent evidence of the existence of phlogiston? Certainly not. So they, in essence, named *the unknown* and concluded that this reified ignorance was the explanation they sought. Freud did much the same with the libido. Unlike, say atoms, it did not yield to a search for an underlying substrate. In the case of functional mental disorders, such a search is rarely attempted. The authors of the DSMs having defined these conditions in terms of clusters of behaviors found it unnecessary to hypothesize the existence of anything more substantive. All that was needed to diagnose a person with a narcissistic personality disorder was to exhibit several of a list of self-aggrandizing activities. Too much boasting, too many manipulative relationships, too much self-absorption and voila, the disorder was at hand.

Another way to look at this phenomenon is to perceive it as part of a quasi-medical sociology. Observant psychiatrists cannot help but notice that their patients are embedded in a social context. Nor can they prevent themselves from discerning how these circumstances impact the makeup of client symptoms. Rather than examining these factors, however, recourse is taken to disguised versions of social explanations. All decked out in biological jargon, these hypotheses suffer from a lack of candor. Remarkably naive because they are pieced together from unscrutinized social assumptions, they pretend to insight into the human condition that are astoundingly incomplete. Encrusted in a pseudo-scientific patina, they seem solid, yet are not. Take, for example, the case of "stress." As is wont with such concepts, it is currently being cycled out of style, but for a while, it seemed the self-evident reason for a host of human ills. Contemporary life was said to be saturated with stress. Everywhere people looked, potential stressors assaulted them. Unless these were well-managed or potential victims adequately inoculated against them, it was clear that trouble would ensue.

One of the first inconveniences of this account was the ambiguity of its central concept. "Stress" has two major senses. It can refer either to external factors that cause problems or to internal reactions to these incitements. In other words, one is either subjected to stress or one experiences it. In either event, the specific referent is unclear. (A closely connected term, i.e., "pressure," suffers from the same dilemma and has similar roots in the forces applied to physical materials.) As employed by popularizer Hans Selye, the crucial factor in mental stress seems to be fear. For him, either that which stimulates apprehension or the resultant emotion may receive the designation. Indeed, experimenting primarily upon animals, he subjected them to what amounted to tortures to discover that this altered their physiological responses. Under this inspiration, Holmes and Rahe[1] later created what became the standard, albeit ad hoc, register of stressors. These included divorce, moving to a new home, and experiencing a major illness. Turning to the interior half of the equation, Cannon's fight–flight reaction became paradigmatic. Individuals undergoing stress were described as either attempting to defeat or flee whatever was causing them anxiety. While this approach possessed a prima facie validity—people do, after all, face dangers they attempt to control—the social nature of these perils was left unexplained. Labeling them stressors merely because they stimulated dread, or stresses rather than fears, did not enlighten us as to why they operated as they did. The stress hypothesis, in essence, treated society as if it were a black box. Considered utterly impenetrable, no attempt was made to discern why some social dangers have the impact they do. These were merely dealt with via a makeshift inventory of intuitive irritants.

Somewhat more sophisticated that the stress model is the trauma hypothesis if only because it is based on more advanced biological information. It too, unfortunately, is sociologically bereft. The trauma concept seems to have made an auspicious medical debut under the auspices of Sigmund Freud. In search of a causative agent for the emotional fixations with which he was struggling, he drew upon his background as a physician to suggest that his clients suffered a fateful injury. In medical lingo, a trauma is a physical wound. It is a material insult to the body, for example, a slashed muscle, a shattered bone, or an exploded spleen. The injuries that Freud detected were, however, of a metaphorical sort. A pivotal example was the "primal scene." Some young children were conjectured to have undergone anguish upon accidentally observing their parents having sex. Misinterpreting this as an instance of father assaulting mother, the small "victim" experienced a psychic insult so severe it could not be consciously endured. This "pain," nevertheless, was not due to damaged brain tissue. It referred only symbolically to a personal injury. There was a hurt, but it did not emanate from a corporeal trauma. Nor were other hypothetical ordeals, such as a fear of castration, actual wounds. Little boys might worry that their fathers would cut off their wee wees because they were seeking the love of their mothers, but there was no physical castration.

In the wake of the Vietnam War, an updated version of the trauma hypothesis emerged. It drew upon the experience of veterans who eventually came to be diagnosed as suffering from a "posttraumatic stress syndrome." An infantryman out in the field who witnessed his best buddy blown away by a Viet Cong mortar might return home to endure inexplicable bouts of terror. Without warning a flashback would transport him through time and space to make him once again feel as if he were in mortal danger. Consciously he knew better, but emotionally he could not separate himself from a debilitating sense of incompetence. Here then was trauma coupled with stress. A dramatic psychic injury elicited a sense of fear so great that it was paralyzing. Fear itself was now identified as a species of trauma. The virtue of this strategy lay in the subsequent connection made between the mortifying event and an alteration in cerebral organization. Freud could not have known, as modern neurologists do, that fear is mediated through the amygdala, a small organ deep inside the brain. It apparently guides laying down mental traces of terrifying occurrences. The distinctive aspect of this process is that the more terrifying the emotion, the stronger the memory. According to current theories, this has the effect of maintaining a recollection of that which is truly dangerous. Were the brain not to have such a mechanism, human beings would regularly blunder into hazards they should have learned to recognize. The amygdala connection not only provides the pathways for these identifications, but also furnishes the motivation to neutralize such threats.

Transported from a literal battlefield to a figurative one that once existed between a parent and a child, posttraumatic stress disorder is now implicated in neuroses. Therapy patients are said to remain terrified due to injuries sustained long ago at the hands of abusive parents. If so, the same sorts of desensitization that work for war veterans should work for them. In fact, many clinicians testify they do. What is more, they are probably correct. Nevertheless, this too simplifies matters to a degree that limits the good done. As sociologically handicapped as supposition about stress, these theories ignore many of the factors that complicate their efforts. First, because most "traumas" suffered early in life are not physical, they are not sustained at a single point in time. Consider the Oedipus complex. If Freud were correct, a little boy's rivalry with his father might elicit threats of harm, but these warnings, not to mention the child's own mental projections, would not have been one-off events. They would have occurred many times, over an extended period. Other so-called childhood traumas are of even less finite length. If, let us say, a mother resented her child for demanding more care than she was willing to provide, the mischief flowing from this could persist for decades. Where then would be the salient moment when the amygdala contributed its labors!

Second, the traumas visited on individuals who afterward suffer personal distress are not accidental happenings, but predictable difficulties. When a bomb dismembers a soldier's buddy, both he and his friend experience bad luck. Or when a drunk driver shatters a child's leg, the odds went against the tyke. To use a somewhat dated figure of speech, these are acts of God. They strike from out of the blue and cannot be foreseen at the beginning of an infant's life. Other kinds of trouble are more expectable. Because they follow from the ordinary structures of human society, many more individuals must cope with them. While it is true that wars, automobile accidents, and lightning are normal and reasonably frequent events, their prevalence pales when compared with the regularity of coercive parenting or hierarchical tyrannies. To disregard how the mechanisms that support human societies create pain is to be willfully ignorant of partially controllable agents.

Third, while traumas tend to be one-way phenomena, the social circumstances that produce most personal distress are usually reciprocal. Rogue automobiles and exploding mortar shells come out of nowhere. All of a sudden, they happen to a person. He or she can be passively ambling down a sidewalk when a cable gives loose and a piano falls on his head. People, to be sure, contribute to automobile accidents by driving unsafely, but the sorts of things that transpire between parents and children unfold as they do because of how both parties act. Almost invariably when a parent treats a child badly, the latter seeks to alter this state of affairs, then the parent reacts to this, and so forth. Most children engage in back talk—at least during some point in their lives—and parents commonly respond with displeasure. In the end, part of the pain the child experiences results from his own intransigence. This means that the child's behavior, not just the parent's, must be addressed if change is to occur. Although learning to be a defensive driver can reduce the chances of an accident, the extent of one's control over adverse interpersonal events is of such a different magnitude as to be different in kind.

All in all, discounting these factors misrepresents what has happened and therefore what should be done. A quasi-sociological narrative that takes no notice of how frequently pain is inflicted, the reasons why it is imposed, and the role of the target in determining its extent is deeply flawed. Such explanations may be simple to grasp, but are perilously off center. By the same token, trauma accounts facilitate a misleadingly superficial moralism. Because specific individuals are accused of meting out particular injuries at definite times, it becomes possible to blame them for the harm induced. They are said to be "abusive," and their cruelty becomes the central concern. All the same, this sort of censure can be seriously wrongheaded.

None of this, however, should be taken to mean that there are no intersections between trauma and loss. Karen Wager-Smith of the Scripps Research Institute reports that when "we look at a brain's reward circuit in animal models of grief and anhedonia, we find a similar molecular program to that of physical injury and pain. It looks as if the loss of a major source of rewarding stimuli leads to a tiny focal injury in the reward circuit, and while the injury is being repaired, molecules are produced that change pain thresholds." In other words, people who experience loss may indeed endure the equivalent of a physical trauma to sections of their brain. Moreover, the very chemicals that induce injured persons to isolate a wound so that it can heal also prompt those who endure a loss to insulate the part of their brain affected by it. In Wager-Smith's words, "this would enable them to dismantle [their] prior behavioral strategy and build a new one." As we shall shortly see, this fits perfectly with how grief operates with respect to overcoming a loss. In cutting ties to what is lost, the physically based pain of the loss prompts a mental withdrawal that permits a person to let go of the past so as to prepare for the future.

Moral Arbiters

Talk about "abuse" has become so rife that it is scarcely recognized as moralistic. That some forms of behavior are "wrong" seems so obvious that their condemnation is regarded as an objective fact. Who, possessing a single ounce of human decency, would deny that putting out a cigarette butt on the naked skin of a bawling infant is obscene? Or who assert that raping a fourteen-year-old girl is not ethically abhorrent? These are unquestionably blameworthy acts. Nevertheless, physical, emotional, and sexual abuses imply moral judgments. People must decide what is acceptable. The problem is they also decide differently. Rulings as to what is abusive vary with time and place. Thus, in some societies, an older man is required to induct a teenage girl into the mysteries of sex. In others, a clitoridectomy is considered a sign of beauty, not a vicious disfigurement. And in still others, a man is expected to beat his wife even if this leaves her terrified. We, in our society, find such conduct repugnant. Nevertheless, we need to be honest enough to own up to our commitments. Utilizing linguistic ruses to induce their acceptance unlatches the gate for an Adolf Hitler to justify the Holocaust on the grounds that the Jews "abused" the hospitality of the German people. In fact, Hitler made this claim. Remarkably, some feminists behave little better in collapsing male gazes at shapely female posteriors into a species of "visual rape." This takes a form of conduct about which people have firm convictions and confounds it with another in order to hijack the attitude toward first for use against the second. Nor has it proved beneficial to describe normal schoolyard teasing as a variety of emotional abuse. These are not facts; they are ideological imperatives that escape detection by employing switch and bait tactics.

Subtler in their moralistic manipulations have been the DSMs. Exploiting a pretense of science to promote a favored code of conduct, they have shamelessly camouflaged ethical verdicts as mental disorders. While giving the impression that they objectively catalog the personal and social ills to which individuals fall prey, they in fact condemn specified behaviors, most of which have long been evaluated as morally abhorrent. The enterprise is essentially a shell game where "social descriptions," "disorders," and "moral lapses" are shuttled past one another with such deceptive speed that the inexperienced observer hasn't a chance of figuring out what is going on. Dazzled by the practiced sleight of hand of a phalanx of authoritative mountebanks, the ordinary person relinquishes his judgment to those who claim to know best.

Surely the preeminent illustration of this moralistic, medicalized, pseudo-sociology is what happened to the diagnosis of homosexuality. During the nineteenth century, and half way into the twentieth, cultivated individuals had no doubt that homosexuality was a perversion. Long condemned by the church as a sin, with the advent of modern science, medicine lent its prestige to this ostracism. No less a figure than Freud revealed a preoccupation with it in his writings. Apparently alarmed at the prospect of "latent" homosexuality, he devised an elaborate psychological explanation for why some men succumbed to the transgression. Attributed to an Oedipus complex gone wrong, gays were hypothesized to develop affection for other men because they could not successfully identify with their fathers. Fundamentally in fear of castration for lusting after their mothers, they solved their predicament by identifying with the female parent. This, Freud opined, was a distortion of human nature. Besides inflicting psychic pain, it prevented men from living up to their potential. It, therefore, constituted a neurosis.

For almost fifty years, Freud's conclusion reigned supreme. Most psychiatrists did not give a second thought to the necessity of redirecting a homosexual's libido toward a more appropriate object. This, by his own testimony, was the case with Robert L. Spitzer. Delegated by the APA to head up a task force aimed at revising the DSM II, he spearheaded the introduction of the revolutionary DSM-III. Initially oblivious to difficulties with the diagnosis of homosexuality, one day he found himself confronted by a throng of psychiatrist-protesters. This being the 1970s, protesting had become part of the national scene, and homosexuals joined the crowd in demanding instant transformations. The activists wanted nothing less than legitimating their condition by deleting it from the official list of mental illnesses. When one of them asked Spitzer what evidence he had that homosexuality was a disease, the good doctor could come up with no immediate answer. Upon reflecting on the matter, and doing a little reading, he decided that he could not in good faith certify the condition as a mental defect. Now inclined to do what he had been implored to do, but not completely sure of his ground, he nonetheless failed to commission original research to settle the matter. What he did instead was to poll the members of the APA to determine what proportion believed homosexuality a paraphilia. When a modest majority voted against continuing the old diagnosis, he had his mandate and the new manual discontinued the old entry. Still unprepared to eliminate the disorder entirely, a new psychosexual category appeared in its pages. Denoted "ego-dystonic homosexuality," from this moment forward, homosexuality counted as a disorder only if the person exhibiting it experienced discomfort. Only individuals who expressed a persistent concern with altering their orientation received the modified verdict.[2]

Now imagine a similar scenario with regard to the measles. Would doctors consider surveying themselves to determine if it were a disease? If they had doubts, wouldn't they assign competent personal to investigate whether an infectious agent was responsible? The reason this was not done with homosexuality was that the participants understood they were not dealing with a physiological defect. Imagine too that a person was told her cancer would be designated a disease if, and only if, it made her unhappy, and if, and only if, she engaged in active efforts to remove it. The absurdity of this speaks for itself. But more importantly, it reveals that members of the APA were willing to tie themselves into knots rather than admitting they were making a moral determination. Having, like their fellow citizens, been influenced by changing social mores, they could not acknowledge this out loud, for to do so would be tantamount to renouncing their entitlement to decide the issue. Once exposed as possessing moral credentials in no way superior to other persons, psychiatrists might have to defer to community standards rather than impose "medical" ones. Their solution, and it was ingenious, was to insist that "functional" medical disorders were at stake. People either were, or were not, operating according to predetermined biological specifications, and they, as experts on medical matters, were best positioned to judge the matter.

The way the authors of the revised manual explained the situation was this: "In the DSM-III each of the mental disorders is conceptualized as a clinically significant behavioral or psychological syndrome or pattern that occurs in an individual and that is typically associated with either a painful symptom or impairment in one or more important areas of functioning. In addition, there is an inference that there is a behavioral, psychological, or biological dysfunction, and that the disturbance is not only in the relationship between the individual and society" (notice the language used). The manual is said to be dealing with "significant" behaviors and "important" areas of functioning. Potential patients are described as in "pain" or "impaired." Moreover, their conduct is proclaimed to be "dysfunctional" or "disturbed." But aren't these moralistic designations? They clearly exhibit an evaluative component that renders them less than scientifically neutral. And what about the notion that the behavioral, psychological, and biological are to be isolated from the social? How is this to be effected? To judge by the following items, very imperfectly.

Lest one have reservations about the moralism demonstrated by psychiatry, one need only undertake a cursory examination the tome produced by Spitzer and his colleagues. Time and again, it attempts to settle vexing social questions by imperiously decreeing that a troublesome behavior is a "disorder."[3] Rather than admit to a fundamental ignorance, it employs what amounts to *word magic* to affect insights it does not possess. While the ostensible concreteness of its diagnoses makes it appear that the medical roots of particular behaviors solve a host of moral quandaries, none are. The "conduct" disorders are particularly instructive. They are so baldly moralistic that it is difficult to pretend to a physiological connection.

The DSM-III's first paragraph discussing the conduct disorders (which incidentally apply to children rather than adults) begins thus: "The essential feature is a repetitive and persistent pattern of conduct in which either the basic rights of others or major age-appropriate societal norms or rules are violated. [Moreover] The conduct is more serious than the ordinary mischief and pranks of children and adolescents." In other words, if children are very, very bad, a doctor is free to certify that they are suffering from a mental disorder. Among the diagnostic criteria for these labels are the following: (1) physical violence against persons or property, (2) repeated running away from home, (3) persistent serious lying, (4) an avoidance of blaming or informing on companions, (5) thefts outside the home, and (6) chronic violations

47

of important rules at home or at school. As they say nowadays, it does not take a rocket scientist to recognize that these symptoms are of a different sort than those used to identify the measles or a cancer. They represent value judgments, and no more.[4]

Adults are eligible for a separate diagnosis. For them the question is whether they possess an antisocial personality. Here the patient must be at least eighteen years old. If onset of the offending activities is indicated before the age of fifteen, symptoms exactly analogous to those of children apply, whereas the strictly adult criteria include the following: (1) an inability to sustain consistent work, (2) a lack of ability to function as a responsible parent, (3) a failure to respect the law, (4) irritability and aggressiveness as indicated by repeated physical fights, and (5) a failure to plan ahead, that is, impulsivity. Once more, most people would interpret these as moral rather than medical. The same applies to the other personality disorders. Thus the narcissistic personality is (1) preoccupied with fantasies of power, success, and brilliance; (2) is prone to exhibitionism; (3) feels entitled to special favors without having to reciprocate them; (4) engages in interpersonal exploitativeness, and (5) participates in relationships that alternate between the extremes of overidealization and devaluation. Histrionic personalities, who are mostly women, are, by contrast, given to (1) self-dramatization, (2) a craving for excitement, (3) overreaction to minor events, (4) irrational angry outburst or tantrums, (5) vanity, (6) overdependence, and (7) manipulative behaviors. Finally, passive-aggressives, whose diagnosis was later withdrawn due to vehement protests, were typified by (1) procrastination, (2) dawdling, (3) stubbornness, (4) intentional inefficiency, and (5) "forgetfulness."

If this is still not sufficiently moralistic, among the psychosexual disorders are the paraphilias. Their essential feature is that unusual and/or bizarre imagery or acts are necessary for a person to attain sexual excitement. A word of caution is in order in that these patterns are repulsive to most contemporary Americans. Conditions such as fetishism, zoophilia, necrophilia, pedophilia, voyeurism, exhibitionism, and sadomasochism are, it is to be hoped, not the norm. They are "unusual" and strange enough to qualify as "bizarre," but how does this transform them into "illnesses"? Immoral? Yes. Candidates for incarceration? In the case of pedophilia, certainly. Requiring medical treatment? The argument has not been made. Indeed, behaviors such as pedophilia have proved remarkably resistant to such interventions. Where, furthermore, is the proof of a physiological substrate? So far it is AWOL. It has not even been demonstrated that these performances might not be the norm in other cultures.

The difficulty with this galloping moralism is that it overreaches. To cite one instance, it has opened the door for activists to insist that both the "racism" and the "battered woman" syndrome should be included in the DSMs. Take the racism model. Based on no additional information beyond that which was available to the authors of the original manuals, civil rights militants describe persons who hate African Americans because of their skin color as exhibiting a personality disorder. Don't such bigots display signs of disturbed functioning every bit as much as histrionics? Aren't they too rigid, vicious, and out of touch with reality? What is more, the advocates of this listing have no difficulty in developing an inventory of symptoms every bit as compelling as those for other personality disorders. To this the DSM gatekeepers must have reacted by wondering where it would all end. Might not someone diagnosed as a racist claim that he was not responsible for a hate crime because he was the victim of an irresistible compulsion? Obviously he needed medical treatment rather than a jail sentence. Indeed this scenario is so plausible that it has been the basis of several episodes of the television program *Law and Order*.

What then do the disorders inscribed in the DSMs have in common? For many entries it is no more than that a majority of physicians have agreed they fall within their purview. Conventional moralists at heart, they are prepared to lend their prestige to censuring socially troublesome conduct. But only up to a point. The moralism and the lack of a demonstrable physiological etiology of many so-called mental disorders are indisputable. But so are conditions that are not included. Unfortunately, given the reigning definition of psychiatric disorders, a baseball player's inability to hit a curve ball could qualify for citation, as might being unlucky in love. Nor do the diagnoses that are embraced teach us much about their social precursors. Being essentially evaluative, they do not, of themselves, explain why they have been incorporated in the compendium. Nor is it likely are their social connections would be clarified when these were from the outset denied. All that seems clear is that the product before us represents the current state of a cultural evolution. As honored members of a modern Western society, physicians happily assimilate its standards. In fact, neither the demands of science, nor the requirements of humanity, dictated that their commitments would unfold as they did. It was a particular history that pushed their guidebook in the directions it took, even though much of this was accidental. Had not sociologists, for instance, abdicated their responsibilities, the heirs of hospital superintendents might not have had the opportunity to make their ethical opinions decisive.

Before closing this section, it must be observed that psychiatrists are neither remarkably moral nor immoral. Nor are they uniquely socially informed. Admittedly more intelligent than most, neither their training nor their personal experiences prepare them for the role of moral arbiters. Would-be doctors endure an undergraduate and graduate education that tests their ability to memorize reams of data. Courses in biochemistry, anatomy, and physiology are enormously complex, but are not geared toward explicating interpersonal relationships. Physicians may on their own read history, literature, and economics, but their on-the-job experience is limited to hospitals, clinics, and private offices. How does this add up to understanding politics, marital disputes, or bureaucratic hazards? Furthermore, although doctors vow not to cause harm, what has this to do with identifying life's moral intricacies?

Sociological Lapses

At this point it would be nice to report that the social sciences have been waiting in the wings with the perfect solution. This would be nice, but inaccurate. Sadly, many of its practitioners have been mired in a pseudo-scientific moralism just as seductive as the medical variety. Also given to a trendy leap in the dark, they failed to live up to the original promise of empiricism. Rather than explore the social antecedents of personal distress, many have been preoccupied with macro-social speculations. More invested in reforming society than understanding the mechanics of social organization, the archetypal sociologist, for instance, does not ask why people become unhappy. Indeed, the neo-Marxists within the discipline think they already know. They are convinced that capitalism is the cause of most human hardships—that it is responsible for such assorted ills as exploitation, alienation, and commodification—but these answers lie within the realm of ideology, not empirical investigation.

Social science began in reaction to the Industrial Revolution. Educated observers began to feel uneasy in a world where the old verities were disappearing. Fewer people were living on the land, with many more earning a living in newfangled factories. Worst of all, the insecurities of accelerating change appeared to be destroying the social solidarities of yore. Laymen felt cut off and unprotected in a way that demanded attention. To this intellectuals responded by calling for greater concern with social issues. Highly idealistic, they trafficked in utopian schemes more notable for what they rejected than what they demonstrated. Of these, Karl Marx was to become most prominent, but Rousseau, Comte, Saint-Simon, and Nietzsche also contributed to the mix.

The result was a legacy of melodramatic rebelliousness. Hysterical charges of oppression collided with ethereal visions of salvation in a manner that was to culminate in such heady promises as those of the postmodernists, the feminists, and the antipoverty warriors. Prone to dividing the world into heroes and villains, reformers clamored to don the white hats of good guys. More concerned with how social movements work than with whether these do any good, they assume that their own motives were so pure that anything they chose will inevitably be best for everyone.

Where does this leave sociology, in particular, relative to explaining "mental illness"? Many of its devotees have preferred remedies that identify a culprit worthy of being hated. The Marxists, of course, have their villains. Capitalists are obviously rapacious rogues. Utterly bereft of compassion, they compete to deprive the poor of their last vestige of happiness. Greedy beyond rational measure, they cheat their workers and leave them with just enough time and treasure to survive from day to day. Thus falsely persuaded that they were at fault for their troubles, proletarians inexorably become depressed and anxiety-ridden. Reduced to selling out their own souls, they treat themselves as objects of commerce, thereby condemning themselves to empty, hopeless lives.

Psychologists and anthropologists often appropriate a different set of scoundrels. One of these is the "schizophrenogenic" mother. She was once thought responsible for driving her children crazy, typically by trapping them in a double bind. As Gregory Bateson explained, some mothers were so incapable of empathy that they demanded their children behave in contradictory ways. Thus, when a child expressed love, the mother pushed him away, but when he held back, she accused him of not caring. Either way he could not win, with the result that he retreated from reality. A close second in cruelty was the refrigerator mom. She was so emotionally cold that her children never experienced what it is to share feelings with another human being. In this case, it was Bruno Bettelheim, who theorized that the consequence was childhood autism. These youngsters found that the best way to stay alive was to cut themselves off from other human beings and barricade themselves in an "empty fortress."

Also popular was the contention that mental illness is a myth. When the psychiatrist Thomas Szasz contended that people with "problems in living" were being shunted into a psychiatric slavery, social scientists provided an enthusiastic audience. Clearly, physicians had invented disease entities such as schizophrenia as a means of discrediting troublesome individuals. R. D. Laing was evidently correct in asserting that the so-called mentally ill were guilty of nothing less than possessing insights denied by the ostensibly sane. In their innocence, they, like the child who saw through the sham of "The Emperor's New Clothes," exposed the foibles of the powerful and therefore had to be silenced. David Rosenhan provided the "proof." As a respected Stanford psychologist, he sent a bevy of confederates into mental hospitals with the instructions that they pretend to be experiencing hallucinations and delusions. After being admitted, they were to revert to their normal selves. If mental illness really were a disease, they would then presumably be released. But this did not happen. The students' protestations of sanity were interpreted as additional signs of disorder, and they remained behind locked doors. Rosenhan and his admirers quickly concluded that there was no there, there. If psychiatric conditions existed only in the eye of the beholder, they were nothing at all.

For most sociologists, this was not news. Their governing analysis of mental illness was as a species of "deviance." To be deviant was to violate social norms. Crazy people obviously did this with panache. They ran naked through the streets even though there were rules against this. They talked to themselves in public—without the benefit of cell phones. They disrespected the rich and powerful—without so much as a by your leave. As a result, psychiatrists, to their shame, medicalized this deviance. Themselves among society's ruling elite, they created a pseudo-scientific mythology to excuse oppressing people because they were different. All that was needed was stop persecuting people with these arbitrary standards, and their panoply of artificial diseases would evaporate like a morning fog. Once medicalistic categories were renounced, the conditions the supposedly identified would fade to nothingness.

In the vanguard of the forces arrayed against medicalization were advocates of labeling theory. They contended that there were two sorts of deviance, the primary and the secondary. The first sort referred to rule-breaking per se and the second to the consequences of being designated a rule-breaker. It was the second sort about which they fretted. Originally applied to explaining the workings of criminal justice, labeling theory argued that many individuals became criminal only after they had been swept up into the courts and prisons. Thus someone who committed a minor offense, after having been labeled a felon, might thenceforward regard himself as one. With his self-image permanently damaged, he would fall victim to a self-fulfilling prophecy. Convinced he was bad, he would in effect rub this in everyone else's face. Except, declared the labeling theorists, there was a means of ending this cycle. Since a person's spoiled image was created by the justice system, it could reverse the injury by refusing to label him in the first place. Rather than empowering police officers to apprehend wrongdoers, social resources could more profitably be allocated to providing fragile egos with the supports required to grow stronger. Prevention, not punishment, was the key.

For a while, labeling theory was so widely admired that Thomas Scheff appropriated it to explicate mental illness. This condition too was more prevalent than necessary because of secondary deviance. Almost everyone, alleged Scheff, behaved strangely from time to time. But if left alone, these idiosyncrasies would peter out with little harm done. If, however, they were thrust into the mental health system, the label thereby acquired would drive them into madness. A combination of losing their freedom, and being treated as if they were crazy, would make it impossible to behave normally. In the worst cases, they would become "institutionalized." Convinced of an innate weakness, they would become utterly dependent on the persons holding them in captivity. Here too the solution was simple: stop sending people to mental health facilities—especially against their will. Radical deinstitutionalization was the way to reduce an essentially iatrogenic plague.

To his immense credit, Scheff did not stop there. Unlike many of his colleagues, he decided to investigate mental health at greater depth. Firsthand experience soon convinced him that schizophrenia was not a con job. It really was an illness that caused tremendous distress to those who descended into it. More than this, Scheff entered training to become a therapist. In the process, he discovered that some of the perspectives pioneered by mental health professionals were sociologically valid. Especially impressed with the works of John Bowlby, he decided that disruptions in attachment processes were responsible for much personal anguish. Regrettably, this dalliance in the territory of sociology's self-professed enemy consigned him to a loss of professional prestige. Now speaking a language with which most of his colleagues were unfamiliar, he was no longer as widely quoted.

Here one encounters another irony. Despite their lack of sociological sophistication and a fascination with moralistic directives, psychiatrists have been in the forefront in exposing the nexus between society and personal distress. Going back to Freud, a plethora of his contributions can be interpreted sociologically. Thus, despite naive speculations about "primal hordes" and "civilization and its discontents," he was acutely sensitive to what was happening between himself and his clients. From this, he forged a pathway to understanding transference and the repetition compulsion. Shortly thereafter, although hated by Freud, and therefore ejected from the psychoanalytic community, Alfred Adler came even closer to the truth by identifying power, as opposed to sex, as the most potent source of individual pain. His inferiority complex was nothing less than prescient. Later Harry Stack Sullivan correctly emphasized the role of socialization and interpersonal relationships in creating personal difficulties. Similarly, a contemporary of Sullivan, Karen Horney blazed the way to comprehending interpersonal negotiations.

Then, of course, there was John Bowlby. His researches into the importance of mothering, and subsequently into attachment and loss, were remarkable. Although he at first encountered skepticism, his empirical bent enabled him, and his collaborators, to unearth significant clues to what can go wrong in people's lives. Anthropologically sophisticated, and aware of both micro- and macro-dimensions, he pointed psychology and sociology in entirely new directions. Happily, the work of Elizabeth Kubler-Ross and George Brown later supplemented his. Her investigations of death and dying demonstrated the predictable stages of mourning, while his studies into the consequences of childhood losses helped explicate the vulnerability to adult depressions.

Besides the contributions of these individuals, it would be remiss not to acknowledge the advances inaugurated by other innovative schools of thought. More interdisciplinary than previous developments, the marriage and family movement led the way to treating natural groups. Before it arrived on the scene, many therapists recommended against working with families on the grounds that this contaminated efforts to help individuals. However, once families were admitted to the consulting room, alert practitioners became aware of such dynamic features as triangulations and enmeshments. Closely allied to this was the emergence of alcoholism counseling. Although many traditionalists eschewed treating addicts in the belief that they were not prepared to make significant changes, their insistent demands for help stirred fresh currents within the helping professions. This, in turn, brought about a greater appreciation of the social roles played by addicts and their families. Although theoretically incomplete, clinical observations about "family heroes," "mascots," "codependents," and "enablers" introduced a flood of new data.

Next, it must be confessed that sociologists have been historically derelict in their duty to study social emotions. On the false assumption that feelings are strictly psychological, these have frequently been ignored. Content to delve into the cognitive realms highlighted by symbolic interactionists, these social scientists mistakenly believed it unnecessary to understand how emotions coordinate human activities. Nowadays this mind-set is crumbling. Sociologists today realize that emotions are interpersonally transmitted. This has opened up fresh prospects for understanding the connection between private passions and interpersonal losses. Today's investigators are therefore better situated to appreciate how intense emotions facilitate—prevent—the reorganization of social relationships and not incidentally create—remove—personal distress.

The application of social insights to personal distress was postponed not merely because of psychiatric self-interest. While it is true that physicians allowed their professional allegiances to override their scientific aspirations, they received covert assistance from many social scientists. Themselves closet moralists, the latter voluntarily donned blinders analogous to those of their medical colleagues. More intent on criticizing contemporary social arrangements than in pursuing the less romantic task of investigating the unconscious dynamics of human groups, they evaded the sometimes frightening task of dealing with personal pain. As a consequence, breaking out of this self-imposed prison is long past due.

Fortunately, several noted sociologists have identified the importance of interpersonal losing as an element in emotional difficulties, even if they have not explicitly recognized it as "losing." One of these, namely, Allan Horwitz, is among the most perceptive of contemporary investigators into mental illness. He, as well as Peter Conrad, has been very clear in pinpointing the weaknesses of the medical model of personal distress. Instead of merely decrying illegitimate efforts to medicalize deviance, Horwitz has sought to make subtle distinctions and thus to clarify the limits of the medical enterprise. More specifically, he has sought to identify the social factors that precipitate personal distress.

In *The Loss of Sadness*, Horwitz and his coauthor Jerome Wakefield sought to illuminate the nonmedical aspects of loss. They attempted to make it plain that loss and sadness are normal aspects of the human condition. When people get sad, this does not automatically mean that they are experiencing the symptom of a psychiatric disorder. Even when they remain distraught for long periods of time, there may be perfectly good reasons for them to do so. What is more, feeling sad is an essential aspect of grieving, and grieving is required when people experience serious losses. In this case, feeling sad helps them to let go of what is lost.

Horwitz and Wakefield state that even when the nature of a loss is not apparent, this does not mean there was no loss. Nor does it mean that a person should fail to experience the sadness appropriate to bereavement. There must, in their opinion, be a distinction between the sadness caused by real-world losses and that caused by physiological dysfunctions. While they admit that the latter occur, they suggest that they are less prevalent than the diagnostic practices of psychiatrists seem to indicate. These sociologists insist that things go wrong in life, some of which provoke distress. Thus, people in love may separate. Similarly, long-term workers may lose their jobs. That which they had, and expected to possess, is suddenly gone, hence they experience the despair of loss. This, however, is not illness.

But Horwitz and Wakefield go further. In exploring the social causes of depression, they write, "Numerous sociological studies indicate that stressful social arrangements typically lead to distress that both emerges and fluctuates in accordance with social conditions. Indeed, the three major general processes that predict high rates of distress correspond to low positions in status hierarchies, losses of valued attachments, and the inability to achieve valued goals." This is surely true. The quality of a person's social ranks, relationships, and roles make an enormous difference. And yet Horwitz and Wakefield fail to distinguish, as clearly as they might, between the consequences of loss and losing. This is an oversight that must be corrected.

The two also implicate the centrality of defeat to the experience of losing when they allude to the concept of "stress." Stress occurs under threatening circumstances, and there is little more threatening than the prospect of a social defeat. All too often, people back down from a social encounter and lose a contest vis-à-vis other human beings because they experience harm and/or dread the possibility of serious harm. To be blunt, they are too frightened to seek the social victories that produce personal contentment and hence do not achieve it.

Notes

1. Mean stress values equal: divorce, 73; marital separation, 65; jail term, 63; death of a close family member, 63; personal injury or illness, 53; marriage, 50; fired at work, 47; marital reconciliation, 45; retirement, 45; change in health of family member, 44; pregnancy, 40; sex difficulties, 39; change in financial state, 38; foreclosure of loan, 30; son or daughter leaves home, 29; trouble with boss, 23; vacation, 13; Christmas, 12.
2. For another take on the medicalization of "sexual disorders," see Jones, J. H. *Alfred C. Kinsey: A Life*. New York: W.W. Norton & Co., 1997.
3. The DSM-IV recognizes this problem. It states, "[A]lthough this manual provides a classification of mental disorders, it must be admitted that no definition adequately specifies precise boundaries for the concept of 'mental disorder.' The concept of mental disorder, like many other concepts in medicine and science, lacks a consistent operational definition that covers all situations."
4. Even more moralistic is the diagnosis for oppositional defiant disorder. It includes indicators such as (1) often loses temper, (2) often argues with adults, (3) often actively defies or refuses to comply with adults' requests or rules, (4) often deliberately annoys people, (5) often blames others for his or her mistakes or misbehavior, (6) is often touchy or easily annoyed by others, (7) is often angry and resentful, and (8) is often spiteful or vindictive.

3

On Losing

Several Things You Will Never Encounter:
- A gaggle of baseball fans doing the wave while gleefully chanting "We are number seventeen!"
- A single woman confiding to her best friend that she hopes to find a man who is a "nice, sensitive loser."
- Parents proudly bragging to the neighbors that their children are failing miserably at school.
- A glowing television biography of an exemplary "loser"; a person so bereft of accomplishment that he or she never achieved a single memorable thing during their entire lifetime.
- A job hunter making it clear that his or her only qualification for a position is that they "screwed up" every employment opportunity they were ever given.
- The president of the United States pinning a medal on a woman for having proven herself the most inept garbage collector in recorded history.

Sore Losers

Everyone hates to lose. Whether are old or young, male or female, tall or short, blond or brunet, smart or stupid, people aim to win. They want to get what they want, when they want it. They also long to be respected. They definitely do not propose to get less than the next guy. Sometimes people settle for a tie, but not if they expect to come out ahead. While it is true that some would-be saints defer to the needs of others, they too want to be the best at what they do—that is, to be more altruistic than others. Even the mentally retarded want to win. The grins on the faces of those who come in first at Special Olympics events testify to this. Conversely, people do not boast about their failures nor savor memories of finishing last. Occasionally individuals look back in amusement at particularly foolish incidents, but they rarely volunteer to reprise them. Indeed, it is so palpable that people detest losing, we take this for granted. However in failing to notice something so universal, we do not factor it into our theories of human behavior.

To state the obvious, losing hurts. Indeed, losing can hurt very badly. As a result, it contributes greatly to human distress. Losses are not physically traumatic, at least, not in the sense of causing observable tissue damage. But they do, it seems, inflict some physiological harm in the neural pathways altered by their occurrence. Even so, much of the bodily harm is produced indirectly. Some losers commit suicide because their pain is unendurable. Moreover, significant losses can compromise the immune system. Still getting the worst grade in class does not cause a visible wound to the brain. Likewise, although bringing up the rear can initiate a gnawing sensation in the gut, this is not because the stomach's integrity has been violated. Undoubtedly, the sting of losing is so general that we do not ask why it hurts. To the contrary, we are so inured to the phenomenon, it seems to require no explanation. Yet it is unlikely that lower animals experience the same sorts of reaction. Crabs, in all probability, do not suffer a wrenching knot in the midsection when driven off a patch of sand by another crab. That we do have immense repercussions for our personal satisfaction.

Conversely, people love to win. Winning is fun. Winning provides a warm glow that has sometimes been described as better than sex. People lust after victories and enjoy consorting with winners. Whereas losers are shunned, those who finish first have bevies of friends. Meanwhile, if losing is traumatic, winning is therapeutic. It makes pains disappear and provides a physiological barrier against disease. It is therefore not surprising that people seek victories. More unexpected are other responses to losing. Consider what it means to be a "good loser." While "sore" losers kick up a fuss, good ones accept their predicament graciously. They do not demand a recount, nor punch the winner in the nose. Instead of getting angry, they adjust to an awkward situation and proffer their congratulations to the victor. Yet young children, who have not yet learned to be good losers, support the theory that these adult courtesies are acquired behaviors. People learn to be nice to those who beat them despite wanting to do otherwise. Even so, good manners are widely attained. This suggests that learning to tolerate defeat is a widespread phenomenon; one as normal as the childish inclination to rebel.

Also remarkable, given our predisposition to abominate losing, is how often everyone does. Sooner or later, the most consistent winners stumble upon a bad day. One year a Muhammad Ali is the best boxer in the world, but several years later his movements are halting. No longer able to float like a butterfly or sting like a bee, even had he not been afflicted with Parkinson's disease, time would have robbed him of his title. It might be imagined that this would prompt people to reduce their exposure to loss. After all, the fewer times they open themselves to the possibility of being beaten, the less frequently will they have to deal with its pain. In fact, this is what people do. Nevertheless, in their quest for victory, they also do the opposite.

Let us start with avoidance. When people foresee a loss, they commonly evade it by arranging to be someplace else. The game of tennis furnishes an example of this penchant. As a zero-sum activity, when it is played someone wins while someone else loses. The result is that potential players do not pair up indiscriminately. Usually those on opposite sides of the net possess abilities not too different from one another. Were this otherwise, the inferior player would face a humiliating defeat. Unequipped to give a good account of themselves, they would tremble at the imminence of disgrace. Rather than allowing this to happen, they choose a more appropriate opponent, that is, someone against whom they stand a better chance. Similar strategies are adopted in the game of love. Willard Waller pointed out years ago that when dating, people seek partners with assets similar to their own. Men hate to be shot down by a *Perfect 10* who considers them beneath her station. Nor do women relish waiting for the phone call from Mr. Wonderful that never comes. Far better to remain within one's own league. The potential rewards may not be as great, but it is more comfortable not having to worry about living up to elevated expectations.

It would therefore seem strange for people to create opportunities to lose. And yet they do. Why else have human beings devised so many venues for interpersonal rivalries? Nowadays the self-esteem movement has condemned competition as gratuitously harmful and recommended cooperation in its stead. Forward-looking little leagues no longer keep score and at the end of the season award all of the participants' trophies. Nevertheless even the youngest players know better. They can tell the good hitters from the bad and the winning teams from the losers.

I discovered this while still in graduate school. At the time, I did an observational study of a New York City grammar school. One of the classes monitored was a kindergarten. Before entering it, the teacher cautioned me that in her room competition was against the rules. There were no grades, and none of the children were praised for doing better than others. It soon developed that she was as good as her word. Whenever a pupil boasted about an achievement, she gently guided it toward a more constructive activity. All the same, the students set up ranking schemes of their own. After carefully checking to make sure she was not in their vicinity, they took out their workbooks to determine who accomplished the most. Needless to say, the one with the largest number of pages completed was considered the "winner." At one point, a small group became particularly secretive. Huddled in a circle so that others could not see, they compared the length of their stockings to see who had the longest pair. Needless to say, the winner was overjoyed, while the losers looked glum.

When it comes to devising ways to determine who is best, people are amazingly inventive. Thus, we have created all manner of sporting events. Contestants will race any sort of vehicle or straddle any sort of creature to determine who crosses the finish line first. Automobiles, boats, skateboards, skis, horses, dogs, pigeons, or cockroaches will all do. People even enthrone winners by betting on which raindrop will slide down a window fastest or who can spit the farthest.

What is the purpose of all this? Why concoct circumstances in which most of the participants fail? The answer turns out to be a cliché. "Hope," we are told, "burns eternal in the human breast" because it does. Hope keeps gamblers trooping to Las Vegas and prompts small-time operators to stand in line to "invest" in state lotteries. The players intellectually understand most will lose, but the mere rumor of a huge payoff sets hearts fluttering. In short, people risk losing because their desire to win is so fervent. They recognize that the odds are against them, but don't care. They want to be best, too much to consider the alternative. Just thinking about the possibility of coming in first warms their insides. The same is true with love. A person in quest of winning this sweepstake will kiss squadrons of frogs despite recurring discouragement. As they say, "It is better to have loved and lost, than never to have loved at all."

To this must be added another characteristic of losing. Most people consider the condition temporary. When things go wrong, they anticipate a turn for the better. As good losers, they defer to the winner, but bide their time for a more propitious moment. Later on they will be stronger than whoever has beaten them today. Back in the early 1950s, the Brooklyn Dodgers were the lovable losers of organized baseball. Even when they did well, they came up short. Worst of all, they developed the infuriating habit of losing to the archrival Yankees in the World Series. To their fans they were "Dem Bums." Nevertheless, at the end of each disappointing season, a familiar cry would go up. "Wait till next year!" was the perennial chant. Next year they would get lucky. Next year their skills would improve and take their rightful place as winners. To the rest of world, the Dodgers were also-rans, but this did not render their supporters supine. Nor did it mean that they were prepared to give the Yankees a free ride. Yes, they hoped for success, but more than this, they were prepared to inflict losses if they could. And then it would be their turn to gloat!

Loss

Loss and losing; the words are similar, but the concepts seem worlds apart. "Losing" is something that happens in competition with somebody else; there is a contest between you and them, and you beat them or they beat you. The more soundly you win, of course, the better off you usually are. A "loss," on the other hand, represents something you once had but that is now gone. Once upon a time, this thing or person belonged to you, but no longer does. This too, needless to say, is terrible. Yet beyond this, what is the connection? Is there something loss and losing have in common? The answer is that they are indeed closely associated. They are, as it were, opposite sides of the same coin. But before we investigate this bond, let us examine the nature of loss a bit further. The best place to begin is with John Bowlby. Although decades old, his studies on the topic remain the gold standard. Originally fascinated by the phenomenon of mothering, he set out to demonstrate that good mothering was essential for mental health. In a society where women were rapidly being liberated to join the workforce, he was certain the quality of the linkage between them and their offspring was critical to adult functioning. The deeper he delved, however, the more he encountered the issue of "separation." It loomed large in the future prospects of infants, especially when coupled with "loss."

Today it seems strange, but a half century ago most experts were certain that young children did not experience depression. They were not believed to possess the mental or emotional equipment necessary to go through the same sort of suffering as grown-ups. More resilient than vulnerable, they were thought to bounce back from calamitous events without sustaining long-lasting damage. This was one of the first myths Bowlby sought to explode. Children did get depressed. Even infants became deeply sad. In fact, they might become so melancholy that the emotion became life threatening. The very young, he discovered, were susceptible to marasmus. If the circumstances of their life were sufficiently dire, they lost the will to live. They literally refused to eat and wasted away until they expired. Nowadays this is often termed a "failure to thrive," but Bowlby made it plain that at least sometimes it was a manifestation of deep depression.

What Bowlby and his associates were also able to demonstrate was that childhood grief was correlated with significant separations; ergo, the title of his tripartite treatise, *Attachment and Loss*. He theorized that if the bond between a parent (usually the mother) and a child was broken, the toddler would mourn its passing. If the loss was sufficiently calamitous, the endpoint might be mortality. Yet even if it were less devastating, it created an emotional vulnerability that could express itself years later. The child who survived this desolation might later find it difficult to cope with the endemic losses of adulthood. Instead of adjusting to unfortunate situations, he or she might enter a mysterious depression. Naive observers judged this reaction to be inappropriate in that the magnitude of recent events seemed inadequate to provoke it. They would be unaware that a long dormant pain augmented the current hurt. Were this true, it would explain many depressions by linking them with no longer visible social circumstances.

Bowlby quite logically began to inquire into the reasons why childhood separations were so destructive. Entering the realm of ethology, he noted the similarity between the behaviors of human and animal babies. Konrad Lorenz had recently popularized the phenomenon of imprinting in which a newborn creature, usually a fledgling bird (geese in his case), glommed on to the first large organism moving in its vicinity. If this were a human being, the infant nevertheless followed along as if this were the parent. It was in this manner that Lorenz himself became the surrogate mother for a string of tagalong goslings. What also seemed to be true is that imprinting occurred during a window of opportunity. If the potential parent-figure appeared before or after a certain moment, nothing happened. It was only during a biologically imposed period of sensitivity that bonding occurred.

With human beings there was no imprinting per se, but a sequence of what Bowlby dubbed "attachment behaviors." Child-watchers were long aware of what was called "stranger anxiety." Along about their seventh month, babies cried when an unfamiliar figure appeared before them. Before this time, they made little distinction between persons they knew and ones they did not. Both were allowed to pick them up and feed them with little fuss. Afterwards, for a period of a year of more, strangers aroused intense fear. Their mere sight sent a child scurrying for mommy, there to hold on with terrified fervor. Bowlby realized that this clinging behavior was critical. What was at stake was not merely a dread of outsiders, but a threat to the child's attachment to specific individuals. Babies developed strong bonds with particular others and utilized these as a source of security. Bowlby speculated that this was an evolutionary device for protecting newly mobile infants from the hazards faced in a hunter-gatherer society. In what he identified as the human zone of environmental adaptedness, unattended infants were vulnerable to a host of dangers. Snakes might strike out from the underbrush or eagles swoop down to carry them off to the jungle canopy. Then too, if lost, they might be in jeopardy from unrelated human beings. The safest course was to stay close to one's mother and hurry to her side whenever an unfamiliar hazard appeared. Were this the case, it would make perfect sense for separation to feel devastating. From the child's point of view, it seemed life threatening and was therefore to be avoided.

To this information, Bowlby was to add data about actual childhood separations. He and his colleagues learned that when children were parted from their mothers as by her hospitalization, the children suffered. If, after the two bonded, she were physically absent for a sustained period of time, the toddler protested against her nonappearance and eventually entered a grieving process. The child looked for all the world depressed, and if the mother subsequently reappeared, she was greeted not with joy, but anger. It was as if the child were saying the following: Where have you been? How dare you desert me! Longitudinal studies later determined that these youngsters were indeed more vulnerable to depression. Although no one intended injury, the mother's departure was a loss—almost a death—that left its mark.

Even this, however, was not enough for Bowlby. He commissioned further studies to determine if there was something in the nature of the parent–child bond that made some attachments more secure than others. Struck particularly by the ethnographic studies of Mary Ainsworth, he concluded that "responsive" parenting was this element. Ainsworth, in her observations of Uganda mothers, noticed that some women were better caregivers than others. The good ones were more in tune with their infants than their less effective peers.

They noticed their babies' discomfort and made efforts to relieve it. The two central components of responsiveness were an empathetic sensitivity to the child's situation and the motivation to do what was needed on the child's behalf. Were this not so, it could reasonably be said a parent was not there for her baby. Despite her physical presence, in a real sense her child was alone. With needed protections unavailable, the neonate might as well be unaccompanied. This was then experienced as a loss. Because when he or she cried and no one came, the child resorted to precisely the same reactions as those whose mothers disappeared into a hospital.

These grief reactions also became a focus of study. Bowlby was aware that Freud had earlier written about the association between depression and mourning. In his monograph *Mourning and Melancholia*, Freud argued that depression was akin to grief. Now Bowlby took up the challenge and sought to put this observation on a more scientific footing. Taking a fresh look at the available materials, he systematized what he encountered. Grief, he decided, followed a predictable course. It began with a period of denial. At first a child faced with a loss refused to belief it. Mommy was not really gone. Maybe she was just around the corner or hiding under the couch. Children often began by looking for a parent suddenly out of sight. They turned their heads and craned their necks hoping to get sight of her. Sometimes they picked up pillows and looked underneath; sometimes they pushed people aside to see if she were concealed behind them. If this did not work, the child entered a protest phase. He or she began to cry and demand that mommy reappear. Were this to fail, the crying grew louder and took on an unmistakably angry tone. Were someone else to attempt to comfort the child, he or she struck out at this Good Samaritan. Instead of experiencing relief, the protest was now directed at the would-be helper. The message was thus: How dare you not bring my mommy back! Or perhaps the following: How dare you take my mommy away? These remonstrations were quite persistent, with the child impervious to efforts at allaying them.

Eventually, however, the protests petered out. Gradually they diminished in intensity and extent, and the child grew quietly unhappy. One incident recounted by Bowlby was of a child who sat quietly bouncing a ball against a wall and then catching it. Time after time, it performed the identical ritual. What it seemed to be doing was tossing away a surrogate for its mother and then recovering it. This Bowlby interpreted as a symbolic effort to come to terms with what had happened. The child was, as it were, repeatedly recreating both the loss and its attempts to undo it, thereby resigning itself to the pain. This seemed to be the principal issue in mourning. The grieving person grew terribly sad and in so doing detached themselves from that to which they had been bound. Over and over, the mourner reviewed what had been lost thereby diminishing the anguish of not being able to rescue what was gone.

Only then would a child cross the threshold into the final stage of mourning. Getting there invariably took time and did not arrive without his or her first surviving waves of distress. But eventually acceptance came. The separation was now final. The lost person would not return. The moment at which to revisit the land of the living had at long last appeared. The focus was now on the future, not the past. What was gone was gone for good and might as well never have been. It was this change in mind-set that made the homecoming of a hospitalized mother so distressing. If a child had accomplished an emotional detachment, it was not relieved by her reappearance. Quite the reverse, this specter from ancient times awakened protests long since put to rest. Instead of being able to turn to new relationships, suddenly the child had to resurrect the old. In the same manner, incomplete childhood grief might strive for finality when later elicited by an adult experience reminiscent of the previous loss. Hence the etiology of some adult depressions.

Partial confirmation of Bowlby's ideas came from the research of George Brown. Working with adult women in London, he was able to establish that many had experienced grief and had actually endured childhood separations. The sequence Bowlby hypothesized was not always recapitulated as predicted, but the match was close enough to elicit acknowledgement. Further corroboration was provided by the efforts of Elizabeth Kubler-Ross. A physician involved with dying patients, she too detected an identifiable progression during mourning. Working in institutions for the terminally ill, she discovered that patients who were aware of their condition traversed a sequence of stages similar to those observed by Bowlby. Conceptualizing these as denial, anger, bargaining, depression, and acceptance, she likewise discerned this pattern in the relatives of her patients. Whereas the patients needed to make peace with their imminent demise, those who loved them mourned their prospective and then eventual deaths. Death even more than separation was a loss. A person who died was gone and therefore the ties to him or her had to be severed before the survivors could resume their normal lives. Since her book *On Death and Dying* was first published in 1969, its impact has been sustained. Professionals in the field of thanatology may not agree on the particulars, but the general outlines of her scheme have been confirmed in practice. This, in turn, has provided additional credence for Bowlby's speculations and enlarged their area of application. These have actually gone further afield, being fruitfully employed to explain such things as the predictable stages that afflict divorce. Here too a relationship has been torn asunder and therefore elicits grief. As those who have endured marital dissolution know, the denials, the anger, and the sadness can be as extreme as any following a physical death.

Losing

When we contemplate "losing," we usually think about games or perhaps wars. Individuals enter a conflict and the battle seesaws back and forth until a decision is reached. There is at first the potential for winning, but it evaporates, and the losing is all the more severe for having obviated a hoped for victory. Whatever a player wished to achieve is not attained, and the pain of this shortfall is appalling. Losing takes many shapes, none of them pleasant, but some are as catastrophic as it is possible for a human experience to be. The loser of a total war can be deprived of their home, family, and life. Unlike a game of tennis where there is a tomorrow, for them there is not. All that is left are acres of rubble and miles of desiccated dreams.

If this were all there were to losing, the condition would deserve its bad reputation, but sadly its implications are even broader. People lose contests for social status, come up short in quest of social roles, and are defeated in the pursuit of love. They can, in short, fail to realize any number of significant objectives. Generally how significant these are decides how bereft someone becomes. Typically the more far reaching the consequences, the greater the pain. By the same token, the more important the goal, the more energetic the efforts to prevail. Conversely, the more energetic the struggle, the worse the ensuing disappointment. Almost anything that people desire can be an occasion for losing, but some kinds of objectives are so widely, and predictably, sought that they regularly generate reverses. Many of these have to do with the way societies are constructed. The impulses that drive individuals into establishing these groups also leave them choking on the dust of others who come off better than they.

Let us consider social hierarchies. Even young children are familiar with the concept of social rank, the notion that some come out first and others follow—that some are on top and others at the bottom. Long before they are old enough to leave home, preschoolers engage in competitions to determine who will be the "boss." The winners then attempt to give orders with which the losers are expected to comply. This prerogative, though considered the due of the victor, will nevertheless irritate the loser. They may even rebel by insisting "you're not the boss of me!"

What these youngsters understand is that hierarchies are ordered arrangements. Each person in a hierarchy has an ordinal position relative to the others, and these are associated with comparative advantages and disadvantages. To indicate that someone "comes first," usually indicates that he is "better off," while to say someone is "on top" more emphatically makes the point. In the second formulation, the inference is that greater power is associated with being at the apex of a pecking order. People strive to occupy positions from which they can look down on others. Everyone—at least in his or her imagination—wants to be King of the Mountain. This compulsion comes so naturally as not to be worth mentioning. But this is precisely why it must be mentioned. The reason people fantasize about "ruling the world" is that the prospect is pleasant. Some literally risk their lives in the hope of attaining precedence. History provides ample evidence that it is physically dangerous to rule a state, yet nations are never short of potential candidates.

Also implied, but frequently overlooked, is that there are regular contests for priority. People not only desire to govern the world, but also fight for their share of the spoils. As already indicated, struggles for hierarchical status are zero-sum games. It is impossible for everyone to prevail, for were everyone on top, there would be no top. Much of the pleasure of winning comes from an awareness of getting the better of someone else. The winner has what the loser wants, and this alone is heartening. Conversely, losers hate losing. To be on the bottom is exasperating. The boot of the winner is in your face and their tongue sticks out in your direction. What could be more infuriating? How better to inspire efforts to reverse the decision that led to this impasse?

To repeat, we human beings are hierarchical creatures. We inherently recognize how painful losing is because we have experienced the feeling or, at minimum, feared we might. Utopian social theorists write rapturously about a future in which everyone is equal, where no one is envious of their neighbors and therefore where conflicts cease. This, however, is an absurd dream. It ignores a universal human propensity. The only way that it could come to pass is if people stopped being people. Ironically if they did, they would not need to engage in reveries about being rescued from their predisposition for conflict. They would not need to fantasize about total equality were they less vigorously impelled toward inequality.

Less recognizable as a font of losing is the human predisposition toward social roles. Human societies are not composed of a collection of indistinguishable clones. People differ not only in size and shape, but also in the tasks they perform. At the very moment that sociology emerged as a distinct discipline, one of its founders, Emile Durkheim, propounded the importance of a social division of labor. Obviously, in modern mass societies, people differ in the jobs they occupy. There are butchers, bakers, and candlestick makers; mothers, fathers, sisters, and brothers; men and women; and the old and the young. Each of these categories is associated with a variety of discrete duties. Moreover, these tasks tend to be complementary. Farmers grow food that they (indirectly) exchange with factory workers who reciprocate by participating in the construction of the tractors farmers require to till their fields. Each benefits from this sort of transaction, and in the end, it is a multiplicity of comparable transactions that enables large-scale societies to survive. Every modern society is composed of a huge assortment of task-defined bricks. These are, despite the carping of critics, their essential building blocks.

Task differentiation actually goes back to the dawn of humankind. Hunter-gatherers were obviously divided into hunters and gatherers, but they also developed other specialties. Grave goods and wall paintings suggest that the role of shaman was present early on. Meanwhile observations of contemporary nomadic bands indicate that particular skills, such as that of honey-gatherer, are concentrated in the hands of identifiable individuals. It also made sense that as tool making became more complex, some persons, being more competent than others, engaged in more tool preparation.

Assuming that there is a social division of labor, the question arises as to how specific tasks are allocated. Among social insects, biology is the determining factor. Worker ants are sterile females who perform a diverse series of jobs depending upon their age.

Shortly after they hatch, they participate in feeding and grooming their egg-bound siblings, but later on they take part in foraging expeditions. No one has to tell them when to do what. The program they follow is built into their genes and activated by chemical transmitters passed along by nest-mates. Some ants, for example, the male drones, are predestined to mate with queens preordained to produce thousands of offspring. But human beings are different. Our biological heritage is not this constraining. The talents and predispositions we inherit influence, but do not decree, the roles we perform. The specifics of our divisions of labor are evidently shaped via interactions with other human beings. Although we too respond to chemical agents such as pheromones, their functions are trivial when compared with those of social insects.

What then is decisive in human role formation? People, it happens, engage in what are best described as role negotiations. They make demands, and counterdemands, that in most cases eventuate in a mutual decision to partition their chores in a particular fashion. Human roles are shared with role partners. The role of *husband* is dependent upon that of *wife*, and vice versa, while that of *teacher* is contingent on that of *student*, and vice versa. More than anyone else, these role partners mold the types of jobs the parties respectively hold. They are the ones who tell each other what they should be doing, and what, in short, is expected of them. They are also the ones who inform each other about whether they are doing this correctly. This, of course, does not always run smoothly. Role partners can be uncomfortable with what is demanded of them. In this case, they may protest these requirements. Such resistance can, in fact, modify what is asked. This in turn, may induce counterdemands that adjust a partner's further responses. What, in effect, emerges is a contest to determine their respective roles. But we have already become acquainted with a potential consequence of this sort of rivalry—that is, some players win and others lose.

Roles are not all of the same caliber. Some have bigger payoffs than others. While a division of labor may benefit society as a whole, this does not ensure that everyone benefits equally. Indeed, some may not profit at all. They are sacrificed for the greater good of the community. Nevertheless, few submit without demurral. In the real world, they may dissent with considerable vigor. In essence, they fight for better roles. Thus, they make efforts to become physicians rather than garbage collectors or business executives in preference to street persons. These labors occur out in the marketplace and within the confines of the home. Witness how children compete to see who will wash the dishes or take out the trash. Eventually some will emerge better off than others. They then take satisfaction in their good fortune, whereas those who suffer defeats nurse their grievances. They have lost and do not like it.

To experience reverses in role negotiations is no small setback. Confinement in a suite of unsatisfying tasks is tantamount to being a major league loser. People hate such outcomes. They hate them so intensely that when they are their victims, they may describe life as "meaningless." Nothing seems worthwhile when every day is filled with reminders that one is not doing what one once dreamed of doing. People ask, "What is the point?" "Where is this leading?" Then they slink off into a corner to brood about the injustice of their fate.

Another manifestation of losing is being unsuccessful at love. Bowlby's starting point, after all, was interpersonal attachments. What first attracted his interest was how small children react to emotional separations. Clearly, this assumed that there was a bond to be broken. Full-blown adult love can be still more problematic. It may, for instance, fail to develop. A person can spend a lifetime seeking a soul mate who never appears. Dozens, and perhaps hundreds, of hopeful encounters terminate in disappointment. A potential partner is too smart or stupid, too attractive or ugly, too honest or deceitful, too successful or impecunious. Worse still, he or she possesses all the right characteristics, but finds the potential lover unacceptable. Somehow the rating–dating game never concludes with a balanced equation. When this occurs, the bottom line is not a shrug of the shoulder and a relieved "who cares." Unrequited love hurts. It is a form of losing, and those who experience it feel like losers. As long as they desire love, but are frustrated in the chase, the feeling is inexorable.

Love can also inflict defeat after a person has entered a relationship. Because there is no guarantee the individual with whom one hooks up is "the right one," losing can occur in the midst of an attachment. Bad relationships do not meet needs or fulfill dreams. Those who belong to an ill-matched couple may not be alone, but may as well be. People who hate their partners, or are hated by them, feel like losers. If they are honest, they will not deny the pain, and if they cannot find a way out, they will feel inadequate. To be trapped in an abusive relationship is demoralizing. Human beings who are beaten, or ridiculed, have their self-images undermined and their self-confidence ruined. They begin to wonder if they are capable of winning and may subsequently engage in behaviors that make it less likely they ever will.

Up to this point, we have been reviewing the chief structural determinants of losing, but cultural factors also create difficulties. In sociological terms, a social structure is an enduring pattern of interpersonal relationships. It is an observable configuration of social dealings that prescribes who should do what with whom. Hierarchies are obviously social structures in that they rank people and determine relative subservience. Social roles are also structures in that they organize social tasks. And so are the personal relationships that govern who will have sex with whom. Cultures, by contrast, are learned and shared patterns of behavior. They include such things as languages, social norms, value judgments, belief systems, technological developments, and esthetic standards. Culture, as it were, specifies how people do what they do, whereas structure tells them with whom to do it. A social norm, for example, indicates that some foods are to be eaten with a fork and not a spoon, while a belief system teaches that an anthropomorphic God must be propitiated lest the crops rot in the field. Unfortunately, not all cultural expressions are created equal. Some are better at satisfying human needs than others. While what works to protect a community differs with the time and circumstances, some styles of life are more destructive than others. To assert that the adverse ones convert people into losers is not a stretch. Obviously, against their wishes, they are trapped in dysfunctional patterns that make it impossible to be happy. This is particularly so for belief systems that misrepresent the nature of reality and moral doctrines that prescribe noxious forms of conduct. In both cases, people are led to inflicting self-injuries.

More particularly, people live in cognitive communities. Much of what they know about the world comes from what other people tell them. Whether it is a question about what lies on the other side of the ocean or how television sets work, they do not have firsthand experience, but count themselves knowledgeable because others in their society know. While it is impossible for individuals to be everywhere, and hence must depend on the senses of others, a tendency to rely on the authority of third parties is built into human nature. If the right person makes the right sort of allegation, people are primed to believe. The most obvious illustration is religious faith. Who finds it strange that the children of Baptists grow up to be Baptists, while the children of Roman Catholics adopt Catholicism? The pattern is so widespread that it is taken as natural. But why does it occur? Isn't it because children are prepared to take their parents' word on such matters? Or if not their parents, that of the minister whom their parents regard as a religious expert? Children assume the adults controlling their world know what they are talking about. Most of the time this works fairly well, and not just for religion. Science too depends on information transmitted on faith. Although most scientists are adamant that their observations can be empirically tested, in reality this hardly ever happens. Lay people do not attempt to verify what competent researchers assure them is true or not. For them electrons are as much of a mystery as phlogiston ever was.

Nevertheless, difficulties emerge when people associate with the wrong crowd. If the cognitive community to which one is pledged is unworthy of the faith invested in it, the consequences can be devastating. If, for instance, a charismatic leader assures their followers that an alien spaceship is waiting to pick them up just beyond the comet Hale–Bopp, ritualized mass suicide may result. Similarly, if a cult leader persuades their disciples that they are an incarnation of Christ, the end product may be a conflagration in which their children perish. What too of the Islamic fundamentalists who believed Osama bin Laden when he declared the United States of America would crumble once a jetliner flew into the World Trade Center? Or on a less apocryphal note, what of the inner city boys who on the assurance of their friends devote their time to practicing basketball rather than studying their schoolwork? They believe one day they will be millionaire superstars, but isn't it more likely they will be disappointed? In the final analysis, they, and those like them, lose. Because their choices are ill informed, their imagined successes never materialize. When placed in competition with others privy to better information, they come up short.

Another cultural landmine is the misleading moral rule. Although people often confuse the moral with the factual, the two are distinct. Moral rules are prescriptive; they instruct people on how to behave, whereas cognitive beliefs are descriptive; they teach people about what is the case. People may decide to honor one moral recommendation rather than another because the facts are this way rather than that, but as David Hume observed a "should" cannot be inferred from an "is." Nonetheless, one thing the moral and the cognitive have in common is that both derive their clout from community sanctions. People belong not only to cognitive communities but also to moral ones. Baptists not only have convictions about the life of Jesus but also have commitments about how to behave. They agree to respect the Ten Commandments and are unyielding in their support of family values. Roman Catholics, as fellow Christians, uphold many similar principles, but their clergymen are bound by regulations regarding celibacy Baptists are not. Shifting gears a bit, citizens of the United States partake of a social order that takes democratic values seriously. Having in grammar school learned the first part of The Declaration of Independence by heart, they are steadfast in their belief that all men (and women) are created equal and have a right to "life, liberty and the pursuit of happiness." None of the above imperatives, though they differ in emphasis, is troubling. What they prescribe rarely results in loss. In fact, decent moral commitments typically enhance the lives of those who subscribe to them.

Some imperatives, however, are appalling in their impact. Nowadays few Americans think of Nazism as a moral order, but during the 1930s, German school children were taught that it embodied the highest form of human ideals. To show fatalistic courage in defense of the German nation—a nation that represented the zenith of human development—was the noblest achievement to which anyone could aspire. This may sound ludicrous, but the Hitler Youth believed. They believed so fervently that when the Third Reich was about to crumble, they put up a tenacious defense in the ruins of Berlin. Whereas the older combatants had long since become disillusioned, they continued to exhibit faith in the ultimate triumph of their cause. Analogous moral commitments motivate the sacrifices of Palestinian suicide bombers. Their faith in Islam is so strong that they sincerely believe that killing and maiming dozens of innocent women and children is virtuous. Jews and Christians are regarded as so vile that clearing them out like vermin is worthy of instant transport to heaven. Yet in the end, they are as dead as their victims. If this is not a form of losing, what is?

Losing is capable of taking many shapes. Human societies are replete with multiple opportunities to inflict defeats. The fact that we are social creatures enormously enhances our personal powers, but it does so at the cost of exposing us to painful setbacks. Both happiness and unhappiness are woven into the fabric of our social institutions. The good and the bad are not accidentally associated, but the product of the same social mechanisms. Disentangling them is therefore no easy chore. Sadly, sometimes it is even impossible.

The Loss/Losing Nexus

Loss and losing are two sides of the same coin. The disparity between them is not so much in the nature of what happens as in the perspective from which events are viewed. As previously indicated, in the case of loss, something you once had is now gone, whereas with losing there is a contest during which you come out second best. What is this, however, but the difference between fighting for something and fighting against something? With loss, you struggle against giving up that which has been in your possession, while with losing you struggle to obtain that which you desperately want but do not yet possess. In both instances, an attachment is at stake, the distinction being that it has existed in one, but is merely contemplated in the other. Emotionally speaking, there is little difference. That which one hopes to attain is, in a sense, an internal reality, and hence its "loss" can be as wrenching as that which has been more substantive. Feelings are provoked not merely by the tangible, but also—and often with as much potency—by that which is only imagined. The significance of this is that much of our social lives emanates from inner fantasies. Relationships are almost as much in the imagination as between the parties. The upshot is that what they project is frequently that to which they react. Another person's character may therefore be more of a construct than a reflection of who he or she actually is.

Put another way, losing is a form of loss, while loss is a species of losing. First of all, to lose is to experience a loss. That which one was hoping to win has, in a manner of speaking, become part of the self. In framing the goal, it is integrated into a person's psychic equipment. That which is strongly desired thus possesses an authenticity that can be reassuring long before it is attained. Savored in dreams and daylight reveries, it gives life its zest. In a very real way, people are their aspirations—which implies that if they have none, they are nothing. To suddenly find, for instance, that a heart murmur will keep one from joining the military, when one has dreamed of being a soldier since grade school, can be devastating. It can throw one's plans into turmoil and, unless a satisfactory substitute is found, can send one into a monumental funk. Second, a loss is a type of losing. When a bond is ruptured the prospect of standing alone can inspire heroic efforts to reestablish the connection. If this goes badly, the person will feel as if they have lost a battle. Before one's partner went away, they were built into ego's life plans. Upon their loss, the activities in which the two once engaged become impossible. They, as much as the physical other, are gone and cannot be retrieved.

Another of the things loss and losing have in common is that both are painful. Frustrating in the extreme, each forces a person to live with a situation one loathes. They are also both saturated with conflict. People fight against them with an intensity that can be consuming. Finally both are resolved through similar mechanisms. The sequence that Bowlby describes applies equally to loss and losing. If a death cannot be resolved except by mourning that which is gone, losing a role negotiation or a hierarchical battle cannot be resolved without protests and grief. Adjusting to failure entails letting go of an aspiration every bit as much as loss can require letting go of a deceased companion. In the one instance, the process addresses external events whereas the other it focuses on the internal. In fact, both attachments and aspirations are primarily internal. What must change to come to terms with either is primarily inside the self.

Consider the case of bad roles. Persons trapped in bad roles do not start out attempting to develop unpleasant assignments. The social tasks to which they aspired were intended to meet important needs. They wanted to be loved, expected to be admired, and desired physical comfort. And then they found themselves—for the sake of argument—cast in the role of *scapegoat*. Their job within their family of origin was to divert blame from the others. No matter who did what; when things went wrong, they were held responsible and punished. Given this job description, who would seek such a mission? Who would not resist it? Once it is foisted upon someone, despite their best efforts at evasion, a part of them dies. Alternative roles are everlastingly aborted. They expired in the very process of being born. They thus have to be mourned. Indeed, somewhere down the line, a bad role has to be mourned if it is to be superseded. Unless it is, better roles never see the light of day.

Similar considerations apply to hierarchical losses. No matter what their station in life, people aspire to better things. Their eyes look upward when they speculate about where they would like to be. Then the hard facts of life intervene to close off ascending pathways. Once again a potentially bright future dies aborning. Here too a person will find no peace unless they can adjust to diminished prospects. The ache of being a loser becomes intense unless a person finds a way to create emotional distance between themselves and the failure. While this may mean accepting a lower status, it can also presage effective efforts at upward mobility. Still, sometimes it is impossible to win contests for hierarchical priority until one disengages from relationships in which victory is precluded. The sort of thing that can happen is that a child becomes entangled in a battle with a parent who, because of their own insecurities, never allows their offspring to rise up. Only severing this relationship will allow the child to test its mettle against others better prepared to acknowledge its successes. It is changing its attitude toward the parent—as opposed to the parent changing its attitude—that permits a reversal of fortune.

Which brings us to relationships. Bad relationships, like inferior roles and reduced ranks, require the drastic surgery of a mourning process. Unless loyalty to a partner who does not merit loyalty is relinquished, a person's attachment can be a manacle that prevents personal satisfaction. Love that is not loving can be toxic. A selfish partner is like a vacuum cleaner that sucks up everything positive in the environment, while an abusive one converts what should be a cooperative enterprise into a sadistic brawl. Yet unless a person undergoes a period of mourning, they may, like an apprehensive child, cling to the very person who arouses their fears. An anxious attachment, rather than a voluntary one, seems to afford protection, but delivers the opposite.

All these prospective reactions to losing are akin to those associated with loss. The emotional components of the mourning processes that undo these ties are almost identical. Unless these are experienced, and worked through, losing will continue to rankle as much as would a loss that is never addressed. Nonetheless, one of the central elements of mourning is fear. People are frightened of both losses and losing. With loss, the dread is that a security-providing attachment will be torn asunder. It is alarming to look forward to an uncertain future deprived of the sanctuary of a trusted relationship. Facing the world alone is, in fact, dangerous. As members of a social species, we are intuitively aware that we are safer when someone is available to cover our backsides. With losing, the terror is that what we planned would make us happy will not be. Absent a clearly visible alternative, we imagine the worst and agonize that an appropriate social niche may never open up.

Thus bad roles are only marginally superior to no roles at all. No role means dangling in limbo without functional attachments to people who are willing to exchange their services for the ones we provide. A bad role, by contrast, allows for interpersonal commerce, but not the sort desired. To illustrate, in exchange for assuming the blame due them, the role partner of a scapegoat may agree to provide love, but the cost to the beneficiary is to endure penalties they do not deserve. Likewise a low rank can be frightening in that it entails a powerlessness that leaves a person vulnerable to more potent adversaries. To be relatively weak is to be comparatively defenseless. It is to be aware that others have the ability to attack with impunity. Finally, enmeshment in a bad relationship can be as alarming as being without a relationship. A violent role partner is a perceptible source of danger. He is literally capable of murder. Yet the absence of a relationship can feel intimidating, for whereas a brutal partner may promise to reform, a phantom partner promises nothing. To be alone without love is to be isolated and dependent upon one's own resources. Needless to say, not everyone is sufficiently confident to weather the latent fury of a heartless universe.

A second potentially overwhelming emotion associated with mourning is anger. The protest phase leading up to grief is characterized by this feeling. Anger attempts to undo that which was unwanted. If fear is the normal response to danger, anger is the normal reaction to frustration. It is the emotional tool charged with changing the world in a more pleasing direction. Moreover, the more intense the frustration, the more ferocious the anger. Since both loss and losing countermand important goals, both elicit rage. So do dysfunctional roles. The worse the role, the graver the frustration, and therefore the more muscular the anger. It is as if a person trapped in an untenable role declares that "this shall not stand!" They may then go on the attack to ensure that this pronouncement is respected. The same sort of progression may unfold when hierarchical negotiations turn sour. The result here is similarly unwanted and thus triggers an emotional rejoinder aimed at canceling what happened. Overt anger does not always work, but is a natural human retort. Resentment is also aroused by an unrequited infatuation. An unresponsive other is thus put on notice that this behavior is unacceptable and invited to reconsider. This rarely induces love, but occurs nevertheless.

The third major emotional response postulated by Bowlby is sadness. Indeed, sadness and loss seem virtually synonymous. It is difficult to imagine the one without the other. Losing, however, incites no such association. Losing is more closely connected with the battles in which it occurs. Sore losers are not sore because they are sad but because they are angry. Nevertheless, losers do become depressed.

Once they have exhausted their options, the despair can be palpable. Those who follow sporting events are familiar with "the big mo." They recognize that winners get extra motivation from winning, whereas losers become dispirited. In their despondency, their energy levels decline, and plays they might have been able to make in the flush of optimism fall apart. Losers do not complain of being sad; instead, they withdraw from the combat just as do individuals in mourning. The same factors pertain to role loss. When someone recognizes they cannot correct a dysfunctional role or retrieve a fantasized one, melancholy is common. Who is not forlorn when their hopes are dashed? In the circumstances of ordinary living, it may not be possible to display sadness, but that does not confirm its absence. As with athletes in the midst of a game, an overt admission of gloom can be an invitation to pile on. Those who aspire to limiting the damage therefore affect an insouciance that is not genuine. They assume an artificially bright demeanor that seems to say, "I remain a person to be reckoned with so you had better back off lest you lose our next encounter." Flaunting sadness, by contrast, produces either desertion or a further show of aggression. In both cases, the despondent person no longer provokes fear and may therefore be treated any way the winner chooses.

Comparable events follow hierarchical losing. Individuals who are forced to occupy the lower rungs of a ranking system frequently relinquish the impulse toward social mobility. It is no accident that poor people suffer from depression significantly more than their betters. Fatalism robs them of the initiative needed to get ahead and confines them to the bottom of the heap. Plainly, when efforts at proving oneself end in defeat, it is disheartening. After a while, one suspects that nothing will work and hence one gives up. Lastly, failed relationships too occasion misery. Listening to any country music radio station will corroborate that losing at love is heartbreaking. Gloom and doom are the wages of an unrequited quest. A forlorn lover may conclude that contentment is impossible. With the rose-colored glasses of love replaced by smokier lenses, alternative relationships fail to beckon, and they sit in a dark corner nursing a warm beer while reviewing the missteps that led to this awful fate.

Fear, anger, and sadness are the terrible triumvirate of the mourning process. They are also the key to resocialization. People recover from a severe loss by grieving that which is gone and then returning to engage a world now viewed through refreshed eyes. A parallel phenomenon occurs with losing. Whether it is a role, a rank, or a relationship that is lost, resocialization is the appropriate mechanism for cutting one's ties to what never can be, so as to pursue the possible. Unless a person puts losing behind them, old battles keep being replayed with the same old results. Fear and anger that have been resolved are, in essence, a prelude to sadness that severs the bonds preventing a person from moving on. Only when they are relieved of the burden of past failures is it feasible to engage in the interpersonal negotiations that establish better roles, higher ranks, and sounder relationships. Resocialization is the sovereign cure for a spoiled socialization. Because only socialization—that is, a learning interface with other human beings—produces roles, ranks, and relationships, only allowing it to proceed anew, without being slowed by previous impediments, can replace the bad with something better. Only putting the past in the past allows a better tomorrow to develop.

The Social/Suffering Connection

By now it should be obvious that human distress arises from more than medical disorders. When people are anxious or depressed, this does not necessarily implicate a chemical imbalance in the brain. Their suffering is not per se evidence of a mental disease. Social circumstances, when they misfire, are *also* pregnant with personal distress (please note the italicized term "also"). Psychiatric conditions such as schizophrenia, bipolar disorders, and endogenous depressions create terrible anguish, an anguish that needs to be addressed by competent medical treatment, but they are not the only source of human misery. Loss and losing too are productive of immense suffering. Standard accompaniments of the human condition, they predictably introduce displeasure into the lives of almost everyone—and massive concentrations of despair into the lives of some. There are three social routes through which suffering is instituted.

1. Bad roles, ranks, and relationships hurt. When dysfunctional, each fails to meet critical personal needs. They do not succeed in delivering the love, security, respect, resources, or stimulation required for a satisfying life. The scapegoat role, to highlight one dysfunctional status, is replete with mortifying incidents. First, it is dangerous. A scapegoat's personal security is at risk whenever one of their tormentors goes too far in assigning blame. Second, they are deprived of respect by perpetually being portrayed as unworthy of it. Ostensibly having inflicted injury on those they love, they renounce any claim to being taken seriously. Third, why would such a person be loved?

So unloving themselves, why would others reciprocate with greater affection? Fourth, for similar reasons, why would their victims bestow resources upon them? Why would they want to share their treasures or assist them in accumulating their own? Fifth, a scapegoat does not motivate others into participating in mutually invigorating activities. Alleged to be the cause of their distress, they are more likely to avoid them than participate in reciprocally stimulating behaviors. Their attitude will probably be thus: let them stew in their own juices.

Hierarchical disappointments are even more perceptibly painful. The term "loser" bears dour connotations for valid reasons. Losers can count of being at the tag end of whatever is happening. They get chosen last at stickball, are likely not to have a date for the prom, and wind up living in dangerous neighborhoods. Hierarchical failures amass the fewest resources, are allocated the least desirable mates, are not heeded when they make suggestions, and are not relied upon in moments of danger. Why would such a person feel good about themselves? Human beings are not ecstatic when their group ostracizes them. For better or worse, people are more like wolves than birds of prey. For them, being social means being hierarchical. And being hierarchical means feeling distressed when someone finishes behind their peers.

Needless to say, but nevertheless requiring statement, bad relationships hurt. People suffer when they are not loved. If we are a hierarchical and a role-playing species, we are also one that specializes in attachments to specific others. When these bonds turn bitter, we suffer. While bears and tigers mate once a year and then hastily separate from their consorts, men and women participate in long-term love relationships. These may not endure for the eternity of which the partners dream, still they aspire to. Nor do people fancy friendlessness. Given their druthers, almost every human being chooses a time on earth warmed by the love of concerned family and friends. Isolation is tantamount to misery.

2. The mechanisms, through which people develop and maintain roles, ranks, and relationships, when these go wrong also produce distress. Role partners negotiate divisions of labor, rivals for hierarchical preference test their mettle against each other, and potential soul mates participate in courtship processes that may, or may not, work. When these procedures succeed, the participants benefit from the experience. When they do not, these are difficult to endure. Role negotiations, contests for hierarchical priority, and courtships can be bruising affairs. They are not sedate episodes during which people sit and reason

quietly together. To the contrary, there is a lot of pushing and pulling, and a fair amount of bashing of skulls. The stakes are so great that the participants often take things to extremes. Worse still, roles, ranks, and relationship, once established, must be kept in good repair. As a consequence, clashes can persist long after the issues have apparently been settled. Sanctions, frequently harsh sanctions, are administered to make certain the contestants do not stray off the reservation. And because pain is inflicted, pain is experienced. The means through which social stability is achieved are anything but emotionally neutral.

Role negotiations sound civilized. The term "negotiation" appears refined, but in practice is more akin to warfare. People lie, cheat, and steal, if the potential gains are great enough. Similarly, they engage in coercion, manipulation, and emotional blackmail if the need arises. So intent are the parties on winning that they do not notice when a partner has been injured. Deeply affected by the jeopardy they feel, they underestimate the vulnerability of the other. The result is overkill, with the loser assigned a smaller portion than that is required to make certain it is less than that of the winner. Even afterwards the winner may demand evidence that the loser's task is less satisfying than their own. Too cheerful, a demeanor invites reopened negotiations and generates an adjusted settlement less favorable to the loser. This, of course, is achieved by inflicting more pain, because only this induces the loser to make further concessions. In some cases, role negotiations are literally "no-win" situations. As with the double bind, one of the partners, usually the more powerful, changes the ground rules at the moment of consummation. Asking for one thing, when it is conceded, the opposite is demanded.

Hierarchical tests of strength are correspondingly jarring. Since they are the central means of being certain about which party is stronger, it is generally necessary for both to go all out. Only a full tilt effort can conclusively establish that the victor is worthy of their triumph. Only then is the loser persuaded to defer to their conqueror. But head-on collisions hurt. And no wonder. They are meant to hurt, for it is when they are sufficiently painful that a threat of their renewal discourages further challenges. Nevertheless, some time later on, when a chink is detected in the armor of the winner, they may break out afresh. The memories of pervious hurts fade and ambition once more reigns. In the meanwhile, in order to remind the loser of their loss, thereby keeping its sting alive, the victor demands periodic signs of deference. The loser must openly acknowledge their inferiority. But proclaiming for all the world to see that one is unworthy is a near death experience. Few self-administered pains hurt more.

Even the apparatus through which relationships are launched can be painful. Thus, dating is not always fun. A dinner and a movie can be excruciating when they are with the wrong person. Other aspects of the courtship process are similarly unnerving: "Does she like me as much as I like her?" "Did I say or do the right thing?" "Do I really want to be with this person for the rest of my life?" And then there are the negotiations through which the deal is finalized. Like all negotiations, these entail a give-and-take that can be unequal. Even at their best, to get something, one must give something. And giving is rarely easy, no matter how advantageous the potential gain. Worse still, when it comes to intimate relationships, the negotiations never end. Some mutual decisions are perpetually in dispute. Couples are often advised that they should never allow the sun to set on an argument. Kiss and make up lest the wounds fester. Yet fester they do when the issues are important.

Whether losses are sustained in hierarchical, social role, or relationship contexts, they can initiate cascade effects. Losing typically begets further losses. Efforts to seek revenge for a defeat or prevent an uprising by the loser frequently create the circumstances for additional setbacks. Reputations are altered, grievances are implanted, and perceptions are distorted as a result of the emotional, cognitive, and volitional consequences of these incidents. Losers, to cite one scenario, come to feel vulnerable and therefore instigate unnecessary defenses, whereas winners can assume they possess entitlements that lead them to invent unnecessary provocations. Even alliances can be modified such that people pick fights in order to keep their coalitions in good repair. They literally come to the aid of a friend, whether or not this is justified, simply to make sure that he or she will be available when there is a need. The upshot is that conflicts capable of being discontinued are not and that mistakes open to correction are intensified. One fight triggers another, which provokes a third, until the players are lugging around gunnysacks of complaints they have little hope of assuaging.

3. Ironically, the third sorts of mechanism through which loss and losing mete out suffering are the corrective devices to which they yield. The grief that enables a loss to be softened is not a joyful experience. The fear, anger, and sorrow that epitomize it are unwelcome harbingers of a better time to come. They too hurt. Indeed, they may

hurt so much people prefer death. In the throes of mourning, people are not aware of where they are going so much as where they have been. What once was intrudes on the agony that is. In many ways, mourning is the quintessential example of human suffering—far more representative than mental illness.

Resocialization is an unhappy process. Relinquishing a dysfunctional role may be necessary for a person's well-being, but is no walk in the park. As a variation of the mourning process, it is, by definition, a time of discomfort. In point of fact, it can be so painful that people spend a lifetime sidestepping it. As we will see in the next chapter, it can feel more like death than death itself. Paradoxically, many kinds of distress usually given a medical interpretation are better understood as aspects of resocialization—or of resocialization gone wrong. Specifically, anxiety and depression often have their origins in resocialization. The mystery and intransigence that surround these erstwhile disorders have their roots in the difficulties inherent in personal change.

Escaping from a hierarchical defeat, just as with role loss, entails what is analogous to a bereavement. If a person is to avoid being trapped in a losing situation, they may need to acknowledge the loss, endure its ignominy, let it go, and then move on to more fruitful opportunities. Part of the difficulty with our human compulsion to surpass others is that it is not always possible to prevail. In this case, remaining locked in a losing proposition can use up a person's assets. It would therefore seem to make sense just to move on. Nevertheless acknowledging defeat is hurtful and leaves the loser feeling like pathetic debris. For a while, the only practical defense may seem to be an emotional retreat. But this too is self-defeating. It can feel so terrible—so bleak—that an immediate restoration of "health" may seem essential. Indeed until the person receives an infusion of vigor from having won, their preparations for victory may themselves remind them of previous reversals and therefore induce a renewed withdrawal.

Dealing with a troubled relationship is equally troubling. Negotiations with an uncooperative person are exasperating. If a resolution never comes, efforts at achieving one can be maddening. One wants to bash the other person over the head, but knows doing so will make the situation worse. A frustrated attachment can therefore leave a person vacillating between buoyancy and rage. Sometimes they will have the presence of mind to persevere, but at others an emotional firestorm will take over and events spiral out of control.

Moreover, if and when it becomes clear that success is not possible, despondency may be the reward. Because a lost love is more discernible than that is a lost role, the resultant despair can be among the worst a person has to endure. To identify it as suffering is a colossal understatement.

Hobson indicates that the temporal connection between anxiety and depression is a mystery to medical science. He acknowledges that clinical practice reveals that the two cycle in tandem, but does not know why. If the resocialization paradigm is on target, the reason is plain. Because anxiety and depression are phases of the same process, it would be odd if they did not arise in the same context. Anxiety, being nothing other than a fear whose cause is dimly perceived, it arises when the prospect of loss comes into view. Meanwhile, depression, being a form of sadness, enters the picture when it is time to cut one's losses. The explanation of why they rotate back and forth is that what is lost may not be lost all at once. A person may, as it were, mourn substantial losses in pieces. Attempting to endure a really significant bereavement at one fell swoop can be life threatening. The pain is so intense that suicide may intervene before a person reaches the other side of the chasm. The consequence is a confusing oscillation between dread and gloom that can last for years.

Not mentioned by Hobson, but a routine part of this picture is anger. Less passively reactive than fear or sadness, and therefore less likely to be identified as a stand-alone disorder, rage figures so prominently in the lives of people who come for therapeutic assistance that it is among the items monitored each time a client comes to visit. A therapist literally asks how frightened, sad, or angry a person is before moving on to more pressing matters. Freud, as it happens, was aware of this nexus. Indeed, he believed that depression was akin to internalized anger. In this, he was mistaken; nevertheless anger is an inevitable part of the anxiety/depression mix because losses regularly elicit anger. As Bowlby knew in discussing the protest phase of loss, people resist defeat. They do not meekly accept reverses, but attempt to keep them at bay. Anger is one of their primary tools for doing so. It is the chief emotional means of grabbing fate by the throat and forcing it to a different conclusion. Like it or not, because anger is a standard feature of resocialization, outbursts of fury can be expected to disrupt the smooth unfolding of personal improvements. This means that a failure to track its course can slow the corrective process and make for additional suffering.

Loss/Losing and the DSM Disorders

To return to Hobson, he begins one of his chapters by observing that "any ill that is mysterious stands a better chance of being poorly dealt with than one that is understood." His illustration is schizophrenia, but the affective disorders are also good candidates for misinterpretation. The depressive and anxiety disorders are among the staples of psychiatry, nevertheless addressing them as if they were biologically set the therapeutic train running on the wrong track. Since an estimated 4–6 percent of the entire U.S. population (more than 16 percent in some calculations) develops an anxiety disorder at some point in their lives, while a reported 7 percent endure depression annually, this is not trivial. As Horwitz suggests, every year tens of millions of people are advised that they suffer from a chemical imbalance when they do not.

But let us begin with anxiety. Among the listings in the DSM-IV are panic attacks, phobias, posttraumatic stress, generalized anxiety, and obsessive compulsion. Of these, only the last presents strong indications of a genetic etiology. The others, which include social phobias and agoraphobia, are clearly related to interpersonal encounters. Panic attacks, of course, come suddenly and with irresistible power. It may be all a person can do to organize a retreat. Phobias, on the other hand, are of greater duration. That which is feared is a specter with an all-pervading potential to arouse angst. Posttraumatic stress has already been discussed. It entails fears that hark back to an identifiable stressor, whereas generalized anxiety is notorious for an inability to be specific about that which is alarming. A person in its grip will describe a "free-floating" fear that makes no sense. Yet as with other cases of anxiety, the sorts of precipitants psychiatrists anticipate are equivalent to personal assaults. Rapes, muggings, and domestic violence all qualify. If, however, loss and losing are the core of the matter, no single experience of violence may be responsible. Ongoing destructive relationships can leave a plethora of traces subsequently obscured by the nature of resocialization. Bowlby's paradigm, it will be recalled, begins with denial. This reaction causes difficulty in identifying the source of fear. It can seem so diffuse that there seems no legitimate basis for concern.

Turning to depression, Hobson describes it this way. "If [a] gloom has no obvious cause or goes on and on for a clearly abnormal length of time, it crosses into the realm of mental illness." For him, the depressive disorders are tied to an *irrational* sadness, just as the anxiety disorders are linked to *irrational* fears. "Both," says he, "are mysterious emotional problems." Consider for a moment the peculiarity of this assertion. Hobson manifestly contends that specific emotional states cross over into mental illness when physicians do not understand their cause. In other words, the fact that they are a mystery to the psychiatrists requires that they be awarded exclusive rights to treat them. What is most irrational here is the perverse logic of this conclusion. "We don't understand therefore stand back and let us take over." This implies that should physicians misidentify the source of a client's problems, their error must be enshrined in the medical classifications to which other helping professionals must defer.

Returning specifically to depression, psychiatrists make a distinction between bipolar disorders, major depressions, and dysthymic conditions. For the first of these, there seems to be good genetic data justifying a medical response. Manic depression is not only a florid state, but also an apparently physiologically based one. Major depressions, however, are less well understood. They are characterized by a quick onset, a deep trough of despond, and a relatively rapid return to normality. Psychiatrists may not comprehend this sequence but, just as with other medical conditions, depend upon the body to cure itself. In fact, some major depressions probably are biologically based. It would be surprising if the physiological factors that control the grieving process did not sometimes go awry because the somatic machinery failed. Nevertheless doctors do not possess a reliable means of distinguishing these cases from the ones where resocialization is responsible. Many major depressions are merely instances of an intense period of mourning for a dysfunctional role, a hierarchical loss, or a bad relationship. If psychiatrists are insensitive to these factors—and generally speaking they are—it should come as no wonder they are mystified.

Dysthymic disorders, by contrast, tend to be persistent. Unlike the major depressions, the sadness attached to them does not become overwhelming. Their major drawback is that they refuse to lift. As yet no good physiological explanation has been found. The resocialization model, however, offers an alternative. If, instead of a mourning process proceeding to its conclusion, it becomes hung up on an obstacle to change, then it may indefinitely lock into a bad place. If, for instance, a person's fears are too terrifying to be faced, they may make it impossible to let go of the past via a full-fledged episode of melancholy. Should this occur, there may be sadness, but its lack of depth indicates that the ties to what was lost have not been broken and therefore the provocation for sorrow has not been removed. The consequence will be a long-lasting, albeit low-level, depression that never accomplishes its mission. And because there is no acceptance of the loss, there is no opportunity to move on to more satisfying attachments.

While Hobson (along with most psychiatrists) acknowledges that "various forms of depression have both a genetic and an environmental side," in doing so he trivializes the social aspects of depression (and incidentally anxiety). He continues his exposition by suggesting that, "on the environmental side, we know that various kinds of stress—including parental neglect, physical or sexual abuse, and other forms of maltreatment—promote depression." As already discussed, the concept of *stress* has limitations in explicating social relationships. It does not truly clarify the nature of role relationships, hierarchical ranking, or interpersonal bonding. How then can it explain emotional reactions that go wrong? Indeed, it is because this scheme has difficulties that its advocates take recourse to moralistic thinking. Talk of "abuse" and "maltreatment" is not medical, but moral. Were these the final word, all we would learn is that these behaviors were adamantly condemned.

Less frequently diagnosed maladies, such as the conduct disorders and paraphilias, also disguise interpersonal links to losing. In these instances, it is how individuals attempt to cope with their losses that draws the negative response. Thus, children who engage in deeds that bring them to the attention of psychiatrists typically are enmeshed in conflict-ridden relationships. Commonly at the mercy of role partners who assert their own superiority, they find themselves in a situation where it is imperative they don't win. Nevertheless, rather than undergo resocialization—which, while we are on the subject, is exceptionally difficult for children—they become embroiled in fighting against the loss. Being children, their resources are limited; hence they resort to stealing in an attempt to get even, running away as a means of evading persecutors, or fighting with peers as a substitute for throttling adult antagonists. None of this, of course, works. Worse still, it irritates the potential allies of their tormentors. The upshot is that they confront a growing coalition of control agents, and their losing is intensified. Merely to moralize this state of affairs, and engage in exhortation aimed at those responsible, is insufficient. Unless one takes the time to survey the larger picture, and discover the actual causes, this amounts to no more than a linguistic exercise.

Regrettably, the paraphilias are, if anything, further moralized. The forms of sexual gratification they represent are no more than anathematized. Pedophilia, for instance, is so abhorred that the mere thought of allowing a person this avenue of self-expression is repugnant. Recognition of the safety needs of children understandably forbids it. And yet where is the damaged biological substrate supposedly precipitating this outlet? Ironically, the fact that child molesters are remarkably resistant to contemporary therapeutic regimes argues against a nuanced understanding of the phenomenon. People want answers. They demand immediate mechanisms for preventing this behavior. What is more, analogous factors attach to exhibitionism, fetishism, voyeurism, and even necrophilia, all of which can be understood within a loss–losing framework. What these practices have in common is that each can be interpreted as an alternative satisfaction to compensate for losses not otherwise open to repair. It is virtually tautological to assert that sexual perverts do not participate in conventional heterosexual relations. A reasonable conjecture is that the normal give-and-take of adult sexuality lies outside their purview because they find the vulnerable equality of good sex unavailable. Frightened of losing during such encounters, they seek "safer" venues. Why else would a person desire intercourse with children or the dead?

Obsessive-compulsives also seem terrified of losing. Their ritualized defenses against disaster imply nothing less. Repetitive and stereotyped actions have for millennia been used to control the unknown. Many religious ceremonies are based on them. Individuals who count the cracks on the sidewalk or engage in persistent hand-washing have personalized this strategy. They symbolically employ a predictable behavior over which they have complete control so as to ward off defeats over which they have little. Paranoids too seem intent on mastering impending losses. Their focus, however, is on the potential source of defeat. Unable to cope with opponents they cannot identify, they misplace their concerns and become hypervigilant regarding persons who are perfectly safe. This false concreteness seems to afford protection, but, in fact, compounds the probability of loss. While there is reason to believe paranoids and obsessives suffer from a biological defect, the bizarre form their conduct takes bespeaks a global human loathing of defeat. Their tactics are flawed, but their desire to forestall catastrophe falls well within the normal range of response to losing.

While the personality disorders are not officially characterized as diseases, they too manifest reactions to potential loss. Whereas obsessives essentially employ magic to manipulate the universe and paranoids fortify their territory against erroneous opponents, those with personality defects resort to incompetent social negotiations. Most of their objectionable behaviors can be interpreted as imperfect forms of self-assertion. In other words, they attempt to win by utilizing means that generally result in loss. Never perhaps having developed adequate methods of getting ahead, they do the best they can. The narcissist is thus universally disliked because they try to outdo others by want amounts to boasting. Witness the DSM descriptions of such a person. They are said to feel entitled to special favors they do not reciprocate. This, to be blunt, describes a taker, not a giver. Their way of coming out on top is to accumulate all they can without benefiting those who benefit them. This is an unbalanced form of social negotiation that, once detected, produces indignation. Even if it succeeds, the triumph is likely to be fleeting. So is a resort to interpersonal exploitativeness. Taking advantage of others' weaknesses is ill calculated to recruit enduring allies. Nor is exhibitionism especially popular. The person who devotes inordinate amounts of time to bragging about themselves is not entertaining. Most potential collaborators prefer to spend their time with those who notice their virtues. The preoccupation of the narcissist with fantasies of power, or relationships that oscillate between overidealization and devaluation, is similarly indicative of an ineffectual person.

The histrionic personality, by contrast, is given to expressions of alarm. Their irrationally angry outbursts and episodes of self-dramatization are designed to inform the world of the magnitude of their distress. "Look at me," they seem to be saying, "see how much I suffer from this accumulation of unwarranted losses." Others may judge them as overreacting to minor events, but for them these are so numerous as to be major. Onlookers are required to feel sorry for them, and therefore to defer to their needs, but they must not, on that account, assess them as inadequate. Although often overly dependent on the good graces of the more powerful, to admit their relative weakness would be intolerable, for this would invite exploitation. The result is a tendency to manipulate and agitate. If a show of emotions can surreptitiously achieve their goals, then they will be the winner. Nevertheless, just as with the narcissist, this strategy is not noteworthy for its ability to win friends or influence people.

The antisocial personality is probably the most perceptibly substandard mode of interpersonal negotiation. Its guiding principles are thus: If I cannot beat you, I will at least injure you. I will steal what you have, assault you with a lead pipe, or lie to you with impunity. Because you are so wretched, it is acceptable for me to come out ahead by breaking rules stacked in your favor. What need has the antisocial personality to hold a regular job or engage in responsible parenting? These onerous tasks are reserved for the real losers. Why also plan ahead? The winners of this world are so undependable that to rely on their promises is foolish. It makes more sense to take what one wants and let the devil take the hindmost. That this sort of orientation will get one labeled an "outlaw" may be foreseen, but discounted. Losing feels preordained—in many cases due to an infancy dominated by parental tyranny—hence the best one can do is flaunt one's losses and celebrate them as victories.

Exploring the histories of antisocial personalities can be a wrenching experience. They have often endured so many losses that one cannot help sympathizing with them—however hopeless this compassion may be. With passive-aggressives, this reaction is more productive. They too have been tyrannized, but instead of concentrating on vengeance, they emphasize self-protection. In their negotiations with more powerful others, they too perceive direct confrontations as perilous. Their answer is to appear inactive while simultaneously seeking circuitous paths toward their goals. They procrastinate not because they are lazy, but because if they go slowly, the other may give up and allow them to move in the direction of their choice. Likewise stubborn, not because they are constitutionally incapable of flexibility, but because if they cannot do what they desire, they refuse to do what their oppressors desire. Indirection is the specialty of the passive-aggressive. They are forgetful or inefficient, not from a natural incompetence, but a need for plausible excuses. Their role partners are so demanding, yet so unreceptive to legitimate explanations, that they seek pretexts that are difficult to refute. Although this strategy, like the other personality disorders, places limits on the possibility of success, its perceived advantage is in placing limitations on potential losses. The passive-aggressive has the consolation of rarely having to give up and of frequently frustrating dominant others who cannot identify the author of their exasperation.

Finally, but not exhaustively, are the chemical dependencies. These too can be mechanisms for coping with loss. The most representative is alcoholism. Imbibing strong spirits has a long pedigree. Distilled alcohol has for millennia been used for sacred and profane purposes.

The most important reason it has is its profound effect on the human psyche. Ethyl alcohol gets people intoxicated. And when they are, some experience euphoric reactions, whereas others undergo an amnesiac effect. Either way, when they get drunk, people can forget their troubles. For at least a while that which is difficult to endure is pushed aside and life feels brighter. One of the features habitually handled this way is the pain of loss. After a bad day at the office, many bureaucrats consciously depart for the nearest "watering hole" to join in what is euphemistically called a "happy hour." The object is to "drown" one's sorrows. With a little buzz on, they deceive themselves into believing all is well.

It is sometimes alleged that alcohol does not work. The problem is it does. It is a superb mental analgesic. Unfortunately it has less advantageous side effects. First, a forgetfulness about one's losses can perpetuate them. Constantly postponing the time of reckoning pushes the due date beyond the period of rectification. Windows of opportunity do not stay open forever; hence chances bypassed in a drunken haze may never open up again. A surfeit of alcohol can also dull the senses and slow the reflexes. A person under the influence is unable to win, whether or not the opportunity arises. Second, alcohol has deleterious physical properties. A dependence on it destroys both liver and brain cells. Nowadays conventional wisdom tells us that alcoholism is a disease like any other, but this is only partially true. To begin with, were it like any other, it would be unnecessary to insist it is. Next, although there is a biological defect, this is primarily after the fact. Alcoholism is more like an injury than a disease. It occurs after one has had too much to drink for too long. This is more similar to a poison than an infectious agent.

Sometimes it is suggested that alcoholism is a genetic disease, but this too is misleading. Some individuals are born more vulnerable to the impact of alcohol than others, but this susceptibility is imperfectly correlated with addiction. Often it is those who get drunk least easily that wind up drinking to excess. Ostensibly able to hold their liquor, they do not realize until it is too late that they have become addicted. By the same token, many cultures so effectively dictate when and how to drink that drunkenness is the exception. Thus Jewish and Italian traditions, both of which celebrate alcohol as a food or a ritual substance, produce little alcoholism, whereas American Indians, who before the advent of Europeans possessed few potent spirits, having no previously established cultural protections, found themselves decimated by intemperance. In other words, alcoholism can become a disability, but almost always when it is not personally or socially controlled. As a means of coping with loss, it is therefore overdone.

A Caveat

All this said, loss and losing are not totally divorced from medicine. There are reasons why the effects of social defeats have often been confused with biological disorders. To begin with, many genuine illnesses are precipitated by instances of loss and losing. The stress that is experienced at these inflection points can be more than that a vulnerable person can bear. Schizophrenia is perhaps the best example of this danger. Not only are the chemical signatures of the brains of those suffering from the disorder different from normal persons, but twin studies have revealed that schizophrenia is at least partially genetic. Children separated from their mentally ill parents are liable to develop the condition themselves. They do not need to be exposed to parental manipulations to contract it. Nevertheless, their likelihood of exhibiting schizophrenic symptoms is not total. Some separated children remain normal for a lifetime.

This suggests several things. First, it is unlikely that the disorder is completely biological. But second, neither is it strictly due to socialization. Were it the latter, there would be no correlation between parents and their offspring once they were separated, whereas were it the former, the correlation would be complete. Being raised by a normal mother and father would, in the absence of physiological causes, thoroughly inoculate a child from the effects of being raised by malfunctioning parents. In this case, there would be no instances of loss and/or losing created by defective parenting because this sort of parenting would not have occurred. On the other hand, the fact that the twin children of schizophrenic parents can have different outcomes suggests that socialization is not completely irrelevant. It may well be that twins raised by different sets of parents encounter different levels of stress and therefore have different outcomes. The evidence thus suggests that there is probably an interaction effect between genetic and interpersonal factors. It is not one or the other that is responsible, but a combination of the two.

The most likely explanation of this fact is that schizophrenia derives from a genetic vulnerability. For those with the necessary biological susceptibility, the stresses of significant instances of loss and losing apparently trigger physiological reactions that occasion the hallucinations and delusions characteristic of the disorder. This may be the reason schizophrenia so frequently erupts during the teenage and early adult years. For many of these young people, this is a period when the transition to personal independence likely introduces insurmountable obstacles. They unexpectedly find that they are unable to meet the challenges of creating individually satisfying roles, ranks, and/or relationships and consequently suffer the tensions of losing. Powerless to win, perhaps their brains go on overload.

Thus, as described in the first chapter, when I was a clinician, I witnessed a promising young man descending into catatonic schizophrenia. When his minister father violated his own long-standing principles by divorcing my client's mother, Tom could not reconcile these behaviors with his personal religious commitments. Since Tom derived these convictions from his father, he could not solve the dilemma that his father's actions presented. It was at this point that the teenager exhibited the catatonic immobility from which he never fully recovered. Tom, as it were, experienced an irreversible occurrence of losing vis-à-vis his father. This was, in effect, an emotional trauma that altered his susceptible brain chemistry. Thenceforward, his brain no longer functioned in a normal manner.

Similarly, although John Bowlby and George Brown have demonstrated that depression often has interpersonal roots, major depressions can have biological causes as well. It is therefore possible that some serious depressions are as genetic in origin as is schizophrenia. They too may derive from obscure genetic vulnerabilities. This also seems to be possible with respect to bipolar disorders. Their characteristic oscillations between depression and mania suggest more than a narrow reaction to loss and losing. It is even conceivable that they derive from physiological defects introduced by hormonal abnormalities, infectious agents, and/or environmental hazards. The fact that our knowledge of potential causes is limited prevents us from being sure of what is involved. It is accordingly a mistake a priori to exclude one possibility or another.

In any event, the distress inflicted by instances of loss and losing can easily exacerbate the symptoms of genuine disease entities. If those suffering from schizophrenia and/or bipolar conditions have their abilities to function damaged, then these impairments can presumably be made worse by external social situations. Hallucinations, for instance, might be aggravated by social maltreatment. Perhaps being yelled at by an insensitive outsider is more than a vulnerable person can bear. They may then hear voices they would not have experienced had they been treated more sensitively. Correspondingly, a biologically depressed person may become more depressed if a new loss is piled on top of their already despondent state.

Then too, the behavioral patterns typical of genuine mental diseases independently generate instances of loss and losing. Impaired social functioning can clearly make it more difficult to win in competition with better functioning individuals. Symptoms such as hallucinations, delusions, or mania unquestionably stimulate social performances that generate interpersonal defeats. To illustrate, people often ridicule those who appear different, which makes it more problematic to develop functional roles, ranks, and relationships. Fair or not, others take advantage of the weaknesses demonstrated by those in the grip of mental illness. As was demonstrated by Hollingshead and Redlich a half century ago, those suffering from schizophrenia tend to move down in social class. Unable to hold remunerative jobs, they must frequently settle for reduced circumstances. By the same token, they are less able to manage intimate relationships. Less attractive as potential marital partners, they are also less able to participate in the necessary give-and-take of interpersonal intimacy. As a result, they suffer relationship losses on top of the distress caused by their physiological symptoms.

If this is so, then biology can cause losses, whereas losses can influence biology. This means that there can be a reciprocal relationship between the two such that it is difficult to disentangle their effects. While they may be distinct, there is no guarantee they will be. There may even be times when it is challenging for professional observers to discern whether particular behaviors have their origin in an out-of-order physiology or a dispiriting interpersonal clash. Given that we do not have easily administered tests to determine whether one or the other is the primary cause, diagnoses will continue to differ. Physicians are naturally more inclined to perceive physical etiologies, whereas nonphysicians tend to favor social explanations of troublesome behaviors. Who is correct may be impossible to establish. Indeed, in some cases, both may be.

Such perplexities are comprehensible, but are not without negative consequences. When mistakes are made, they can perpetuate a despair that might be responsive to more suitable interventions. Care must therefore be taken to separate the physiological from the nonphysiological. Since this is not always possible, practitioners of every stripe must be alert to counterevidence. Someday the mechanisms for making accurate diagnoses will be more sophisticated than they are at present, but in the meantime both possibilities must receive attention. It will not do to be exclusively medical or social, since both are significant. The current work emphasizes the implications of loss and losing, not because they are exhaustive, but because they are frequently underestimated. Medicine matters, but so do dysfunctional roles, ranks, relationships, beliefs, and morals.

4

Resocialization

Johnny skins his knee. The pain is intense; the flow of blood surprising. He runs to his mother screaming for protection. She takes him in her arms and surveys the damage. Then she bends down to kiss the booboo to make it feel better.

Suddenly all is well and Johnny smiles through his tears. (A familiar childhood scenario)

A Sovereign Remedy

If loss and losing are endemic to human existence, it would be remarkable if there were no way to relieve them. Damage that allowed no means of repair would be so injurious as to threaten the survival of our species. It therefore makes sense to expect a standard mechanism for *resocialization*. Similar mechanisms are certainly found for other ills. Thus, although a mother's touch is not of itself curative, it can feel remarkably so. While her saliva has antiseptic properties, the feel of her lips comforts a child. Obviously this technique was not invented in modern times. It reaches back to the dawn of time, apparently an evolutionary device for reassuring the young. Resocialization too seems to be an evolutionary innovation. It is normal, natural, and not the invention of contemporary therapists. Nor does it require therapists to initiate or supervise. Resocialization has been occurring on its own for eons and, as long human beings continue to experience loss and losing, will surely persist.

Resocialization plainly takes place in response to the death of others. It has also been documented with respect to divorce. In addition, it arises spontaneously with regard to dysfunctional roles, hierarchical failures, and relationship disasters. Some instances are utterly predictable, but nevertheless underappreciated. To illustrate, in Western societies, the teenage years are fraught with Sturm und Drang. Late adolescence is notorious for mood swings and histrionics. Not-quite adults oscillate between railing at their parents and feeling sorry for themselves. What is less well recognized is that this is a period of role change. Individuals who had been considered children endure a transformation into adulthood. In order to achieve this, however, they must relinquish their previous status and develop new forms of interaction. This entails cutting their ties with the past via a period of mourning and then renegotiating behavior patterns with fresh role partners. If this is not understood as resocialization, it is because it happens in situ. So much is swirling within teenagers' life space, and so much of this is emotionally extreme, that the sequence of events is obscured. Nonetheless, a dispassionate examination of events will be rewarded by the revelation of a coherent process. Observers will notice how youngsters repeatedly deny their situation. They will also discern fierce anger directed toward parents. Then too they will observe an exaggerated sadness that accompanies periodic failures. Finally they will perceive a host of new relationships in which previously missing forms of cooperation appear. Not the least of these, of course, are employment and love relationships.

Although natural, resocialization is not automatic. People resist it or, having crossed its threshold, become stuck before emerging out the other end. As is commonly acknowledged, not everyone survives the adolescence unscathed. Some never grow up, whereas others are so damaged that newly acquired roles are badly deformed. They get married, but not happily; they obtain a job, but not a legal one. If we look toward enduring another's death, it is easier to comprehend what can go wrong. When a loved one dies, not everyone traverses the requisite stages of mourning. The period of denial can be prolonged, the protest phase severe, and the depression interminable. A heartbreaking example occurs when a young child dies. Because contemporary parents expect their children to outlive them, when one passes away, the pain can be beyond endurance. If, let us say, a child is crushed in an accident, the image is more than many mothers can tolerate. For a long time they may prefer to fantasize that a beloved daughter has merely gone on a lengthy vacation. When the fatal collision is finally admitted, the rage can be monumental. However reasonable the explanation of the event, forgiveness is withheld. And then, of course, there is sadness. This may be so profound and all-embracing that it becomes the experience's most salient characteristic. Thenceforward, everything seems tinged with bitterness. Such mothers are rarely prepared to move on. Fresh opportunities never excite their interest, and future successes never taste as sweet as primeval memories.

The resocialization subsequent to role, rank, or relationship failures is potentially as defective. It too can be blocked at any point in its progress. Among the possible impediments are intense emotions, false beliefs, incompetent plans of action, and obstructive role partners. People who have experienced a loss may not recognize this as a defeat, may protest against it by employing destructive means, may refuse to feel as sad as they must, or can create new patterns that are less satisfying than the old. The result is that dysfunctional roles are locked in place, or worse yet, more defective ones succeed them. By the same token, efforts at social mobility, or finding sustainable love, can eventuate in lower status or abject loneliness. In order to work, resocialization must be adroitly navigated. Those who would come out of it better off require the strength and know-how to deal with an extended sequence of challenges.

Fortunately, effective resocialization can be facilitated. People can be helped to traverse minefields that, left to their own devices, might leave them in tatters. Friends and relatives, for instance, can offer emotional support for the more frightening aspects of the process. The mere presence of a trusted other is often enough to stiffen the resolve of a person shaken by a devastating loss. Such an ally provides the courage to confront past demons. Then too, an experienced companion can supply guidance. They can explain what is about to happen, thereby reducing the terrors inherent in the unknown. This, by the way, is the secret of psychotherapy. Counselors and therapists perform their magic by serving as trustworthy ciceroni. Their training enables them to facilitate resocialization by furnishing the knowledge of how change occurs and the nerve to deal with its alarms. If, on top of this, a helper's life history has imbued him or her with an acquaintance of the sorts of thing that break down and a desire to extricate strangers from situations that once horrified them, they can pass muster when clients put their tenacity and expertise to the test.

Despite this potential support, resocialization is discomfiting even when it proceeds smoothly. Its protest and depression phases are inherently so painful that no one cheerfully volunteers to endure them. A useful analogy, albeit one that risks confusing medical with social complaints, is the parallel between resocialization and the symptoms of disease. The common cold can serve as a model. Today we know that a virus invading nasal passageways causes this illness. In one sense, the disease is the damage meted out by these biological assassins. Yet it is not this destruction that raises the most havoc. Paradoxically the healing process inflicts more discomfort. When the body releases histamines and T-cells to fight the intruders, the resulting congestion is unsettling. The victim coughs, raises phlegm, and has difficulty breathing. These are what over-the-counter cold remedies promise to keep in check. They are the hated indicators of being sick. But they are also signs of getting well. Loathed though they are, they terminate once the attacking viruses have been vanquished.

In many ways, resocialization is like this. Its phases are also signs of a battle being fought and hopefully won. Nevertheless they too are disagreeable and may be conceived of as a problem in need of relief. Just as cold-sufferers seek medications to repress their symptoms, so may those immersed in resocialization. Because they despise feeling angry, frightened, and sad, they demand chemical preparations to inhibit these feelings. They may also consult helping professionals whose expertise lies in suppressing the effects of bad roles, ranks, and relationships. Regrettably should these interventions succeed, resocialization may never proceed to a satisfactory conclusion. Instead of being facilitated, it is obstructed such that what was lost is never released or replaced. Many millions of human beings live out their lives in the limbo of incomplete resocialization—including many satisfied that this is the best they can expect. But whether or not they realize it, they are missing the freedom that comes from dealing more directly with their losses. At minimum, they deserve insight into what they must choose between. Without this, they may assume that disaster lurks behind what is actually an opportunity. Lacking it, they never realize it is feasible to cut their losses.

The Repetition Compulsion

At first Sigmund Freud was surprised. He expected his patients to embrace the interpretations he offered. He further expected them to learn from these and steer clear of the circumstances that got them in trouble. To do otherwise was irrational, and yet irrationality is what he observed. Time after time, his subjects persisted in the relationships in which they were enmeshed. If they had abusive parents, they maintained their contacts with them. If their fathers maltreated their female patients, they selected husbands who continued to maltreat them. Clients experiencing anxiety about sex because of the primal scene continued to experience anxiety even after the origins of this fear were explained. Those fixated on Oedipal traumas persevered in latent homosexuality. The conventional wisdom among those unfamiliar with psychoanalysis is that when a therapist helps a patient recover lost memories, the symptoms vanish. Yet this is not what Freud witnessed.

After World War II, when Freudianism was at full throttle, a spate of Hollywood movies depicted what was thought to occur. In one of these (*Mirage*, 1965), Gregory Peck played a nuclear scientist who found himself gripped by anxiety and amnesia. Not sure of who he was or what he was supposed to be doing, he stumbled through most of the film uncovering clues as to his identity. Eventually he had an "aha" moment during which he remembered having been present when a revered mentor fell to his death from a skyscraper window. He also suddenly recalled that this father figure was revealed to be a traitor to his country. With this recollection, everything else fell into place. His anxieties lifted and he understood exactly where he was and why needed this quest. He was "cured." Gone were his neurotic symptoms, and he was exposed as the normal everyman we always suspected Gregory Peck to be.

Freud himself discovered early on that this was wrong. Recovering long concealed memories was not sufficient—nor were brilliant analytic interpretations. Before patients could change, before they were released from bondage to unfortunate behaviors, they had to reexperience the traumatic incident(s) that interfered with normal development. Franz Alexander, one of Freud's disciples, dubbed this the "corrective emotional experience." Only when an analysand emotionally returned to an earlier scene of damage could it be reworked. Absent a passionate reliving of the past, all that transpired was a cold-blooded and therefore sterile, review of interesting reminiscences. No more than an intellectual exercise, this was useful as a parlor game; nothing else. When the actual rage-filled, anxiety-saturated past was revisited during a therapeutic session, the consequences were different. It was these moments that clinicians sought to arouse, for they were the ones that moved patients forward.

Contemporary filmmakers, many of whom experienced personal contact with psychotherapy, have learned this lesson. In the movie *Analyze This*, Billy Crystal portrays a psychiatrist shanghaied into treating a mobster played by Robert De Niro. After encountering the usual client resistance, the story reaches its climax when the gangster is forced to remember the circumstances of his father's death. Confronted with a restaurant setting similar to the one in which his father was gunned down, he tearfully recalls his anger at his father and his unwillingness to alert him to the danger. Now entirely immersed in the past, his long-submerged guilt pours forth. The moment of trauma is resurrected, finally to be interred. The movie then has the integrity to send the De Niro character to his bedroom to cry over his loss. This depression, unfortunately, lasts no more than a few weeks—the demands of dramatic continuity being what they are. In this, it regrettably underestimates the period of sadness typical of resocialization. Nor is a discrete late childhood event the standard source of unexplained anxiety. Nevertheless, an honest effort is made to display the emotional aspects of Freudianism.

Less well depicted is what Freud called "the repetition compulsion." He also noticed that patients recycled the past during their daily routines. Outside of the consulting room, they did not so much recall the past as relive it. It was as if a script lifted from earlier in their lives was reenacted in the present. Theirs was like a theatrical role that required endless revivals. Not by inadvertence was this described as a compulsion. His patients seemed driven to repeat previous experiences despite conscious intentions to do otherwise. Time and again, without any awareness of what they were doing, they recapitulated relationships with sadistic or neglectful parents. This impulse was so strong that Freud assumed that it must be pleasant. In some peculiar sense, his patients were attempting to fulfill crucial desires. Just as their dreams were vehicles for wish fulfillment, so apparently were these reconstituted behavior patterns.

In this, Freud was almost correct. His patients were compulsive, but what they reiterated was not in quest of pleasure. The need was to correct what had once gone wrong. They were seeking a return to the time when their dysfunctional roles, ranks, and relationships were created. The goal was not to delight in historic defeats, but to reopen lost negotiations and produce a better result. Unsatisfied with the lifestyles then thrust upon them, they sought to go back and undo what they did not have the power to do the first time. Instinctively, they understood that only a return to the scene of the crime offered the prospect of change.

What most did not realize was that the past could not literally be undone. It was, after all, the past. Often all the repetition compulsion accomplished was to recapitulate previous disasters. Once emotionally returned to a prior state, a person endured the same weaknesses as brought forth defeat the first time. Now the victim of a renewed panic or an out-of-control rage, he or she forfeited the mental composure of their adult self and rejoined former battles with all the aplomb and wisdom of an inexperienced child. What the person did not appreciate was that all that could reasonably be achieved was severing ties to ancient struggles. If in going back to the past, it was recognized that victory was not feasible under the then prevailing circumstances, a person could renounce the conflict and move on to something more promising. Antediluvian losses would not literally be undone, but relegated to an unlamented past. Once properly mourned, they could be provided with a burial that stuck.

In fact, the sort of process Freud stumbled upon has found validation in modern neuropsychiatry. Allan Hobson might be surprised by the suggestion, but recent discoveries about limbic system explain much about the repetition compulsion. He notes that it is likely "that a prime purpose of sleep is to consolidate and file new information within the brain's vast data storage system, and that dreams are an incidental by-product of this process." He further states that "during sleep portions of . . . hippocampal memories . . . are filed in parts of the cerebral cortex and elsewhere, and ties between the hippocampal memories and these cortex memory pieces are created or strengthened. In this way, information gained during the last waking period is consolidated with previously stored cortex information of the same sort, making it easier for you to come up with new ideas and to work with this consolidated pool of information in the morning." Hobson also reports that the amygdala is essential to the emotional aspects of these memories. It coordinates their storage and ensures that their memory will not be lost. Because emotions warn of danger, these memory traces are more hardwired than most because as Hobson emphasizes, "You don't want flexibility here."

Where does this leave us with respect to compulsively generated behaviors? To understand them, we must recall that Freud believed dreams were therapeutic. In dreaming, people resurrected their problems and sought solutions. These might then be applied to their waking lives. This is why Freudians instruct their clients to record their dreams and relate them to their therapists. The insights thereby uncovered are in Freud's phrasing "the royal road to the unconscious." Now let us assume that neurologists are correct and memories are constantly being updated while we sleep. Assume further that emotional memories are especially difficult to update. If we, at this point, apply the repetition compulsion, let us see what happens.

When a person enters a relationship similar in emotional tone to one in which important roles, ranks, or relationships were developed, they will feel what was once felt. Then, if the amygdala is doing its job, come nightfall, it will route today's emotions to the same niche where their counterparts were stored. These will therefore become accessible to modification. Next, if what happened today is the same as what happened in the past, there should be no change. But if the present does not recapitulate the past in every detail, if it instead unfolds with an emotional twist whereby what was once terrifying is now more manageable, the previous memory may be reworked. Furthermore, indications of this change should appear in a person's dreams. Where once they might have had nightmares of fighting an overpowering father, they may now have dreams of cooperating with a more loving one.

If the above suppositions are correct, the repetition compulsion is itself a sovereign means of creating an emotionally corrective experience. In prompting a person to reenact the past, affects are elicited that allow destructive emotional memories to be amended. It is sometimes imagined that there is a yawning chasm separating neurophysiology from the social sciences. This is untrue. Socially based phenomenon, such as resocialization and psychotherapy, owe much of their design to the biological nature of human beings. It is a truism—or should be—that whatever human beings do has a biological foundation. As animals, everything people think or feel has a brain correlate. The micro and macro levels of science are not at odds. To the contrary, they provide complementary views of the same events. The sociologist can describe how mourning unfolds at a conventional interpersonal level, whereas a neurologist explains it at a neural level. Both perspectives can be accurate, with neither inherently more valid than the other. Indeed, each proffers information that enables the other to better explicate what is happening at its level.

Nonetheless, caution is in order. Brain science may be applicable to personal distress, but this does not imply that the best person to solve personal problems is a brain scientist. Neurochemistry may have a role to play in alleviating individual discontent, but is not well situated to supervise resocialization. Pointing out to a person what is happening at cortical synapses is not the sort of intervention that facilitates the reorganization of brain traces. A sports analogy may be appropriate. When a baseball player loses his or her ability to hit a curveball, they experience anxiety. They will worry about whether their skill is unalterably lost and in perseverating about this will make things worse. The question that must be addressed is to whom should they be referred for help? Should the referral be to a physician or a coach? The physician, as the expert on neurochemistry, can prescribe a tranquilizer. This may make the ballplayer feel more relaxed, but will it boost his or her batting average? Most observers would agree that an experienced coach, one who can spot the kinks in a swing and suggest modifications in a batting stance, has a better chance of correcting the problem. Whether or not neurons have misfired, it is the macro dimension that is likely to prove appropriate. The same logic applies to resocialization. Although a depressed person may manifest changes in the balance of neurotransmitters, what he or she needs is someone to guide them through an incomplete mourning process. Once this is achieved, their neurotransmitters will come into alignment on their own.

One of the reasons therapeutic assistance is appropriate for role, rank, and relationship problems is that a reliable interpersonal connection creates the environment that makes resocialization possible. Psychotherapy turns out to be a superb medium for eliciting the repetition compulsion. The quiet womb-like ambience of the therapy session provides the requisite safety to reexperience dysfunctional social patterns. Added to this, a concentrated focus on the client's distress provides permission to be egocentric in a way not permitted in more mundane transactions.

Another phenomenon discovered by Freud is operative here as well. It is transference. Initially Freud was impressed with the intensity with which his patients seemed to fall in love with him. No matter how hard he attempted to stay neutral, his attentions were interpreted as romantic, and he was idealized by vulnerable souls who became emotionally dependent upon him. Eventually it was also clear that many demonized him with as little provocation. Only after years of experience was it possible to distinguish that they were projecting pervious relationships into the present alliance. They were, for instance, transferring patterns of animosity that existed between themselves and their parents onto Freud. He was now perceived as possessing the same motives and qualities as them.

Yet is this not what also happens in the repetition compulsion? The difference is that one occurs in the consulting room with the therapist, while the other takes place on the outside with inexperienced role partners. This can therefore be turned to advantage. A trained therapist was less apt to react antagonistically than an ordinary person who does not understand why he or she stimulated an out-of-place response. The therapist can also profit from learning about a client's dysfunctional past at firsthand. In observing problematic interactions close up, they can detect what previously went wrong and suggest methods for fixing it. They can, in essence, arrange experiences unlike the original relationship. These can then be integrated into rearoused emotional memories such that neural circuits are redirected. Out in real life, it may be more difficult to do the same, but even sophisticated laypersons can be more tolerant of projected reactions than those unaware of the nature of resocialization.

Denial

With loss and losing as prevalent as they are, and with resocialization its normal remedy, how is it possible that the association of these phenomena with personal distress has escaped notice? If human intelligence arrived at its present state tens of thousands of years ago, why haven't troubled persons recognized what should be obvious? The answer lies with the nature of loss and losing, and resocialization. Were losing less painful, it would readily leap into view. Likewise, was resocialization easier, its course would be common knowledge. The mysteries of human distress are mysteries because their source lies in the spectacular human capacity for denial. That which is unpleasant or frightening is banished from consciousness and made to appear nonexistent. It literally becomes invisible or is provided with an ideological cover story to disguise its features. In any event, the discomfort remains to provoke attempts at explanation. These accounts, whether spiritual or medical, then become institutionalized. Individuals and groups develop an interest in preserving them. In the end, millions of people are convinced that they understand what is going on when they are actually collaborating in a conspiracy of silence. Should anyone have the temerity to challenge this arrangement, they will be accused of ignorance. As a result, few do.

Be that as it may, let us take closer look at the first stage of resocialization. People trapped in dysfunctional roles, ranks, and relationships are typically unaware of their plight. They experience discomfort, but do not appreciate its source. The last thing they intend to do is to plumb the depths of their feelings. Doing so might liberate terrors so horrendous as to seem beyond survival. The trouble with this is that before resocialization can occur, that which went wrong must be reexperienced. It must be felt, not merely understood. But the emotions associated with past losses are not people friendly. To describe them as painful is to underrate their severity. It must be remembered that bad roles, low ranks, and unsatisfying relationships commonly have their origins in childhood. As a consequence, the negotiations that produced them tended to be skewed. The now adult, but then child, was at a power disadvantage with respect to persons who, consciously or not, were unfair. This meant that he or she could be overawed by a partner disposed to be coercive. But the emotional reactions to such mismatches can be extreme. Acute fear and violent anger may shake the frame of a child subjected to the unequal blows. Worse than this, they surely will have experienced the terrors, rages, and depressions inherent in being a "loser." As a child, they would not—and could not—have had the resources to stand up to them. As a consequence, they had to be expelled from consciousness. Only this would have enabled life to proceed with a modicum of security.

Yet what of the adult who was once that child? What is he or she to do with the emotional remnants of long lost battles? Can a person about to enter resocialization allow themselves to reexperience them? One might imagine that such a person would be better prepared to deal with what a child could not, but this ignores a decisive factor. When an adult descends into the arena where childhood struggles took place, they once more feel like a child. The coping skills that accumulated during the intervening decades desert them, and they flee with all the dispatch of petrified immaturity. A mere glimpse of long-buried fears, rages, and depressions smacks of death, and they hastily reinstate the defense mechanisms that allowed them to grow up.

One of the last things an adult trapped in a bad role wants to perceive is that he or she has been imprisoned in a dysfunctional lifestyle. We human beings are future oriented. We live on hope. Whatever may be wrong today, we have plans to make things better tomorrow. These may exist in solely fantasy, but we depend upon them to console us as we bear our present misery. Recognition that we do not know how to escape would rob us of our faith in the future. We might become fatalistic and give up. But to give up is to guarantee failure. The upshot is that people wallow in flights of the imagination that could easily be debunked had they the desire to do so. Nor do people want to be reminded of the circumstances that coerced them into their current straights. This would renew a desperate desire to reverse the results of adverse role negotiations and therefore risk the possibility of again losing. Once was bad enough. Why tempt the fates when the latest outcome might be worse than the first?

Nor does a hierarchical loser want to relive old disappointments. He or she would rather invent a rationale for accepting their current status than hazard a brutal rebuke. Yes, it is true he is a "common man," but what is wrong with that? Common people are the salt of the earth. They produce the goods and services upon which their superiors feast. Besides, who would want to hang out with snobs who pretend they don't put on their trousers one leg at a time? They are so phony that their mere presence is repulsive. This, of course, has the effect of separating the winners from the losers and therefore protecting the latter from reminders they do not have the strength to beat these effete show-offs. In associating with their peers, they can pretend to have no weaknesses. They can wipe the specter of defeat from their minds and take pleasure in fantasized triumphs.

Love too thrives on an anticipation of success. A bad or an absent relationship can feel too lonely, or dangerous, to tolerate. As a result, people settle. They assume they have done the best possible and limp along with as much dignity as they can muster. Some take refuge in daydreams of meeting the perfect soul mate, while others convince themselves that a current partner is better than they are. Nevertheless dysfunctional relationships encourage visions of true love. The outcome of such ambitions is daily seen on *The Jerry Springer Show*. People stumble from one horrendous liaison to another totally oblivious of the character of the person with whom they are associating. Constantly deceived by dreams of true devotion, they betray, and are betrayed, with the blithe optimism of childish naïveté. They more than metaphorically lurch through life with their eyes closed. Determined not to perceive their predicament, they arrange unending strategies for remaining ignorant.

Whatever the springs of a person's losses, if they are serious, they will discover the means to tolerate them. Making it to adulthood is evidence of having crafted a slew of workable defenses. As a consequence, these are available during the opening phase of resocialization. This assortment of long-practiced mechanisms will not have to be reinvented, but will be close at hand at the slightest whisper of bad news. The impulse to reexperience galling defeats is thus be by an equally powerful impulse not to be threatened by them. Sufferers of grave losses typically fluctuate between a desire to move forward and a compulsion to withdraw. Bystanders may be confused by this inability to take a stand, yet it follows logically from the emotional plight of the sufferer.

One of Freud's greatest contributions, one elaborated by his daughter Anna, was the defense mechanism. Coming from a psychological perspective, he sought devices grounded in mental operations. In this, he was not disappointed. The psychological tools he depicted were so acutely rendered that even today—with Freudianism in decline—we take them for granted. Perhaps the most controversial is repression. Based on his belief in the unconscious, Freud posited a process in which what is too painful to be conscious is thrust into a remote corner of the mind. A person becomes so unaware of it so as to conclude it does not exist. The primal scene, for instance, may be so deeply submerged that a client honestly avers it never happened. Critics of this hypothesis assert that the unconscious is a figment of Freud's imagination. They claim that a person cannot perceive what is not real. In place of repression, they substitute "suppression." Freud himself portrayed the latter as a semiconscious process. A person who employs it is aware of thrusting something from consciousness and is therefore capable of recovering it to awareness. That which was suppressed does not cease to exist; one's attention is merely withdrawn from it. In either case, these contrivances were well suited to achieving denial. Both enable a victim to avoid seeing what she does not want to see. For my own part, I am convinced repression occurs. Some painful memories are pushed so far down into the psyche as to be incapable of recovery without help. Thus, when a person denies that their mother rejected them, they may mean it. They may not merely refuse to share the truth with an inquisitor. If so, that which is repressed may be more difficult to retrieve than that which is suppressed.

Freud also popularized the term "denial." When used with reference to the first phase of resocialization, this encompasses all of the mental and social devices employed for not recognizing losses. In its restricted manifestation, it signifies that something is not so. Asked if their mother hated them, the patient says, "No!" Moreover, they do so adamantly. They are not claiming they cannot remember, but maintaining they know the answer is negative. Furthermore, a person can deny they are angry or frightened. They can passionately declare this with the clear intent of persuading others it is true. The same declaration may also be intended to persuade themselves. Because they do not want to know, they use language to announce there is no point in looking.

Among the other Freudian defenses are *projection* and *rationalization*. In projection, a person denies something is true of themselves by concluding it is true of someone else. They may literally perceive it in the other and not in themselves. It is the other who is the liar, not he or she. The other person is frightened, not they. Projection enables a person to displace that which would be unacceptable in the self onto another who is then condemned. It is a marvelous mechanism for denial because a person does not have to disavow the problem or refuse to seek a solution. They can simply fob these off in a different direction. This permits them to feel self-righteous without having to recognize their limitations.

Rationalization provides similar benefits. Here the displacement is in terms of the reasons something is done. A person might, for instance, launch an assault on a role partner for hoping to obtain a selfish gain. This, however, might justify the target in retaliating. If instead one claims to be pursuing a humanitarian goal, the other will be egocentric in resisting. In the case of rationalization, the stated reasons are not the real ones, but socially acceptable alternatives. They are put forward in an attempt to avoid losses by persuading potential adversaries that what ego is doing makes sense. This mechanism operates as a form of denial because when it succeeds, those involved, including ego, agree that what is so really is not.

Two further Freudian defenses are *sublimation* and *identification with the aggressor*. Both of these move in more social directions. As with rationalization, but more so, sublimation achieves its end by persuading others that what a person is attempting is valuable. They are a philanthropist at heart, one who is set on doing others good. In telling the truth, they are not trying to get even with a rival, but seeking honesty for its own sake. In sacrificing their time to assist a friend, they are being helpful and are not in quest of eliciting guilt. Sublimators are "good" people. Everyone knows it. The sublimators make sure they do. Sometimes sublimators really are good. But what counts is that with this reputation secure, they do not have to defend their conduct.

In identification with the aggressor, denial succeeds because the one-time loser recruits an adversary to run interference for them. A person who has endured years of abuse, instead of fleeing their tormentor, seeks to be like them. Rather than renounce the violence of the oppressor, he or she emulates it. Now they identify themselves as a winner by mentally associating with someone who terrified them.

In their imagination, they too have for years intimidated potential competitors and looks forward to doing so in the future. They are not an insignificant victim, but the trusted ally of a conqueror. As such, they too are a conqueror, and the pains of any wounds once sustained are transmuted into exercises designed to create greater strength.

Ever since Freud, social psychologists have explored other mechanisms for achieving internal security. Among the best validated are *selective perception* and *cognitive dissonance*. It seems people are more sensitive to evidence that confirms what they already believe. They do not look for facts that contradict their convictions, nor recognize these when they are waved under their noses. A trusted political leader who lies is not be perceived as dishonest, while a pet theory that fails to work is nevertheless perceived as hugely successful. Thus, when it became known that the Head Start Program did not improve the long-term academic prospects of poor children, these data were not disseminated by those who ran the program, nor believed by citizens who voted for it in hopes of promoting justice. Neither has research that indicates resources spent on schools are largely irrelevant to student success been widely accepted. Educators and politicians alike, in spite of numerous failures, vie to increase school funding in the mistaken belief that this elevates achievement scores.

Leon Festinger's theory of cognitive dissonance takes this tendency a step further. It suggests that people are uncomfortable with mental contradictions. Because they want their beliefs to mesh, they do not acknowledge inconsistent information. In one of the best documented cases, the members of a doomsday cult, while perturbed when their prediction of the end of the world did not come true, were not thrown off stride. After a period of licking their wounds, they regrouped and put forth a new interpretation of what had happened. They were not wrong; they had merely made mistakes in their calculations. In other words, people are capable of denial even when confronted with solid evidence of error. Ingenious mental gymnastics, and a blatant unwillingness to accept what is, come to their rescue, and they continue to uphold that which puts them in the best light.

Sociologists too have investigated defenses against loss. Less often applied to explaining how individuals deny personal defeats, these are less well appreciated by the general public. They are nonetheless enormously important in perpetuating an ignorance of distressing information. Thus, human beings regularly collude in maintaining their denials. They are also prone to coercive means of enforcing disclaimers. A private ability to ignore what is in plain sight is enhanced by conscripting allies to reinforce beliefs or by intimidating others into validating what is required to be true. A modest example is "civil inattention." People routinely overlook embarrassing details about their immediate environment. Nowadays with cell phones in the palms of every teenager, people walk down the streets, holding loud conversations with unseen associates. Although it would be simple to eavesdrop, most strangers do not. They prefer to pretend these others are not there in the expectation that their own privacy will likewise be honored. When this inattention is directed at the losses others experience, they are spared the embarrassment of having their setbacks publicly advertised.

A more important social protection derives from our ability to employ *accounts* and *excuses*. Accounts are stories that people use to explain why what happened did. Excuses are similar, but they go further in providing a reason why the actor is not responsible for what transpired. Both derive their power to defend from the acceptance that others proffer. What members of a society consider believable stems not just from what is correct, but from what they have been taught is correct. This propensity to authenticate particular narratives is a cultural artifact that differs from one community to the next, depending on the prevailing consensus. A miniature example occurs every day in the lives of most Americans. When two acquaintances greet each other on the street, one is apt to ask, "How are you?" The second is just as likely to reply, "Fine." This then concludes their transaction. The rejoinder is taken as satisfactory even though it explains almost nothing about the second person's situation. The supposition is that their condition is predictable and therefore unworthy of pursuit. Despite the fact that almost everyone has something of interest occurring in his or her life, the answer suggests that the person is content to have their privacy respected. Indeed, the form of the first person's query implies that they hope for this reaction. In America, "fine" is a conventional account itself deemed sufficient. In the Middle East, however, the initial question would have elicited a lengthy narrative regarding the second person's health.

Other accounts are more complex, but they too imply a common understanding of how the world works. Thus, one person may ask a second why a third did as he or she did and receive as an explanation that he or she is "evil," "rich," "tired," or "drunk." Why did so and so rob the bank? Well, they are wicked. It is in their nature to do terrible things. Before 9/11, most people considered this sort of justification inadequate for world events. They would have demanded an account based on the childhood traumas of the perpetrators or national interests. Since the Al Qaeda attack, thanks to George W. Bush's speeches, an incomprehensible villainy is treated as sufficient. Although some of his critics attribute this to a lack of ratiocination, their favored accounts are as simplistic. Why do people commit crimes? Well, they are the victims of poverty. If it is pointed out that most poor people do not commit crimes, this in no way diminishes their confidence in this justification. Having many times heard it from people they trust, they do not question it.

When an account is employed to reduce culpability, it becomes an excuse. In the United States, in recent years, excuses have become rampant. Why did the Menendez brothers murder their parents? Well, they were reacting in self-defense because they believed their sexually abusive father was about to kill them. Why did the Los Angeles rioters throw a brick at the head of Reginald Denny? Well, they were reacting to the madness of the crowd and could not control their impulses. Why did Osama bin Laden develop a homicidal hatred of the West? Evidently the hegemonic United States unfairly exploited the Islamic world and precipitated the deaths of thousands of his coreligionists. In each of these cases, what would otherwise have been judged criminal became normal and therefore not blameworthy. The perpetrators would certainly deny they had done wrong. With the enthusiastic backing of a large percentage of the public, they would claim they were not engaged in "losing" behaviors and therefore should not be punished. Indeed, if a large and powerful faction coalesces around an excuse, those to whom it applies have not lost. Wasn't this the case when William Jefferson Clinton was found not guilty of high crimes and misdemeanors? Clinton could afterward go before the nation to proclaim he had successfully defended the constitution. Instead of hanging his head in disgrace, his allies buttressed his denials and made it possible to disregard his missteps. Thanks to them, he was not a loser.

What constitutes an excuse, however, can vary. A singular example is the case of drunk driving. Several decades ago, an inebriated driver could claim he or she was not responsible for an accident because their senses were impaired. Even when death ensued, because they were incapable of control, the tragedy was not their fault. It was an act of God that could have befallen anyone. After teenage driving became common, all this changed. Mothers Against Drunk Driving emerged to argue that drunkards should not be behind the wheel. Because their presence resulted from a voluntary decision for which they were responsible, they should pay a price. The upshot was that traffic laws were more rigorously enforced, and many motorists who previously elicited sympathy found themselves behind bars.

Social myths, ideologies, and narratives matter. They condition who will side with whom and therefore, in the case of conflicts, who is likely to defeat whom. They also provide plausible denials in some cases and socially endorsed rationalizations in others. Thus the attractiveness of political spin. Politicos expend considerable effort at influencing how ordinary people interpret events. This is why after a presidential address dozens hasten to the nearest television camera to explain why what the viewers just witnessed was wonderful (or the reverse). Because we human beings live in cognitive communities, we depend upon authorities to mold our understandings. When those in charge tell us what is real, we are primed to agree. Even in ordinary circumstances, when those with whom we interact present themselves as being a certain kind of person, we generally accept their version of reality. When they tell us they are smart, artistic, or compassionate, we suspend our disbelief and give them the benefit of the doubt. The effect is to allow people to get away with denials. In dealing with symbolic representations rather than things themselves, we make it possible to rewrite history so as to make it more palatable.

Similarly miraculous disappearing acts are achieved via normative means. Because we human beings belong to moral communities, their features are used to disguise what a person does not want to see. In this instance, force frequently comes into play. People intimidate and manipulate others into assisting them in a cover-up. Outsiders will agree to distort the facts lest they be exposed to disagreeable social sanctions. Take the situation of a scapegoat. When they are blamed for sins they did not commit, they may acknowledge them as their own because the alternative is to undergo significant punishments. But in consenting to a lie, they are allowing their oppressor to repudiate their own transgressions. This other will have intimidated the scapegoat into defending a falsehood and thereby employed moral censure to keep them from conceding their innocence.

Morality can seem so pure that we fail to notice that it is a form of social power. Anger, guilt, shame, and disgust are brought to bear to force an issue or shield an untruth. Paradoxically, morality is one of the safest refuges for villains. By turning the tables and accusing others before they can blame the scoundrel, the latter's crimes vanish from the radar screen. Additionally, the more dominant a person, the more effective this camouflage. Skilled manipulators, practiced liars, and well-connected power brokers possess leverage. They can arrange events so that others are at a disadvantage and hence are unprepared to instigate a counterattack. Relative clout allows them to hide in full view. Military dictators, to cite an extreme illustration, rarely understand the personal motivations that prompt them to tyrannize entire nations. Happily for them, their control of which rules get enforced ensures that most of their subordinates are sycophants. Who would have dared suggest to Hitler that his hatred of Jews stemmed from an abhorrence of his father?

Protest

Once a person has begun to penetrate their denials, the protest phase of resocialization commences. This is fundamentally the stage during which a person attempts to undo the ravages of faulty negotiations. While there are differences in the details of how ranks, roles, and relationships are constructed, there are crucial parallels. The coercion and manipulation that typify unfair interpersonal bargains habitually produce strong emotional reactions. These then tend to be denied because they contribute to losing. When intense emotions are employed intelligently and appropriately, they advance a person's agenda, but when not, they may make things worse. Since people in need of resocialization are trapped in dysfunctional roles, ranks, and relationships, it is a safe bet that they at some point were betrayed by their feelings.

The most central emotions that need to be reworked are fear and anger. In combination, these provide the protest phase with its pivotal qualities. What is being disputed is, after all, the iniquity of previous negotiations. What went wrong then was essentially that a person was frightened into giving up. He also grew impotently angry, but fear frustrated their ambitions. In order to correct what transpired, an individual now hopes to intimidate his or her former role partner into withdrawing illicit maneuvers. This other will then be less intimidating, hence ego will no longer be afraid to demand what was originally desired. In the case of childhood separations, angry stipulations once directed at a parent may be reactivated. Because the youngster was, and the adult still is, afraid to be alone, they want to obtain long-sought protections. This is a protest in that the child, and now adult, hated the former situation and insists it be rectified.

For the protest phase to succeed, today's anger and fear must somehow alter the results of yesterday's anger and fear. Emotions that were over the top, and therefore had to be denied rather than achieve their goals, must be brought under control and turned to good effect. Since it is literally too late to reverse a loss incurred years before, obtaining what was once wanted is too much to hope for. What can be realized, however, is an emotional readjustment. When the neural traces of ancient terrors are tamed in the present, the anger they incited can be diminished, thereby allowing a person to contemplate letting go. Feelings that were once too strong to be managed can be softened such that a current panic does not result in running away or rage end in a temper tantrum. An old loss may not be converted into a victory, but by tamping down the emotions it set off, new losses do not emerge. Likewise, by withdrawing salience from the relationships where losing occurred, the need to defeat old adversaries will decline. Only after this can, the prospect of future victories comes into view. Less desperate regarding what was lost, a person can better assess their situation and prospects. If this is so, the issue becomes how to manage long unmanageable fears and anger. But first we must pause to examine how intense emotions operate.

As ubiquitous as emotions are, they are not well understood. This too is one of the mysteries of resocialization. The process has not been recognized because strong feelings interfere with their own apprehension. Indeed, the stronger they are, the more they cloud the mind. People in the throes of fierce passions act as if they were dumb. They seem to go on automatic pilot, thereby sabotaging their most prized plans. This, not to put too fine a point on the matter, is one reason why people in distress have been evaluated as crazy. Nevertheless, emotions are not beyond human comprehension. They have been an essential component of animal behavior for geological epochs and are therefore a natural phenomenon capable of study. Happily, neurologists, in their investigations of the limbic system, are beginning to unravel their secrets.

What remains to be appreciated is the social nature of emotions. There is a tendency to consider feelings as strictly internal, but this is dangerously misleading. While emotions have their seat in the brain and do rile individual guts and psyches, they also have profound interpersonal effects. Human beings could not interact socially were they not subject to emotional influence. Anger is perhaps the best example. People do not get angry merely to entertain themselves. They get mad in order to change the behaviors of others. When they direct their ire at a particular person, the intention is to motivate him or her to do what is wanted. In fact, if nothing happens, one grows angrier.

The general pattern of the emotions is this. To begin with, emotions have goals. The purpose of fear is to protect against danger. Its goal, in other words, is safety. Meanwhile the purpose of anger is to remove frustrations. Its goal is the fulfillment of strongly desired aims. Sadness—since we will deal with it shortly—specializes in cutting ties with that which has been lost. Its goal is effecting a separation. To mention another vital emotion, shame seeks to focus negative attention on other persons. Its objective is to control social behavior by preventing others from serving as role models by inducing them to hide out. Lastly, disgust is a reaction to hazardous materials. It aims at getting people to avoid spoiled foodstuffs or ripe excrement. Because it is so efficient at this, it has also been appropriated to expedite social control. When individuals behave badly, they are treated as if they were too loathsome to approach, so as to persuade them to alter their conduct.

Not only do emotions have goals, but also these tend to continue in force until they accomplish their endpoints. As long as a person is in danger, she or he usually remains frightened. Only after safety is assured will calm return. Likewise, when a person is angry, as long as their frustration has not been assuaged, it continues to demand satisfaction. This propensity has enormous implications for resocialization. People trapped in uncomfortable social positions may remain irritated for years. Having sustained a hated loss, they entered upon a long-term vendetta. The fact that angry people do not give up easily imbues their protests with tenacity. Ironically, it also prevents them from letting go of what is lost. By the same token, sadness does not terminate until that which needs to be relinquished is cut loose. As long as a person nurses the expectation of a restoration of the status quo ante, the pain of loss remains.

The mechanisms the emotions utilize to achieve their goals are also intelligible. They are logical, comprehensible, and capable of being effectuated. The two principal avenues through which they operate are communication and motivation. Emotions communicate both with the self and with others. Thus, anger informs both the self and others that a major frustration is in progress. Anyone who has been angry will recognize the feeling that something is wrong. It may not immediately be apparent what has been thwarted, but a tropism in this direction alerts those who take the time to scan their environment. The ferocity of anger also brings this craving to the attention of others. Anger, whether internal or external, screams out to be noticed. It is a dependable signal that something is so acutely amiss that urgent consideration is imperative.

Yet were this all anger accomplished, it would be fruitless. The emotion also motivates action—and motivates it robustly. As with communications, this is directed both toward the self and others. Obviously an angry person is an obstinate person. He or she wants what they want and want it now. Angry people fight hard for what they desire. They are energized. That which they crave is so important that all their faculties are mobilized to obtain it. At the same time, their energies are trained on role partners who are expected to comply. When an irate person concentrates their fury on someone deemed responsible for a frustration, its intensity can be unnerving. As often as not, this other is frightened by this display and seeks to restore safety by fulfilling the angry person's demands. This, to be sure, is not automatic. If anger is misapplied, it can stimulate counter-anger. In this case, the other will treat a person's rage as a frustration and seek to eliminate it. The end product can be a head-butting contest so zealous that both parties wind up with cracked skulls.

For an emotion to achieve its goal, it must be implemented effectively. Its communication and motivational aspects must be performed appropriately for the situation. While all emotions possess a biological template, these need to be modified during the process of growing up if they are later to be successful. Their initial incarnations are "primitive," whereas the subsequent ones are "socialized." Babies certainly get angry and unquestionably get frightened. And when they do, they cry. They can cry so ferociously that their parents rush to meet their requirements and restore their safety. Nevertheless crying does not obtain the same outcomes for adults. Were grown-ups to cry, they would be ridiculed. They must learn to ask for what they want. Unless they are concrete regarding their anger or fears, others will not know how to assist them, nor care. The problem is that when people are intensely frightened or angry, they revert to primitive patterns. With fear, this expresses itself as panic. Out of control, fear results in a headlong rush to escape, often into the jaws of a threat. A terrified person is not thinking clearly about the danger or how to evade it.

Their feet fly into action without suitable calculations. With anger, excessive vigor spills over into rage. The person is taken over by a blind fury. When enraged, we say that people are seeing red because that is all they are seeing. Infuriated people strike out reflexively. They punch or kick, much as an infant might, but with imperfect conclusions. Not thinking rationally, they become vulnerable to the counterattacks of their targets. As a consequence, their anger does not abate. Rage and panic make things worse. They increase frustrations and reduce safety.

With regard to the protest phase of resocialization, panic and rage can be problematic. Frequently complicit in the original loss, they can also prevent its rectification. As long as the intensity of a person's emotions remains unmanageable, they can occasion the repetition of past errors. When therapists allude to clients "working through" issues, it is dealing with these emotions they generally have in mind. They know that if their analysands have not mastered fear and anger, they must now learn to do so. Only then will they be able to achieve safety with respect to lost negotiations or prove capable of laying ancient frustrations to rest.

For the moment, let us set aside the question of how this can be accomplished. What must come first is an examination of the sorts of fears and anger that arise during the protest stage. For starters, it must be emphasized that the most problematic fears are almost entirely provoked by people. During role, rank, and relationship negotiations, their partners—more accurately adversaries—attempt to inflict losses. They engaged in coercive tactics that included threats of harm, physical violence, and deceitful manipulation. All of these were unsettling, especially for children. Each hurt, and some could cause death. But the dangers of unfair negotiations went beyond this. It was not only what the other party did, but also how it was done. Unreasonable negotiation partners are intransigent. For reasons a child cannot fathom, these others did not give up. No matter how desperate their pleas, or protracted their suffering, they would not relent. This introduced an alarming element of hopelessness. These partners were probably inflexible, in part, due to their own losses. Feeling unable to win, they could not afford to give up. Yet how would a child know this? Children have difficulty even comprehending their own motives.

Closely akin to coercion would be a fear of abandonment, and closely akin to abandonment is neglect. When a parent deserts a child, this loss is forced on the victim. Children are programmed to form bonds and resist separations. The latter must be energetically imposed. Neglect differs from abandonment in that it takes place without a parent leaving. A child's needs are so relentlessly ignored, it is as if the parent were gone. Here too the child will struggle to be protected, but to no avail. In both cases, it loses and must fear both aloneness and a failure to obtain life-sustaining support. Some parents compound this problem by sending contradictory signals. As in the classical double bind, they promise security and then punish a demand for it. They literally ask the child to come closer only to push him or her away. Worse still, these responses are usually unpredictable. The child never knows where it stands and must fret about what is to come even when a parent's attentions are appropriate. Such insecure attachments, as Bowlby observed, prompt an anxious bonding in which a child clings desperately to the very person causing insecurity. B. F. Skinner likewise demonstrated that pigeons subjected to intermittent reinforcement schedules, that is, ones where they were unpredictably rewarded, produce the most intense and enduring exertions.

Moreover, children, being children, possess a narrow social purview. Unable to place themselves in the shoes of others whose life circumstances they have never experienced, they cannot begin to fathom events swirling around others. Their insecurities are multiplied by an ignorance of the fights, jealousies, and failures of their negotiation partners. Nor can children comprehend how third parties influence the behaviors of those who hold sway over them. Theirs is inevitably a universe filled with social uncertainties. If secure attachments are not available to alleviate doubts, these too escalate to unsustainable levels. With restricted stores of knowledge, immature mental equipment, and incomplete personal experience, they are adrift in a cosmos they cannot handle.

And then there are a child's own impulses. These too can be frightening because of their potential impact on caregivers. Babies are born greedy. They want what they want when they want it. Reason does not diminish their appetites, nor parental problems eliminate a desire for attention. When coupled with an inability to understand what might set off significant others, this can be a recipe for disaster. A gnawing in the belly, or an overly insistent bowel, may initiate a chain of events that terminates in a painful thrashing. Since these demands are barely under the control of young children, they inevitably worry about facets of themselves they cannot predict. It is not at all unusual for them to seek self-command by punishing themselves for wayward appeals. These attempts at control then become something else to fear. Besides this, their anger is a source of anxiety. Because they want to resist the impositions besieging them, but because this may provoke the counter-anger of powerful others, their frustrations can be self-defeating. Ever alert to such emotional threats, children develop a vigilance that looks both inward and outward. The solution can be to do as little as possible. Even so, life will appear jam-packed with perils.

With so much to fear, losses are bound to accumulate. A tendency to withdraw, in conjunction with the incompetence that accompanies panic, results in a multitude of opportunities lost and battles botched. Frustrations, and thus anger, inexorably mount. Indeed, the more extensive the losses, the more important it will feel to win and the greater impetus to rage and further losses. With this sort of a downward cycle in place, an escape into adulthood will not interrupt these dangers. Fantasies of one day being strong enough to impose one's preferences on others will flounder in the realities of one's adult weaknesses. Instead of developing the maturity to win grown-up conflicts, a history of inept self-assertion produces an isolated anxiety that is self-perpetuating. Having never surmounted the fears that disrupted earlier efforts to prevail, and having never fully socialized their anger, as adults they fume and sputter until fresh defeats force them to abandon the field.

In order for anger to become an effective negotiating tool, some fundamental lessons must be learned. For starters, a person must acquire the internal controls not to act precipitously. One of the primary reasons children lose confrontations is that they get enraged in the wrong way, over the wrong things, in the wrong places, and at the wrong times. First, throwing a tantrum is definitely counterproductive. Screaming, cursing, and pounding one's fists on the table are puerile. The loudness and violence of such explosions demonstrate a lapse of self-restraint that makes a person vulnerable to others who are under better control. Those not on infantile automatic pilot are better able to recognize how to injure others and are therefore much more intimidating. Second, anger that erupts at the mere hint of frustration often attempts to achieve the impossible. No one, no matter how powerful, can win every battle. Potential winners understand that they must choose their clashes with care. If they mobilize for a fight, it should be over something important, regarding which they can prevail. To do otherwise is to squander one's resources. It is to bring too little energy to bear at the point of contact and therefore to lose. Third, the scene of combat matters. Getting angry with somebody on their turf can make all the difference. When people are on familiar ground, it stiffens their resolve and makes them more formidable. Good generals understand that you launch an attack where you have the edge. Fourth, timing matters. If you can help it, you don't go into battle when the other person is most prepared to resist. Winning tacticians look for the advantage of surprise. Similarly, those who know how to use anger wait to express it when the other is receptive.

Because anger tends to precipitate counter-anger, it is essential to know a prospective enemy. What makes him or her angry? What resources can they draw upon? Most vital of all, what are their goals? Children often lose encounters because they recognize none of these. Constitutionally egoistic, they are dreadful role-takers. They may realize some situations are too treacherous to hazard action, but they rarely recognize how to use an adversary's weakness against them. This is not to say that children cannot be manipulative. Their intuitive insights into the frailties of negotiating partners can be uncanny. Nevertheless, their social horizons are so narrow they miss critical cues and blunder into fatal errors. In their inexperience and emotional immaturity, they miscalculate the forces acting on the other and thus cannot redirect these for their own benefit. For example, a child whose father chases it into the bedroom will not realize that his rage has been displaced from a snub that took place earlier at work. It will therefore have no idea about how to assuage his dignity.

Anger is also most effective when used in conjunction with allies. Interpersonal battles are frequently multi-person affairs and hence winners are those with the numbers on their side. As every child understands, if mommy can be recruited in a battle against dad, victory becomes possible, whereas if it is lined up against both parents, defeat is preordained. Nevertheless, children are relatively isolated. They know fewer people than their parents and those they know—their siblings and playmates—are less formidable than the adults with whom they must vie. To put the matter candidly, the deck is stacked against them. In fact, the more effective they are in employing their anger, the more they are apt to inspire adults to enlist additional allies. Leave mom shaken by arguments in favor of staying out late, and she calls dad into the fray. Set both parents back on their heels, and they threaten to bring in the police.

Dependable alliances are so essential to making anger stick that one of the main virtues of psychotherapy is that it furnishes a reliable collaborator. A clinician is supposed to be on a client's side. When the latter feels overwhelmed by recollections of an oppressive parent, the therapist can be there with a dose of reality. In reminding the client that their parents were unfair, the helper offers himself or herself as a partner against them. This provides the client with both the courage to resist and additional arguments with which to counterattack. For those who embark on the protest phase of resocialization without benefit of a therapist, the same services can be brought to bear from friends, spouses, and colleagues. In validating a person's feelings, they too can function as allies. They too can provide resources that were missing in childhood and make possible victories unavailable earlier on.

The protest phase is consequently not merely about protest, but effective protest. Emotions that once interfered with winning must be honed until winning becomes feasible. Unless this happens, a person will not be prepared to move on to the next stage of resocialization, that is, to letting go. In order to relinquish what has been lost without being able to imagine, obtaining something better is psychologically unworkable. It is to stare into an abyss without a bottom, which is utterly terrifying. It is therefore crucial for a person to strengthen their emotional reserves. Years of losing may seem to have demonstrated an endemic weakness, but it is indispensable that one discovers emotional potency can be augmented. A person has to learn that they were not born inherently fearful or innately out-of-control. Both fear and anger can be mastered when someone understands how.

Some years ago, I wrote a book on anger management. It described a five-step process called integrated anger management. Although concerned primarily with rage, the mechanisms elucidated also apply to intense emotions such as fear. The preliminary step is to ensure safety. An emotion, whether anger or fear, that becomes primitive goes ballistic. In the midst of an unmodified rage, people commit murder, and under the influence of unrestrained panic, they commit suicide. Intense emotions are so witless that they perpetrate acts completely at odds with a person's interests. It is therefore imperative to keep them from becoming too extreme. An angry person must be calmed down and a fearful one bucked up. One way to achieve this is to remove a person from the presence of that which is provocative. If a frustration has become unbearable, leaving the room may lessen it. Or an antagonistic spouse might, for instance, be excluded from a therapy session. Similarly, if a fear has gone into overdrive, the danger inciting it may be made less visible. A client's attention can, for example, be diverted so that he or she does not obsess on the possibility of losing a job. Even without the aid of a chemical assistant, it is possible to reduce the strength of a passion so it does not do damage. Once this is accomplished, it is possible to move on to the next step.

One of the notable discoveries of psychological clinicians has been desensitization. If a person is exposed to a tolerable emotion—one that has not flipped into a primitive state—and this exposure occurs under safe circumstances, eventually the feeling becomes less threatening. That which seemed beyond control ultimately becomes controllable and therefore less apt to go awry. Another way to depict this process is as "incremental tolerance." If emotions are chopped up into small, manageable doses, these can be faced and in the long run incorporated into the psyche. The memory of what provoked them will be altered and hence that which was frustrating, or frightening, become less so. It takes time for this mental rearrangement to occur, but given the patience and expertise to deal with feelings progressively, they cease to be awe-inspiring.

This, however, is not the end of becoming emotionally effective. In order for feelings such as anger, fear, and sadness to be of value, they must be used. Their communication and motivation functions have to be harnessed so as to facilitate winning. Anger that does not help a person overcome frustration is futile, fears that do not promote interpersonal safety are wasted, and sadness that never tears broken bonds asunder is pointless. Emotions are not ornaments intended to fill people's heads while other things take place; they are vital elements of life. If they do not communicate and motivate properly, the proceedings are clumsy and the outcomes not as desired. But to be used well, what is occurring must be correctly understood. The causes of a person's anger and its potential resolution need to be accurately assessed. Likewise, the sources of fear must be rightly apprehended and potential havens of safety duly noted.

Incremental tolerance having lowered the affective pitch, an accurate evaluation of the circumstances of an emotion should be achievable. A frustrated person can determine the goals being frustrated, as well as who (or what) is doing the frustrating. More than this, it should be possible to plan a successful course of conduct. With a head clear enough to assess the situation of likely adversaries, what motivates them can more accurately be established. Their goals can be discerned and potential allies conscripted. With fear it becomes feasible to determine the nature of the danger and how it can be diffused. Would fight or flight be best under these conditions, and how could these be effected? Before swinging into action, the entire chessboard needs to be appraised. Unlike the mechanical and stereotypical strategies of primitive emotions, what is done must be germane and efficient.

In some cases, an honest review will establish that what is wanted is not possible. A person might have been frustrated because a parent did not deliver the desired affection, but upon closer inspection, it may be obvious that the parent was incapable of it. Under these circumstances, it may be necessary for a person to alter their aspirations. No matter how fondly a goal is desired, or how vital it is to a person's well-being, if it is not achievable, it is not achievable. To continue insisting upon it would therefore be in vain. However painful, the only reasonable response is a change in direction. Relinquishing a long-held objective, however, requires the same sort of emotional processing as letting go of an attachment to a human being. Here too sadness is the appropriate mechanism for surrendering what has been lost. With anger, unless this sort of mourning is endured, a person will continue to fight and persist in being frustrated. With fear, sometimes only abandoning what is dangerous can bring safety.

In any event, integrated emotion management cannot come to a satisfactory conclusion until problematic emotions are successfully put to work. Its fifth and final step is to achieve what is wanted. Only then are the goals of emotions reached and brought to quiescence. With respect to resocialization, however, a final accounting must be postponed. Because the function of its protest phase is to lay the groundwork for what is to come, the tasks it seeks to achieve cannot be completed within the protest stage itself. The fear and anger that characterize it must remain in a state of suspended animation until later resurrected to replace what was lost. When these are eventually reexperienced, albeit under renegotiating circumstances that make them more effective, unhappy childhood outcomes can finally be improved upon. In the meantime, discovering that success in one's original endeavors was never viable must be recognized. The roles, ranks, and relationships that once seemed vital must be perceived as forever beyond reach. Those who enter upon resocialization typically imagine that unless they undo previous losses, winning is out of the question. Perhaps their most unwelcome finding is, therefore, that the opposite is true. They must learn that unless they definitively lose what was lost, they can never win. Seriously dysfunctional roles cannot be tinkered with until they become functional. To the contrary, more serviceable ones must supplant them. Nor are low ranks miraculously transformed into higher statuses. The contests that established these must be bypassed in favor of tests of strength where a person possesses an advantage. Similarly, abusive relationships are hardly ever converted into fairy-tale affairs complete with "happily ever after strolls" into a glorious sunset. In the best cases, they are replaced by entirely different relationships.

A phenomenon common to various forms of psychotherapy, and therefore resocialization, is "peeling the onion." Freud was fond of comparing psychoanalysis to an archeological expedition. His clients were routinely encouraged to plumb the hidden depths of past relationships in order to determine what went wrong. The "fixations" for which they were seeking a resolution were not, however, to be found in a single mother lode of insights. Discoveries came piecemeal, with one preparing the way for another. The reason can be attributed to the Cascade Effect. Because losses tend to succeed each other, when they are revived, it tends to be in reverse order. Thus, successfully protesting one permits a person to penetrate the defenses surrounding an earlier one. Overcoming the anger associated with latter increases an individual's sense of potency such that he or she acquires the courage to confront other areas of vulnerability. In the end, it takes many years, replete with many breakthroughs, before important losses are tackled and surmounted.

Sadness

When someone dies, the proof of death is usually tangible. When roles, ranks, or relationships are lost, they do not expire as categorically. It can take a lot of convincing before a person realizes that what is gone really is gone. The denials can be interminable and the protests protracted. Even as a person learns to discern what went wrong, the hope of finding an ingenious way out can linger. With just a little more effort, or a little more goodwill, who knows what is possible? The upshot is that the protest phase can last for years. Long after it is clear that bad things really occurred, their futility is excluded from consciousness. Indeed, the pain can be so great that accepting it feels like the ultimate loss, that is, a loss of life itself.

"Sadness" is an unpretentious word. It may not sound so bad. "Depression," however, has worse connotations. Still, these are not insuperable. "Sorrow" is probably a little worse and "misery" worse yet. Nevertheless, not until we get to "despondency" does the full impact of the emotion begin to be felt. "Gloom" and "hopelessness" round out the picture. Grief, in short, no matter how normal, is not for the faint of heart. It can, as its intimates discover, be horrendously painful. Not only about death, but since it can literally feel like death, people do not intentionally choose it. Rather it chooses them. Among other things, those in the depths of "despair" suffer an existential aloneness. With no one available to offer help, they feel forlorn, surrounded, as it were, by an empty, inky-black nothingness. As a result, deep in their chests they undergo the gnawing agony of the totally unloved. Since no one else seems to care, they conclude there is no point in caring about themselves. In the throes of sadness, they feel entirely hopeless. Having experienced an unmitigated loss, they perceive no possibility of winning. Moreover, with almost everything except the particulars of their defeat crowded out of their heads, they cannot imagine a way out. Perhaps the best option is to give in to the pain and terminate life. This, they deduce, would terminate their worries. What, indeed, is the purpose of enduring relentless anguish into an indefinite future?

One reason mourning feels lethal can be traced to its origins. Individuals who have experienced losses early in life actually had a close brush with death. The marasmus of which Bowlby spoke applies not only to ruptured attachments, but also to dysfunctional roles, hierarchical failures, and horrific relationships. Each of these, because it entails a dreadful loss, can make a child feel as if there is no point in striving to live. Lest it be forgotten, young children do not have a firm hold on life. When they find themselves choking on their own tears, they do not know why. When they suddenly feel themselves falling, they cannot judge the seriousness of the potential impact. For a young child, night terrors truly are terrifying. The shadows that pass along the wall, or the sounds emanating from the blackness of the street, betoken dangers that may seem mortal. For the very young, death is a specter they are not certain they can keep at arm's length. Inarticulately aware of their vulnerability, they tremble at the prospect of that which they cannot master. In fact, for them extreme aloneness is tantamount to death. And so, therefore, is the aloneness of adults who reexperience childhood losses. Once their ancient wounds are reopened, they too will worry about their safety. Very much against their will, they once again feel like children, hence when they lay their heads down on their pillows, they too dream of falling into a bottomless pit of despair from whence there is no return. The shadows of their impending grief appear to be a vacuum intent on sucking them in, thus the resolve not to allow this to happen.

For some people the realization of loss never arrives. They will not permit it. Theirs is an ache that never wholly disembarks, nor ever quite goes away. It is a subtle melancholy that hangs on through the best of times. Things may never get so bad that they cannot be tolerated, but they never get so good that the gray haze separating them from reality is pulled aside. For others, however, the gravity of loss cannot be evaded. They eventually reach a point where they cannot fool themselves into believing that what went wrong can be fixed. They see the sadness coming, and want to postpone it, but like a Sandburg fog, it creeps inexorably forward on little cat feet. Sooner or later they find themselves enveloped by a pall through which they can barely see. Now they awake each morning feeling listless. Small events that previously felt pleasant lose their delight. Suddenly they do not want to do anything. Content to sit in a dark room and mull over they know not what, anything to which they apply their efforts, they perform ineptly. Life slows to a languid pace. And amazingly, they do not care. They do not care about anything, and that is the nastiest turn of all.

Grief is not something for which we practice, and until recently it was not something anyone studied. When it comes, it does so on its own terms. In the midst of mourning, a person can experience a compelling need to be alone and later on the same day an equally powerful need for comfort. The head is flooded with thoughts, some of which are in focus, but others lie just beyond an unidentifiable shore. In a state of grief, a person will stare into space contemplating a lost instant in time or with a vacant smile shed a tear for his or her own misfortune. Mourners occupy a universe filled with unpleasant dreams. During the day these can be starkly real, but at night more so. What is actually happening is of little consequence and therefore subject to neglect.

What is occurring in a state of grief is that a person's emotions and circumstances are being reorganized. The filing and consolidating processes to which Hobson alludes are in an active mode. So many feelings need to be readjusted and so many plans of action modified that reworking them takes all of a person's time and energy. As fresh memories kaleidoscopically replace each other, they elicit the emotional responses originally connected with them, thereby sanctioning their alteration. Ties are cut because they become available to be cut. Oh yes, it was wonderful to share those intimate conversations over the morning coffee. Even the smell is as it once was, but now it is gone. There is no coffee, there is no conversation, and there is no loving person. They are in the minds' eye, not the here and now. They truly have vanished and cannot be acted toward as if they had not.

This kind of separation from the current reality is an essential feature of depression. The very pain of sadness is a mechanism for ensuring the space to reevaluate and reorganize both emotional memories and long-term commitments. Like the pain caused by a physical injury, it produces a vulnerability that impels a person to seek the privacy of disengagement. Erik Erikson, in discussing the tribulations of adolescent identity crises, affirms their need for a "psychosocial moratorium." They are said to require a suspension of ordinary demands so they can metamorphose into their adult selves. Something analogous applies to the grieving process. Those caught within its dark clutches are, thanks to their discomfort, adrift in a limbo of colliding thoughts and reassessed emotions. In their pain, they become immobile, much as pain might induce them to immobilize a broken arm. Here too external pressures are excluded so as to facilitate healing. In this case, however, the healing entails reviewing, and reassessing, the past in excruciating detail.

If all this angst is burdensome in the case of death, lost roles, ranks, and relationships are more difficult to endure. Because losing is a process and not just an event, it entails many losses. Unlike the case of definitive traumas, there are many more ties to be severed, frequently too many to be excised at once. The result is multiple troughs. Individuals undergoing resocialization endure succeeding periods of depression. Each time they emerge from a pit of despair, they may imagine that their trial is over only to plunge into another decline shortly thereafter. This adds yet another layer of mystery to the process of coping with failure. Since these fresh depressions can come without warning, an unexpected incident can set a person off and they are once again deeply unhappy. This incongruity is intensified by the fact that renewed mourning can arise when things seem to be improving. The paradox is that sometimes a person is not ready to experience a deep sadness until they are strong enough to bear it, and this strength is not consolidated until things are going well. It is the security of success that paves the way to confront the insecurity of further losses.

These collective circumstances should begin to explain the tangle of diagnoses that have surrounded periods of profound sadness. Major and minor depressions come packaged as they do as a result of where and how they appear within the resocialization process. They are not separate entities, but distinct manifestations of the same course of development. While some depressions are biologically produced, the vast majority have their origin in dealing with loss and losing. Once this is understood, it makes it easier to guide people through the shoals and shallows that mark the progression of moving on. They can be instructed on the instinctiveness of the process and helped to recognize that at its bottom is not death, but an upward corridor toward a better future. For many, this awareness can make the difference. It can provide the extra measure of courage they need to press ahead.

Interestingly enough, the details of resocialization provide explanations for some of the baffling peculiarities of depressive disorders. Dysthymia, for instance, can be understood as a long-term, low-level depression that fails to lift because it never reaches completion. Instead of a person descending into the depths of despair, he or she is so frightened of its pain as to not allow it to fully occur. The result is never letting go of a loss, with the consequence that it never stops hurting. A related phenomenon occurs with some forms of cyclothemia. Repeated episodes of sadness may be due to the Cascade Effect regarding losses. Because these are chained together, a person may work through one loss, only to acquire the strength to work through another. Rather than cut one's ties to all at once, there is a roller-coaster effect of feeling worse, then better, then worse, and so forth. If this is so, it may not be due to defective biology so much as to the limits of our ability to sustain the anguish of losing.

Renegotiation

The last stage in surviving a loss is generally referred to as "acceptance." The implication is that after his or her sadness lifts a person is ready for whatever comes next. Accepting a loss means it no longer has to be resisted and that a person's energies are freed up to deal with the new. There is the further implication that with gloom dispersed, hope returns. The former mourner is now looking forward in anticipation, and this will be sufficient to deal with whatever comes.

New relationships and unpredicted victories are the reward of those prepared to welcome them.

All of this is partially true. Emerging from depression does make progress possible. But it does not do so of its own. Resuming a winning itinerary after years of losing is not reflexive. Individuals who have never learned how to win do not commence doing so because they have cut their ties to prior losses. They must first learn how to prevail. And this entails a raft of skills they may not yet possess. New roles, ranks, and relationships do not descend from heaven. Once their dysfunctional predecessors have been banished, improved versions must be created. Nor is there a guarantee that what is merely different will be better. Unless a person is competent at negotiating new social positions, and doing so with appropriate negotiating partners, the losing may start all over again. Individuals who do not know how to bargain, or who are inept at identifying fair-minded collaborators, can plunge into another round of misery.

The final phase of resocialization is the renegotiation phase because enhanced roles, ranks, and relationships come into existence only through such social negotiations. One way or another, the interactions necessary to fill the void left by relinquishing the past have to take place and take place well. The question is how fruitfully these will occur. Under the best of circumstances, children learn how to negotiate by interfacing with parents' intent on helping them do so fairly. Fathers and mothers who love their offspring want them to achieve social statuses in which personal satisfaction is possible. If they themselves feel like winners, they do not resent the victories of their children. They do not feel that these triumphs diminish their own. Nor will they demand roles skewed in their favor, ranks that are oppressively dominating, or relationships that are abusive. To the contrary, they will coach their children on how to be appropriately assertive. Then they revel in their successes.

Most people who must endure resocialization have not been so lucky. They have had to outlast unbalanced divisions of labor, brutal tests of strength, and deceitful relationships. What they may therefore require are trustworthy tutors. In psychotherapy, the clinician occupies this role. She or he not only explains how negotiating is done, but provides an object lesson in useful techniques. The same sort of transference that was a prominent feature earlier in their early collaboration may be drafted to serve this other purpose. The client will not merely talk to the therapist, but make demands of them. Indeed, the more confident the client becomes, the less diffident they will be. This, in fact, will test the therapist's mettle. An insecure clinician may impose their will on the client, but a competent one will allow them to be more forceful. This sort of therapist recognizes that the goal is not control, but interchanges that result in equitable agreements. These may be relatively trivial, for example, regarding the time of meetings, but they serve as models for more important negotiations outside the therapy session.

The same sort of renegotiation training can take place in ordinary life. It is remarkable how frequently people engage in such activities as a means of rehearsal. In sociology, this is called anticipatory socialization. A person arranges their social parameters so as to approach an imagined future by mentally checking a variety of possibilities. College professors do this when they test materials in a classroom that are later presented at professional associations. Daters do this when they go out with partners they know will not be "right." How the two handle choosing a restaurant may set the pattern that later resurfaces when making cooperative decisions with a spouse. As long as gross unfairness is avoided, these dry runs are not only acceptable; they are a standard means for honing essential skills.

These skills will include role negotiations, tests of relative power, and interpersonal courtship processes. Each has its own complications, but these will be dealt with further in the ensuing chapters.

5

Roles

Each man's freedom stops at the tip of his neighbor's nose.
(A libertarian refrain)

The Division of Labor

Americans have grown accustomed to thinking about society as a collection of separate individuals. The image that leaps to mind is collection of unrelated billiard balls sitting on a pool table. Each of these is conceived of as a Leibnizian monad distinct unto itself and untroubled unless there is a collision with another monad. The notion that everyone is perfectly free, except when physically interfered with by an antidemocratic neighbor, is deeply imbued in the national psyche. As long as people do not throw garbage into each other's yards or get into a punch-out when they have a political disagreement, they are at liberty to live life as they choose. "This is a free country, and I can say whatever I want" (with the possible exception of yelling fire in a crowded theater). This is the mantra on the lips of the youngest Americans. Each implicitly believes that if no one gets hurt, each can be absolutely independent of others.

In recent years, the postmodernists have taken this position and pushed it forward with a vengeance. They resent attempts to dictate how others should behave, characterizing these incursions as oppressive. Particularly incensed that elites seek to impose standards on others, they denounce external controls as inimical to freedom. In *The Social Contract*, Rousseau wrote "Man is born free, and everywhere he is in chains." Postmodernists believe this true and have made it their mission, like modern Philippe Pinel's, to strike the manacles from the wrists of an imprisoned humanity.

The problem with this vision is that it is at odds with the realities of the human condition. As social creatures, we human beings interfere with each other all the time. If we did not, we would be no different than autumn leaves blown across a lawn. Our actions would be uncoordinated, and there would be no benefit to living together in large numbers. People are not like bears. We do not wander the woodlands as solitary operators, foraging only for ourselves and acting in concert only to fornicate—quite the opposite. Our social natures decree that the vast majority of us participate in extended webs of attachment. Rather than proceed alone, we join forces in common endeavors. Even when our collaborators are not physically present, we take them into consideration. Sometimes their demands determine our actions and sometimes ours determine theirs, but sometimes a mental conception of our respective needs is all that is necessary to shape our joint behaviors. Indeed our identities are molded by these influences. Who we are, what we want, and when we succeed are all constrained by social linkages. Our survival depends on it. The fact that we, as a species, are as powerful as we are is due to interpersonal coordination.

Remarkably, this coordination is largely achieved without the need for people to touch each other. They do not require physical contact in order to manipulate one another's behaviors. Most of our influence is, in fact, accomplished symbolically. Sounds and sights transmit compelling messages. Language is an obvious medium for such transmissions. However, the way we dress, the place we live, and the literatures we read are also effective. Much of this is unconscious and apparently built into our biology. Making faces, for instance, can be remarkably forceful. Yet if not genetically programmed, why would a child's protruding tongue produce distress? It is as if each of us possesses a cerebral amplifier that makes particular signals especially salient. This ability is so refined that humans affect each other even when physically absent. The mere memory of previous communications can be sufficient to modify individual conduct. Such messages are particularly potent when incorporated in a person's self-image.

Charles Horton Cooley, in pioneering American sociology, made the enduring observation that personal identities are dependent on the judgments of significant others. Children develop what he referred to as a "looking-glass self." In gazing into a parent's eyes, they perceive an image of themselves as envisioned by this other. The well-loved child thus comes to conceive of itself as lovable, whereas one who has frightened its parents may consider itself inherently intimidating. Moreover, socially created beliefs subsequently govern an adult's interpersonal relationships. The loved child is more likely to be at ease with a greater array of peers, whereas the unloved one will be more wary.

Social controls are ubiquitous. Whether internalized, environmentally imposed, or symbolically mediated, they affect everyone—including hermits. Postmodernists notwithstanding, no one is free to do whatever he or she desires. Although these externally inspired limitations can be onerous, they have their payoffs. People may wish to have what they want, but they benefit from being part of a group. Just as low-ranking members of a wolf pack tolerate indignities in exchange for a share of the kill, so human beings swallow their pride rather than be ostracized from the community.

One of the primary ways human associations pay off is via a role-based division of labor. Adam Smith in his *The Wealth of Nations* commented on the virtues of "modern" pin factories.[1] As he explained, back in the old days, blacksmiths manufactured pins. They would spend an entire day preparing the metal, drawing it out, cutting it to size, making points, and producing flat ends. And when they were done, they would have a handful of fasteners. "Nowadays," however, pins were fabricated in factories. A functional division of labor split the assembly process into an assortment of interlocking tasks. One person was responsible for drawing out the metal, and only drawing it out, while a second was delegated to cut it to size and only to cut it. This specialization enabled each to concentrate on a single operation. The result was greater efficiency. In the end, more pins were produced, which were cheaper and of higher quality.

Emile Durkheim took this insight a step further. Like his precursors, he was fascinated by the organic analogy of human society. As did August Comte and Herbert Spencer before him, he compared contemporary civilizations with animal bodies. The latter were not homogeneous, but divided into organ systems. An elementary anatomy lesson disclosed a stomach, liver, lungs, heart, brain, eyes, and muscles. Each of these performed a singular task to contribute to the survival of the larger organism. The lungs oxygenated the blood, the heart pumped this around the body, and the muscles converted potential energy to movement. The brain specialized in thought, the eyes in sight, and the stomach in digestion. Without each doing its job, the whole would collapse. For Durkheim, the pattern was the same with regard to human societies. These too consisted of webs of cooperative organs. Farmers grew food, truckers brought it to market, and vendors made it available to ordinary citizens. Likewise politicians specialized in planning, soldiers in community defense, and scientists in developing knowledge. Here too the continued existence of the whole depended on the collaborative functioning of its parts. Although individual contributions differed, they were complementary. Together they made the social order more potent. In societies, these specializations were incorporated in individual roles. With each person occupying a distinctive niche, all were better off than if they performed identical operations.

Durkheim believed that this organic arrangement was characteristic of modern civilizations. In mass-market societies, people cooperated with one another because they profited from exchanging goods. Dubbing this "organic solidarity," he contrasted it with the "mechanical solidarity" of hunter-gatherers. Durkheim described our nomadic ancestors as cooperating because, with all performing the same tasks, they could understand and empathize with each other. In this, however, he underestimated the degree of specialization found among early humans. *Homo sapiens* began their tenure on earth already prepared to divide communal chores. It is difficult to imagine that hunting parties equipped only with spears would tackle prey as large as mastodons without an efficient means of synchronizing their attack. Some must have been delegated to drive the quarry in a preselected direction, while others to ambush the animals. It is also likely that some were superior at fabricating tools and therefore concentrated on doing so. We know that present-day hunters rely on skilled tree climbers to gather honey. We are also familiar with their reliance on dedicated healers. Why should our distant forerunners have been different? A division of labor based on disparate abilities and a need to harmonize complex activities would have been as useful then as now. Because a stable division of labor facilitated collecting food, building dwellings, and protecting against external threats, its advantage is plain. So too is the fact that we inherited a proclivity to engage in role behavior.

On the assumption that social roles are indigenous to human societies, the next question to be answered is this: What are the prerequisites for a successful division of labor? There are several. The first is *stability*. If functional roles are to be complementary, they must be predictable. It is impossible for two (or more) people to work together if they cannot calculate their respective actions. Just as motorists must be able to foresee where other motorists are headed, so must hunters anticipate the positions of their comrades. By the same token, members of the same household need to understand who is responsible for stocking the pantry. A failure to agree on this could produce hunger pangs. Worse still would be a mother who impulsively decided to abandon her children. If she were not reliably available to nurse her infants, what would become of them? They would occupy a universe so undependable as to be terrifying. On a less discordant note, how could subway systems operate if motormen did not report at regular hours? An excessively dynamic role structure would therefore send everyone scurrying to care for their own needs, thereby wiping out interpersonal cooperation. If only one's own contributions were predictable, it would make no sense to depend on strangers. Beyond this, roles must be difficult to change. They must possess a conservative quality that ensures they are not arbitrarily modified. This, however, dictates that both functional and dysfunctional roles are difficult to alter. For the sake of stability, that which does not meet individual or social needs is frozen in place just as strongly as roles worth preserving. Despite the wishes of all concerned, mechanisms that prevent random change prevent people from improving that which needs upgrading.

A second precondition of a viable division of labor is *complementarity*. For interlocking roles to be useful, they must be different. If everyone performed exactly the same tasks, there would be no point in cooperating. Each person is better off only if an exchange of unique specialties distributes benefits not otherwise available. Were everyone his own carpenter, few would have the opportunity to become skilled carpenters, plumbers, or electricians. Moreover, tasks that supplement each other make for a superior tapestry. Their unique features interlock to reinforce each other. Yet different implies unequal. Because not all jobs are satisfying, some individuals get plum assignments, whereas others get stuck with the dregs. Nevertheless, efforts to ensure complete equality are ill advised because only coercion could manage this, the detrimental effect of which would be greater than the disparities.

Lastly, a functioning division of labor entails *coordination*. For specialized tasks to be beneficial, they must match with corresponding roles. Trains operate best when the motorman and brakeman do not simultaneously exercise their prerogatives. Nor is it possible to erect a skyscraper if the people who pour the foundation arrive months later than the plasterers. To be functional, roles must synchronize in a manner consistent with their design. As with dance partners, if it is not clear who goes forward and who back, who leads and who follows, the consequence can be a pratfall. To drive this point home, the offensive squad of a football team is unlikely to score many touchdowns if the center and quarterback never practice together. Such preparations, however, entail interpersonal demands. The only way to ensure that people do what is required is to insist that they perform in a specified manner. Yet because individuals are not spontaneously cooperative, this insistence must periodically be adamant. More often than the participants like, they are compelled to do someone else's bidding. Clearly, given our desire for freedom, they may be inclined to protest.

If all of this is so, if, in order to be functional, a division of labor must be stable, complimentary, and coordinated, how are integrated roles established? If they are unequal, subject to coercive demands, and difficult to change, why do people assume them? Must a Hobbesian Leviathan impose a straitjacket on a reluctant humanity? Or do people voluntarily assume their roles anyway? To begin with, there is no single traffic cop directing the synchronization of a society-wide division of labor. Nor could there be. With so many actions to be coordinated, no central authority could possibly cope. Nor would a force sufficiently potent be tolerated by a species that wishes personal autonomy. There are, however, numerous centers of coercion. These are the role partners with whom individuals interact. Such persons impose stipulations that sometimes approach being nonnegotiable. They frequently require a person to deliver services whether or not they feel like it. Moreover, as long as these conditions are consistent with an individual's role assignment, their partners will receive the support of other community members.

There is a social psychological tradition that defines roles in terms of the "expectations" of role partners. This, however, is misleading. People who coordinate their activities with others do have expectations, and these are grounded in predictability. Nevertheless a social division of labor is more than predictable; its stability is socially imposed. Role partners "demand" compliance. If a role partner does not deliver what is desired, an "order" backed by force may be forthcoming. Delinquent partners are punished. They are sanctioned—often viciously. Any human being who participates in a social network is surrounded by potential penalties. Encased in a far-reaching role complex, each contributor is subject to diffuse authority. Ironically, rather than this dispersal of power making for a weaker mandate, it makes for a stronger one. Role partner enforcement is more pervasive and robust than that imposed by any prospective despot.

Furthermore, role partner demands do more than enforce roles; they help create them. Social roles do not spring forth unbidden. When children enter the world, they arrive in an already structured place. A multitude of others recruit them into an existing system. For a variety of reasons, these others desire that certain positions be filled. In a sense, the child has no choice; what these others demand is what they demand. On the other hand, it is not a passive vessel. It can, and will, make counterdemands. If outsiders have preferences, so does it. The result is a negotiation from which roles emerge. This being so, in a sense no one is in control. Social roles are imposed, but only partially. They are also collaborative efforts. As a consequence, they cannot be totally foreseen or regulated. Even when adult roles are at issue, neither partner has complete control. A husband may know what he expects of his wife, and she of him, but that does not mean either will prevail. The odds are that both can anticipate surprises.

Finally, in answer to the query about whether individuals voluntarily assume the responsibilities of particular roles, the answer is both yes and no. Children do not invent the idea of a social division of labor. They have no choice but to be inducted into a preexisting arrangement. Nor do they dictate the demands made of them. Still, they have an opportunity to modify these. Their own desires occasion counterdemands that modify the behavior patterns of their elders. Whatever their shape, social roles become the property of their inhabitants. They alter their own identities and hence are adhered to with a tenacity that often exceeds the desires of their partners. Roles are conservative not merely because of the demands of others, but because those who occupy them are similarly motivated. Their internal dynamics, as well as external circumstances, conspire to generate a momentum that is difficult to divert.

To sum up, social roles present individuals with both opportunities and limitations. Were they not to participate in them, there is much they could not do or receive. On the other hand, when they partake in them, there are other things they cannot do or obtain. Contrary to the refrain of radical feminists, no one can have it all. Social networks have up- and downsides. Life is filled with trade-offs, hence the best that can be achieved is a comfortable balance. It must be understood that on one level, people have no choice. To be human is to be involved with social roles, but to be social is to be entangled in interpersonal demands. Misery is thus possible for everyone.

Traits versus Roles

There are a number of different types of roles, each of which has its own pitfalls. Roles can be defined by social positions, bundles of tasks, and individual persons. The first of these, social-position delineated roles, entails relationships that are identifiable regardless of the interactions of the participants. The paradigm for such a role is that of "mother." It is assigned to a woman who has given birth to living child. Likewise a boy will be ascribed the role of brother if his mother also delivers a girl baby. Other family roles have the same character. "Grandmother," "father," "uncle," "cousin," "mother-in-law," and "wife" have a relationship orientation in common. In the case of parenthood, this connection is created by nativity, while the spousal role is generated by a social ceremony, whereas the "in-law" role is a combination of the two. Gender roles are also positional. When an infant arrives, the first question asked is "what is it?" and the appropriate response is either a "boy" or a "girl." This is determined by a furtive peek between the baby's legs. Here the social position is imposed by biology. Once decided, however, how the infant is dressed, held, or named is likely to be foreclosed. Another sort of positional role is that of a king. In this situation being the firstborn son of a father who is a king, and then having him die, settles the matter. Before he expires, of course, the operative role is that of a "prince."

Task-oriented roles are different. They are not fixed by relationships, but activities. "Carpenters" are people who engage in carpentry, "artists" are individuals who create art, and "bankers" are those who engage in banking. Sociologists often make a distinction between a social position and the role attached to it, but in this case, the distinction is without a difference. The position is supposedly a job, for example, that of a "carpenter," whereas the role is the sort of work performed by a person in this position. Weber would have described such a job as a "defined office," and in the modern bureaucracy its parameters are determined by a "job description." The trouble is that even though a job may occupy a discernable slot on an organizational chart, it has no meaning over and apart from the tasks its occupant performs. To speak of a carpenter who does not work in wood makes no sense. What happens with task-defined roles is that we mentally abstract the job from its performance, but the construct has no existence beyond the collection of duties associated with those who execute them.

The third sort of role is more difficult to grasp. It has not traditionally been included within the roster of social roles, but is potentially the most disruptive. Personal roles are defined by the individuals to whom they are allocated. Whereas it is conventional to think of roles as separate from the individuals, this is not always so. Some roles are not interchangeable by persons. John or Mary may each perform the role of carpenter, but not necessarily that of "family intellectual." This sort of role is assigned on the basis of the kind of person John or Mary is thought to be. They are alleged to possess certain qualities, rather than fulfilling certain tasks. What are here designated as personal roles have customarily been described as personal traits. This latter depiction is grounded in the supposition that what is identified is a constellation of individual skills and dispositions.

To illustrate, intelligence is considered a personal trait, and it is, but being the family's "intelligent one" is a personal role. The former is based on IQ whereas the latter is rooted in presumed abilities. The "intelligent one" has been singled out as particularly smart and is required to demonstrate this aptitude whenever company comes to visit. Although they may be of inferior intellect, this is not the determining factor. What matters is their reputation. The same considerations apply to the role of "intellectual." Such a person will have partners impressed by their presumed intellectual activities. They will be expected to read, listen to classical music, and/or engage in years of formal education. All of these modes of conduct are believed to typify someone with superior intelligence.

Another personal role is that of "athlete." It too is associated with particular aptitudes, in this case of a physical variety. Once again, however, what matters is the perception of the behaviors in which the individual is believed to specialize. Many persons who are strong, fast, or agile do not go out for sports. Others do, sometimes for their own reasons, but perhaps at the behest of their role partners. In either event, when they take their place on the playing field, they are expected to do well. If they do not, they are subjected to ridicule or worse. Nowadays it is not unusual for a parent to demand that the family athlete join the football team and work assiduously to become a star.

A different sort of personal role is that of "class clown." Youngsters themselves frequently initiate this niche. In grade school it is not uncommon for an unpopular student to seek attention by entertaining their friends. Perhaps accidentally discovering a gift for making people laugh, they exploit it to the hilt. Once this pattern is established, however, their peers may encourage them to act out, especially at moments of social tension. Although the clown may not always want to be on stage, it is assumed that being funny comes naturally to them. Also required to perform may be the "family beauty." Told from infancy how beautiful she is, she becomes dedicated to primping for the admiration of others. Now transformed into a miniature pageant queen, how she looks is converted into what she does. Sadly, these personal roles are not always grounded in reality. Imagined rather than actual qualities can be at their core. Thus, a family beauty may be beautiful only in the eyes of her family. Sometimes this elicits a personal carriage that can make her appear beautiful to others, but sometimes moving outside the family circle can precipitate disillusionment.

The varieties of potential personal roles are legion. Among these are those of "klutz," "family idiot," "fatty," "rebel," "bully," "scapegoat," and "caregiver."[2] Some of these can be quite fulfilling, but others, such as "scapegoat," are uniformly dysfunctional. It is imperative to realize that unlike biologically bestowed traits, they are socially stabilized. This means they can be altered in a manner not available to traits. Because they are not a part of a person so much as a behavioral package she inhabits, they can be modified by resocialization.

Sociologists generally distinguish between ascribed and achieved roles. This distinction is related to the features just discussed, but is not quite the same. An ascribed role is one that is assigned to a person regardless of what they do. In this respect, it is much like a positional role. Indeed, gender roles, birth order roles, and aristocratic roles are normally cited as examples. An achieved role, by contrast, is grounded in what a person does. In this respect, it is analogous to a task-oriented role. Illustrations of this are provided by "the butcher," "the baker," and "the candlestick maker." Unlike ascribed roles, achieved ones depend on being able to perform. To be a butcher, one must possess skill in meat cutting, whereas to be a duke, all that is necessary is the correct parentage.

In fact, the reality is a bit different. Ascribed roles must also be achieved and achieved ones ascribed. Let us take the role of a king. The death of one's father, the former monarch, may automatically initiate a coronation, but of itself does not make a king. There are assigned duties to be satisfactorily performed by its occupant regardless of how he came to the throne. An utter incompetent such as Edward II of England may not occupy the position for long. In some cases, unfit individuals have been deposed before they took command. Achieved roles, on the other hand, may not be open to independent ascension.

Take the situation of a "college professor." In present-day America, to become a professor, one must first go to college and graduate school. Earning the requisite degrees is clearly something a person does. But this is not all that is necessary. An accredited institution must also hire an individual. Unless a college or university does so, they cannot confer the distinction on themselves. Outsiders finalize the role by ascribing what the individual worked hard to achieve.

Although it may be assumed that the role is not the same as the person, that whether positional, task oriented, or personal, it is distinguishable from the individual, this is only partially so. People identify with the roles they perform. They become one with these role identities. The longer they occupy a particular position, the more likely they are to confuse it with themselves. Nor will they be wrong. Roles are often conceived of as garments that can be donned at will, but this is false. Persons are not autonomous actors that abide apart from the acts they perform. They are flesh and blood creatures who are, in part, what they do. Some cutting-edge moralists claim that we should condemn the murder, but not the murderer. It is the act that is to be abhorred, not the person who commits it. This makes it sound as if the act were a disembodied phenomenon—which it was not. Persons engage in their own behaviors. They plan, initiate, and execute them. When these are horrific, they also deserve to be reviled. The same logic applies to roles. People's role performances are an aspect of who they are. If they carry them out well, they deserve the credit, and if not, they don't. Yes, roles have an external aspect, but they also possess an internal one. In contrast with theatrical roles, they are not artificial and can therefore be at the core of what a person has become.

Among the roles most likely to be subsumed within an individual's identity are *basic* roles. These are developed early in life and are remarkably difficult to change. Gender roles fall within this category. People occupy these so early in life that they cannot imagine living without them. Their obstinacy is dramatically revealed in the experience of transsexuals. Adults who come to the conclusion that the physiological gender with which they were born does not accord with a deeper gender identity nevertheless encounter difficulty adopting the behavior patterns consistent with the gender they seek. Even though they emotionally reject the role hitherto delegated, its details are engrained in the ways they walk and talk. If the switch is from male to female, softening one's interpersonal style will take far more effort than is commonly imagined.

Moreover, basic roles are not only difficult to modify, they provide the foundation for later roles. Because they are orchestrated early in life, they include long-practiced behavioral patterns that subsequently prove useful to adult positions. An example would be the caregiver role. A woman required to nurse an invalid mother will have developed models of care that serve as precedents for the attentions later lavished on her husband. Having perhaps learned to jump when her mother requested a cup of tea, she may transfer this inclination to when her mate is disgruntled with an evening meal. In hastening to adjust his plate, she may not be performing the same tasks as she did with her mother, but these will be familiar variations that require few amendments. Basic roles are persistent in large part because they are emotionally salient. Derived from a period when emotions were especially intense, the negotiations that established them were burned into her psyche. To renounce a basic role feels terrifying. It is like abandoning the pillars upon which all else is built and is thus reminiscent of pulling down a Philistine temple. People refuse to do so because it is akin to excising one's very center.

To complicate matters further, no one has but one role. Everyone occupies many simultaneously. In addition, these are not always compatible. At any given moment, a person must decide which pattern to activate. If these conflict, the ensuing headache may be literal. What is more, the roles between which a person must select are variable. There are numerous options from which to choose. Caregivers, for instance, do not come in a single universal version. Even when a role has a concise label, its dimensions may be imprecise. Exactly how a "rebel" will rebel is not predetermined. To describe someone in these terms, therefore, does not impart sufficient information to predict how they will behave. Social roles are notoriously informal. Diffuse and difficult to pin down, they are impossible to measure. So far a Linnaeus has not appeared to categorize them, hence people hobble along in a quasi-impressionistic manner.

Role Scripts

With roles this turgid, how do role players determine the way to play their parts? What guides them when they choose a particular course of action? That there is such guidance is substantiated by the relative consistency observed in role playing. Despite the fact that there are many ways to be a "mother," potential mothers are not totally adrift. There are boundaries to their behaviors. Nor are outsiders without guidelines regarding how to judge role competence. Some persons are evaluated as good at their jobs, whereas others elicit demands for improvement. From whence do these restrictions derive and how do prospective role players and their partners learn them?

It turns out there are role scripts. These are not recorded in libraries or associated with identifiable authors, but are nevertheless demonstrable. It also develops that such scripts are composed of four elements. These are the cognitive, emotional, volitional, and social. Roughly speaking, the cognitive constituent consists of beliefs that explain the way the world is and how a person fits in. Meanwhile, the most important emotional elements are familiar affects such as anger, fear, guilt, shame, disgust, and love. The volitional components are primarily norms and values. The term "volition" is not commonplace, but indicates that people make decisions to act. They are, in short, motivated to do what they do. Each of these factors, the cognitive, emotional, and volitional are interior to a person. They are, as it were, internal scripts. The fourth dimension, namely, the social, is external. It consists of demands made by role partners. While these are instrumental in internalizing the other aspects of role scripts, they do not terminate once these are in place. Ongoing demands emanating from role partners do not disappear, but operate alongside the cognitive, emotional, and volitional ones.

More than two millennia ago, Plato sought to analyze the human soul. In his masterpiece, *The Republic*, Socrates concluded that it is composed of three parts. They were the rational, appetitive, and spirited. No longer in vogue, these terms appear alien, but they are none other than the three internal aspects of role scripts. The rational matches the cognitive, that is, the part that strives to understand the world. The appetitive is the volitional. It specializes in cravings that press for fulfillment. Lastly, the spirited is the emotional. It is the rah-rah part that brings everything else to life. Without emotions everything appears in black and white, but with them life is a riot of Technicolor. That these distinctions recommended themselves to an ancient Greek bespeaks their centrality to the human condition.[3] The Hellenes too, it must be supposed, were role players.

Although the Jewish-Austrian Sigmund Freud did not allude to social roles, he too, in his personal life, must have been familiar with them. In any event, his tripartite analysis of the human mind has a recognizable ring. It includes the ego, the id, and the superego. The first of these, the ego, returns us to the conscious mind, that is, to the reasonable part of the soul. This corresponds with the cognitive component of role scripts. Next comes the id, the hidden instinctive region of the psyche. It is described as a nether region of dark primitive impulses. The id wants what it wants when it wants it. This sounds extraordinarily like the untamed emotions of infancy. In other words, the id is the domain of unsocialized emotions. Then there is the superego. It is the psyche's conscience. But from whence does this voice of reason derive? Its soft inner demands are reputed to reflect parental requirements. Put another way, it is the internalized manifestation of social norms. The superego is thus a small slice of the volitional component of role scripts. As with many interior rules, it originates from a social source, but becomes an independently functioning part of the self.

Amazingly, all of this is replicated in modern neuroscience. The cerebral cortex has long been associated with the higher mental functions, and this has been confirmed via new techniques that scrutinize the working mind. MRIs and PET scans corroborate earlier impressions of the frontal cortex as involved with reasoning, with the left temporal hemisphere sheltering a verbal center and the right hemisphere specializing in spatial activities. These then are associated with cognitive activities. The limbic system is likewise connected with emotional functions. As earlier noted, the amygdala and hippocampus are among the organs whose emotional assignments have been elaborated. The surprise comes with regard to localization of volitional activities. These appear to be associated with the cerebellum. Not long ago this large convoluted area, not far from the brain stem, was thought only to coordinate motor behaviors. But Hobson writes, "As researchers discovered in the 1990's, the cerebellum coordinates a lot more than motion." Neurologist Jeremy Schmahmann of Harvard Medical School expands upon this by noting "the aim [of the cerebellum] is to take information, smooth it out, and make it harmonious with the intended goal—regardless of whether this is a motor goal or some other goal." But what is smoothing the way for intended goals but "planning." With planning an essential element in volitional behavior, this suggests that the cerebellum is crucial in coordinating decisions to act. Then again, that a motor center is implicated in originating motivated activities should not come as a surprise.

This picture also dovetails nicely with what has earlier been said of the emotions. They seem to occupy a mediating role between the cognitions and the volitions. If, as was indicated, they both communicate and motivate, they deal with both information and action. When an emotion such as fear alerts a person to danger, it helps them understand their situation as precarious. This enables them to apply their higher cognitive functions to determining the nature of the threat and potential reactions to it. When the same emotion impels a person toward fight or flight, it would seem to activate the cerebellum, thereby harmonizing what they have learned with their plans to escape. Their decision to act is now more than reflexive and therefore more apt to succeed. This scenario portrays the emotions as fundamental coordinating agents. This would make them the linchpins of role scripts. Indeed, it has been suggested that the thalamus, which is intimately connected with the amygdala (and therefore part of the limbic system), is the central switching terminal of the brain. It is even suspected as the seat of consciousness.

The scapegoat role provides a useful vehicle for demonstrating how these elements operate. In learning this role, scapegoats are instructed in a variety of causal connections. Their role partners participate in creating cognitive templates that indicate how bad things happen. They point out, for instance, how their behaviors precipitate terrible events. Consider the situation of a child helping its father construct a bookshelf. The child is told to hold up one end of a board, but wavers in this assignment. When its father later makes a mistake in cutting the shelf to size, he, in a towering rage, accuses the child of having precipitated this error. The youngster's innate clumsiness was the root of this miscalculation. The child subsequently comes to believe it is physically inept and the cause of countless blunders. As a consequence, when it is blamed for what goes wrong, it agrees. This disposition, this tendency to understand the world in a particular fashion, sets the stage for its adult role as a scapegoat. As a grown-up, when things go wrong, they continue to assume that they are the source. Such a predilection, however, virtually invites role partners to concur. They will have grounds—which the scapegoat confirms—for blaming him or her and, in the process, keeping the scapegoat role alive. In general, the self-images people acquire guide them in particular directions. Because these constructs persuade them to believe they are capable of only certain behaviors, they select roles dependent upon these aptitudes. Thus, those who learn they are well-coordinated incline toward athletic roles, those rewarded for their intellectual prowess discover a love of learning, and those trained to believe they are Jonahs slide into the scapegoat role whenever someone is needed to divert blame.

The emotional component in the scapegoat script also guides a person toward a range of role performances. That which they learn to fear, loath, or love attracts them in some directions and repels them from others. The messages received from their emotions, and the impulses to action they instigate, make some forms of action more, or less, likely. This is evident in the child blamed for destroying its father's carpentry project. It will not merely endure intellectual blame, but torrents of rage. Given the disparity in size between parent and child, this can only elicit fear. Thus, the child will not only believe itself inept, but be terrified of the punishments to come. As a consequence, it will make certain to obey its father. A mere glimmer of alarm prepares it to evade the assaults apt to follow—thereby inviting them. As an adult, he or she will still be averse to taking chances. Rather than protest when unfairly singled out, they silently abandon their own cause and join in the chorus condemning them. From their perspective, this is a preemptory measure designed to avoid severe criticism, but probably has the opposite effect. Ironically, scapegoats can be harder on themselves than anyone else. Other emotions too shape their role. A child might, for instance, accept blame because it loves its parent. Aware of its parent's discomfort, the child diverts culpability toward itself. This then becomes a pattern repeated with adult role partners to whom they are emotionally devoted.

The primary volitional aspects of role scripts are norms and values. Norms are rules of behavior, whereas values are stubbornly sought goals. The difference between them is that of means and ends. Norms tell people how to do things, while values tell them the sorts of things at which to aim. In most cases, the two are easily told apart, but norms have a way of being treated as values. That which is habitual is frequently perceived as worthwhile in its own right. Notice must also be taken of the fact that norms and values can apply to groups or individuals. Some social norms are directed at entire communities. Moral rules, such as "Do not kill!" are of this sort. Others are more limited in scope. Those incorporated into role scripts are among the latter. It is the individual child, not its siblings, who learns that blame must be accepted even when inappropriate. It is the specific child, not its parents, who is instructed it is "bad" and deserving of punishment. Once these inclinations have been internalized, the victim possesses a mental set that orients it towards becoming a scapegoat. Because it believes this is right, it steps forward as a sacrificial lamb. And it does this as an adult as well as a child. Whether admitting having failed to hold up a shelf or culpability for a spouse losing her job, it assumes responsibility as a matter of course.

The same pattern can be found with other roles, for example, that of "caregiver." The caregiver will have learned that the only thing of value they have to offer other persons is their servitude. Having repeatedly been told how untalented and unlovable they are, the only imaginable reason others would want their company is because they attend to their needs. Such a self-image is obviously restrictive. It scarcely prepares a person to seek relationships other than menial. A caregiver's cognitive script is also apt to contain the belief that others are so helpless, they require their assistance. When her husband demands that she fetch a can of beer, it will not occur to her that he is physically capable of serving himself. On the emotional level, the caregiver is victimized by a fear of abandonment if she does not perform. She may be angry at being exploited, but will have learned to direct her rage at herself. Instead of demanding her own liberation, she angrily accuses herself of ingratitude. She then utilizes her fury to force herself into subservience. Closely related to this, of course, is guilt. A major player in role scripts, guilt is frequently implicated in persuading a person to do as they are told. Rather than endure inner censure, they comply with what would otherwise be distasteful. Translated onto the volitional level, they perceive themselves as inherently bad. Only somebody fundamentally evil would rebel against virtual cripples. This undoubtedly requires chastisement, if privately administered. A caregiver will likewise adopt a host rules for assisting others. Thus, they may have learned to inquire into their needs. Ever alert to their distress, they will have developed an array of techniques for anticipating their desires. As a child they may mop the kitchen floor before asked and as an adult make sure the refrigerator is always stocked with the essentials for entertaining guests.

So far, the social dimension of role scripts has been left out of this account. Psychologists have done a superb job of investigating their internal aspects, but they have neglected the external ones. To be sure, the cognitive, emotional, and volitional elements could not operate as they do were not the brain set up as it is. But by the same token, social roles could not function were people isolated from others. Interpersonal relationships are indispensable for both shaping interior scripts and outwardly cueing their operation. On the cognitive level, because human beings belong to cognitive communities, what they believe is due as much to what others tell them as to what they discover on their own. Programmed to be influenced by authority figures, they often give more credence to what they are told than to personal experience.

Private emotions too are subject to being molded by interaction with others. Environmental influences are organized so as to arouse particular feelings. An example is a parent stirring up fear by placing a child in danger. External influences are likewise essential in sculpting the form an emotional expression takes. Thus, children exposed to parents who throw tantrums may never effectively socialize their anger, but instead develop a pattern that involves tossing furniture around. Especially effective in shaping emotional reactions are the emotions of others. Feelings are contagious. They communicate and motivate not only with the self, but with outsiders as well. An angry parent can thus create an angry or fearful child. On a more upbeat note, love begets love and curiosity begets curiosity.

Norms and values are similarly transferred from one individual to another. Clearly, children are intentionally instructed on how to behave and are sanctioned if they fall short. But just as clearly, there is an unconscious transmittal of prescriptive data. A parental frown notifies a child that it is holding its fork the wrong way. Similarly a grandparent's smile reveals that poetry is enjoyable and to be valued. These environmental pressures make all the difference in the lifestyles a person adopts.

A great deal of attention has, in fact, been paid to how cognitions, emotions, and volitions are socialized. What has been relatively ignored, however, is the cueing aspect of social relationships. Once a person's role partners participate in constructing their inner scripts, they do not disappear. The demands that initiated the internalization process do not evaporate, but remain as reminders. It is as if these significant others collaborate in installing a series of internal switches, then hang around to flip them on or off as needed. These switches—which might be called hot buttons—continue to be available for later role partners to activate. Their observations, requests, and emotional reactions can set off behavioral patterns that have been dormant for decades. Thus, people who become intimate usually discover where each other's controls are located. They become aware of each other's sensitivities and may respect or exploit them. The husband of a caregiver can, for instance, unearth her guilt and then coerce her into pampering him, while the boss of a scapegoat may perceive his or her willingness to accept blame and heap on as much as he can. The behaviors of these partners call forth specific roles, thereby keeping them alive. Furthermore, because the social aspects of role scripts are durable, they provide an additional explanation of why roles, including dysfunctional ones, are difficult to alter.

This role conservatism is reinforced by the stability of role partner roles. These others also have internalized scripts, complete with cognitions, emotions, and volitions, each of which is difficult to modify. Moreover, each of these partners also possesses a throng of role partners who oversee the social aspects of their scripts. In other words, the demands made of ego are influenced by the demands made of a role partner by his or her role partner. Because role scripts have this social dimension, societies consist of webs of interlocking roles. However simple it may be to say that someone should change, both her insiders and outsiders conspire to defeat this intension. So complex are these networks that it is often impossible to discern their full extent.

Nevertheless, role players are not passive. The social elements of role scripts are not solely the domain of their partners. When demands are made, so can counterdemands. The social cues to which people respond are therefore entwined in a two-way process. Social roles are "negotiated" not only when originally created, but also when later activated. If a person finds some pressures objectionable, they may instigate opposing pressures that alter the demands of a partner. This other might be scared off or induced to change their mind in which case, her demands will be modified. The essence of a negotiation is a push and pull that results in a deal that may either be balanced or biased. Consequently, the more powerful, knowledgeable, or resourceful a party, the more probable their roles can be influenced in a constructive direction.

Role Partners

The social aspects of roles and role scripts place enormous responsibilities upon the shoulders of our role partners. Because they contribute so much to the specifics of our roles, they can be the source of pleasure or distress. And yet role partners receive little explicit training for their positions. They do not go to school to learn how to instill roles, nor consult books dedicated to the subject. Parents, to be sure, are instructed on how to raise their children, and teachers are trained to impart role-related skills, nevertheless the role aspects of these assignments are generally passed over in silence. Nor are role partners licensed. Teachers are certified, so are psychotherapists, and, for that matter, so are spouses who require state authorization before they wed. Role partners, however, are recruited on an ad hoc basis. Societies are like huge pickup teams where the only requirement for a particular assignment is showing up. Gatekeepers ensure that only PhDs are allowed to become college professors, but similar qualifications are not imposed on prospective parents, friends, or coworkers. Instead, people find themselves in a Forrest Gump world that resembles a box of chocolates where one can never be sure what one will get. There are definitely no guarantees role partners will be fair or competent.

If the truth be told, there are powerful incentives for role partners to be unfair. As human beings, they too are motivated to win and may not be scrupulous about how. The social negotiations that create and maintain roles can therefore be unbalanced. These bargaining sessions are not like tennis matches with a referee sitting in a courtside chair to guard against infringements of the rules. As often as not, only the role partners themselves know what is taking place. If they do not police their own interactions, there may be no one who can. This is problematic because in the real world power tends to be distributed disproportionately. Since some people are stronger than others, they have the ability to impose their will regardless of another's interests. In the real world, deception is also rife. People manipulate the truth in order to prevail in social contests. Sometimes this is achieved so deftly that the loser never realizes he or she has been bamboozled. Add to this is that deceit and coercion are tempting precisely because so many people feel like losers. Desperate to win, they kick over the traces and utilize any device that provides an advantage. If, as a result, their partners suffer, they find a way to deny the pain they cause. One of the reasons love and friendship are so highly prized is that they provide protection from exploitation. Partners who love each other are less likely to be unscrupulous.

Besides the question of the trustworthiness of an individual partner, there is the added complication that everyone has multiple roles and therefore multiple role partners. Even within a single role, a person may interact with a variety of partners. Take the situation of a schoolteacher. In the classroom, she or he interfaces with their students. Outside it, they also interact with colleagues and administrators. From time to time, they are even required to interface with the parents of their pupils. Each of these will have ideas about how they should teach, but these may not be the same. Their children will demand that they assign as little homework as possible, whereas their parents may ask for as much as is necessary to foster learning. The parents also have an interest in seeing that their children get ahead, whereas the principal has one in enforcing fairness. The principal in their turn may seek written confirmation learning has occurred, whereas the teacher will be more sensitive to the firsthand reactions of their students. In short, the mandates emanating from these manifold sources can be inconsistent. There may indeed be no way to reconcile their requirements. In sociological jargon, this situation is labeled "role strain,"[4] and it can be a font of extreme distress. Sometimes this results in ignoring particular demands, while favoring others. Sometimes duplicity is used to persuade separate partners that their opposing needs are being met.

One of the primary instruments for managing role strain is compartmentalization. People place inconsistent role demands in discrete mental cubicles where they are prevented from communicating with each other. Transactions with one role partner are segregated from transactions with another and their incompatibility disregarded. This technique is on parade every Sunday in churches and temples across the land. Congregants nod in sincere accord with clergymen who instruct them on the wickedness of dishonesty, but when Monday comes, they suffer no pangs of conscience in approving exaggerated advertising copy. Another common mechanism for surviving role incompatibilities is to favor one direction over another. Such decisions are frequently made with regard to the competing demands of family and work. Consciously or not, millions of men and women elect to concentrate their energies on one or the other. Thus, a man may choose to take extended business trips despite his wife's reluctance to be alone, whereas a woman may prefer to spend more time with her children rather than pursue a promotion to the chairman of the board.

Nevertheless, these coping techniques do not ensure comfort. Role strain and role conflict are nearly universal. Both men and women experience tension about family/job competition that never finds a satisfactory equilibrium. Some days are better than others, but eventually an issue comes up where uncertainty reigns. Indeed, some occupations are notorious for presenting insurmountable conflicts. The job of foreman is typical. On the one hand, a foreman must please his bosses, the executives. They supply him with marching orders they expect to be carried out. On the other hand, a foreman must get along with the workers he supervises. Unless he has a reasonably good relationship with them, they can sabotage his authority. More than this, if they hate him, they can make his daily routine a burden. One reason they might detest him, of course, is that he assiduously enforces the dictates of his superiors. If he does not, however, the latter will be disappointed, and they, after all, control his fate. No wonder foremen feel pulled apart. No wonder too they relate to their diverse constituencies by utilizing different styles. Theirs is a tightrope act in which an excruciating fall always looms just ahead.

At minimum, role strain can be confusing. Because a definitive settlement between competing demands may not be possible, their clash is often concealed by ambiguity. Uncertainties are allowed to remain uncertain. Despite the resultant psychic discomfort, this is preferable to outright warfare. To illustrate, people usually find it better to pretend they are getting along with others rather than investigate their potential disagreements. Although this may mean living atop a powder keg, they think this more prudent than setting off a spark.

Unfortunately, role diversity makes for situations ripe with mischief. This begins with our families of origin. We all have parents and siblings who initiate us into the mysteries of group living. Later in life, most also participate in a family of procreation. We marry and become parents, thereby entering relationships with a new clan of role partners. No sooner do we set up housekeeping with a person who had hitherto been a stranger, and we are told we are using too many towels to dry off after a shower. "Folks never did it that way in my family," may become a familiar refrain. Then there are the in-laws and questions of how often to visit or if we should inform them that their curiosity has crossed the line. And, of course, there are the children. They are born both selfish and far from submissive. All of these relationships entail negotiations that can go awry.

Still, the role challenges do not end there. A surfeit of role partners waits outside the family. Occupational, civic, and social responsibilities abound. Earning a living means there are employers and customers to satisfy. Being a good citizen exposes us to political aspirants, court systems, and fellow motorists, all of whom make demands. Then too there are friends, neighbors, and associates clamoring for their piece of the pie. How is anyone to manage so many claimants? The answer is most of us do so only sporadically. Part of becoming an adult is learning things inevitably go wrong. Sooner or later someone is unhappy. And then we go on vacation—to get away from it all. The stress of dealing with diverse petitions accumulates, and we long for a place in the sun equipped with platoons of waiters whose only job is to respond to our demands.

Given all this, a central part of growing up is learning to manage hordes of role partners with rival demands. A mass-market society such as ours requires a long period of socialization, in part, because we must acquire defense mechanisms, not merely against our own impulses, but against those of others. Individuals who exit childhood without developing a thick skin are in trouble. If their sensitivities send them into a tizzy whenever someone is mean-spirited or if, when confronted with role partner contradictions, they collapse in a cold sweat, they are destined for unremitting anguish. Paradoxically, it may be essential to learn how not to listen. Selective perception pertains not only to hiding unpleasant facts, but also to refusing to entertain disagreeable social demands. Since not all can be met, psychological comfort requires that many not be heard. They are treated as if they do not exist and therefore never have to be denied. Needless to say, too much selective deafness can be debilitating. It can exclude beneficial influences. What must be developed is an ability to filter the wheat from the chafe. To be a successful role, negotiator requires good judgment. Another reason human childhood is so protracted is to provide the time to ascertain these distinctions. Indeed, much of our adulthood is devoted to refining this knowledge.

Dysfunctional Roles

With all these complexities, it should not surprise that role negotiations often disappoint, and many result in scripts that fail to meet personal needs. Dysfunctional roles and dysfunctional partnerships are a fact of human life. They are so ubiquitous that they are a major source of losing. The very variability of our roles and negotiations provides the latitude for things to go amiss. Positional, task-oriented, and personal roles can all flounder. They are not what the role player hoped and despite strenuous efforts cannot be corrected. Frequent attempts to improve roles only deepen a person's misery. Because they do not understand what went wrong, or how problems can be fixed, mistakes are repeated in endless loops until hope is lost.

Let us begin with task-oriented roles. Not all are created equal. As previously remarked, some are more satisfying than others. Nevertheless both the enjoyable ones and the nasty ones need to be performed. A functioning society requires not only entertainers who garner glory, but also dishwashers who clean up the mess. In the army, there is an assortment of military occupational specialties (MOSs). These range from fighter pilot, to tank driver, to foot soldier. Some are fairly glamorous, and therefore attract many aspirants, whereas others are gritty and have a high turnover. Among the grittiest were the kitchen police (KP). KP involved carrying out the dirtiest kitchen chores, from washing the dishes to cleaning the grease traps. It was so nasty that traditionally it was not an MOS, but a revolving duty, akin to standing guard. Almost everyone got a chance because almost everyone hated it. Outside the military, the situation is not quite the same. Dishwashing is still not a favored task, but there is no communal roster that allows it to be assigned on a rotating basis. Instead, restaurants depend on individuals who have little choice but to settle for what they can get. Itinerant workers, frequently chemically dependent, will sober up long enough to earn the money for their basic needs and then, when they get fed up, fall off the wagon. They are not happy campers, but desperate souls who have been reduced to doing what they must to survive. Could they exchange their lot for another, many would. Losers, as it were, in a vast social negotiation, they get stuck with the leftovers. Unhappily for them, the social division of labor has worked out with them confined to an unsavory ghetto.

Many other jobs are also disdained. Nowadays garbagemen make good money, but are still garbagemen. They must handle other people's waste and hope that an evening shower removes the stench. Few sanitation workers proudly proclaim their employment when they attend fancy parties. Apt to defend their trade as honest, socially indispensable work, they know it is not prestigious. For them, glory comes from the avocations supported with the proceeds of their day jobs.

In contemporary America ditchdiggers, used car salesman, housekeepers, elevator operators, farm laborers, janitors, and shoe shiners are in a similar predicament. They cannot boast of being successful in the same mold as physicians, college professors, judges, bankers, or architects. Their relatives do not point to them as shining examples of talent or enterprise. And deep inside, they realize this is true. Nor are most persons with dangerous jobs content with their station. People become convenience store clerks, cab drivers, or roofers because their options are limited. Although roofers, like garbagemen, earn good salaries, they perform their duties on hot (or cold) slanted surfaces from which it is not difficult to fall. Fated to carry heavy loads up rickety ladders, they develop back problems and smash their fingers with hammers. Why should they exult in this situation? Why shouldn't they fantasize about winning the lottery?

This said, it remains the case that many personal roles present greater opportunities for despair. Because these lie closer to an individual's sense of identity, when they are wretched, so are they. Occupational posts are generally considered something a person does, rather than who they are. Jobs can be, and are, changed. If a task is too uncomfortable, a person can quit. They can consult the want ads and move on to something better. Even if practical considerations make this impossible, they can dream. In the mind's eye, the most forlorn of losers can imagine being president of the United States. They can comfort themselves with the hope that someday their talents will be recognized, and they will be hired for a scintillating career. Personal roles, by contrast, are difficult to separate from one's self. Frequently conceived of as personal traits, they seem integral to one's being. This person is an intellectual because he is smart. She is a great beauty because she is beautiful. There is no way these qualities can be repealed or sloughed off. They were assigned to a person because of who he is. How could a scapegoat contemplate being something else when their innate propensity to screw things up continuously gets them in hot water? Having for decades been indoctrinated into the extent of their weaknesses, they cannot imagine these being rescinded. Nor can they imagine people failing to blame them. From their perspective, this is not something that their parents specifically did, but something any rational person would do. Flight into a more rewarding relationship is therefore inconceivable.

Paradoxically, the boundaries of dysfunctional personal roles are nevertheless difficult to establish. With no official roster of potential parts and only suggestive labels, it is impossible to be exhaustive about their extent. Personal roles are so idiosyncratic that even when two go by the same title, their details differ. Scapegoats are not all blamed for the same thing, in the same way. Caregivers do not all provide the same services or furnish them to the same recipients. Neither are these roles uniformly distressing. Scapegoats, no doubt, suffer from being condemned for what was not their fault, but caregivers often flourish. True, if they are only allowed to meet the needs of others, their own may be sacrificed. Yet if they are also permitted to care for themselves, they can obtain enormous satisfaction. Mothers who have fulfilling careers outside the home frequently find helping their children the most gratifying thing they do.

Alcoholism counselors have been in the forefront of identifying dysfunctional roles. Among the distinct positions they have detected are the "family hero," the "mascot," and the "codependent." When one member of a family becomes an alcoholic, the others assume complementary roles. Because recurring inebriation prevents a person from completing an array of tasks, they step into the breach. The "family hero," generally the eldest child, assumes the role of precocious adult. He determines to be strong in a manner the alcoholic is not. If the younger children must be guarded against bullies, he will do it. If no one else has cooked dinner, the same applies. The hero aims at nothing less than rescuing the family's honor. If dad never held a job for more than several months, one day he will be an occupational success noted for his dependability. If mom retreated into a bottle while dirt layered every corner of the apartment, she will become a supermom celebrated for her immaculate household. Family heroes try harder. They not only renounce alcohol, but also refuse to give themselves a break. Afraid to backslide or let down dependent family members, they cannot relax. While many have the satisfaction of conventional success, they achieve it by sacrificing simple pleasures. Never pleased with their accomplishments, they engage in a species of internal flagellation that robs them of their just desserts. It is true they were coerced into the role by the emotional abandonment of their parents, but it is also true they chose this form of coping and they who enforce it. Sadly when heroes let go, perhaps because they have lived a life of self-denial, many resort to alcoholism. However much they have looked like winners, they still felt like losers.

"Family mascots" have a different story. Their solution to an alcoholic environment is not to simulate victories, but to withdraw from the contest. Coerced by arid relationships into seeking a modicum of satisfaction, they find this in being "cute." Commonly a younger child, a mascot, is treated like a family pet. With an older sibling in all likelihood striving to keep the family together, he or she finds refuge in an alternative role. Family divisions of labor, like all divisions of labor, work because the parties engage in distinctive, yet symbiotic, tasks. Were all to strive for the same objectives, these would compete and thereby disrupt family dynamics. The mascot therefore does not try to outdo the hero, an assignment that given his or her relative youth they would probably lose, but dotes instead on being taken care of. Encircled by people who are bigger and stronger, they court their patronage. Yet to be patronized is to be treated as inferior. Every time someone tells them how cute they are, or sets them aside so as to perform an important piece of business, they are thrust into an incompetent status. Extolled for their youth and inexperience, they are denied the opportunity to grow in stature. Although pleased to be special, they suffer from being excluded from the adult world. How indeed can a person become a winner if others protect them from the jarring competitions that produce victories? Without practice in attempting what is difficult, they reach adulthood with a skin so thin that they have to hide from ordinary challenges lest they pierce their body armor.

Unlike the previous two roles, that of the "codependent" generally belongs to an adult, usually the spouse. Sometimes also designated "enablers," these persons permit the alcoholic to remain an alcoholic. Not themselves addicted, they are generally in an enmeshed relationship with the addict. Finding it difficult to survive on their own, they build their lives around a chemically dependent person. That person's needs come first, their problems demand solution, and their safety is of paramount concern. Codependents ostensibly want to help. They empathize with their partners and are dedicated to assisting in overcoming their dilemmas. Constantly indicating that they would like them to sober up, they actually facilitate the addiction. They pay the rent, put food on the table, and oversee the children—and free up the time and resources for the alcoholic to keep drinking. Indeed, should their partners regain sobriety, they may tempt them back to intoxication. Sometimes they provide the liquor; sometimes they provide a provocation that must be drowned in ethanol. Although allegedly stronger than their partners, enablers are dependent on an untenable situation. Because they too feel weak, they bind themselves to a relationship that makes them feel relatively strong. Were they actually as tough as they pretend, they would face the realities of their condition and improve it.

Closely related to this role constellation, but often unrelated to alcohol abuse is the "savior/rescuer" syndrome. Parents whose own roles have been unsuccessful often attempt to reverse fortune via the secondhand successes of their offspring. Their children are designated to rescue them by fulfilling the adults' dreams. A mother who is a frustrated actress may thus designate her daughter to become a movie star or a father groom his son to be the professional athlete that he was not. Neither of these roles, of course, is necessarily doomed, except that they may not be consonant with a child's aspirations. Imposed in order to redeem the enforcer, they are generally thought to bring love, respect, and/or security to both parties, but may deliver none of these.

Dysfunctional roles are so numerous and so variable that only a sampling can be presented here. Injurious in a multitude of overlapping ways, one thing they have in common is that they facilitate losing. Individuals trapped in bad roles are precluded from achieving success for a variety of reasons. Sometimes their roles expose them to recurring punishments. Sometimes they reduce their options or blind them to unfulfilled needs. Often such roles are stacked in favor of a partner's requirements. Frequently they foster incompetence. Likewise, the damage inflicted can be modest or severe. Sometimes the problem is that they leave a person "typecast." Consigned a particular set of behaviors, other more useful patterns are ruled out of bounds. In the worst cases, dysfunctional roles prove fatal. Unrepentant alcoholics die. In general, however, flawed roles merely leave a person worse off than they might be otherwise.

Surprisingly, moral variables are regularly responsible for dysfunctions. Life is pervaded with morality plays in which people are designated the roles of hero or villain. Required to be "good" or "bad," their scripts can be so extreme that they are not permitted the normal shades of gray. While some individuals can carry these off, most cannot. A case in point of the former was Robert E. Lee. The son of a politically prominent father who ended his career in disgrace, Lee sought to redeem the family fortunes by being a paragon of virtue. At West Point he was so celebrated for never receiving a single demerit that he was cynically heralded the "marble model." He, to be sure, went on to be worthy of public statues, but this is the exception. Most "saints" and "goody-two-shoes" wind up annoying their associates. Rather than draw acclaim, they are ostracized. Forever exposing their companions to invidious comparisons, they are like the kid down the block one's parents held up as a good example—and was hated for it.

"Martyrs" take invidious comparisons in a different direction. More apt to boast of their goodness than actually be good, they dramatize sacrifices that theoretically benefit others. Specialists in inducing guilt, they pretend to be miserable, but, in fact, revel in ostentatiously giving up personal advantages. Craving admiration, they may elicit disgust. In the end, the martyr is usually forced to live a cramped lifestyle. Constantly complaining they are not appreciated, they too are deprived of peace and contentment. A closely related, but socially more constructive role, is that of "peacemaker." Forever ready to insert themselves in the disputes of their associates, they may genuinely wish to moderate these conflicts. In the main, however, they are liable to be irritating. Even when people require the services of a referee, they resent interference. Geared up for a fight, they turn their hostility toward this uninvited meddler. Like police officers who attempt to defuse family quarrels, the reward may be a full measure of grief. As law enforcement agents know, calls to family disputes are among the most dangerous.

At the opposite end of the spectrum are roles that glorify being bad. Some people delight in being "criminals." They break the law with gusto and chuckle at the discomfort of honest citizens. Among their peers, they are respected for their audacity, but pay a price for their brazenness. Organized constabularies, after all, are delegated to pursue them. These arrest, prosecute, and send them to jail. Many crimes go unpunished, but many do not. The odds are not good and most spend a large fraction of their lives behind bars. Nowadays inner-city toughs rejoice in being labeled "bad." The aspiration is to be the baddest dude on the block. Nevertheless, this sort of notoriety does not recommend itself to most employers. Bad dudes are not good risks. Their reward is thus a truncated occupational career.

Some dysfunctional roles more directly limit a person's potential. One such is that of the "failure." In some families, the way their members get ahead is by stepping over the prone bodies of other family members. The achievements of these "successes" may not be spectacular in a larger context, but compared with the "black sheep," they do well. "Failures," by contrast, are supposed to be uniformly inept. Whatever they touch turns to dross. Should they go to school, they flunk out. Should they start a business, it goes bankrupt. Should they marry, divorce awaits just around the corner. So inured to disaster are those groomed to fall short that when things go well, they get nervous. With muscles pre-tensed for a fiasco, if it does not arrive, the anxiety of anticipation can precipitate one. Better to blow a hole in the bottom of one's own boat than endure the agony of waiting for it to happen.

"Rebels," "geeks," and "hypochondriacs" are also experts in hierarchical misfortune. Rebels are specialists in picking fights. Oppositional in nature, whoever is riding high, they are against. So inclined are they to be negativistic that they will not accept triumphs that are theirs for the taking. In perceiving themselves as outsiders, they cannot imagine being in charge. As a result, they keep fighting even after they have prevailed, thereby arousing antagonisms that snatch defeat from the jaws of victory. Geeks, by contrast, are just annoying. Constitutionally weird, they present a facade incompatible with winning. Because hierarchical success is frequently contingent upon conforming to preconceived ideas of what success looks like, they do not meet these criteria. Geeks insist upon being visibly deviant. Awkward, deficient in social graces, and interpersonally insensitive, they disqualify themselves for power by refusing to appear powerful and wind up losing because others do not take them seriously. Hypochondriacs accomplish a similar feat by obsessing on phantom illnesses. They are the incurably sick ones who cannot be entrusted with influence because at a critical juncture they falter. Seekers after sympathy, the factitiously ill use their putative condition as an excuse for failure. Convinced that they do not possess the credentials necessary for success, they discover weaknesses over which they have no control and for which they should not be blamed. The problem with this tactic is that it permanently exempts them for the fruits of victory.

An opposite strategy plagues the "overachiever." This person sets their sights too high. Consciously misled by an inaccurate assessment of their abilities, they believe themselves capable of feats that lie outside their competence. Overachievers frequently do well because they try harder, but many eventually overreach. Then confused by an unanticipated failure, they make things worse by squandering their resources on ill-conceived efforts to recover. Unable to understand why they failed, they substitute energy for insight. Sometimes such persons become "retreatists." Preoccupied by ritual, they spin their wheels in a vain effort to reverse fate. From the inside they seem to be making progress, but as viewed by others, they are irrelevant. "Wheeler-dealers" confront a parallel conundrum. Infatuated with the possibility of becoming hugely successful in brilliant commercial coups, they risk being too clever. Intending to manipulate others for their own benefit, they instead alienate them. In overestimating their intelligence, they jeopardize being found out by their inferiors. Once unmasked, they forfeit the trust essential for mercantile success and, à la the Gene Hackman character in the movie *Get Shorty*, become caricatures of the prosperous producer.

Among the most precarious roles are those attached to human sexuality. It is no secret that people pair up to participate in procreative activities for pleasure and social prestige. Like the moral roles, these tend to be divided between the virtuous and the promiscuous. Among the promiscuous are the "tart," the "bimbo," and the "Don Juan." The tart is a sexually available woman, whose services may be for sale. For her, sex is a weapon. She uses the promise of intercourse to control her relations with men and frequently as a means of getting even with them. Having perhaps been abused as a child, her goal is to degrade men, but in the process she degrades herself. The bimbo, also a woman, is likely to be an amateur and a dim bulb. She flaunts her sexuality because she believes it is all she has to offer, and, having broadcast this message, is taken at her word. Prepared to be used by men solely for their gratification, she is. The Don Juan is, of course, a man. Obsessed with making sexual conquests, he is skilled in the art of seduction. The real Don Juan counted his successes in the hundreds, whereas the basketball star Wilt Chamberlain bragged of tens of thousands. Apt to be admired in a way prostitutes are not, his is not a life of committed intimacy. And therein lays the rub. The sexually promiscuous of either gender reduce their chances of being part of a love relationship. Focused on genital fulfillment, they relinquish the right to be trusted by a long-term companion. So vacant is the crossroads they have selected that many compulsively seek new partners to relieve their loneliness when not copulating.

Less ribald, but also less dysfunctional, are the roles of "flirt," "macho man," and "monk." Dedicated flirts can experience the exultation of the chase without sacrificing their reputations. If too devoted to teasing, intimacy may be the casualty, but usually all that is at stake is an evening's diversion. "Southern Belles" traditionally raised the latter to an art form. Macho men, by contrast, skate closer to the edge. In pretending to a supremacy over women that is incompatible with modern notions of gender equity, they invite ridicule and defiance. What follows is often humiliation and abuse. When the posturing of the macho man does not produce the expected deference, his rage can be monumental. At the very least, in his efforts to appear strong, he convinces others he is not. This last outcome does not worry the monk. He has withdrawn from the sexual game entirely. Unconcerned with displays of potency, he feigns a sexlessness that may be difficult to sustain. The recent troubles of the Catholic Church demonstrate the pitfalls of celibacy. Even if authentic, especially when apart from a religious vocation, self-denial can repudiate an insistent part of the self.

Naturally the worst sexual roles are those designated perversions. Paraphilias such as "pedophilia," "necrophilia," "zoophilia," "exhibitionism," "fetishism," and "sadomasochism" in deflecting the source of sexual gratification in socially condemned directions invite frustration. Even when physical satisfaction is possible, the social censure may be difficult to bear. Once uncovered, careers are ruined and relationships torn asunder. Besides, complete satisfaction is rarely to be had. The demons that prompt an abnormal outlet also conspire to make it desolate. In earlier eras similar things might have been said about homosexuality, but today the role of "queer" is adopted with pride. The same still cannot be said about that of "sissy boy." Unlike that of the "tomboy," it encourages a violent reaction from male playmates. Boys who cannot stand up to roughhousing are liable to be threatened for their reservations.

Some roles concentrate on diverting others from their troubles. In addition to the "scapegoat," "mascot," and "clown" roles, "entertainers," "artists," and "gossips" save their role partners from themselves by focusing attention on something less menacing. Entertainers tell stories, sing songs, and dance dances. They amuse, instruct, and envelop in activity. In exchange for attention and plaudits, people are removed from their mundane concerns and transported to a better place. For the entertainer, the price may be confinement in an unreal world, one in which "let's pretend" is indistinguishable from truth. The actor Patrick Stewart, Captain Jean-Luc Picard of *Star Trek* fame, has described acting as professional lying, and to the extent it is, an actor can be fooled by his own fabrications. Artists, be they painters, sculptors, or novelists, can also be seduced by their creations. The more compelling these are, the more attractive they are as alternatives to a squalid reality. Gossips are less well organized and less well respected. As purveyors of semi-illicit information, their services are sought out, albeit in semi-secrecy. People are ashamed to be party to their stories, but consume them with enthusiasm. As with entertainers and artists, they can bring color and excitement to a drab existence.

Some roles are pieced together from cognitive tasks. These too have positive and negative dimensions. "Fools," "airheads," and "idiots" are examples of stupidity converted into a way of life. As with "failures," they specialize in doing wrong. Alleged to be unable to tie their shoelaces without help, they nevertheless manage to remain alive long enough to be scorned by those who consider themselves more clever. Invariably smarter than they appear, they are depicted as slower than slugs so their betters can confirm their intellectual superiority. "Bookworms," "professional students," and "geniuses" have a complementary dilemma. Because they are deemed too smart, their abilities are systematically mocked. Bookworms are thought to understand nothing beyond what they have absorbed from books. They are believed to be so smart that they are dumb. This assures ordinary people that they actually understand what is going on, whereas it condemns the genius to irrelevance. The situation is comparable to that of the "dreamer." Individuals who are creatively or intellectually distracted are said to inhabit a world of their own. Because their attention is elsewhere, they are alleged to be out of touch with reality. So impractical does this make them seem that their opinions seem of no value whatever. To all intents and purposes, they might as well be stupid.

Emotional concentrations likewise produce dysfunctional roles. The so-called personality disorders offer evidence of this. "Hysterics," that is, women suffering from a histrionic personality disorder, are too emotional for their own good. Dramatic to a fault, they are as unreliable as geniuses. Trapped in a universe of uncontrolled passions, they are out of touch and thus need not command attention. "Narcissists" are also emotional, but being men, are accused of self-involvement. In their insecurity, they are grandiose, arrogant, and lacking in empathy. Interpersonally manipulative, what exasperates others is the supercilious emotional tone they project. The problems inherent in both of these roles derive from incompetent social negotiations. For men, because their gender roles promote instrumental behavior, they are tempted to improve their situation by pretending to a hierarchical status they do not possess. By puffing themselves up, they hope to bluff rivals into backing down during tests of strength. Were this to succeed, it would enable them to arrange a division of labor to suit themselves, but because they overplay their hands, they lose. For women, whose gender specialization is grounded in expressive behavior, status, and therefore power, is gained by displaying emotional competence. Histrionics attempt to achieve this by demonstrating that they are more emotional than others. The trouble with this technique is that people are more apt to respect an ability to fathom the emotions of others, rather than flaunting a lack of personal restraint. Instead of establishing that they are equipped to mediate interpersonal conflicts, they confirm the opposite.

"Passive-aggressives" would merely seem to be emotionally deficient, but they too are emotionally, and therefore negotionally, odious. Forced to disguise their true feelings, their resentment intrudes into their relationships and makes them unwelcome associates. Indeed, their tendency to withdraw from conflict-laden situations makes it less likely that they will be able to assert themselves during bargaining sessions. The result, of course, is a series of unsatisfactory deals. Also not found in the DSM-IV but similarly provocative is the "cool pose." The bad dudes discussed above are notorious for affecting insouciance. Whatever happens, they make a show of being unperturbed. The goal is to show that they are so strong that nothing unsettles them, but the effect is an empathetic disconnect that makes them fickle role partners.

Lastly, both personal skills and external appearances can be the foci around which dreadful roles accrue. An absence of muscular coordination, motor dexterity, and verbal fluency can each stimulate inferior role assignments. "Spastics" and "klutzes" tend not to be popular. Whatever compensatory skills they amass cannot overcome the rejection that attends their handicap among school-age children. "Jocks," on the other hand, are widely admired. Their disability is the expectation that they are not smart. As long as they score touchdowns, people act as if they were intelligent, but when their talents decline, they are consigned to the ash heap of history. Those with verbal skills, in comparison, may be assigned the prestigious role of group spokesperson or the less exalted one of "motormouth." In the one instance, being articulate is harnessed to social objectives, and in the other it is converted into a sideshow.

Physical appearances when converted into social roles also prove both helpful and the reverse. Just as there is status I being a "great beauty," so there is none in being the "unbearably ugly one." To be judged ugly is a dreadful burden. It disqualifies a person for a host of jobs. Being "ugly" is equivalent to being a pariah. It is an ineradicable advertisement of being stupid, ineffectual, and undesirable. Less polarized are the roles of the "tall" and "short one," but these too can be debilitating. Tall girls and short boys are equally familiar with the trials of dating. "Fat" and "skinny" when adapted into social roles are more disquieting. Fat people are particularly prone to being treated as freakish. Regarded as inherently stupid and lazy, they face greater difficulties than the height challenged. Moreover, being overweight it is thought emblematic of a weak personality. The only saving grace is that fat people are supposed to be jolly.

Gender Roles

So far we have not discussed the dysfunctions associated with positional roles. It may be assumed that because these are ascribed they cannot go far wrong, or at least that people discover a means of coming to terms with them. After all, that which cannot be avoided must presumably elicit an adjustment. To judge from the vociferousness of radical feminists, this seems not to be the case with gender roles. It is alleged that artificial distinctions between men and women have been employed to hold women in captivity. Ever since the Agricultural Revolution some ten thousand years ago, males have utilized their superior upper body strength to deprive females of autonomy. They have locked women away as household chattel, forcing them to dedicate themselves to cooking, cleaning, and raising the young. Absolutely out of bounds have been activities in which authority is exercised. These have been preserved as a male monopoly.

But the feminists go further. They claim that despite the fact that the physiological and mental differences between the genders are marginal, exploitation and oppression have become the order of the day. Sexually abused, mentally manipulated, and physically beaten, women have neither been listened too nor paid for their services. The time has therefore come for a turn of the wheel. Only deconstructing the entire gender edifice can relieve this externally imposed misery. Instead of continuing to distinguish between male and female jobs, androgyny should become the rule. Because modern laborsaving devices have removed the advantages of upper-body muscle power, affirmative action should be imposed to ensure that all jobs are divided fifty-fifty. Women must be allowed to become long-distance truck drivers and men nursery school teachers. Only this is fair.

The problem with this prescription is that it is almost entirely misguided. Indeed, the recommendations imposed by the radicals have become a greater source of misery than the inequities they allegedly correct. To begin with, men and women are different. Their biological peculiarities do not stop with a divergence in sexual plumbing. Modern psychology and neurology have uncovered a host of brain-related differences. The verbal centers in women's cerebrums are larger, their corpus collusom's are thicker, and their fine motor skills are a quantum leap superior. They are even better equipped to work with children in that the young find their high-pitched voices more comforting than male baritones. Because of these variations, when men and women are given a choice, most do not select the same sorts of job. They prefer the work in which they have an advantage.

Years ago Robert Bales's group-based research revealed that men tend to be instrumental in orientation, whereas women tend to be expressive. Men are more competitive and more concerned with completing tasks. Women, however, are more relationship oriented. More alert to emotional discrepancies, they are natural peacemakers. Even feminists agree that women are more inclined to be cooperative than men. What this adds up to is that left to their own devices, the genders gravitate toward different undertakings. This became crucial in light of the Industrial Revolution. Several hundred years ago, the gender division of labor was not controversial. Most men were farmers who worked out in the fields plowing furrows and pulling out tree stumps, whereas most women had charge of the home, making the family clothing and spending hours preparing the meals. Neither side complained of this arrangement because both understood that their respective contributions were critical to the family economy.

The Industrial Revolution overthrew this partnership. Men went off to factories to earn a living for the family, while women stayed home to perform tasks that became ever less challenging with the invention of refrigerators, microwaves, and washing machines. By the 1950s many women did little more than watch television soap operas and gossip with friends. The difficulty with this was that it deprived them of the respect of performing useful labor. Looking around, the alternative seemed obvious. If women were allowed to perform the same jobs as men, they would regain the esteem they lost. Moreover, in earning money of their own, they would not be dependent on the good graces of their husbands.

Left out of this equation is the fact that the genders differ. While some feminists recognize these disparities, they attributed them to socialization and argued that if boys and girls were raised the same way, the distinctions would melt away like snow on a hot summer's day. This has not happened because they were wrong. As women entered the job market, they did not assume the same positions as men. Even when they entered the same fields, they concentrated on different subfields. Thus, while more women have become doctors, they have clustered in family medicine. And while many have gone into real estate, they have focused on domestic, rather than commercial, properties. Other areas, such as the machinist trades, where men have an advantage due to their superior spatial skills, few females joined up despite massive efforts to train them for these jobs. What has essentially occurred is the evolution of a new gender division of labor. Based upon familiar distinctions such as the instrumental/expressive divide, each side gravitated to what made it most comfortable.

The burden imposed by the radical feminists has been to ignore these developments. Trapped in an ideological time warp, they have done more than advise the genders on what to choose; they have lobbied for legislation to enforce their vision. Sadly, to the extent that they succeeded, they multiplied human distress. In disregarding natural human inclinations, not only have they required coercive means, but they also maneuvered millions of people into jobs that left them unsatisfied. The recent rebellion of women against the superwoman model is evidence of this. Originally persuaded that in crashing through the "glass ceiling" they were fighting for freedom and democracy, many have come to the conclusion that this did not bring the gratifications they imagined. Remarkably, many have concluded that their most satisfying undertaking was raising a family.

Perhaps the most destructive aspect of the feminist agenda has been the discord it has sown between the genders. In convincing millions of women that men are abusive rapists, it made it more difficult for men and women to create intimate relationships. Just at a point in history when intimacy has become more voluntary, feminists demeaned the family and introduced the myth of the multicultural family. Falsely claiming that single-parent families are as good as any others, they encouraged the belief that fathers are irrelevant. They have also, in disparaging gender-based roles, promoted a competition between spouses that is inimical to interpersonal trust. This has had the effect of fostering loneliness, but most important of all, of depriving children of the social supports that make for a happy adulthood. Because there is such a thing as human nature, and it differs between men and women, disregarding it has resulted in unnecessary stresses.

Notes

1. A century earlier Sir William Perry made a similar observation. He noted the advantages to be had when "each manufacture is divided in as many ways as possible. In the making of a watch, if one man shall make the wheels, another the spring, another shall engrave the dial plate, then the

2. watch will be better and cheaper than if the same work were put on any one man."
3. In earlier works I have referred to this same role as that of "caretaker," but evolving usage seems to favor this revision.
4. A contemporary version of this is Wilson Trivino's ABC model. Here A stands for attitude, B for belief, and C for commitment. The first corresponds to emotion, the second to the cognitive, and the third to the volitional.
5. Sociologists call an inconsistency between roles "role conflict," and it can have similar effects.

6

Ranks

> *King of the Mountain is a game played in some form or other by children throughout the world. The game tests strength, stamina, and cunning. The game requires a hill of rocks, sand, dirt, or ice with room at the top for only one child who is the king. Since all the other children also want to be king, they do everything possible to dislodge the current occupant from his lofty perch. They may try to do this by physical force—grabbing at the king's ankles, tugging at his arms, and trying to wrestle him down—or they may adopt different tactics and strategies to relax his guard and lure him off. They may challenge him one at a time or charge up the hill all together and attack him from all sides. Sometimes they get so frustrated and upset that they lose their tempers and get violent. But even when they form alliances among themselves to overthrow the king, they know that only one of them can become the new king. Then once the new king has made it to the top, he must defend himself against all the other children, who now want to topple him. (Arnold M. Ludwig, 2002)*

King of the Mountain

Hierarchies come into existence mediated by a unique form of social negotiation. Typically far more violent than the relatively tepid conflicts from which social roles emerge, they rivet the attention of the participants and leave indelible traces. Intensely emotional, they are difficult to overlook or forget. Wherever one looks, people are fighting to move to the head of the line, to become what the historian Arnold Ludwig graphically describes as "the king of the mountain." Determined to win, they produce a social system that is both persistent and potentially injurious. They kick and claw, and make such a ruckus that both those who end up on the top and those who end up on the bottom are never quite the same. What emerges from their exertions is an arrangement that possesses a host of characteristics that lend themselves to personal distress. Even after the dust has settled and they are no longer actively contesting who will sit on the summit, what is left behind consigns many to failure.

Hierarchies are zero-sum games. There are always winners and losers. Whereas roles can be reciprocal, ranks are less so. A husband and wife can benefit equally from the division of labor they establish. If they agree that he will do the cooking and she repair the furnace, however nontraditional this pact, both may feel good about the consequences. Because each helps meet the other's needs, both correctly judge themselves winners. With ranks, this is rarely the case. If each party is competing to be first, when a decision is achieved, one inevitably turns out to be second best. Moreover, the one who comes in behind will have lost. He will not have obtained what was desired and will resent the fact. In role negotiations, both participants can get most of what they crave, but not so in hierarchical ones. The loser may adjust, but this is not the same as winning. One of the clichés of modern business is that all parties to a decision should seek synergistic solutions from which all profit, but this cannot be so with ranks. Similarly, a widespread feminist shibboleth has it that cooperation should supplant competition, but this is equally impossible with regard to hierarchies. Their very essence entails conflict and disparity.

Hierarchies are also transitive. If alpha is better than beta, and beta is better than gamma, then alpha is better than gamma. This is the familiar phenomenon of rank ordering. Hierarchies assign individuals to relative positions, with some "higher" and others "lower." Mostly determined by levels of power, one person is evaluated as more forceful than another, and he or she than another, and so forth. All save the one on the top and a few on the bottom will have both superiors and inferiors. Furthermore, these positions are expected to be ratified in displays of deference. The winner may stand taller, whereas losers tend to grovel. In so doing, they publicly announce their comparative statuses and affirm their acceptance of it. The players may resent having to demonstrate inferiority, but enjoy confirmation of preeminence. In any event, these exhibitions fix their positions vis-à-vis others and establish where they fit in the scheme of things. Once this becomes public knowledge, it is difficult to pretend to be equal to someone who is superior to someone superior to oneself.

Hierarchies are likewise subject to punctuated equilibriums. First proposed with reference to biological evolution, these balances are epitomized by long periods of stability interrupted by short bursts of change. Although, at any given moment, a particular ranking system may seem inviolable, sooner or later it is upset. Those at the top, who now seem unchallengeable, will one day be successfully opposed and come tumbling down. Sooner or later the midgets nibbling on the ankles of the king topple him so that one of their numbers can fill his shoes. Nothing is more certain than that hierarchies are only semi-stable and that periods of peace will be interspersed with episodes of strife. Nor is anything more assured than that despite the risks of competing for predominance, there will be no shortage of challengers.

These facts are as they are in part due to the mechanisms that create and maintain ranking systems. The central focus of these is "tests of strength." To utilize a Weberian ideal type, if hierarchy is considered in its simplest manifestation, it consists of a number of identifiable individuals each of whom is situated in a pecking order relative to the others. How they got where they are must now become the gravamen of our inquiry. If we concentrate on the top, the question is how did number one emerge on top? Surely someone else must have held this position before him. So how was this other displaced? This is where tests of strength come in. Just as with baboons and chimpanzees, delving into the history of human status ladders typically reveals a point at which the individual who was to take over the mantle of leadership successfully defied its pervious occupant. The two faced off to determine who was the toughest, with the victor taking over the top spot. Among baboons and mountain sheep, these contests are almost exclusively physical. Rams butt their heads to determine who will give ground. Baboons fight savagely bringing their huge canines to bear. They bite and scratch until one runs off. The results can be fairly bloody; even fatal. Usually, however, the loser concedes and either leaves the troop or is relegated to a subservient position.

Among human beings such physicality is not irrelevant, but is not the whole story. People have multiple means of demonstrating who is stronger. Because our sources of power vary with the situation, the mechanisms employed fluctuate with the time and place. At their most fundamental, these are remarkably similar to the tests utilized by other primates. William Foot Whyte, in an ethnographic study of pre-World War II Italian gang members in Boston, was privy to just how elementary these can be. In his *Street Corner Society*, he described how Doc, the gang's leader, took over from the previous leader by challenging him to a fistfight and then beating him up. His predecessor subsequently left the gang, and Doc gradually consolidated his hold over the remaining members. Much as in King of the Mountain, he who stood on top was deposed when he proved unable to demonstrate that he was still the toughest.

Before moving on to other methods of establishing priority, another feature of this process must be highlighted. This is the emotional significance of achieving victory. Fights are not everyday occurrences. When one person takes his or her fists to another, something extraordinary has happened. People sit up and take notice; they are moved by the event. The parties to the battle cannot themselves help experiencing emotions such as fear and anger. However powerful each conceives himself, he or she knows that defeat is possible, and this makes the person nervous. More than this, the opponent will be a source of frustration. As long as this other refuses to back down, he or she is depriving the person of a victory. No surprisingly, the bigger the prize, and the more robust the desire to win, the more intense these feelings are. Even after a contest has been decided, they will not be forgotten. As a peak experience in the career of each contestant, it colors their lives forever after. In the dark of a cold winter's night, one will recall his or her bravery in the teeth of a grave peril, while the other will shudder at a danger that refuses to recede from consciousness. Additionally, the winner's sense of satisfaction is amplified by the joy of victory, whereas the loser's trepidations are augmented by the misery of defeat.

The spectators to these events will also be moved. As fellow human beings, they understand what is at stake and vicariously participate. Aware that they too might be drawn into the fray, they experience fear and anger regarding a struggle that may soon spill into their laps. Perhaps imaginatively placing themselves in the roles of the participants, they become almost as emotional. If these outsiders identify with one of the combatants, they may maintain a rooting interest that gets the blood up. Then should one party triumph and the other fail, the winner will become a source of awe and the loser one of derision. Suddenly the victor is someone to be feared—or courted. He or she has demonstrated an ability to inflict defeat, which might someday be visited on the bystanders. Whereas the loser can safely be shunted aside, a winner cannot. He is now someone of whom to be wary. He is someone who will have acquired a *reputation* for being strong. Thence forward deference must be shown lest he take offense and unleash his clout in the observer's direction. This sort of reputation is a potent force for maintaining stability. Because it persuades others that it is not feasible to challenge him, they do not. The result is that for a while, no further changes occur. For his or her part, the winner is the beneficiary of a temporary respite. Because others are intimidated, all the victor needs to do is remind them of his or her ascendancy. And since the other's apprehensions are emotionally based, he or she can count on their continuity. Then too a winner's own confidence will motivate him or her to assert him or herself. Besides emitting signals of potency, he or she will make claims that can only be denied by challenging their position.

Unlike King of the Mountain, this is not a game. There will be no mirth-filled resumption of hostilities. Because all of the participants understand that someone might get hurt, they refrain from fooling around. Children practice what is to come; they do not actually engage in it. Authentic contests for supremacy, in contrast, instill a diffidence expressed in succeeding group activities. He or she who has assumed command henceforth is in a position of dominance with regard to other situations as well. His or her reputation, as it were, leaks over into these other occasions. One of Whyte's classic observations was of a series of bowling matches. He noticed that when Doc was not present, Frank—a natural athlete—won more than his share of these. But when Doc was playing, he did not. On the way to the alley, Frank ribbed Doc about how this time he would beat him, but at the moment of truth, he faltered. In contemporary parlance, Frank was "psyched out." His anxieties at trying to defeat a hierarchical superior got the best of him. Since tests of strength are designed to instill fear, this is a universal occurrence. Indeed, hierarchies are maintained by the "halo effect" of well-publicized victories. Leadership is not confined to the specific area tested, but expands to create a ranking system with far-reaching consequences. In Whyte's example, this was manifested in the respect accorded Doc's intellect—already deemed stronger than anyone in the gang, a developed consensus that he was the source of its cleverest ideas.

As internalized signposts denoting strength, reputations for supremacy enjoy a broad writ. In *Fiddler on the Roof*, the milkman Tevye exults that when you are rich, "people think you really know." When asked a question and you make a mistake, you do not have to worry because others will not challenge your wisdom. The prerogatives of money surround you with a corona that the less prosperous do not possess the courage to pierce. Chester Barnard commented on the same factor with regard to business executives. Although as human beings they cannot know how to solve every problem they might be called upon to address, their solutions are accorded a respect that exceeds their insights because they are the bosses. Even Frank Baum was aware of this. The author of the *Wizard of Oz* wrote of a carnival charlatan able to hold the Emerald City in his thrall with razzle-dazzle that made him appear mysteriously compelling. Ironically, this is the case with stereotypes. Group supremacy is maintained, in part, when one faction has a reputation for greater power than another. As simplified generalizations, stereotypes announce the putative abilities of group members and therefore make claims about what they can, or cannot, accomplish relative to others.

To return to the potency compared in tests of strength, with human beings this goes well beyond muscle power. Intelligence too can be the basis for establishing a pecking order. People compare their IQs to determine who is smarter and then defer to the one who demonstrates the quicker wits. Indeed intellect is usually assumed to be more legitimate than brute strength. Even so, most people do not recognize this as a means of intimidating others, despite the fact that they are often intimidated by it. Nevertheless, on an unconscious level, they understand that bright people can work out unbeatable strategies. Still, as distinct from physical strength, intelligence is more difficult to confirm. As a consequence, people resort to all sorts of devices to provide evidence of mental superiority. They ostentatiously solve puzzles; they quote from classical tracts, and they flaunt a vocabulary opaque to their listeners.

People also seek to overawe competitors with their beauty, prosperity, talents, goodness, and age. Amazingly, beauty can be intimidating. It can be disquieting to stand next to someone radiantly attractive. Strangers automatically consider this other smarter, nicer, more competent, and therefore "stronger." If there are "goodies" to be distributed, in almost every case, she goes to the head of the line. As Tevye knew, the same is true of wealthy people, hence their pretentious displays of affluence. A fancy car, a royal palace, and even two thousand–dollar suits can frighten rivals off. Unable to keep up, they fear being outspent. It is no mistake that cartoonists frequently depict rich people as physically larger than others or that for years the public was fascinated with the high jinks of a well-off Dallas clan. By the same token, who voluntarily plays tennis with a Pete Sampras? His abilities are so much greater than ordinary players that his backhand can make them feel like pygmies. Competence and talent may seem neutral, but because they can be ranked, they furnish the materials for hierarchical precedence. Goodness too seems an unlikely candidate for tests of strength, yet because people follow the lead of those deemed morally superior, some contests evaluate comparative righteousness. He or she who can appear more saintly thereby convinces others that his or her judgments are superior. Even age can be converted into strength. Historically it has been associated with experience. In the remote past, before societies became literate, the older members of the community were storehouses of knowledge. They were deferred to because only they remembered how to cope with sporadic crises. Today this attitude survives in the concept of seniority. It is therefore not unusual to consider relative years on the job before deciding who should be laid off. Grade school children too are familiar with this. Almost all know what it is like to be stared down by an upper classman.

Given this assortment of comparative strengths, when individuals find themselves at a disadvantage in one venue, they frequently seek another area in which to compete. If a lack of height precludes dominance in basketball, they practice their spelling skills so they can win an impending Spelling Bee. They may also resort to a tactic that is a human specialty. Being social creatures, people are familiar with the power of numbers. We understand that an isolated person can rarely withstand the assaults of a determined group of persons. As a result, before we commit to a test of strength, we line up allies who may assist in defeating our opponent. Baboons have also been observed employing this approach, and so have chimpanzees. Primatologist Frans de Waal's account of chimpanzee politics at the Arnheim Zoo is a masterpiece of exposing what is involved. Nevertheless, people are the true masters of this strategy. Our species would still be digging roots in East Africa were we not skilled in assembling coalitions.

Politics has been defined as the art of the possible, but it is actually about forming and utilizing interpersonal alliances for the purpose of exercising power. Advantageous far beyond the confines of government, politics is found almost everywhere human beings congregate. Business organizations are rife with them, as are professional societies, religious institutions, civic groups, and casual friendships. People are forever in search of support to augment their personal assets. One of the ways this is achieved is through a demonstration of individual merit. On a military level, this was once accomplished by convincing potential recruits that a would-be leader possessed the clout to bring victory. Among the German tribes that defeated Rome, warlords established their credentials, not by birth, but through battle. A "duke" (i.e., war leader) had to be a physically capable warrior, but more than this, he needed to be a deft strategist. Only in this way could he become a magnet for fighters in quest of success. His proven abilities became the catalyst in enhancing his capacity to do so.

Allies can also be attracted by economic strength. Wealth begets hangers-on. People want to be in the company of rich people, in part to bask in their reflected glory, in part, in hopes of deriving an economic benefit. In ancient Rome, wealthy patricians patronized less affluent plebeians, thereby acquiring a dependable cadre of supporters. Lest we forget, bread and circuses quieted the multitudes and redirected their energies. Nowadays wealth is more closely associated with commercial or industrial enterprises. These provide rich people with the ability to organize the activities of others. In paying their salaries, they buy their loyalty and expertise. Wealth can also be converted into weapons. In the Middle Ages, only the aristocracy possessed the wherewithal to purchase the plate armor that made them knights. Money also enabled them to discipline the infantry needed for effective battle strength. Today's plutocrats do not themselves gird for combat. Their taxes merely pay for the tanks, fighter planes, and bombs that make conquest possible. In financing national armies, however indirectly, they thereby acquire influence over policy and, in essence, leadership positions in a vast association of colleagues.

Moral leadership too can translate into alliances. Extraordinary goodness seems magical. In an uncertain world, it promises a special relationship with providence. Saints reputedly have the ear of God and presumably His best wishes. Crossing them is therefore dangerous. It is more sensible to curry their favor. Popes may not have money, or military prowess, but contrary to Stalin, in a pinch, they can field many divisions. So too can moral crusaders such as Ralph Nader and Noam Chomsky. Their inspirational musings have convinced innumerable idealists to join their ranks.

A further complication in the establishment of hierarchies is that in contemporary societies power generally entails an anonymity not characteristic of the ideal type. Small-scale ranking systems operate on a face-to-face basis. Their tests of strength occur between individuals who look each other in the eye and take a direct measure of their respective strengths. This classical model can be found among children on any playground. In choosing sides for stickball, the players are familiar with their relative abilities and select teammates according to their capacity to contribute to victory. In a Gesellschaft society, however, that is, in a mass-market society where most people are strangers to one another, this is not possible. The parties continually interact with others whose assets are unknown. Ignorant of their histories or social attachments, they make do with secondhand and thirdhand data.

Muzafer Sherif, one of the mid-twentieth century's leading social psychologists, in scrutinizing the behaviors of children at summer camp, encountered a surprise. When these youngsters were asked to rank each other's toughness at the beginning of the season, they did so on the basis of relative size. By the end of the summer, however, most changed their minds. Asked the same question, they now graded their bunkmates according to a demonstrated ability to beat up their fellows. Having in the interim witnessed numerous fights, they realized that some of the smaller campers were, in fact, the hardest hitting. Since their earlier assessments were made before this information was available, they based their judgments on symbols of strength. Because size seemed a good indicator of power, it dictated first impressions.

Something similar occurs in society at large. A booming, buzzing jumble of strangers is difficult to sort out, hence the resort to symbolic indicators. Most significant are those related to social class. In dividing communities into upper, middle, and lower classes, people sift through the comparative positions of throngs of unfamiliar faces. Often based on no more than how someone looks, they suppose that one individual is superior and deserves deference, while another is inferior and can safely be slighted. The way they are dressed, the accents in which they speak, and the neighborhoods in which they live become surrogates for actual tests of strength. Among the most persuasive indicators are those that demonstrate military, economic, or moral resources. In a class-oriented society, the economic are now the most prevalent, ergo the popularity of large houses, expensive jewels, and designer clothing. People are also partial to emblems of their alliances, consequently their fads in fashions and political shibboleths. Dressing the same as others or mouthing identical slogans as they is taken as signs of being on the same team. But just as in Sherif's case, mistakes are made. Because symbols are not literal strengths, they can be manipulated so that others come to the wrong conclusion. This is why people buy counterfeit Rolex watches or lease automobiles beyond their budgets.

Another consequence of contemporary anonymity is that many alliances are forged between individuals who never meet. They support one another, not because of personal loyalties, but from a shared set of commitments. When two persons have internalized similar norms and values, they tend to behave in analogous ways. If confronted with role partners who diverge from these patterns, they come to each other's defense without ever realizing that they do. They also vote for the same political candidates, contribute to the same charities, and denounce the same sorts of deviance. Members of a common coalition despite themselves, they reflexively spout judgments that intimidate outsiders. To illustrate, individuals raised thousands of miles apart, but in the same market society, may simultaneously believe in the sanctity of private property. When one finds oneself menaced by government expropriation, one's chestnuts may be pulled from the fire by a political activist applying pressure to the judge living across the country. He or she may never learn of this, but be its beneficiary nevertheless.

Roles and Functions

Hierarchical positions are also impacted by social roles. One of the tasks partitioned in a division of labor is authority. Some job descriptions explicitly specify leadership functions. A person may be appointed a team leader or the vice president in charge of marketing. Teachers, to cite familiar example, are delegated to run their classrooms. They decide on the curriculum, impose the examinations, and grade the results. Students may complain that an instructor is high handed, but cannot object too vociferously lest a phalanx of their role partners close ranks and come to their rescue. Nor may the school's administrators like them, but as long as they stay within their allocated responsibilities, will rule in their favor. Role partners thus serve as source of "anonymous" support. Although an educator and his or her principal know each other, they do not consciously decide to back each other. This determination is built into their roles.

Roles cannot, however, substitute for tests of strength. Merely appointing someone to a leadership position does not ensure he or she will be able to carry it off. Unless individuals possess the competence to assert themselves, their authority may be flouted. Standard operating procedure when one official succeeds another is for his or her new subordinates to test his or her mettle. A teacher who has never exercised classroom discipline may thus be in for a rude surprise. Expecting automatic obedience, he or she will instead meet with determined, and frequently surreptitious, resistance. For student teachers, this is a rite of passage. They are traditionally greeted with cross talk, random out-of-seat movements, and spitball contests. Unless they are equipped to put down such mini-rebellions, they will be hard-pressed to organize learning activities. New leaders who understand that their followers will test them often begin by forcing the issue. Whether or not it is necessary, they alter inherited procedures. Since inertia will impel some of their subordinates to defy this modification, the stage is set to discipline them into submission. Once this is successfully accomplished, it serves as an object lesson for others.

Given this interconnection between roles and ranks, the fact that there is a resemblance between role scripts and the mechanisms that stabilize hierarchies should not astonish. To begin with, roles and ranks are both negotiated. The "what" and the "how" vary, but not outrageously. With roles, a division of labor is constructed; with ranks it is scale of relative power. Roles assign complementary tasks, whereas ranks determine who decides group plans or enforces these. Moreover, role negotiations entail mutual influence between partners who may not always be fair or gentle, whereas ranks emerge from clashes that tend to be more severe and therefore more emotional. Each provides opportunities to lose. In addition, once established, the positions they produce, whether for good or ill, tend to be self-perpetuating. Role scripts channel role behaviors down familiar paths, while reputations for power achieve something similar for ranks. These reputations too have cognitive, emotional, volitional, and social elements. The primary difference is that they apply to relative power as opposed to particular duties. The issue is comparative strength, not who is to specialize in specific skills.

On a cognitive level, role beliefs indicate what individuals can do, whereas ranks are allocated, in part, based on viewpoints about who can beat whom. Although this information may be deduced from direct observation, sometimes it derives from myths, legends, and ideologies. These are typically dedicated to enhancing, or destroying, reputations for strength. They regularly illustrate why certain classes of individuals harbor certain powers. When positive, the heroes are inherently intelligent and constitutionally moral, or, when negative, irredeemably devious. Marxists, for instance, assure their disciples that capitalists are innately selfish and therefore permanently motivated to exploit workers. Thanks to their inherent defects; once they are to be defeated, they must be obliterated. Only this can eliminate antagonists whose strength originates in a perverse compulsion to control everything in sight. Meanwhile, male chauvinists are convinced that women are intrinsically soft; hence when assigned a female boss, they are prone to disrespect. Unwilling to credit strengths to the "weaker sex," they may misread their talents. Especially pernicious are the stereotypes applied to African Americans. Alleged to be biologically dull-witted, they have been denied jobs, homes, and the equal protection of the law. Because they were also believed incapable of courage, during the Civil War, Northern generals at first refused to employ blacks as soldiers. Even proven bravery in battle did not change some minds.

On an emotional level, reputations for power are intimately related to the inculcation of fear. Because tests of strength can be brutal—baboons are not the only primates that inflict wounds in the course of asserting themselves—they are intimidating. An awareness of this prompts vigorous efforts to instill terror. Slaves, for instance, were whipped to ensure that the mere sight of "the man" would be awe-inspiring. In the process, white skin became a symbol of domination. Since society is imbued from top to bottom with manifestations of relative superiority, it might be supposed that most people walk around in a state of suppressed dread. Yet this is not so. In reality, most anxieties are effectively submerged. They influence behaviors, but hardly ever from the front of the mind.

On a volitional level, reputations for strength are integrated into every society's norms and values. Individuals are instructed on how to assert themselves in particular circumstances and relative to whom. Thus, parents teach their children how to address their inferiors and betters. They also coach them on how to order the weak about or obey the strong. Among the upper classes, for instance, it used to be considered well-mannered to treat servants like pieces of furniture. Even small children understood that they could expect services without expressing appreciation. Indeed, the very notion of inferiority may be incorporated within a value system. If poor people are considered a lesser species, then inflicting pain on them is of less concern than doing so to full human beings. Such an appraisal obviously facilitates proving one's strength by lessening the difficulty in meting out injury. In removing pangs of conscience, it reduces inhibitions and therefore can increase the force delivered.

On a social level, tests of strength, like role negotiations, are a persistent phenomenon. In the wake of a battle over power, neither the winners, nor the losers, fade out of existence. Their respective reputations for power remain available to be reinforced. This indeed is the purpose of symbols of domination and deference. People go out of their way to remind others of their comparative status. Winners inflict small insults because they can, and losers endure these because they must. A particularly important means of reaffirming hierarchical superiority is conspicuous consumption. Social leaders are notorious for inventing means of flaunting their control of a community's resources. Riding around in a bright yellow Ferrari advises all and sundry that I can afford this vehicle and you cannot. It is a declaration that I have got it and you do not, and furthermore, there is nothing you can do about it. In short, you had better stay in your place whether or not you like it.

Like social divisions of labor, hierarchies produce an unequal distribution of personal satisfaction. Even more than social roles, they impose ways of life that individuals would not choose, but cannot reject. The reason for their perpetuation with respect to roles derives from the social efficiencies they promote. Specific persons lose, but the community gains. Similar functions justify the survival of ranking systems. Socialists and romantics, of course, have for centuries denied this. They proclaim that in their instinctive state human beings are inherently equal, but have recently been enslaved by corrupt civilizations. Also convinced that this wrong can be corrected by a return to our natural cravings, they are adamant that this will occur once the hegemons are stripped of their ability to quash others.

The problem with this analysis is that it has not been born out by the facts. So far, an alleged primeval equity has never emerged anywhere. Proclaimed efforts to promote it—as in the Soviet Union, China, Cambodia, Cuba, and Tanzania—all ended in despotism and/or poverty. Likewise fanciful tales of preliterate communities subsisting in splendid egalitarianism have invariably failed to be confirmed. When studied in depth, these too are revealed to be immersed in conflict. Nor is there convincing evidence that our remote ancestors lived in communal concord. Everywhere we look, a careful inspection reveals hierarchies. This is especially so for large-scale societies. There must be a reason for this, yet determining the function of these arrangements is not simple. Human organizations are not teleological in the sense of being consciously planned. Individual persons have purposes, but civilizations do not. The latter evolve. They come into being, and persist, because of the interlocking actions of millions of contributors. None of these control the whole and therefore none dictate its operations. Some, it is true, are more influential than others, but no one—or group—is so potent as to intentionally organize the totality. There is, in consequence, no purposeful function to be discovered.

What can be found are the reasons why some social arrangements survive, whereas others do not. What seems clear is that, as a common feature in the lives of numerous social animals, ranking systems must contribute something to their perpetuation. In any event, there is no dearth of suggested advantages. Among the things hierarchies seem to do are (1) allocate scarce resources, (2) motivate individual effort, (3), coordinate complex activities, (4) provide for group protection, and (5) influence sexual selection. There isn't complete agreement on any of these, but the evidence for each is compelling.

One of the longest standing sociological explanations of resource allocation and the motivation of individual effort is that of Kingsley Davis and Wilbert Moore. They note that among the scarcest resources is talent. To this they add the assertion that social effectiveness is dependent upon gifted persons employing their abilities for the good of all. But then they ask, Why should they? What incentives have they for exerting themselves? Their answer is that only if they are allowed a disproportionate share of their contributions will they be motivated to do what they can. In the end, they get more than others, but those who receive less obtain more than otherwise. Because some work harder than they would without a reward, more is available to be distributed. Respecting the selfishness of the more able therefore results in everyone being better off. If this is so, then maintaining hierarchical inequality is a matter of enlightened self-interest.

An especially intriguing theory comes from anthropology by way of evolutionary psychology. James Boone has hypothesized that resources have a signaling power that promotes lineage survival. Citing the earlier contributions of Amotz Zahavi and Alan Grafen, he suggests that "wasteful displays" among animals publicize the fitness of the advertiser. A peacock with an unusually large tail thereby parades his exceptionally good health. Since only a vigorous male could produce such a spectacle and still preserve his life despite the handicap of having to carry it around, he flaunts evidence of being good breeding stock. His genes survive because females read the symbolism of his feathers and choose him to inseminate them. Boone argues that the same logic is perceptible among people.

In many small societies, the most prosperous members wantonly destroy their surpluses. Instead of consuming what they produce, they convert it into apparently pointless displays. Energy is devoted to creating intricate costumes or throwing extravagant feasts. In the process, they accumulate brownie points with the rest of the community. In essence, they prevail in tests of strength regarding the extent of their wealth, thereby inspiring deference. "The point of this," says Boone, "is revealed in times of famine." In wasting today's resources, an elite preserves a surplus for hard times. In his words, "in a fluctuating environment a family or lineage can increase their probability of survival through bad years by maintaining continuous access to a much higher harvest rate than they would need to survive during normal years." When the crunch comes, their inferiors starve, but all they must do in order to endure is reduce the proportion of their output that goes to showing off. Their displays, therefore, keep them from skating too close to the edge, while, in maintaining the deference of others, they protect their oversupply from pilferage. What is more, in subsidizing potential allies and attracting desirable mates, they safeguard the conditions required to continue meeting their needs.

Using the Hopis as an example, Boone explains how mythologies further this strategy. Higher status clans produce an excess largely because they farm the best lands. But, claim the legends, they own these because their ancestors were the first to occupy them. Later arrivals had to settle for less productive areas. Having learned this in childhood, the poorer members of the village understand that they are not entitled to challenge the property of their betters. Hence, in times of scarcity, they may be required to migrate in search of provisions. In the olden days, there are stories of displaced families having all of their men slaughtered and all of their women enslaved by the tribes into whose territory they wandered. Status, as a means of controlling resources, can therefore be a matter of life and death. In contemporary America, the stakes are not as high, but conspicuous consumption has similar roots. By "wasting" materials, the rich not only demonstrate the breadth of their control, they preserve a core of possessions around which their lineages can rally. In times of economic downturn, the family trinkets ensure a comfortable style of life.

Perhaps the nastiest incarnation of an unequal distribution of scarce supplies is during a food crisis. In a country such as India, millions perish in periodically devastating famines. This burden, however, is not equally shared. Typically, the wealthy continue to eat, while the poor starve. This not only profits the elite by physically maintaining their lives, it also preserves the social order. If the poor were to rebel, they would not only steal food from their superiors; they would instigate conflicts that might reduce the food base of all. People would be killed in the process of fighting for a larger share, but, more importantly, efforts to produce more would be disrupted. Disregarding social regulations would thus imperil the entire society, not just its lower orders.

The coordination of complex activities is presumably a more altruistic function of hierarchies. It facilitates the creation of widely enjoyed benefits. While some divisions of labor operate autonomously, that is, as long as the role players have internalized their parts, others do not. The synchronization of their efforts is so delicate that a unified vision must be imposed by centralized control. World War II could not have been won had the generals in various theaters of operation independently requisitioned the supplies they desired. Were this so, Douglas MacArthur would have expropriated the lion's share, thereby depriving the European invasions of the men and munitions needed to defeat Hitler. Franklin Roosevelt and George Marshall prevented this. Abdicating their responsibility for leadership would thus have been equivalent to a death wish. The same reasoning applies to large-scale construction projects and complex manufacturing processes. This also applies to retail operations, where decisions must be made regarding which products to stock and promote. A chaotic mishmash would be lethal to the bottom line.

Ralf Dahrendorf calls the process of maintaining central control *imperative coordination*. In these circumstances, orders are given and obeyed. Since those at the top of the food chain concentrate power in their hands, who is better positioned to make such decrees? Even when they do not impose the best plans, the mere fact of a unified blueprint can make the difference between success and failure. This has been so since the days of our ape ancestors. Indeed, we see it in chimpanzees. When a troop must decide on a direction in which to forage, it is the alpha male who dictates the choice. In so doing, he keeps all together to more effectively exploit their environment. Similar undertakings occur in hunter-gatherer societies. These too harmonize their migrations when respected leaders constrain group decisions.

Superior group protection is another consequence of hierarchies. Both within the community and with respect to external threats, the existence of a recognized power source is advantageous. Three and a half centuries ago, Thomas Hobbes launched sociology by asking how societies managed to prevent internecine warfare. His answer was that people are so individually greedy that only a Leviathan could compel them to behave civilly. In his era, this was a King whose personal strength was magnified by the obedience of his subjects. Presumed to be more powerful than those he commanded, he could impose justice upon them. Nowadays, hereditary leadership has dwindled, but the judicial and executive functions of government have not. Presidents can still send in the National Guard to quell urban riots, and judges can sentence murderers to jail. Although they may not be personally prepossessing, these leaders occupy positions in a chain of command that permit them to engage in actions comparable to alpha chimps. Once a male chimpanzee has established his dominance, he takes an interest in suppressing intragroup conflicts. When two of his subordinates get into a shouting match, he hastens to intervene and will chasten whichever animal attempts to defy his mediation. The result, as with humans, is to reduce the level of destructive violence.

Relatively powerful leaders are also expedient with regard to external hazards. Whether the danger is a leopard or a band of poaching chimps, an alpha chimpanzee can rally his group to resist. Although individual subordinates might flee, his presence stiffens their resolve and coordinates an effective counterattack. But isn't this what Winston Churchill did for England during the Battle of Britain? In his nation's darkest hour, when Hitler seemed about to hurl a cross-channel assault against a demoralized people, he rallied their efforts by promising "blood, toil, tears, and sweat." His personal example infused millions of others with the courage to persevere and prevail. The ultimate effect of having a bold leader was victory and evasion of Nazi slavery.

Lastly, hierarchies influence sexual selection. When rams bash their horns together, the reward is a harem of ewes. Winning offers an opportunity to pass genes along to the next generation. The function of excluding less potent males from breeding is to maintain the health and well-being of the entire population. Among human beings, the connection between power and generativity is not so clear. Most societies promote a pair bonding that limits the fecundity of dominant males, but human females seem to prefer "strong" men. Muscle, economic, and political power all make them attractive bed partners. Henry Kissinger is famous for declaring that power is the best aphrodisiac. Numerous sports figures also attest to this via the availability of nubile groupies. More importantly, Arnold Ludwig, in his survey of twentieth-century national leaders, remarks that "monarchs and tyrants, who wield the greatest power, show the greatest sexual promiscuity, infidelity, or polygamy." Even Mao Zedong, his body flabby from sloth and his teeth green from poor dental hygiene, could command a revolving cast of virgins to attend him when he deigned to bathe.

Few of these functions, it must be emphasized are intentionally pursued. They are by-products of the nature of hierarchies. Having evolved long before the emergence of humanity, they derive from the intuitive impulses of billions of participants. Friedrich Hayek warned against "constructivist rationalism," that is, the belief that social institutions are deliberately, and cleverly, put together. He acknowledges that they are constructed, but insists they are inadvertently erected by masses of players who never perceive the entirety of their labors. Unable to predict what is beneficial, a trial and error process gradually presses them in favorable directions. Nevertheless, many serious mistakes are made along the way. Hierarchies are imperfectly functional. While they add to human contentment, they also make hefty contributions to personal misery.

Leaders and Tyrants

Leadership positions are coveted. More people prefer to exercise control rather than be controlled. Males, in particular, expend huge stores of energy in competing to be at the top. Over the millennia, this has evolved into an extensive array of hierarchical arrangements. All entail ranking, but the mechanisms for maintaining control differ dramatically. And so do their implications for personal contentment. If we limit ourselves to modern national regimes,[1] we can follow Ludwig's lead in classifying their leaders as monarchs, tyrants, visionaries, authoritarians, and democrats. Some of these are despotic and others egalitarian; some centralized and others decentralized. For our purposes, they also differ in their degree of brutality. Some consciously protect the welfare of the governed, whereas others are oblivious to the needs of the little people, and still others are detrimental to them. In democracies, because large constituencies amend the decisions of the leaders, their administrations tend to be comparatively gentle and relatively enlightened. Moreover, democracies also incorporate stable mechanisms for deciding succession. Democratic leaders are elected in and out of office and therefore have less incentive to eliminate competitors physically. Electoral politics can get quite dirty—including what Bill Clinton characterized as the politics of personal destruction—but they tend not to descend to the concentration camp mentality of totalitarian regimes.

More centralized polities, such as monarchies, often depend on tradition to provide legitimacy. The king is the king because he inherited his position according to procedures that can be traced back to the Middle Ages. Because he (or she) does not face the challenges of coup conspirators, it is generally possible to be more lenient. Absolute monarchs have been celebrated for their greed, but much less frequently for their bloodthirsty demeanors (Ivan the Terrible was an obvious exception). Authoritarians, such as the apparatchiks who governed the Soviet Union after Stalin, owed their legitimacy to being faithful to a bureaucratic apparatus. Having moved up slowly within a pedestrian system, they were renowned for a plodding inflexibility. Nevertheless, as long as their followers played by the rules, they could be tolerant. It is appearances they worried about. As long as these were respected, a great deal of corruption survived under the surface. Visionaries are significantly different. They are intent upon imposing a mental image upon reality. A Kemal Ataturk, in his determination to modernize Turkey by making it more like its European rivals, brooked little dissent. Things had to be done his way, yet his interest in the welfare of his people was genuine. As with most leaders of his kind, the only way to impose the radical reforms is by disregarding the entreaties of dissenting subordinates. This means they can, with a clear conscience, inflict considerable pain on those who resist.

Tyrants,[2] however, are in a class by themselves. They revel in inflicting misery. Although they may pretend to defend the interests of the nation, it is achieving and retaining personal power that drives their agenda. Arrogant to a fault, they so totally believe in their own mandate that they respect few limits. No level of brutality, including mass slaughter, is beyond their ken. Often personally brave, many have distinguished themselves in combat. Idi Amin, whatever his defects as head of state, was a fearless soldier before he took control of Uganda. Even after his assumption of power, merely being willing to expose himself to assassination, demonstrated a daring beyond that of most human beings. No doubt, he took a cruel revenge on those who challenged him, but he was no coward.

Tyrants are also famous for their casual approach to the truth. Adolf Hitler has not been alone in intentionally employing The Big Lie. He had no compunctions in declaring that he attacked Poland in self-defense or in libeling the Jews for an alleged complicity in Germany's defeat in the Great War. But then neither did that "tyrant-in-waiting," Osama Bin Laden, in spreading the word that Israelis flew the planes that obliterated the World Trade Center. Then too Saddam Hussein apparently spent few sleepless nights in contrite remorse for invading Kuwait. In fact, a decade later, he blamed Americans for inducing him to do so. He also submitted documents to the United Nations claiming not to have engaged in nuclear arms building, denying even activities thoroughly verified years earlier. All of this deception is aimed at permitting the tyrant to get away with whatever he pleases, regardless of the consequences to others. If thousands of Poles were killed when Warsaw was bombed, the leading Nazis were content to let their souls be damned. What counted was that no one interfered with the carnage. If a few lies can divert potential adversaries from contesting a tyrant's actions, they are a small investment in maintaining his superiority. Stalin said that one death is a tragedy, but a million is a statistic. He understood that if propaganda can disguise the body count, aggression is more palatable and hence less difficult to arrange. When he was chided for suggesting to Roosevelt and Churchill that slaughtering fifty thousand military officers would control a postwar Germany, he passed the proposal off as a joke. What he dared not mention is that he had already employed this tactic against the Poles.

Another common characteristic of many tyrants is a touch of madness. Most people want their leaders to be special. Most want them to be good. They, at least, assume that they are brighter than ordinary people. This frequently turns out to be untrue. Many brutal rulers have crossed the threshold into craziness. Ludwig documents a rogue's gallery of insanity. According to his calculations, 41 percent of twentieth-century tyrants suffered from alcoholism and a full 55 percent from paranoia. Large numbers also exhibited signs of drug addiction and mania. All told, he estimates that 91 percent could be diagnosed as having a mental condition. Ironically, these diagnoses did not include depression and anxiety. Apparently, inflicting pain on others offers protection from fear and sadness. (Visionaries are also prone to insanity. Their levels of depression and anxiety are high, but at 68 percent, their paranoia is stratospheric.)

This mental instability finds an outlet in the pain visited upon those at the mercy of the tyrant. Stalin, who certainly exhibited symptoms of paranoia, was responsible for tens of millions of deaths. Like a good visionary (albeit one with totalitarian streak), he sought to impose collective farms on the Soviet people; hence, when the Ukrainian kulaks protested, he sent his forces to collect extortionate taxes. When this resulted in famine, he prevented the wheat coercively shipped north from being sent back. The consequence was millions of deaths. Nor did Stalin grieve the countless thousands falsely executed in the wake of his show trials. That their families might also suffer the tribulations of exile to Siberia was likewise a matter of indifference.

Other tyrants have been as callous. Robespierre knew he had to protect revolutionary France from the nation's deposed aristocrats. But his reign of terror, like Stalin's, drew in more than counterrevolutionaries. The guillotine did not care whether the head it severed was that of a peasant or duke. Nor did Pol Pot investigate the alleged crimes of the tens of thousands he expelled from Phnom Penh. Because they were city dwellers, they were automatically guilty of sabotaging Cambodia's traditional culture and deserved to be eliminated. There were some two million who were. Even long rows of gleaming skulls did not prevent the lessons from proceeding. The same almost happened in Rwanda. The leaders of the Hutus came close to arranging the genocide of all the Tutsis. Less efficient than their precursors, the tables were turned on them and tens of thousands of Hutus also died.

Nevertheless, the most dreadful gift of tyrannical leadership is war. Rulers who induce their peoples to engage in aggressive warfare sow the wind and reap the whirlwind. Their legacy can be generations of impoverishment and misery. Entire regions have been depopulated for the greater glory of a sovereign intent on burnishing his image. The ultimate excess of those who enjoy total power, warfare inflicts unspeakable hardships on combatants and civilians alike. Bullets rip away at flesh, and bombs tear down homes. The catalog of desolation has so often been enumerated that it need not be rehearsed here. We must not, however, neglect some side effects of battle. These include forced expulsions such as those of the Tartars from the Crimea or the Chenins from Chechnya. Then there are the Holocausts such as those afflicted the Jews and Armenians. No wonder losers become demoralized, and this demoralization can eventuate in poverty and despair generations later.

One of the most paradoxical miseries of hierarchical immoderation is the threat posed to hierarchy itself. Given the misery that can flow from tyrannical regimes, it might be supposed that eliminating ranking systems would make sense. Whatever the advantages of imperative coordination or stabilizing the division of scarce resources, the ravages of some tests of strength should cancel them out. Why not then heed Rousseau's advice and get rid of the entire apparatus? If people are trained to cooperate with one another, superfluous competitions cannot escalate out of control. What this leaves out, however, is the danger of hierarchical collapse. If maniacal rulers inflict millions of casualties, so can an absence of hierarchical controls. Anarchy is chaotic. It is akin to a Hobbesian war of all against all.

Every so often, a Dark Age has interrupted the progress of civilization. The Mycenaean culture celebrated in verse by Homer was in his odes revealed to have fallen. The Iliad and the Odyssey were not written down because their bard was illiterate. Not so the heroes of whom he sang. Their communities sank into disrepair in the wake of northern invaders (and perhaps the volcanic destruction of Thera). The warrior kings who provided the backbone of their form of life sailed away never to return. In their absence were left communities of squabbling barbarians who, in their disorganization, could not sustain the population or luxuries of their predecessors. Forgotten were the abilities to both write and engage in long-distance trading. The consequence was a decline in the store of human happiness.

These familiar facts were repeated when Germanic barbarians administered the coup de grâce to the Roman Empire. When they marched across the Rhine to evict Roman aristocrats from their villas, they too sounded the death knell of literacy. Without schools to teach these skills or bureaucrats who knew how to use them, scribes were confined to isolated monasteries. Gone too was the storied discipline of the Roman Legions and with it the engineering skills that constructed an unrivaled network of paved roads. Commercial activity soon ground to a halt, and money fled from circulation. The Roman Emperors might have been obtuse and bellicose, but they managed to keep the system afloat. Once gone, millions perished from starvation and disease. Their misery too needs to be considered. And so does that of the millions of their descendants who eked out a living in a marginalized medieval Europe. The primitive technologies at their disposal owed substantially to the hierarchical incompetence of their rulers.

Less well-known is the hierarchical disorganization of the Mayan civilization. Several centuries before the Conquistadors arrived, what had been a thriving society fell into its own Dark Age. Whether as a result of intercommunity warfare or too intense an exploitation of a fragile ecology, the population crashed and cities fell into disrepair. Advances in literature and astronomy were forgotten, vanished with the princes that were their patrons. So complete was the collapse that later generations of Americans were completely insensible to their triumphs. Closer to home, and therefore more visible, is what happened to the Confederacy. After the South's loss, reconstruction descended like a pestilence upon the land. Margaret Mitchell mourned a society that was "gone with the wind," and this was not an exaggeration. Roving bands of Klansmen took the law into their own hands and the economy plummeted to new lows. By the beginning of the next century, a region that had been a cradle of the American Revolution became a political and economic backwater. The victim of an elite that lost its self-confidence and of a larger populace deprived of inspirational guidance, the area treaded water—content merely to keep blacks in their place.

One of the worst instances of hierarchical disintegration occurred subsequent to World War I. Unprepared for the dissolution of four major powers,[3] an entire continent shuddered in stunned disbelief. Submerged nationalities emerged to quarrel about the most insignificant border disputes. The worst ravages, however, were reserved for Germany. Like most of its neighbors, the first crisis was impending starvation. With old patterns of trade smashed to pieces, food could not move from the countryside to the cities or across newly established borders. Only the stability of the United States made it possible to deliver relief. But then came the revolutions, the insolent bands of thugs, and a hyperinflation capped off with depression. The Kaiser and his generals had run off and what remained was an idealistic republic that could not control its people. Eventually, Hitler offered himself as the solution. Promising a "leadership principle" to suppress the anarchy, he did return hierarchy, albeit with a vengeance most came to regret.

Caste and Class

More common and pervasive than government hierarchies are the anonymous ranking systems of caste and class. Officially leaderless, these institute lose categories of graded positions. People have a general idea of where they fit, but not necessarily of how they stand relative to specific others. Ask most Americans their class and they reply "the middle class." Provide an opportunity for them to identify themselves as "working class" and millions make the switch. Ask what class Bill Gates belongs too and most incorrectly chime in the "upper class" as opposed to "lower upper." Since they are below his level, they do not distinguish between old money and the "nouveau riche." Ask where Madonna fits and many also declare the "upper class." Unaware of the difference between celebrity and social class, they confuse fame with status. Ask them to distinguish between caste and class and most cannot. Such distinctions are lost on them because they are hardly ever considered during the course of daily living. Associating primarily with others on the same level as themselves, people do not worry about the larger differences.

Caste, as opposed to class, has almost vanished from the United States. Caste systems are characterized by limited social mobility. The group one is born into is the one in which one remains for a lifetime. In medieval Europe, an Estate system came close qualifying for similar rigidity. Its serfs were tied to the land with a limited opportunity to move into higher strata. They were peasants in the literal sense of the term, bound to work as petty farmers and laborers. Few became merchants, and fewer still rose into the aristocracy. The latter was theoretically impossible. Blood and Divine blessing, neither of which was available to serfs, supposedly conferred nobility. In India, the situation was more restricted. Someone born into the priestly caste, that is, the Brahmins, was destined to be a Brahmin, regardless of personal failures. Similarly, a person born a Sudra, that is a peasant farmer, was destined to remain a Sudra, regardless of his personal virtues. (The Kshatriyas, that is, the warriors, and the Vaishas, that is, the merchants, were also predetermined by birth.) Moreover, a Brahmin was always superior to a Kshatriya and a Kshatriya to a Vaisha irrespective of their individual accomplishments. To most Americans, such an arrangement seems foreign, yet it has been mirrored in the country's racial order. Especially during slavery, but also during Jim Crow, no matter how qualified a black, he or she was deemed inferior to whites. Whether a doctor or a minister, an African American had to step aside for the most impecunious white. Deference was owed and extracted.

Caste systems are maintained both ideologically and coercively. Those at the bottom are forced to remain in poverty and impotence, while those at the top are protected by religious ideas and punitive customs. In medieval Europe, most people believed in a Great Chain of Being. Decreed by God, it relegated all living creatures to predestined stations. God, of course, was at the summit, and creatures like earthworms near the bottom, but kings were closer to the angels than were serfs. Should a serf disagree, his master could with impunity slice him in half with a broadsword. In India, the metaphysics was stricter still. Souls were consigned to particular ranks based on the moral worth accumulated in previous lives. A belief in the transmigration of souls and karma shaped a certitude that the position one was born into could not be altered. Just as a donkey could not become a horse, it was impossible for a Sudra to become a Brahmin. But if one tried, the penalty for defying a law of nature was death. In America, religion too dictated the subservience of hereditary bondsmen. Had not the Bible recorded the curse placed on Ham and his descendents? Predestined to be hewers of wood and drawers of water, they were serving just as the Lord specified. Besides, blacks were closer to being children than adults and therefore required white supervision, particularly if they were to be saved by conversion to Christianity. Later Social Darwinism made similar claims, albeit based on a presumed biological atavism. In either case, the sentence for a black man casting a lascivious glance at a white woman was lynching. Even when Teddy Roosevelt took the simple step of inviting Booker T. Washington to the White House, the condemnations reverberated from sea to sea.

In a sense, caste systems can be conceived of as resting upon intergroup tests of strength. To the degree that individuals are attached to a specifiable level, their fate is tied to its. If their peers have prevailed over others, they will be treated as if they had as well. One of the primary ways this was achieved is through conquest. Much of the European nobility tracked its lineage back to leaders of the German tribes that vanquished the Romans. When their remote ancestors moved onto the estates of their predecessors, they, and not God, established a tradition that carried forward for millennia. Even more successful in monopolizing the upper strata were the Aryan invaders of India. Already graded as priests, warriors, and merchants upon their arrival, they thrust the indigenous populations into the Sudra and untouchable ranks. In America, a European invasion had comparable effects. Ultimately forced onto reservations, Amerindians were reminded of their inferiority by such sayings as, "The only good Indian is a dead Indian."

African Americans have been the victims of the other primary means of instituting caste, namely a forced migration. Kidnapped from the continent of their forebears by armed merchants who bought them from native slavers and transported across an ocean they did not possess the means to recross, they were then deposited on plantations where they were managed as if they were cattle. Deprived of the means of defending themselves against their masters, they learned to be subservient. Continuously under the threat of the lash, they knew that their only option was surreptitious resistance. Indeed, confronted with overpowering force, many accepted the reputation imposed by whites and came to believe in their own inferiority. Literal losers in interpersonal clashes, they adopted a worldview not unlike that of classical slaves. In the Roman Empire, prisoners of war were the primary source of new slaves. Since their lives were already forfeited on the battlefield, they were regarded as walking dead and therefore whatever the punishments inflicted upon them, these were improvements. Correspondingly, antebellum Southern slaves were often grateful for the favor of not being whipped. Needless to say, this was not a fortunate condition and neither was that of freedmen treated as if they were still slaves.

Social class, in contrast, is grounded in social mobility. Because its rankings are based primarily on economic, rather than martial, considerations, to the degree that it coexists with a market system, it is inherently flexible. In market economies, value is determined by what people are prepared to buy. Anybody who can meet the desires of consumers can stockpile a portion of their resources for themselves. Efficiency and ingenuity, not birth, are the hallmarks of success. The result is that market-based societies feature a circulation of elites. Captains of industry come and go. Marketing geniuses skyrocket to unprecedented heights and then arc downward. In the Middle Ages, elites too were replaced often because some families were decimated in war, but in modern times, the clashes are less violent. As Richard Herrnstein and Charles Murray have documented, nowadays there is a correlation between success and educational achievement. Obtaining the skills needed to be competent in the marketplace has replaced military prowess as the foremost ticket to relative strength.

Melvin Kohn's insight that "self-direction" is the key value of the middle-class parents provides a window on what is now important. Leadership in a market system depends on being able to make independent decisions in an environment of uncertainty. A person must be able to make good choices, that is, ones that are economically and socially viable, if he or she is to influence potential subordinates. Among the qualities required is an ability to take risks. Even though a person cannot be certain that a particular choice will work, he or she must be willing to move forward, all while taking responsibility for what happens next. If failure ensues, he or she must be flexible enough to fix what is broken. One of the more painful things anyone can do is admit failure, yet such admissions—at least to oneself—are essential to understand what must be corrected.

Above all, members of the middle class must be competent planners and adroit organizers. In their occupations, they typically pull people together and motivate them to work in concert. As professionals, middle managers, and entrepreneurs, they set objectives, work out procedures, and initiate activities. They also create marketing campaigns, design innovative pieces of equipment, and intervene to settle subordinate conflicts. All of this takes skill, knowledge, and emotional toughness. Should these qualities prove absent, would-be leaders may not be able to sustain their positions. More qualified individuals lower down on the social scale will challenge them; hence, they stand a good chance of being deposed. Because leadership that does not provide benefits destroys the social cohesion upon which it rests, it is inherently weak. Leaders must thus produce, and this generates insecurities. Although a person may sit high in the scheme of things, an awareness of personal limitations makes for unease. It impairs an otherwise favorable situation. For those in the lower orders who manifestly lack what it takes to be in charge, their deficiencies are likewise a source of discomfort. Conscious that others are more potent than themselves, they are attacked from within and without by accusations of inadequacy. Worse still, they may have no idea of how to improve their situation. Having been raised, as Kohn documented, to be obedient conformists, they experience anxiety when exercising initiative. Rather than take risks or develop preparations for the future, they stand pat; forever ready to complain about the proposals of others. They are thus handicapped in the race for success.

The indignities and privations that attend slavery and caste systems need no elaboration, but those within class systems are less obvious. Almost as pervasive, they are less visibly connected to social suppression. Although members of higher social classes rarely engage in the sort of overt exploitation that permeates more rigid hierarchies, those obliged to occupy the lower rungs understand they are losers. They routinely compare their fantasies of success with their achievements and shudder at the disparities. Much of what they suffer results from the relatively small portion of social resources they control, but more derives from their reaction to being losers.

Poor people must be content with the worst living conditions that their communities offer. Relegated the shabbiest housing, the least appetizing foods, and the most unfashionable clothing, their lives abound in symbols of bankruptcy. In contemporary America, where the supply of commodities outruns that of earlier generations, they nevertheless obtain less than their more prosperous rivals. Available to them in quantities perfectly capable of sustaining life, their relative dearth injures the spirit. Consider housing. The worst inner-city slums provide better protection against the elements than the hovels of the rural poor several centuries ago. All the same, they are dirty, noisy, and crowded compared with the accommodations available in the suburbs. Yet who keeps these places dirty and noisy? Isn't it the residents themselves? Isn't it they who interfere with each other's peace? And isn't it they who fail to make the most of the bounty found in the aisles of the most pitiable supermarkets? The ingredients for delectable and nutritious meals are all there, at remarkably low prices, for those determined to take advantage of them. That most of those at the bottom of the class system do not is testimony to their demoralization. Fatalistic, and desirous of instant gratification, they squander money they don't have on frozen pizzas and six-packs of beer.

Richard Sennett and Jonathan Cobb write of the hidden injuries of class. Most of these have to do with a damaged self-image and a tendency to retire from competition. While the victims of class may blame their deficits the malice of higher-ups, they actually result from the dynamics of losing. Losing hurts and therefore calls forth efforts at self-protection that can be more damaging than the original defeat. The solution, according to many reformers, is to abolish competition. This would safeguard the self-esteem of the less capable by fostering beneficial cooperation. Yet if hierarchies are natural and constructed from ubiquitous tests of strength, this is a pipe dream. Societies do not have to promote inequality a la Davis and Moore. Unfairness inevitably results from our innate impulses to power, impulses shared by rich and poor alike. If this is so, then self-defeating security devices are inevitable. They are not imposed by the winners, but by the nature of winning and losing.

Among the defenses of the poor is oppositionalism. Because losers not only despise losing, but also the winners, they are inclined to contradict their betters. Instead of trying to determine what will benefit themselves, they automatically disagree with their enemies. Regrettably, this sometimes implies objectives that are against their own interest. The joy of seeing a superior sweat outweighs the inconvenience of not obtaining a needed good. How many unions have opposed management no matter what it offered because they suspected dishonesty and then paid the price in jobs lost when the company folded? The same sort of attitude is on display in the loudness of the working and lower classes. Those who believe they are not being heard often compensate by raising their voices. But this alienates, rather than impresses, potential allies. Rowdy types love the decibel level of wrestlers when they declare an intention to fracture the sculls of their foes, but this same tactic directed at a shop foreman puts one's job in jeopardy.

Among the more vexing corollaries of social class is poor health. Losing creates physiological stresses that express themselves in illness and disability. Virtually any health problem one cares to mention is more serious among the poor. They boast a larger proportion of heart attacks, cancer, tuberculosis, and schizophrenia. They also have higher rates of alcoholism, smoking, and chemical dependency. Each of these contributes to shorter life expectancies and longer periods of disability. Less apt to commit suicide, they are also less likely to seek medical treatment. Regardless of their access to health providers, they are uncomfortable in the presence of the highly educated and hence are frequently hostile to their recommendations. Because physicians belong to the upper middle class, they are dismissed as pompous know-it-alls; hence, self-medication often replaces legitimate prescriptions.

Losing similarly has baleful consequences for family relationships. People who feel like trash detect conspiracies everywhere. Those closest to them, who should be their strongest allies, are instead perceived as devious rivals. Rather than a spouse being a source of comfort, he or she is a constant reminder that she or he is a poor provider. Likewise, rather than children being cherished emissaries to the next generation, their successes highlight one's own failures. These others must therefore be cut down to size. Ensuring that they are lower on the social scale enhances one's relative prowess. Men thus become macho bullies and women critical harpies. Children rebel against these oppressors and vow never to make them proud. Trapped between a romantic desire for unconditional love and a cynical fear of betrayal, all are too wary to give freely of themselves. Constantly afraid of being cheated, they do not negotiate in good faith, thus depriving themselves of the advantages of collaboration.

Also more likely both to commit and be victimized by violent crime, social class losers are encircled by insecurities. Others who covet their treasures steal the little they have. At home and on the street, they are knocked down and stripped of personal goods despite their protests. But when they attempt to appropriate what others have, they are exposed to retaliation. Dissed, jostled, and physically threatened, they recognize that tomorrow may be worse than today. What is more, they are not well educated. Often school dropouts, they cannot count on developing the skills to lift them to a higher level. Convinced that formal education is a sham designed to humiliate them, they prefer to rely on street smarts. When this does not work, they blame the system.

Situational Stupidity

Hardly ever remarked upon is the nexus between social class and irrationality. Viewers laugh at the antics of the guests on talk shows such as Jerry Springer's, but politely abstain from attributing their follies to social status. This would be tantamount to snickering at the physically disabled. In fact, social status is intimately connected with predictable mistakes in logic and evidence. In what may be called "situational stupidity," individuals are pressured by their societal positions to ignore facts or jump to unsupported conclusions. Instead of using their brains, they go on an automatic pilot that often guides them to a crash landing. This defect, however, is not confined to those at the bottom of the heap. Corresponding forces also betray those at the top.

Individuals at the summit, be they tyrants, corporate presidents, or professional auditors, have positions to protect. They know that others crave what they have and are laying in wait to ambush them. They also know they must continue to perform lest a false step be interpreted as vulnerability. Nevertheless, they are human and understand better than others that there are chinks in their armor. To cope, they turn to mechanisms that deny these limitations and/or cultivate the means to offset them. Richard Stengel, in his study of flattery (*You're Too Kind*), writes that successful people are more susceptible to flattery. Prepared to assume that the positive things said of them are true, they believe. This, however, subjects them to manipulation. Rather than accurately assess a situation, they are led astray by subordinates out to further their own agendas. In other words, because they are blind to their own inadequacies, they can be influenced to make faulty judgments. They are, in short, inclined to stupidity because their exalted positions insulate them from unpleasant truths.

Successful people also have a tendency toward arrogance. Inclined to overestimate their abilities even without external prompting, they are deceived by previous triumphs into believing that they know more than they do. In consequence less receptive to good advice than is warranted, they surround themselves with toadies, sycophants, and yes-men. Utterly unaware they are being told what they want to hear by subordinates who fear they will be blamed for bad news, they never suspect there are volumes of information to which they are never privy. Such was the fear of offending Hitler that while his empire crumbled, he moved phantom divisions on his maps, divisions that had long since been reduced to shells of their former selves.

Other leaders are let down by a tendency to be complacent. Grown indolent due to a series of unbroken victories, they feel entitled to the positions they hold. Finding themselves standing on third base, they are convinced they hit a triple. Such persons are frequently the beneficiaries of tradition. Nevertheless, reputations derived from the accomplishments of prior generations are in danger of being found out. Louis XVI of France inherited the mantle of Louis XIV, but not his abilities. Both may have resided at Versailles, but one built it as a tool to control an unruly aristocracy, while the other was seduced into believing that he was more secure than he was. When the bill for his self-indulgence came due, it was paid in blood at the chopping block.

Elite stupidity is also a product of the practices needed to manage large groups of people. When leaders present their schemes to potential followers, they are constrained by the limits of symbolic communications and the variability of their constituencies. As a result, they simplify their messages. If these are to be persuasive, they must avoid befuddling complexities. What they say must seem totally unambiguous, even though it may be the reverse. Crystal clarity would reveal that where the leader wants to go is not what others have in mind. In fact, since they are almost certainly a diverse crowd, not all have the same aspirations. Being unequivocal would thus disclose dissensions in the ranks. Seeming to be clear, however, allows potential acolytes to project their own interpretations on what is communicated. Opposing factions can therefore agree with the leader, without agreeing with each other. Moreover, complexities confound, whereas minimalism seems too down-to-earth to be wrong. From a leader's point of view, the danger is of being seduced by his or her own generalities. He or she too may be reassured by apparent certainties, with the effect that his or her plans are based on misinformation.

Leaders are often brought low by the ideologies that solidify their claims to priority. Communists fell off their perch when communism failed to deliver, and self-proclaimed messiahs have tumbled into obscurity when their predicted millennia proved false. Now largely forgotten, at the conclusion of World War I a blossoming demagogue, and model for Mussolini, the poet Gabriele D'Annunzio turned the tiny port of Fiume into an international flash point. A genius at public relations, he rallied Italian public opinion into demanding its annexation by referring to the recent armistice as a "mutilated victory" and Woodrow Wilson as a "Croatified Quaker." When he warned of a "marching army" of disaffected Italians, this had the effect of calling one into existence and enabling him to take over the town. But when the mostly Slav city was later turned back to Yugoslavia, his fortunes sank as quickly as they had risen. In America, political spin was also able to salvage Bill Clinton's presidency. Repeatedly told by politicians and media gurus that his lascivious behaviors did not rise to the level of "high crimes and misdemeanors," his reputation survived—but barely.

Those at the bottom of the social pyramid are enticed into foolishness for different reasons. Assaulted by losing from a myriad of directions, they do not want their pain exacerbated. Rather than stare directly at the train-wrecks of their lives, they look away. Similarly, rather than expose themselves to additional frustrations, they do not prepare for the challenges of leadership. A staple of late night talk shows are man-in-the-street interviews that disclose how ill-informed the general public can be. Ordinary people cannot locate the Pacific Ocean or identify a picture of the majority leader of the U.S. Senate. The Civil War is said to have occurred during the twentieth century, and the first president's name is recorded as Abraham Lincoln. Audiences giggle and wonder how anyone could have escaped compulsory education without assimilating these simple facts. The answer is that when they were students, individuals destined for social class oblivion were bored. They did not care about their lessons because they were convinced these were irrelevant. In this, they were correct, but because of a self-fulfilling prophecy. Having failed to study because they could not imagine getting ahead, they fell behind when others became aware of their ignorance. Nor do they enjoy reading books to fill the gaps in their education. Even educational television leaves them cold. In the end, their own choices prevent them from learning what is needed to be a good planner.

Disorganized, fatalistic, and present-oriented, denizens of the lower classes grab for what is immediately at hand, not what would bring long-term advantage. The truth is that they do not calculate what is needed, that is, if they can avoid it. Logic is wearisome when it lays bare a string of errors. Juvenile fantasies of grandiosity are more soothing than invidious comparisons with winners. A tattoo of an eagle on his bicep can make a man feel like a general when he knows that he does not have the credentials to be a military officer. For similar reasons, the orgasmic roars of a rock concert can convince a bathroom diva that she is as much a star as her heroine on the stage. Since more accurate predictions would be embarrassing, why bother with them? Skin piercings do not make for a conquering hero, so why think ahead to how others will receive them? Memorizing the lyrics to dozens of songs will not convince a manager to represent her, but dwelling on this would spoil the moment. The problem with these propensities is that they make it less likely a person will develop strategies that work.

Low status is also correlated with emotional immaturity. Losing is emotionally intense. It elicits overpowering terrors and rages. As primitive emotions, these typically fail to achieve their goals, but worse than this, they interfere with rational thought. Enraged people try to break down doors; they don't stop to figure out where the key might be. Terrified people hide under the bedsheets; they do not compute the best avenue of flight. Inclined to jump up and down or chew on the carpets, they do not reflect on the actual situation or their options. Nor are emotionally undeveloped individuals good at empathy. Grievously injured by their setbacks, they tend to be self-involved. Continuously ruminating about their reverses, they have neither the time, nor the penchant, for examining other's circumstances. Their sympathies are reserved for themselves, with nothing left over for outsiders. This isolates them in a unidimensional universe. Seeing things from one perspective, these are almost invariably misperceived.

Social losers can also be remarkably selfish. Aware of a comparative absence of success, they begrudge others theirs. This makes them dreadful role partners and unreliable attachment figures. Caught up in their private soap operas, they betray others without compunction or regret. Insensitive even to the pain of others, they break promises to gain a tiny degree of leverage. And then they feel insulted when accused of treachery. Always sure they have been cheated, they cheat others before they get a chance to do so and then throw tantrums to cover their tracks. The question is, with friends like this, who needs enemies? And with friends like this, is committed love possible? The emotional turmoil of the slums is such that people desperate for love and friendship habitually undermine their relationships.

Inanities also emanate from the rigidities of being a loser. People uncomfortably familiar with mistakes hate to admit them. The truth may be kicking them in the rump, but their nose is firmly planted in a direction where it can be cut off to spite their face. Stubborn to an extent that surprises their closest associates, they do not alter course. To do so might give their enemies satisfaction and that would be intolerable. Disinterested observers plead with them not to be foolish, but they do not listen. It can seem as if they are not smart enough to recognize an impasse, but it is their histories, and not their higher cortex, that deceive them. It is long-established anger that impels them to fight impractical battles and hold onto outcomes that cannot be undone.

Bureaucracies

As the Industrial Revolution hurtled into an era of automation and mass production, the miniature backroom workshops where most manufacturing once occurred disappeared into textbooks. Supplanted by huge factories and gigantic corporations, bureaucracies became the standard means of organizing industrial and commercial enterprises. In earlier times, only the church, the army, and some government agencies were managed this way. A broader need to coordinate large numbers of workers changed all this. It introduced a level of formality that had previously been rare. Rules and regulations, precise job descriptions, and files and records became the order of the day. Workers were closely supervised as to what they did and from whom they received supervision. Weber's portrayal of this as an iron cage was apt. With the introduction of bureaucracies, people had far less latitude than they once did and were more under the thumb of identifiable bosses.

This development instituted new discomforts, but offset them with unheard of efficiencies. To this moment, no other means of organizing battalions of employees has been able to compete. But this does not signify an absence of difficulties. Bureaucracies too create personal distress in a variety of ways. Everyone in modern societies is familiar with red tape. Named for the material with which nineteenth-century British government officials bound their records, the term now refers to the endless regulations that can make dealing with large organizations a trial. Regardless of their ability to substitute simple remedies, people feel compelled to follow mindless procedures. Form so-and-so requires a signature from official X who can only be approached by standing in line Y, except today when he is at outstation Z. Sorry, you will have to come back tomorrow and begin again by ferreting out where requisitions AA and BB are kept. There are circles within circles and legions of officious gatekeepers who revel in the authority to implement the system. Some years ago, IBM, then the epitome of a rule-bound organization, found its primacy in the computer business challenged by an upstart producer of personal workstations. Eager to put Apple in its place, its managers found it impossible to develop the requisite machine in-house. The checks and balances then in place required a series of approvals that it would take years to navigate. Instead the company opted for a processor that could be put together from components already on the shelf. What was not foreseen is that this would make room for clones. Dozens of small competitors rushed to join chase and in the process denied IBM the market dominance it sought. No doubt the company's managers were distressed that practices utilized to maintain organizational control prevented effective competition, thereby dooming them to a reduced status within the industry.

Bureaucracies are also notorious for displaced goals. They start out trying to achieve one thing but wind up pursuing something very different. Federally supported welfare agencies are a case in point. During the Great Depression, aid to families with dependent children was inaugurated with the explicit understanding that it was intended to be temporary. Figures as prominent as Franklin Roosevelt fretted that giving people money for doing nothing would deprive them of their independence. In time, however, these reservations were forgotten. Civil servants submerged in a sea of regulations began to conceive of their task as delivering funds as expeditiously as possible. When the welfare roles rose, they did not throw up their hands in despair, but congratulated themselves on providing what was now portrayed as an "entitlement." It took decades for it to become evident that this attitude bred dependency. But it was not the bureaucrats that made this discovery. Political reformers imposed it on them. To the end, the former resisted legislation that would return the program to its original goals. A related difficulty is that bureaucracies can be "too efficient." They can achieve barbaric ends. Hitler became maniacal in no small measure, thanks to the vaunted efficiency of German officialdom. He could order the Holocaust because his subordinates made the trains operate on time. Not only did these deliver steel to be turned into howitzers, but human beings to be converted into lampshades.

What bureaucracies are not noted for is creativity. The rules are the rules, and they must not be tampered with. Most bureaucrats proceed along well-worn paths; they do not explore unknown territories. It is small outfits, like Apple, that invent new technologies in an unknown enthusiast's garage. Control entails predictability; hence, variation is anathema in the well-oiled corporation. Large organizations frequently come to dominate the marketplace by purchasing someone else's innovation. This was true even of Apple when it grew up. It appropriated the idea of icons from a disrespected research group at Xerox—thus the MacIntosh.

Another aspect of large organizations, albeit not exclusive to them, is politics. Whenever large numbers of persons are engaged in the same project, the question arises as to who will be in control. Who will decide what the group does? The coalitions that contest these decisions are not confined to governments. Newcomers are often surprised to find that most companies harbor intense rivalries. They suppose that everyone agrees on the organizational mission and it is just a matter of implementing it more effectively. They are therefore startled to find colleagues more concerned with factional success than overall effectiveness. Nevertheless the competition for primacy can be so fierce that innocents are ground into submission. Those intending to mind their own business find their jobs sacrificed on an altar dedicated to someone else's ambitions.

Robert Michels formalized some of these intricacies in his Iron Law of Oligarchy. Having stumbled across the fact that the theoretically democratic leaders of unions sought to monopolize power, he hypothesized broad pressures that concentrate control in the hands of a few. These individuals use a variety of techniques to ensure dominance. For one, they keep secrets. Information others might use to gain power is systematically withheld. Newsletters, for instance, are edited to promote the positions higher-ups favor. If something is embarrassing, it is not reported. For another, they groom their successors. Individuals who agree with their attitudes are singled out for goodwill. This makes certain that their policies are perpetuated. It also freezes out the opposition. If others are correct, they still do not prevail. The effect is to propagate error and lessen overall satisfactions.

When bureaucracies are embedded in the marketplace, some discipline is exercised over their follies. If they stray too far from what customers want, competitors rush in to fill the void and they find themselves out of business. The pain of the resultant dislocations can be fearful, but in the end, social needs are more adequately addressed. Government agencies are more subject to the whims of ideology. Because who gets elected, and therefore who decides, is determined by an ability to persuade the voters, appearances count more than actualities. Farm subsidies provide a wonderful example. For almost one hundred years, these have been earmarked for rural areas with disproportionate influence in the Senate. Initially designed to save family farms from economic ruin, they did not stem the tide of commercial agriculture. Today less that 2 percent of the population is family farmers. Present subsidies go mostly to agri-corporations, often as incentives not to produce crops. The milk supports are a prime instance. They keep consumer prices artificially high and channel excess inventory into products that are subsequently destroyed. The spigot is not turned off, partly in sympathy with farmers and partly because of backroom deals to buy the votes of legislators from places like Vermont.

But even governmental hierarchies are not invulnerable. The Bolsheviks commandeered the Russian State early in the twentieth century, but their mismanagement eventually caught up with them and the Soviet Union dissolved. Nevertheless this took the better part of one hundred years. Ideas change slowly—in the case of India's caste system, they lasted for millennia. Think too of the adulation that sadistic leaders inspire. The Russian people loved Joseph Stalin. When he died, their grief was genuine. Many considered him a father figure and could not imagine life without him. Their vision of the world was so warped by ideological controls that they did not realize how many millions he killed. Repeatedly assured he was protecting them from class enemies, they believed he had spared them worse indignities.

As hierarchical subordinates in a coercively imposed social order, they could not face the truth. They had to believe they benefited from their leader's efforts. To think otherwise might have impelled them to a suicidal resistance. The upshot was that even after their oppressor's departure, they continued to inflict his organizational arrangements on themselves.

Notes

1. Paul Roscoe notes that these have variously been described as "kin-based, theocratic, despotic, militaristic, tropical forest, managerial, oligarchic, caste, class-based, group-oriented [and] individualizing."
2. Daniel Chirot draws a chilling, yet compelling, portrait of twentieth-century tyrants. Ranging through Latin America, Africa, Asia, and Europe, he leaves no doubt about the dangers that are possible.
3. Germany, Russia, Austria-Hungary, and the Ottoman Empire.

7

Relationships

Falling in love with love is falling for make-believe, Falling in love with love is playing the fool. (Rogers and Hammerstein) Some say love is for the lucky and the strong. (The Rose, Bette Midler)

Intimacy

The way it is supposed to happen is this: two stranger's eyes magically lock onto each other across a crowded room. Instantly they understand that they were fated for one another. Theirs is love at first sight; a romance ordained by heaven. Without knowing anything about each other outside of what they see, they are certain that henceforward—to and beyond the grave—theirs will be a mutual devotion so strong that nothing will ever come between them. Furthermore, they appreciate that everlasting love can cure all personal defects. Because they will be cherished, they expect to be released from whatever demons have troubled their souls. Subsequent to a whirlwind romance, they will be free to express the tender feelings they always knew they possessed. Petty jealousies will be forgotten, irrational anxieties banished, and their deepest ambitions realized. As Bette Midler opined, with the sun's love, the seed they have planted will grow to be a magnificent rose.

Sadly, Midler was wrong. Falling in love is not for everyone. Although almost everybody is capable of "falling in love with love," this does not necessarily apply to falling for other human beings. Fantasies of "unconditional positive regard" abound. Some fine day a prince (or princess) will walk into one's life and see the beauty to which others have been oblivious. This "soul mate" will provide a protective envelope so cozy as to exclude the cold winds of reality. Her very touch will infuse a strength that keeps dangers at bay. The problem is that intimacy requires strength. Midler notwithstanding, love is for the lucky and the strong. One of life's most tragic ironies is that the people who could most use love, that is, the one's deprived of it in their youth, are least likely to get it. Having been stifled as children, they desperately seek affirmation in the arms of a rescuer, but in their desperation, push others away. Forever needy, they demand love without being able to return it. Like the black holes at the hub of galaxies, they do not glow with light, but instead suck in every once of energy that comes within range.

Real love entails a mutual giving; hence, it requires two partners capable of this. Each must be strong enough to sustain periods without being the center of the universe and be sufficiently autonomous to share themselves without fear of depletion. In all probability once having been loved, such persons know what intimacy feels like and enjoy passing along its gifts. Real love entails mutual understanding; hence, the impossibility of love at first sight. While there is such a thing as lust at first sight, that is, of an all-consuming sexual attraction, real love is of another person and therefore contingent upon knowing him or her. But such an understanding takes time. Human beings are complex. No one is a pane of glass utterly transparent to a lover's gaze. It takes years to appreciate another's intricacies. Furthermore, real love is the product of bonding. Lovers must travel through predicable phases before they achieve a durable attachment. In the "falling in love with love" phenomenon, there are undoubtedly paroxysms of joy, but these are generated by internal hopes. Actual love is in response to another frail human organism. People develop strong connections not only despite, but because of each other's limitations. But, to reiterate, learning this takes time. Only after undergoing a courtship process that tests their respective mettle do they genuinely come to care for someone who had previously been a stranger.

Committed intimacy[1] is dangerous. People who pledge to be there for one another in sickness and in health eventually have to endure some sickness. They must surely endure moments when this other behaves badly. There will even be moments when they behave badly. Human beings are not angels. Sometimes they get selfish; sometimes they are thoughtless. Sometimes individuals who love each other get so angry they want to hurt one another. The difficulty with intimacy is that it provides both the provocation and the opportunity to do so. In contemporary society, heterosexual intimates tend to live together. Usually they share the same bedroom. Physically present when the other is naked, they experience each other at their biological worst. Lying side by side, they are also able to deliver blows where a partner is most vulnerable. A spouse who is truly irate has the possibility of suffocating a sleeping enemy. Were intimates completely spontaneous, it is doubtful any would survive long enough to raise a family. What is essential is restraint. Not all feelings can be acted upon and not all acts allowed to go to completion.

More dangerous still, because it is both prevalent and tempting, is emotional violence. Intimates quickly learn where their partners are vulnerable. They discover what this other fears and what makes him or her sad. They also learn this other's fondest dreams and which have been realized and which not. Intimates perceive when the other has been frustrated and, if they desire, can increase this frustration. Propinquity furnishes many occasions for sabotage. Secret maneuvers can be implemented to reduce a partner's chances for success. Exacerbated fears, for instance, may be employed to terrify a "loved one" into submission. Likewise, guilt can be instilled to change a partner's decision to one more congenial to the manipulator. Although less physically damaging than overt violence, these exercises are as destructive. More difficult to discern, they tear away at a person's innards without her recognition of what is occurring. As a consequence, more difficult to resist, they can also be more enduring. Emotional fetters are hard to handle. Easy to disguise from the self and the other, they arise with greater frequency. Love is supposed to be exalted, but it is not always fair. Despite professions of eternal troth, relationships are regularly torn by private warfare. Instead of helping each other, spouses can beat each other into the ground. Only when a partner is suffering do they rest content.

What then can reduce these threats to personal satisfaction? How can potential partners learn to trust one another and make no mistake about it? Trust is critical. People hesitate to enter dangerous relationships or remain in them, unless they have reason to believe they are relatively safe. There are several possible mechanisms for limiting the risks. The first is *commitment*. Interpersonal bonds stand a better chance of lasting when both parties promise to dedicate themselves to the relationship. People who take promises seriously, because they believe in promise keeping, are more likely to exert an effort to stay together. Motivated not merely by a desire to please the other, but also by a desire to live up to internal principles, attempts to forestall, or to repair, foreseeable damage occur without prompting. Those for whom relationships are sacrosanct only as long as these are satisfying discover a host of alternatives. They betray without compunction and therefore inflict insidious injuries. On the assumption that they can always find someone better, they refuse to make compromises or recognize the justifiable concerns of the other. Terminal romantics, such persons, in their self-centeredness, make long-term romance impossible.

A second protective factor is *knowledge*: knowledge of the self, the other, and their mutual circumstances. People who do not know what they are getting into tend to get into hot water. Because they don't understand what they want, what others have to offer, or what it is possible to share, they harbor unrealistic expectations. Frustrated when they do not receive the impossible, they reject that which is possible. People need to be aware of their desires and limitations if they are to pursue the achievable. They also need to be aware of the desires and limitations of potential partners if they are to link up with someone who can provide them with satisfactions. They similarly need to be aware of the pitfalls inherent in intimacy. Unless they recognize the potential frictions that go with being close, they may blame an innocent other for what no one could have prevented. Bedazzled by their own imaginations, they bounce from one unfulfilling experience to another.

A third protective factor is personal *maturity*. People who are not emotionally mature cannot control their passions. They wax hot and cold out of synch with external provocations. Encapsulated in a bubble of primitive emotions, they oscillate between titanic rages and a chilly remoteness. Sometimes terrified by insubstantive shadows and at other times bold beyond what is prudent, they manufacture their own troubles. Utterly unfamiliar with Goleman's emotional quotient, they alternatively attack or shut out those closest to them. Unable to tolerate modest frustrations or endure miniscule anxieties, they overreact. Impracticable when reasoned with, they induce others either to retaliate or depart the scene. Themselves bewildered by the furies swirling around their heads, they resort to what comes naturally, but which, because it is primitive, makes things worse.

One of the reasons intense emotionality is hazardous to intimacy is that it interferes with productive negotiations. A fourth protective factor is therefore an *ability to negotiate* successfully. No matter how well suited a couple, there will always be disagreements between them. No two people ever run on identical schedules. At some point, their desires diverge and they have to find a means of reconciling their differences. While psychologists have discovered that there is no optimum technique for achieving agreement, deals that are satisfactory to both parties have to be within reach. If one wins, and the other loses, especially if this occurs at regular intervals, grievances accumulate. Sooner or later there is an explosion and a parting of the ways. Some people negotiate quietly and reasonably, whereas others do so with fire and thunder. What matters is not the pyrotechnics, but the results. If these are agreeable to both sides, neither will be motivated to take advantage of their closeness.

In a real sense, intimacy is the product of ongoing negotiations. Just as social roles and hierarchies are negotiated, so are interpersonal attachments. These too result from a give and take between the parties. The difference is that with roles and hierarchies, these encounters are contests during which scarce resources are allocated, while with relationships, once an alliance is established, both parties may get more than they started out having. Intimate relations likewise involve compromises. Each side may have to forfeit something dear, but when the bonding process works, both receive compensations. Successful relationships are inherently synergistic. The mere fact of having acquired a dependable ally can be of incomparable worth.

The opening phase of relationship negotiations also differs in being more byzantinely choreographed. Unlike the straightforward interpersonal demands exchanged by role partners or the tests of strength of hierarchical rivals, courtship rituals are lengthy, anxiety-ridden, and occasionally exhilarating journeys. Usually launched between two strangers who cannot be sure of the outcome, each can decisively terminate the adventure if they wish. With supplementary partners waiting in the wings, their eyes periodically stray so as to make judgmental comparisons. Whereas role partners seek a complementary division of labor and hierarchical rivals strive for the highest prospective status, potential intimates look for a specific person to whom to commit. They do not necessarily want the best possible person, but the best possible person for them. As we shall see, what is desired is moral equality. Intimates must wish for both to succeed. If one ranks higher, or has a better job, jealousies can undermine their alliance.

Strangely, this equality is not equivalent to sameness. More imperative than a division of labor between the genders is one between spouses. A husband and wife cannot afford to be rivals. If their relationship is based upon competition, sooner or later one will outdo the other, thus generating envy. One way to reduce this is for them to pursue different objectives. If the tasks in which they specialize differ, both can be successful without impinging on the other's accomplishments. Each can be happy for the other without feeling impelled to do him or her one better. The traditional gender roles provided archetypes for such a partition, but recent developments have made these problematical. This, however, does not obviate the need for a separation of tasks. It merely transfers the responsibility for developing a workable arrangement onto the shoulders of couples themselves.

Friendly feelings are also essential for effective role taking. Intimates must not only understand where their mates are coming from, but they also "feel" where they are coming from. They have to empathize despite differences in gender. Men can never know exactly what women are feeling, and vice versa, but they can come close. People who love each other sense each other's pain without being verbally informed of it. To like someone is to care about her welfare—and to care is to take notice. To care also implies the motivation to help. Loving couples do not unthinkingly exploit their partners. One of the worst consequences of modern feminism has been to generate suspicions between men and women. This has made it more difficult to recognize the other's needs and to assist in fulfilling them. The good news is that the feminists are wrong about the nature of the sexes. Intimate collaborations between the genders are possible, but they depend upon each side being able to experience things from the other's perspective.

A complicating factor, of course, is sexuality. Passion is not the same as love, but sexual passions can be powerful. People are sometimes motivated by their hormones. Over and above the bonding that occurs between individuals is a desire for sexual release. This means that upon occasion, they do not worry about being faithful or trustworthy; they merely demand satisfaction. Moreover, since male and female sexuality is not the same, their mismatches are a source of tension. The war between the sexes has been going on since the beginning of time and will probably endure until we are extinct. Jealousies and misunderstandings are therefore preordained. Nevertheless, although these cannot be extinguished, they can be contained. Just as other aspects of our humanity can be understood, so can our sexualities. And allowances can be made; allowances, not ignorance or mindless tolerance.

Relationship Negotiations

Contemporary attachment theorists have characterized adult bonds as being fourfold in character. Some relationship behaviors are said to be *secure*, some *resistant*, others *avoidant*, and still others *disorganized*. In the first case, when people establish stable linkages, the process of creating them is portrayed as having worked successfully. Rather than their attachments being disrupted, the participants have an opportunity to make trustworthy commitments. In resistant situations, however, one or the other fights against the attachment. Instead of allowing the bonding to proceed, anger from failed attachments intercedes to dictate a desire to get even. The other person's overtures are thwarted and instability prevails. In avoidant situations, a person actively steers clear of getting involved. From the outside, it may seem he or she is indifferent to personal attachments. Apparently self-contained, such a person is to all intents immune to the loneliness that plagues others. But appearances are deceiving. The reality is of someone who has concluded that it is impossible to lose if one does not play. Attachments are shunned lest one come to care and then be disappointed. Lastly, in the case of disorganized attachments, a person swings unpredictably from one extreme to another. He or she apparently does not know what is wanted and therefore is never satisfied. Of these modes of interaction, only the first is satisfactory. Only it leads to dependable relationships or provides their benefits.

Some years ago, the psychoanalyst Karen Horney foreshadowed this analysis. Her concern, however, was not with attachments, but neuroses. She observed that her clients either *moved toward others*, *against others*, or *away from others*. In the first case, they became dependent, often overly so. In order to deal with their insecurities, they sought protectors. When confronted with a frightening situation, they placated whoever promised shelter. In the second case, they protested against their dilemmas. Primed to blame others for their misery, they angrily attacked people who got too close. Uncomfortable in passively trusting their fate to the mercies of others, they sought to defeat potential rivals before they were themselves defeated. In the third case were clients who avoided entanglements. They sought safety in isolation. As long as they were alone, they could guarantee their own security by remaining alert of perilous intrusions.

The parallels between Horney and the attachment theorists are evident. They clearly deal with analogous modes of social interaction. Why this is so can be discerned by creating a matrix. If it is assumed that there are two major dimensions to social negotiations, their interactions can be seen to produce four categories. The first dimension is *direction*. Negotiators can move either toward or away from each other, that is, they can agree to cooperate or they can compete. The second dimension is *activity* level. The parties can either be passive or aggressive; they can choose to fight or not to fight. Putting these together produces a table with four cells. *Active and toward* is liable to produce stable relationships. *Active and away* gives us conflicted rivalries. *Passive and toward* is dependent and disorganized. *Passive and away* is avoidant and alone. Together these define the possibilities open to individuals when they seek to delineate their relationships with potential attachment figures.

Confidence in this analysis is provided by the applications to which it can be put. Robert Merton is celebrated for theories about deviant behavior. The best known of these was originally called anomie theory, but has more recently strain theory. Based upon the notion that members of a community differ to the degree that they accept a society's values and the resources they possess for achieving these, it uses these to predict subsequent behaviors. If they support a society's values and have the means of obtaining them, they become *conformists*. They buy big houses and fancy cars and do not become deviant. In terms of the above analysis, they are *active and toward*. What they perceive as desirable, they approach with vigor. As a consequence, they improve their chances of success.

Merton's *innovators* and *rebels* correspond to the *active and away* pattern. Both of these groups are dissatisfied and make spirited efforts to alter their surroundings. The innovators develop new goals and techniques to replace the old, whereas the rebels are content to destroy the old. *Retreatists* are likewise disgruntled with their present circumstances. They, however, are *passive and away* in their response. Instead of trying to make a difference, they withdraw from what they do not like and erect defensive barriers. Finally, the *ritualists* go through the motions. They do not reject what is; they simply fail to embrace it. *Passive and toward* in their orientation, they exhibit the external manifestations of conventional objectives, but do so without investing their internal energies.

Remarkably, the same sort of analysis can be applied to the personality disorders. These have already been described as referring to modes of social negotiation, but it is also possible to classify their bargaining strategies according to their directions and activity levels. The antisocial personality is easy. This sort of person is *active and away* in his or her relationships. He or she enthusiastically fights against other human beings perceived as enemies. Paranoids too are *active and away.* The difference is that they are much more specific in identifying their foes. Narcissists are similarly *active and away.* Like the antisocial types, their acrimony is broadly based, whereas their means of resisting is more specific. Determined to inflate themselves, while manipulating others for their own benefit, they are active in building themselves up as opposed to tearing others down. Passive–aggressives, in contrast, are *passive and away.* From their perspective, adversaries hedge them in. Desirous of getting even, but fearful of retaliation, they dare not do so openly. Their compromise is to resist with as little visible effort as possible. Dependent personalities, however, are *passive and toward.* They seek the help of others, yet depend upon them to do the work. Clingy and needy, they overestimate the goodwill of potential protectors, while underestimating their ability to defend themselves. Obsessive-compulsives likewise are *passive and toward.* As with ritualists, they go through the motions—over and over again. They do not rebel against that which is; they merely invoke its external shell as a reflexive protection. Histrionics, in comparison, are *active and toward.* They buy into the standards of those around them and attempt to dramatize their exemplification of them. Unduly spirited in their approach to life, they overdo what might otherwise be considered conformist. Schizoid personalities are more problematic. They are *active and away* in the sense that they reject the "normal" world and institute bizarre substitutes. They are also *passive and toward* in that they submit to the judgments of others in a manner that paranoids do not, but they do so with a casual indifference. Decidedly different from others, they are more akin to "disorganized" negotiators. Unsure of whom they are or what they want, they swing between diametrically opposed poles.

Three further patterns need to be introduced with regard to personal negotiations. The first of these is Dean Pruitt's Dual-Concern model. He posits a universe in which negotiators have four options. Each may individually be concerned with promoting his or her own interests (and only these interests), or in promoting only the interests of their partner (and only those). Or he or she may be indifferent to their collective interests, or choose to promote the interests of both. The last is the dual-concern stance that Pruitt advocates. He believes that if two individuals act as partners, they can problem-solve so as to maximize the benefits that accrue to both. But this requires that they understand their respective needs and value them equally. Intimate relationships, in particular, demand a mutuality of objectives. It is working in tandem that provides the synergistic leverage that makes coupling advantageous. Because teams are unstable when their goals are skewed, it is essential that both sides profit from the alliance. The *dual-concern* model can also be assimilated to the *secure attachment* and the *active and toward* models. Thus, in its preferred mode, the participants are oriented toward each other and are secure in their efforts to assist one another.

Second is the previously alluded to double bind form of negotiations. Often associated with schizophrenia, this configuration is perhaps more insidious within normal relationships. Typical of this pattern is a parent who will offer closeness only to deny it when its actuality makes it feel threatening. A mother, for instance, may complain that her daughter does not demonstrate sufficient affection, yet will become cold when an embrace is offered. Most likely, she fears closeness—fears probably instilled in her own childhood and by now deeply repressed. Similarly, a father might demand that a son act more like a man only to slap him down when his subsequent assertiveness arouses the older man's insecurities. The opposite of a dual-concern model, in this pattern, inherent contradictions prevent a viable conclusion. Instead of a win-win situation, it becomes a no-win negotiation. The parties then bounce back and forth utterly oblivious to how one (or both) are sabotaging their joint endeavor.

In the third arrangement, winning is also obviated. Here one or both of the parties is "ambivalent." In this case, the goals of either may be unclear. Sometimes they want one thing, sometimes another. To be ambivalent is to be torn by competing aspirations. It is to be unsure of one's priorities, and often to oscillate between them. Instead of making a predictable demand, what is asked varies with unfathomable motivations; motivations that may be in conflict and are sometimes impossible to resolve. Because either party may be confused about what he or she wants, the other will be more perplexed. Rather than make a deal, the two chase each other's tails until their mutual frustrations erupt into recriminations that make it impossible to come to an agreement.

The moral of these distinctions seems to be that working collaboratively with a negotiating partner to achieve shared ambitions will usually achieve the best results. It ensures the maximization of needs—fulfillment with the fewest difficulties. Nevertheless, there is a potentially dangerous naïveté built into this assumption. It presumes that one's interlocutor is a worthy partner and that the balance of power between the pair is equitable. In our complex world, however, neither of these prerequisites may be met. As a result, what is best depends on the situation. Not all negotiations should be treated the same. Indeed, to do so might create regrettable outcomes.

If the person with whom one is dealing is dangerous, moving toward him or her can be a mistake. If this other is given to coercive, neglectful, or double bind tactics, it is doubtful that he or she should be regarded as a friend. Dual concerns are all well and good, but not if the other party is unconcerned with a partner's needs. In this case, considering him or her an enemy is justified. The problem with paranoids is that they detect enemies where they do not exist; even so the world is populated with real foes, real evils, and real pitfalls. Some people intentionally inflict pain upon others, and moving away from them is therefore rational. Moreover, this can be accomplished through fight, not merely flight tactics. Working energetically to defeat an horrific other may be the most effective means of avoiding catastrophe. More than this, it can be heroic. Active efforts to limit the scope of a Hitler were mandatory, not merely acceptable. A failure to exert power against such an adversary is tantamount to allowing him to win.

How active a person can be is contingent on the other's relative power. Spitting in the face of a Nazi guard when one is an unarmed civilian is not laudable; it is foolish. When an adversary has all the advantages, discretion is safest. Passive–aggressives who have suffered under the boot of tyrannical role partners behave as they do because in their world it was the only practical means of survival. Were they to be more forthright, they would have incurred punishments they could not resist. On the other hand, if one's power is equal or greater than an adversary's, one can be both more overt and more restrained. For a while, it was recommended that people be "assertive," as opposed to "aggressive" or "passive," in their relationships. They were supposed to speak up energetically on behalf of their interests and not hostilely attack or quietly accept whatever came their way. Assertive tactics turn out to work well when one has the clout to make others listen. One can then be explicit and refrain from being punitive because the listener does not have the power to strike back. In this case, it is risk-free to offer a detested message and do so without excessive force. However, aggressive policies become necessary when the other can fight back and must be put in his place. Here, if one is to win, every ounce of energy may need to be marshaled. Passive strategies, however, are imperative when the other has so much power that one might be crushed. In this case, evading attention is warranted.

With regards to intimacy, the most appropriate sort of negotiating stance is thus coming into focus. As long as the person with whom one is seeking an attachment is a decent human being, moving toward him or her makes sense. Such a partner has the capacity to be generous and to engage in role taking. He or she can be concerned with the interests of a companion and therefore has the potential to collaborate in a dual-concern model. Becoming actively engaged with such an individual can pay handsome dividends. This is especially so if this other's power is on a par with one's own. In this case, neither submission nor dominance interferes with bargaining. Neither party will be tempted to enforce selfish wishes because this is less possible. Individuals who regard each other as hierarchical equals are also unlikely to be neglectful. Aware that this other can pack a wallop, his or her wishes command respect. But because this other's power is not overwhelming, it is not intimidating. A person will therefore feel safe in asserting his own wishes.

Out of bounds should be relationships in which one or the other party is a bully. Choosing the wrong person with whom to explore the possibilities of intimacy can have dismal consequences. A great deal of misery is generated within pairs that are not well matched. This makes the selection process critical. Individuals must be able to recognize those who bode ill. Generally, the only way to handle them is to give them a wide berth. Nor is it a good idea to seek an active engagement with someone who is distinctly more, or less, powerful than oneself. The temptation to unfairness then becomes too great. Worse still, one party will feel inferior and the other superior. Instead of being able to relax in each other's company, they have to be wary. Forever open to invidious comparisons, each will discover grievances that are exacerbated when one takes advantage of a superior strength, while the other becomes aggressively defensive.

Sex

Men and women are different. Nevertheless, what should be an enduring cliché has become a subject of contention. Even within the realm of sexuality, the equivalence of the genders has become a political football. In some quarters, the missionary position has been interpreted as an expression of male dominance, and women have been urged to demand being on top as a matter of conscience. Yet sex, as opposed to heterosexual bonding, has pitfalls over and above those incurred by establishing intimate attachments. The specifically sexual differences between men and women create conflicts, which, when they get out of hand, can be as destructive as rank and role problems.

In recent years, Freud has been excoriated for asserting that "anatomy is destiny." In his view, men and women seek different objectives because they are hardwired to do so. With respect to their sexual desires, there is little doubt he was correct. Because men and women are often physiologically and evolutionarily at cross-purposes, conflicts flourish. Whether in bed or during the hunt for bed-partners, their differences create disputes that generate complaints. Foremost among these are the frictions inherent in the "double standard." From time immemorial, men have been reckoned the more promiscuous sex. Eager to amass conquests, but shy of commitment, they have sought to seduce—and frequently abandon. Women, in opposition, have generally been more loyal and more selective. While a few have earned reputations as "sluts," the majority are more circumspect in their dalliances. In some eras, they have even demanded ironclad commitments before they have deigned to offer their favors. The double standard endorses this disparity. It commends men when they are successful in their quests and condemns women when they stray. A man may be deemed more of a man when unfaithful, but a woman forfeits her status as a lady and becomes a whore. Feminists have therefore encouraged women to play the field. Determined to strike into the teeth of an injustice, they have argued that if men can get away with it, why shouldn't they?

The reason for the differences, however, is apparently a matter of basic biology. Women invest hugely more in having children than men. Not only do they bear them; they are responsible for nursing them through their first years. Furthermore, a woman is more limited in the number of children she can conceive. Men can spread their seed over broad pastures and then disappear into the next county, whereas women have but one pregnancy at a time. It is thus more important for a woman to be careful in her selection of a mate. Choosing the wrong one with whom to copulate can leave her alone with an infant whose genes may not be suited for survival.

All of this translates into differences in what the genders find attractive and in how they engage in sexual activities. Men tend to be visually fixated. When they see a beautiful woman, they become aroused. Generally the first thing they notice is her waist to hip ratio. If this is in the neighborhood of 6.8–10, they are stimulated. Evolution seems to have decreed this a rough and ready measure of a woman's ability to bear children. Women who boast clear complexions and symmetrical features also attract men. These qualities appear to indicate good health. In essence, men are turned on by women who offer evidence of fertility. Biologically impelled to pass along their genes as widely as possible, they are visually alert to potentially good sexual partners.

Women, given their divergent objectives, employ a different set of indicators. More verbal and tactile in orientation, their priority is finding a man who can assist in raising children. The desire is for a strong man who can both protect and provide for her and her young. Less concerned with physical attributes, she seeks proof of social superiority. In our market-oriented society, this is frequently provided by economic success. Women are literally attracted by men who are financially well off. They also seek men who are prepared to commit; that is, men who are ready to tell them how much they are loved. This division between the genders is most noticeable in their choices of pornography. Men obviously favor nudity. They want to see feminine curves in the flesh. But when *Playgirl* Magazine attempted an analogous strategy with women, it failed miserably. What sells among women are romance novels. These bodice rippers specialize in a virile young man rescuing a damsel in distress and then pledging his eternal troth. Love, that is, commitment, is the issue, not fertility or bedroom gymnastics.

The anthropologist Helen Fisher has attributed these differences to a "sex contract." She, and others, have speculated that in the environment of human adaptedness, it was essential for men and women to band together to raise children. Due to their big brains, human infants are slow to mature. Born more dependent than other animals, they take years to learn the skills necessary to stay alive. During this period, they rely on their parents to feed and protect them. But a mother in a hunter-gatherer society is unable to provide these services on her own. Tied down physically by the need to carry her youngsters around, hunting clearly becomes impossible. Men who are able to move about more freely can track down game, but where is the incentive to share their prizes with women and children? The answer, says Fisher, is sex. Women offer the satisfaction of their bodies in return for a portion of the bounty. This is why, in contrast to virtually every other species, human females have a menstrual, versus an estrus, cycle. Sexually receptive at almost any time of the year, they can please their mates virtually at will. This creates an emotional set that is distinctive for each gender. Although sex is pleasurable to both, it is the man who seeks the favor of the woman and the woman who offers her genitals as a gift to the man.

In any event, calls for androgyny have been fiascos. Thus, when urged to be as profligate with their attentions as men, most women demonstrated an inability to follow through. They have not taken to calling men for dates, but continued to entice them into doing the calling. Nor has an easy sexuality provided women the same satisfactions it does men. As a result, a reaction set in that men have been demanded to be more like women. A virtual industry arose to accuse men of sexual harassment. Once upon a time, harassment consisted of bosses coercing female subordinates into coitus in return for keeping their jobs—the Hollywood casting couch being a notorious example. But times have changed. Today when a man looks lasciviously at a woman, he can be charged with "visual rape." In other words, when a man scans a woman to evaluate her sexual attributes, if she objects, he is automatically guilty. Although he cannot know in advance what she will find acceptable, even when she dresses in a manner gauged to attract attention, he is vulnerable to condemnation. The point is that where once women were advised to be more sexually assertive, men are now commanded to be less so. The problem is that in both cases, the genders have been asked to behave counter-instinctually. Only a supposition that sexual uniformity is both normal and moral could produce such gridlock.

Since sexual activity is a common ingredient in heterosexual intimacy, reducing its inherent frictions can contribute to personal contentment. When men and women fail to recognize their differences and expect the other to be what he or she is not, they set themselves up for frustration. Men who hope to satisfy their wives need to understand their emotional and tactile needs. Similarly, women who want happy husbands must recognize their visual desires and emotional limitations. Each party will occasionally be driven to distraction by the other's opacity, but this need not escalate to open warfare. The good news is that couples who are firmly bonded tend to make allowances for each other. Because they care, they are more sensitive and flexible than otherwise.

Choosing a Partner

With the need to choose an appropriate partner more crucial than ever, it is astonishing how poorly understood the process is. Most Americans remain in the thrall of the myth of romantic love. Where once medieval troubadours sang of the magic of courtly love, contemporary authors turn out odes to the magic of passionate relationships. Love is something that is supposed to strike from out of the blue. Instructions on evaluating potential suitors are deemed irrelevant. When the time comes, one will simply know. Mr. or Mrs. Right will send out unmistakable vibes that will be received because they fit so well. Besides, the constituents of love are supposed to be a mystery. They cannot be taught because they are intrinsically beyond understanding. In fact, it is the mystery that is supposed to make love so enchanting. Were it reduced to calculable formulae, it would lose its greatest virtue.

Back in the 1930s, Willard Waller introduced the concept of rating–dating. As American folkways changed to favor personal choice over arranged marriages, he recorded how these practices evolved on college campuses. Among these was the phenomenon of dating. Teenagers had taken to going out with members of the opposite sex, chiefly on weekends. Putatively for fun, these expeditions entailed such activities as going to the movies, taking a drive to a lover's lane, or eating dinner at a nice restaurant. Boys and girls often coupled up by "going steady," but as frequently scrounged through a revolving door of "possibilities." One of the functions of this process was to sort out potential mates. Some contenders were clearly superior to others. In comparison, they "rated" higher. Eventually, a preference emerged. One partner stood out as best and the pair became an "item." If everything worked out, in due course the two got married.

In fact, this is not quite what Waller found. He discovered that individuals were not looking for "the best" potential partner, but one on a level comparable to their own. They required relative equality; not equivalence. If one were better than the other, the other might feel inferior. Neither would be comfortable and sooner or later would split up. The necessary moral equality could be achieved by both being unusually attractive or uncommonly smart, but they could also find parity if one were rich and the other beautiful. Although ranked excellent in different dimensions, each would be aware that their companion brought a significant asset to the relationship.

This issue of parity spawned the related question of whether individuals should seek a partner who was the same or different from themselves. Conventional wisdom endorsed both options. Sometimes it was said that "opposites attract," but also that a couple must "share interests." No detailed consensus emerged and daters were left to sort out the truth on their own. In fact, both parts of the equation are true. Potential intimates benefit from being similar in some areas and different in others. One important similarity goes counter to American mythology. Men are supposed to be attracted by dim-witted women; the dumb blonde being the pinnacle of their ambition. Desirous of being fussed over, they dream of being the unquestioned intellectual leader in the household. The trouble with this is that research regularly demonstrates it wrong. In reality, couples tend to be equally matched on IQ. And no wonder. A smart man with a dumb wife will not feel understood and conversely a dumb woman with a smart husband will feel slighted. Neither will be able to communicate with the other, and they ultimately will move apart.

Another area in which similarity predominates is values. Intimates need to agree on what is important, particularly in the moral domain. If one believes lying is wrong and the other does not, the stage is set for interminable disputes. When he lies with a clear conscious and she feels betrayed, he will see no reason to placate her, except with a few more untruths. Neither will understand why the other is upset, but because their value commitments are deeply ingrained, they will not be motivated to change them. A divergence in attitudes can also be troublesome with regard to life goals. If one wants to live in the country and the other in the city, a compromise may not be reachable. Or if one dreams of a house filled with children, while the other is determined to brook no encumbrances, a resolution may also be out of the question. The result is that when people match up, value complementarity is one of their most important aspirations.

Researchers also find homogamy with regard to social class. People from the lower orders tend to choose mates from the lower classes, whereas those from higher strata choose partners with a comparable background. Once more the myths are wrong. People joke about how it is just as easy to fall in love with a rich person as a poor one, but this is not so. Their values, experiences, skills, networks, and knowledge are bound to clash. Social class is not merely about money; it is more fundamentally about lifestyles. A person who is self-directed may have difficulty adjusting to someone who prefers conformity. Of even more significance when it comes to intimacy are disparities in marital customs. Thus individuals of upper middle class origin tend to favor companionate marriages. Each spouse regards the other as an equal and a best friend. They habitually talk out their differences and come to a common conclusion. Moreover, much of their socializing is done in the other's company, hence they spend a good deal of time together. Working class individuals, however, tend to subscribe to a dissimilar pattern. Theirs are often skewed marriages. The man fancies himself the master of his domain, but, in fact, cedes running the household to his wife. Given to macho posturing, he claims to be the boss, while she quietly manipulates the family behind the scenes. When he socializes, it is frequently with his buddies at a bar. When she does, it is with her family of origin. If asked, she cheerfully admits that her mother is her best friend. Thus, when persons with diverse upbringings get together, their expectations can generate disappointments.

Another area in which similarities are found is in the party's interests. They tend to like many of the same things. Nevertheless this is also an area in which differences abound. There will be occasions when couples share their pursuits, but others when they will not. While it can be fun to go on ski trips together, it can be disastrous to spend every waking minute doing the same things. If there is no division of labor, the two will habitually toil in the same vineyards. The opportunities to compete thus multiply and so, therefore, do potential conflicts. Nor is too much togetherness productive of privacy. No matter how comforting it can be to be close to a loved one, sometimes it is essential to be alone. Only then can one maintain a sense of identity. What is optimum, therefore, is an assortment of interests, some of which overlap, but others of which do not.

Somewhat more complex is the issue of role complementarity. Intimates are not only bonded; they inevitably constitute each other's most significant role partner. Particularly with regard to basic, personal roles, they will be each other's most available foil. It is therefore imperative that their roles fit together. Not sameness, but a pairing of tasks is required. Sometimes this necessity is recognized in the observation that a loud person has a quiet spouse or that a shy one has a gregarious partner. Each seems to make up for something missing in the other and they vicariously enjoy their respective propensities. Nevertheless, the way roles interact is more complex than this. What each person does for the other may enable this other to perform a familiar script. Indeed, the partner may constitute an essential element of this script, namely its social constituent. His demands are what keep his partner's role operative and intact.

Consider the plight of the scapegoat. With no one to pick on him, it might not be possible to continue accepting the blame for things never done. What is needed in a partner is a "bully." This way the bully has someone to harass and the scapegoat someone to provide the customary harassment. Or consider the perpetual caregiver. She needs someone to take care of. If someday she encounters a "prince" who feels entitled to continuous fawning, she will be in her element. The two will feel as if they have discovered a soul mate who completes them by filling in a missing component. These intimates recognize that they are different, but also feel part of an accustomed whole. And they will be correct. Most probably, they are assisting each other in recreating childhood scenarios.

Many couples partake of what might be called a "repetition-compulsion relationship." They return to the unfinished business of the past, sometimes to correct it, but sometimes to perpetuate it. When the previous business was fulfilling, they are in luck. Having perhaps been loved in childhood, each can reestablish the sort of bonds that once provided emotional nourishment. When, in contrast, the earlier roles were dysfunctional, restoring their potency can be painful. Heroes get trapped into being endlessly heroic, rebels are confined to eternal loops of rebellion, and clowns are fated to provide amusement for legions of insatiable fans. Afraid to strike out in unfamiliar directions, unresolved emotions impede innovative ventures. Now tied to someone with corresponding apprehensions, the two reinforce patterns that long ago proved inadequate. Instead of their relationship expanding their respective spheres of experience, it restricts them within a palisade of anguish.

Unless a person wishes to be imprisoned within a folie à deux, self-knowledge is indispensable. Ignorance of a dysfunctional role may be indistinguishable from a sentence to reiterate it. Not only is it necessary to recognize the role, but its associate role must also be recognizable. Those who cannot perceive the signs of unfair demands are destined to fall prey to them. Partner selection must thus begin with personal maturity. When someone does not possess the emotional strength for an accurate self-assessment, the chances of joining forces with a loser escalate. A downward cycle is initiated from which release is problematic.

Because love is not a universal curative, the requisite maturity must be achieved before settling on a partner. People do not automatically grow up when exposed to someone who adores them. If their childhoods have relegated them to a dysfunctional set of roles, it is they who will have to go through resocialization. Should this be achieved before the rating–dating process, a pristine clarity of vision will attend their subsequent effort. Should it await entanglement within a relationship, it is critical that the partner be committed to resocialization. In the best circumstances, this can eventuate in an alliance for growth or, in the less favorable, in a decision to follow separate paths.
   A fortiori, efforts at rescue rarely succeed. When one person takes pity on another and devotes herself to helping him overcome his limitations, the results are generally disappointing. As with the self, resocialization is the only practical avenue to growth for the limited partner. But resocialization requires the personal investment of the one in need of development. An outside person can facilitate change, but she cannot go through the emotions that must be experienced to produce it. When the helper is part of an intimate relationship, there is an additional complication. Sympathy normally flows from the strong to the weak. It thus implies that the facilitator is more than equal. Yet solid relationships are grounded in equality. If the helper is superior, in the long run the helpee will grow restless. Ironically, if the weaker party does expand to match the stronger, the former may feel threatened. Since the relationship was founded on disparity, when this disappears, the helper's reason for being attracted may also vanish. She may actually be offended at being treated as an equal by her former subordinate. This is the fate of many enablers.

Courtship

   The negotiations that end in committed intimacy are unique in that they pursue a relatively prescribed course. The details of this itinerary vary from one society to the next, and one individual to the next, but its broad outlines are fairly predictable. Whether its mileposts occur before or after marriage, they produce an emotional bonding that is later difficult to tear asunder. The mental templates of each party are so altered during the process that another's presence is woven into the fabric of their shared futures. Since this progression usually begins with an encounter between strangers, that is where our account must start. Before we enter this journey, however, a distinction must be made between courtship and flirting or pickup behavior. Courtship is about establishing a love relationship, whereas the latter are about initiating sex.

Nevertheless courtship can begin with flirting. Before people join together, they must first come to each other's attention. For reasons that need not be specified, they decide that a particular other is a potential mate. They must then get to know this person. Since they are not familiar with each other, they generally start out by trying to persuade the opposite party that they are better than they are. Utilizing the impression management techniques elaborated upon by Erving Goffman, they advertise themselves as smarter, more attractive, nobler, better educated, richer, and more worldly wise than is the case. They dress up for their dates, take special care with personal hygiene, and watch their language. When they talk, they boast of their accomplishments, and when they walk, they do so with better than ordinary posture. He spends lavishly on their dinners, and she eats calamari as if she always had.

Should these theatrical performances continue without modification, both would be deeply disappointed. If they were foolish enough to fall in love with the images they purvey, they would later be unable to keep up the charade. Sooner or later the truth would creep out. As a result, rather than seduce a stranger into valuing what they are not, each is wise to introduce the other to his real self and hope this proves satisfactory. Indeed, this usually does happen, albeit gradually. One of the major reasons why contemporary dating involves eating out is so that the parties can talk. When they do, they get down to biography swapping. Each tells stories about their past adventures and present relationships. The two get to hear what the other does, what he or she likes, and how their respective families are organized. At first, these narratives are generally limited to socially acceptable accounts. But in time, they incorporate less savory elements. Something embarrassing is shared and then the speaker waits to see how this is received. If the other person responds in kind, the coast is clear to proceed. If not, the relationship may end then and there. It is as if one person has given the other a club with which to beat her about the head and expects to be given a similar club in return. The parties must equilibrate their revelations so that these are balanced and neither has an advantage over the other. Because moral equality is fundamental, if they are to become happily attached, their actual histories must be harmonized.

Assuming that the parties like what they hear, they will proceed with the next order of business. This is, in fact, a task that will pervade their association. They must ascertain each other's trustworthiness. What they tell each other will be evaluated to uncover indications of danger. Is this other a recently discharged mental patient, or worse, a newly released serial killer? Does he regularly tell lies to exaggerate his achievements? Does she keep her promises? Besides what is said, what is done is evaluated. Does he habitually come late? Has she beaten her dog? Is this other person a slob, a neat freak, or merely an economic disaster area? Most important of all, what are the odds of this person inflicting injuries? A total insensitivity to one's vulnerabilities can be disquieting.

Trust is such an important commodity that it is not left to mere observation. During courtship, potential intimates test each other. They arrange circumstances to see what a partner will do. Thus, a secret may be revealed to see if confidentiality will be violated. Or money may be lent to determine if it will be repaid. Men frequently take women out to fancy restaurants to ascertain what they will order. If a date is totally indifferent to the constraints of his budget, he will at least have learned that she is high maintenance. Women frequently test men by teasing them. If he responds in fury to a joke about how he is dressed, she will have discovered he has the potential to be abusive. One of the best techniques for testing each other is to take a road trip together. The stresses of travel have a way of exposing the best concealed foibles. Should these precautions not be taken, discontents await. Partners who refuse to look for signs of trouble—or alert to them—are entering a relationship based on fantasy. They are asking to be tortured by a partner who, in actuality, remains a stranger.

If thus far, all continues to go well, the next step is frequently infatuation. The potential partners discover that they more than like each other. He or she will now seem special. Freud described love as entailing an overestimation of the loved object, and this applies to infatuation. For many people, the feelings that now occur are the essence of what it is to be in love. They feel happy; very happy. Their friends tell them they "glow," and though they may be loath to admit it, they do. A song from *My Fair Lady* has a smitten lothario crooning that when on the street where his sweetheart lives, he is several stories high. With his feet no longer in contact with the ground, he is lost in dreams of unfulfilled longings. For those in love, the objects of their affection also glow. They seem perfect; almost too good to be true.

People in love believe they can live on love. They moon over songs on the radio; they feed each other little morsels of food, and they invent saccharine terms of endearment. But as wonderful as this condition is, it is no miracle. The feelings they experience will not, as they imagine, last a lifetime. But they are the central feature of a bonding process. As distinct from the mechanisms that create communal hierarchies or social roles, courtship incorporates an emotional reorganization grounded in love, not fear or anger. The biological foundations for this transformation have scarcely been laid bare, but their reality is certain. After the infatuation, the nature of a relationship is categorically altered.

Evidence of this transformation is provided by what comes next. Although it is unwelcome, it is as predictable as what precedes it. This is the lover's quarrel. At the height of the infatuation, both parties assume they are so in harmony that they will never disagree. Indeed, the other's qualities are so flawless as to preclude criticism. Then one day this changes. The scales fall from one or the other's eyes and an imperfection that feels like a betrayal is exposed. One's beloved is revealed to slurp when consuming his soup. He or she forgets an important anniversary or thoughtlessly makes a reservation at a restaurant earlier discovered to be a dud. People deluded by the whimsy that love entails eternal bliss can come crashing to earth from the simplest of letdowns. If they require love to shield them completely from harsh realities, they are doomed to have their thin skins abraded. More realistic souls are in for a fight. When they call a partner's defect to his attention, the response can be harsh. A loved one will no more welcome an accusation of imperfection than his consort enjoy delivering it. This too will feel like a betrayal. Nevertheless the critical feature of their collision is this: before the infatuation stage had these blemishes surfaced, they would have precipitated an immediate separation. Afterward, they stay together to work out their differences.

This first quarrel is but the opening salvo of what will be a lifelong series of negotiations—that is, if they remain together. Because no two individuals are ever perfectly matched, and because the world always throws up obstacles to mutual problem-solving, if they remain attached, they must develop the tools for settling disputes. They must learn how to inform each other of their concerns and how to resolve them. This cannot be a one-sided procedure. Both must participate and both profit from it. Not all disagreements need be split down the middle, but in the long run, there should be an approximate balance. Each must have to make concessions, but each must also obtain indulgences. As earlier suggested, some people believe that a couple should never let the sun set on a fight, yet this is absurd. Significant discrepancies cannot be resolved on a predetermined schedule. Those who are prepared to stay in close proximity—without resorting to dirty tricks—will find that pretend settlements fall apart. Tenacity, born of an intention to continue as a couple, is essential to engineering mutually satisfactory conclusions to major differences.

Research has counterintuitively shown that there is no best way to conduct intimate negotiations. Some people shout at each other, while others are so subtle in their signals that only they detect them. What matters is working things through so that their grievances do not linger. Skill at negotiating is probably the single most important contributor to a successful relationship. It is surely the best guarantee of limiting potential losses. The reason this is so important is that the issues to be resolved are important—and numerous. They include mundane items such as on which side of the bed each will sleep, who gets to use the bathroom first in the morning, and what color towels to purchase. Other simple questions, such as what to eat for dinner, when to visit the in-laws, and how often to go to the movies, can be vexing if not approached in good faith. Among the more serious differences to be decided are when to have children, in what religion to raise them, and whether to move for the sake of a job. These sorts of issues are not reserved for the beginning of a relationship; they crop up with disconcerting regularity.

One reason they are disconcerting is that they entail anger. Because each partner wants to win, even minor concessions can be frustrating. A couple can easily begin bumping heads in an escalating ballet of mutual recriminations. It is therefore crucial that both know how to manage their anger. They must be mature enough to express what they feel, but not in a manner that goes out of control. This is essential because only through honest anger can they inform each other of their respective interests. It is via the intensity of their wrath that they communicate how significant a particular objective is. Mere words can be faked, but the level of frustration is more difficult to counterfeit. Regulated irritation is thus vital to dual-concern negotiations. It helps certify that the compromises made will genuinely balance.

The courtship process does not allow for shortcuts. Unless each step is satisfactorily navigated, the bonding process is probably in jeopardy. Smiling photographs cannot substitute for knowledge, trust, or love. Nor can they replace reasonable interpersonal agreements. Those for whom love is a superficial game are setting themselves up for heartache and isolation. Strong relationships provide dependable companions; sham associations deliver veiled losses.

Divorce

Once upon a time, marriage was forever. Rarely were the bonds of matrimony broken, except by death. About fifty years ago a trend began that did not abate until almost the end of the twentieth century. One of the fruits of the Industrial Revolution was a prosperity that permitted unprecedented freedom. No longer did individuals have to belong to a couple to have their elementary needs met. Adult men and women alike could go it alone. Almost all could get jobs that provided sufficient income to set up independent households. Men did not need to cook for themselves. They could microwave TV dinners or order a pizza. Women did not need to beg for a husband's largess. They could have their own bank accounts and credit cards. Why then stay married if the institution was not living up to expectations? Many decided that it did not make sense, and the divorce rates rose exponentially. Within a few decades, 50 percent of all marriages were terminating in divorce. This, it must also be acknowledged, was a little misleading, for only one-third of first marriages later dissolved. The difference was made up by the dissolution of second, third, and fourth marriages.

By the end of the century, almost everyone knew someone who had divorced. It might, therefore, be supposed that they concluded marriage was temporary; that one entered an alliance on a contingency basis and when it ran its course, one stepped aside with scarcely a second thought. Nothing, however, could be further from the truth. Today when people marry, they still expect it to be for a lifetime. And when they divorce, they suffer. Other people may have difficulty keeping their vows, but almost no one believes this will apply to them. Having entered what is intended to be a permanent relationship, their judgment is obscured by its rosy glow.

There is also a generalized belief that divorce does little damage. Or that if it does, the negative consequences can be limited. Mature adults are thought capable of moving on to something else with as little upset as traversing a speed bump. What is left out of this perspective is that divorce is a failure. It is an instance of losing of enormous magnitude because it flies in the face of what almost everyone craves. Eternal love is almost universally desired. To be cared about by someone who will never lose his ardor is too comforting a dream to be jettisoned. It provides a sense of importance and safety that few other illusions do. Hence when this goal falls apart, the pain can be devastating. Unexpected and unwanted, it is a defeat of epic proportions. For most people it is, if not the worst, then nearly the worst, disappointment they will ever endure.

Divorce is such palpable evidence of losing that its connection with bereavement has been recognized for some time. Psychologists, sociologists, and physicians all agree that the grieving process described by Bowlby and Kubler-Ross applies to the dissolution of marriages. One of the most complete accounts has been provided by Robert Weiss. Working at Harvard, he pioneered support groups to assist divorcees in surviving the pain. Observations from these confirmed that when marriages died, the survivors experienced denial, anger, bargaining, sadness, and finally acceptance. The chief difference was the duration of mourning. In the case of an uncomplicated death, a year or so was needed; in the case of divorce, three years came closer to the average. The reason for this discrepancy is that death is more final than divorce. The deceased do not rise to walk again, but separated mates can appeal for a second chance. As a consequence, it is harder to let go when one cannot be certain this is for good.

The denial phase of divorce can be protracted. People do not like to admit when a marriage is going bad. They notice that they are having fights, but assume this is a normal feature of every relationship. The partners make excuses for themselves, for their mates, and for their circumstances. Yes, Joe lost his temper, but he has promised never to do it again. He even purchased a makeup present. Sure, times have been hard, but the economy is about to pick up. Once we both have jobs, things will smooth out. Efforts may even be made to reform an errant partner. A self-help book here and a marital counseling session there, and all will be well. Because so much is on the line, these stopgap measures can persist for years. Indeed, it is not unusual for couples headed for a breakup to proclaim their happiness—and mean it.

When the rupture comes, when one or the other walks out, the one left behind may be shocked. Their denial may be so complete that when asked for a divorce, its antecedents are not discernible. The active party may have been simmering for years, but her partner will have no clue. In summoning the nerve to leave, the actor's understanding of the situation crystallizes, whereas the recipient is mystified.

Eventually both come to understand that a definitive breakup is imminent, but this can be after a lengthy period of temporizing. The other did not really mean it. This separation is only temporary. If I make this concession, she is sure to relent. Repeated failures to reconcile may be necessary before it sinks in that none will work.

When an impending divorce can no longer be denied, anger is the frequent reaction. Indeed, the venomous anger spewed between separating spouses is difficult to match. For sheer hatred, nothing equals the fury of a loved one scorned. Divorce is more than a loss; it is a betrayal. A partner who failed to keep up his end of the bargain has violated a sacred promise. This commitment was to be forever. It was supposed to underpin of a lifetime of mutual assistance. What happened? How could this other be so vile? He was not supposed to be that way. He was not meant to rob me of the years I invested in our relationship. So-and-so is a louse! He is among the worst human beings ever! I loathe him! If only the ground would open up and send him straight to hell!

Parties to divorce are not easily placated. What was love transmutes into a passion for vengeance. Personal ambitions are forgotten in an obsession on getting even. The anger phase of letting go can therefore be prolonged. Unlike death, the object of one's antipathy is available for retaliation. They can be hurt. Moreover, they are probably providing additional provocations. Surely unwilling to admit their guilt, they have made a host of unfair demands. They may even have the temerity to seek vengeance. Such a person deserves whatever they get. Sadly, this compulsion to seek reprisals can draw in third parties—most notably the children. Potential allies in their parent's hatred, they can be recruited to do what a spouse cannot. They can also be withheld from the other party as a form of punishment.

The bargaining in divorce takes many shapes. Thus, it can be about whether or not to separate. Marital counseling is often the venue for prospective reconciliations. Deals are made in the hope that this will reverse the slide a parting of the ways. The parties may agree to communicate, to provide each other with small services, or to compensate for past indiscretions. They may even draw up contracts that specify their respective duties. For the most part, however, these are vain exercises. A lack of trust intercedes to undermine the best of intentions. Ultimately the bargaining will not be about how to stay together, but about how to arrange their farewells. At this point, lawyers, as opposed to counselors, become the mediating agents. Now the question is not who will do what, but who will get what. Material objects that were once of no importance become symbols of unfairness. Suddenly it is imperative that the book uncle Charley sent for Christmas goes to her, while the broken down motorcycle goes to him. Alimony, child support, and property ownership acquire a significance second only to life itself.

In due course, even these confrontations subside. For most people, the skirmishes surrounding divorce do not rise to the level of *The War of the Roses*. No one dies, but many are scarred. It is in this condition that they limp into the depression phase. Repeated frustrations in wrecking vengeance or obtaining adequate concessions eventuate in a recognition of defeat. There will be no acceptable compensation for what has gone wrong. This is a loss; a terrible loss; a tragic and horribly sad loss. It is an episode in life that demands effusive grief. When divorce started to become common, it was regarded almost as a dalliance. Rich matrons trooped to Reno for six weeks of relaxation before their decrees were finalized, then they returned home to a swirl of parties celebrating their liberation. It took almost a generation for it to be understood that divorce was not a happy event. People in its midst withdraw to lick their wounds; they do not immediately throw themselves into a quest for another partner. If they go out on dates, these are generally dismal affairs. Because their minds are on past events, these are what they talk about. Not good company even for themselves, they are scarcely attractive companions for potential intimates.

The last phase of this progression is, as with mourning, acceptance. Sooner or later, his or her anguish lifts and a person returns to ordinary living. The bonds established during courtship are broken and alternative attachments become possible. Because even bad relationships entail an emotional connection, terminating them is a wrenching experience. Only when this has been done can tranquility be restored. Sadder, but wiser, a person who has traversed the requisite way stations may be able to make better choices. Having reviewed what went wrong, it may be possible to sidestep future travesties. Then again, it may not. Even the agonies of divorce can be navigated with one's eyes shut. People determined never to grow up can avoid learning from their losses. The proof of this is available in the divorce statistics. They reveal that second, third, and fourth marriages are more susceptible to break up than first marriages.

The Children of Divorce

If mythologies have developed regarding the consequences of divorce for adults, more have accrued with regard to children. Designed by adults for adults, the effects of these split ups upon children were an afterthought. Because the central objective was to set the spouses free, what happened to the little ones was of less concern. Indeed, the initial tendency was to deny that anything untoward happened to them. They were regarded as resilient creatures who would adjust to whatever came along. Howsoever grievous their immediate distress, time would reduce the pain and in later years it would be forgotten. If anything, divorce would be a boon. No longer crushed between quarreling parents, their universe would become more tranquil. Now safe from potential abuse, they would be free to blossom. Their gains would also be multiplied by witnessing adults taking charge of their lives. A mother's (or a father's) courage in the face of adversity would be an example that could later be emulated. Moreover, the custodial parent's improved spirits would make their household a happier place in which to grow up. With love more available than previously, they would flourish.

John Adams said that facts are stubborn things, and they surely are. The rationalizations in favor of divorce were shown to be exactly that when information about its consequences began to surface. As the offspring of divorce matured into adulthood, it became evident that many were not doing well. In almost every measurable category, they lagged behind their peers from stable intact homes. They did less well at school and topped out earlier than equally intelligent classmates. Their jobs were less satisfying and less remunerative. More emotionally fragile than others of their cohort, they required additional mental health interventions. Even their physical health suffered. Most telling of all were their relationship difficulties. They had a harder time trusting members of the opposite sex, and when they did, were more likely to end up divorced. In general unhappy, most did not know why.

To Judith Wallerstein, we owe a great deal of our insights into the texture of the lives of these children. One of many to investigate their condition, her longitudinal studies make compelling reading. Her accounts put faces on the statistics and turn private pains into accessible public documents. As should have been anticipated, but was not, divorce entails losses for children too. They are denied one or the other of their parents, but more than this, they lose the security provided by their parents' marriage. As a result, they too must endure grief. The difference is that they are children. They do not possess the resources or personal strengths of adults. Emotionally immature, they have not yet mastered intense passions. When assaulted by the concentrated feelings that accompany losing, they are less able to cope. Anger, fear, and sadness are enormously threatening to them, and thus more difficult to work through. Nor have they the power to influence others. What their parents decide to do is largely beyond their ability to control. They certainly cannot force them to stay together. Nor can they prevent adults, themselves in pain, from visiting their frustrations on them. The adults are the giants of their universe. They can get away with transgressions merely by imposing them. The best their offspring can do is protest.

Lest it be overlooked, parents in the midst of divorce can be self-involved. Entangled in their own fierce emotions, they have little energy left over to devote to their young. They may not even notice when their children are in distress. If anything, they will be motivated not to notice this. Were they to recognize how tortured their offspring were, they might be consumed by guilt. Already overwhelmed by other feelings, this would be more than they could handle. The solution is to pretend otherwise. Subconsciously children are commanded to be brave. Don't cry! Don't whine! Everything will be okay. Mommy and daddy still love you! It is reactions such as these that fostered the original belief that children are resilient.

These attitudes complicate a child's ability to navigate the denial phase of mourning. He or she is being asked not to see what he or she already does not want to see. One of the first reactions of most children is to blame themselves when they discover the impending split. Daddy (or mommy) is about to leave because I have been "bad." If only I stop being naughty, the departing parent will cease being angry and change his mind. Explanations that it is not the child's fault fall on deaf ears. Biologically conditioned to view the world from their own perspective, they misunderstand adult motives. Ordinarily this functions to motivate conformity with adult demands, but in the case of divorce, it sets up guilt that is difficult to assuage. A related problem is that from the child's point of view, mommy and daddy belong together. Having never known a period when they were not a couple, their togetherness seems a fact of nature. That they may once have lived separate lives is unimaginable. It would be as if the sun refused to rise in the morning.

Something so horrible must be averted. It is an intolerable idea that has to be protested as vigorously as possible. A child will grab a departing parent's arm and kicking and screaming attempt to drag him back into the house. Furious crying can also be employed to force the issue. "I will hold my breath until I am blue in the face and then you will be sorry!" Parents may encounter this sort of resistance with a bemused indifference or a livid counterattack. Some try to explain why things are as they are. Others demand good behavior. Possessing the strength to enforce their will, but themselves feeling impotent in an atypical situation, many overdo their responses. Orders that the child desist are so energetic that they require it to suppress, and in the end repress, this anger. If the child is to continue eating and maintaining a roof overhead, its true feelings must be submerged. For many youngsters, this makes it impossible to work through their distress. Required to be good, they have no alternative but to impose an ironclad denial. In later years, a repetition compulsion may erupt to direct their rage at inappropriate targets. One of the favorites, of course, is themselves. Forced to turn their anger inward, they resort to extreme punishments to extinguish reactions they cannot help experiencing. This is a major source of failure for the adult survivors of divorce. Convinced of their own evil, they are determined to deny themselves undeserved rewards. How can a person who has inflicted so much misery on others be allowed to be happy? As the enforcer closest to the scene, he or she must make certain that justice is served.

Bargaining too is complicated for children enveloped by divorce. Their primary objective is the reattachment of their parents. But as peripheral protagonists, they do not possess the ability to compel compliance. At best mediators, never arbitrators, they can fiddle with parental exchanges, but little more. Often functioning as a Greek chorus, they make suggestions, most of which are brushed off with barely any consideration. The movie *The Parent Trap* has become a perennial favorite because it depicts the secret fantasies of many children. The idea of manipulating estranged parents so that they realize they were meant for each other has crossed many minds, yet few have been able to turn it into reality. Not for want of trying, children discover that their brilliant maneuvers do not have the anticipated effect. Having misinterpreted what is happening, their interventions wind up being beside the point.

This leaves children with a need to deal with the depression that goes with mourning. Unable to undo their losses, they must endure the sadness of being utterly defeated. The problem is that children are not equipped for such misery. Their need to be cared for by a pair of strong parents is so relentless that admitting being vanquished will feel close to dying. Nor will parents already feeling guilty about depriving them of an intact family welcome overt misery. Children are thus required to get over their melancholy. They must feign contentment and/or accept efforts to cheer them up. Once more denial becomes a necessity. The time needed to sever one's ties with what has been lost is therefore not permitted. As a consequence, that which is gone is never fully relinquished. It remains as unfinished business and is experienced as a low-level melancholy. The brightness will go out of a child's existence for reasons that become less evident as the parental rupture recedes into the past. Coerced into a facsimile of life-as-usual that cannot compensate for what has gone wrong, rectification must await adulthood.

What this adds up to is that the final phase of mourning is rarely achieved by children. A phony acceptance replaces the genuine article and they make do. Never quite understanding the tragedy visited upon them, they cannot move into a future free of a taint from the past. Never privy to an example of parents who were able to resolve their differences, they do not learn how to do so. Likewise unable to rely on the commitments of adults to protect them, they find it difficult to trust commitments. Their own weaknesses exposed by a calamity they were unable to prevent, they are saddled with a self-image that includes a grave defect. Although the children of divorce may dream of one day waking up to a clean slate, they remain encumbered by old baggage. As adults they will have to revisit the mourning process and complete it more satisfactorily. If they do not then find a way to let go, the damage done to their innocence will continue to blight their prospects.

As if this were not bad enough, a divorce can be a wound that keeps on giving. Far from being a discrete trauma, it can inflict pain beyond that of the separation. To begin with, children can be pawns in parental battles. They can be physically kidnapped, have their minds poisoned regarding the absent parent, or be required to serve as a substitute mate for a bereft custodian. Moreover, when spouses cannot take out their rage on each other, they may displace it onto youngsters who cannot resist. The latter will be blamed for sins they never committed and disciplined for neglecting duties outside their capacity to perform. They are also forced to endure the unanticipated hardships of divorce. Sociologists talk about the feminization of poverty. In this they refer to the decline in income consequent to a family breakup. Because mothers usually retain custody of their offspring, they bear the lion's share of expenses. But because women generally earn less than men, and fathers contribute only modest sums to child support, the financial condition of the rump family is substantially worse than the intact one. The upshot is that not only women, but their children make do with less.

Added to this insult is the disappearance of the father. He is frequently too angry with his former spouse to enjoy the contact with her required to maintain his relationship with his children. If he later remarries, he may, in fact, transfer his attentions to the children attached to this new alliance. They will be the recipients of his time and financial largesse. This becomes particularly burdensome when the children of his former marriage move toward adulthood. Because court ordered payments are likely to terminate, they will probably not have their college educations underwritten by their biological father. For years denied the benefit of his presence, his masculine demands, and his protective concern, they end up virtual orphans, dependent upon their own initiatives to make their way in the world. Even when their father remains in contact, relationships can be strained. A periodic weekend visitor, his function may become that of a large playmate. Meanwhile the custodial adult will be treated to an endless string of complaints. Already blamed for dad's disappearance, she will be attacked because she is a safer target. Having demonstrated her trustworthiness in remaining with her brood, she can be abused with impunity, whereas if he is offended, he might decide to leave forever.

One of the truths regarded as a fiction when the divorce rates soared was that it is important to stay together for the sake of the children. The conventional wisdom asserted that there was more harm in perpetual parental conflicts than a separation. It now turns out that this was mostly wishful thinking. Research indicates that children are often oblivious to parental disputes. They are aware of the frictions, but if these are not too severe, they are more concerned with their own activities. Regarded almost as background noise, unless they are abused, these arguments can seem normal. Thus, when parents sacrifice for the good of their young ones, this may not be in vain. It may be an example of a commitment honored despite the difficulty in doing so. The security so imparted may pay dividends during a child's majority.

Reconstituted families too can be a problem. Some people imagine that remarriage fully corrects the damage of a bad beginning. The new family takes the place of the old, and life continues without missing a beat. The trouble is that what has happened has happened. Past hurts do not suddenly disappear. Nor do previous attachments fade to nothingness. This is especially so for children. When their custodial parent decides to take up with a new partner, this is not an occasion for joy. Mother may want her new boyfriend made welcome, but his arrival has an entirely different significance for them. She may be looking forward to love she has missed, but they are staring into an abyss. If this strange man refuses to go away, the bond he establishes with their mother will freeze out their father completely. Whatever fantasies of reconciliation they retain will go aglimmering. Why should they greet him with civility? And why submit to his discipline? As they will remind him, he is not their daddy. Should this man bring children of his own into the family, *The Brady Bunch* notwithstanding, they are liable to be perceived as rivals. Making second families work is possible, but is a difficult proposition.

Finally, there is the myth of joyous single parenthood. Feminists have been wont to portray the woman who intentionally raises children on her own as a courageous pioneer. Determined not to be exploited by the egotism of men, she understands that she can manage nicely on her own quite. What is at stake is merely a choice of lifestyles. Broadminded people know that this alternative is an extension of multiculturalism. The parochialism of Western society historically mandated marriage, but sharing love is more important than keeping up appearances. The woman who wants children should simply go ahead, regardless of the attitudes of the naysayers. Unfortunately, this exercise in tolerance neglects the needs of children. While some can prosper with only a single parent to shelter them, most cannot. Fathers are not accidental baubles to be dispensed with as a matter of convenience. Different in kind than mothers, they permit a synergy in parenting that redounds to the benefit of the young.

As with the children of divorce, the children of single parents suffer in almost every measurable category—only more so. Deprived of a father because one or the other of their parents did not care to have him involved, they may feel defective, that is, as unworthy of love. As with divorce, they may blame themselves for what they do not have. In any event, both the mother and her children are apt to feel relatively powerless. Poorer than their peers, they will feel beleaguered in a world where others can count on assistance they cannot. Those in this predicament generally proclaim themselves satisfied with their condition, but their tribulations belie their words. The work of David Blankenhorn and David Popenoe amply document the pitfalls. They reveal that unstablity in family arrangements produce a debilitating personal disorganization. Once more education, occupational success, and subsequent relationships suffer. To be blunt, bringing children into this world should not be a matter of personal satisfaction. It should at least consider the consequences for those who have no say in the subject.

Note

1. Please note that what will be discussed below is adult, heterosexual intimacy. Homosexual intimacy, and that between parent and child, are no less important, but require separate presentations.

8

Beliefs

In medieval France priests and judges maintained that animals could be possessed by Satan. On the gallows in the French countryside, cows and pigs were hung by the neck until dead to release the devil within.

Because the meat of convicted stock was sinful, cow corpses were burned, not butchered. Thus, people starved while watching farm animals slaughtered, but not used for food. (Duh!, Bob Fenster)

Cognitive Communities

Every day sees more magic. Across the globe, billions of human beings engage in activities that are almost supernatural. Using no more than a few sounds, or perhaps a few squiggles on a piece of paper, a woman sends her husband to the supermarket, and he returns with precisely the items she intended him to purchase. Similarly, with no more than a string of noises one friend explains to another how stingy his or her deceased father was and the second constructs an accurate mental picture of someone he or she never met. None of the people involved in these events believe them special, but no other creature on earth could replicate them. Other animals also communicate with each other. Monkeys give distinctive howls when they detect a predator, and dogs can be trained to roll over when a master gives a predetermined command. Neither species, however, has as broad or flexible vocabulary of signs. Monkeys boast a couple of dozen innate signals at best, whereas dogs must be trained to react as desired to a handful of specifically designed markers. Unlike human beings, they do not possess a syntactical intellect that enables them to rearrange a large, but finite set of indicators into an infinite array of unpredictable propositions. As communicators, people are nonpareil. The information we convey to one another is so adjustable that it covers materials no other animal can touch.

So flexible are human messages that they can relate details about things neither present, nor tangible. Linguists[1] often cite the following example: "My father was poor, but honest." This sentence is in the past tense. It refers to things that were, but no longer are. People nevertheless find it easy to match it to the reality it is intended to transmit. The sentence also alludes to a biological relationship. For someone to be a father, he must have participated in a procreative act. Though this too is not present, it is bundled into the meaning of a single word. Likewise alluded to are the ethereal concepts of "poverty" and "honesty." They are used to indicate a person's financial and moral status. Yet these markers imply so much that it is impossible to explicate them without resorting to many paragraphs. Still, they too are thoroughly comprehensible. If this does not seem special, consider this: How would a dog communicate these details to another dog? Could any amount of training teach one how to impart the notions of "parenthood" or "integrity?"

Indeed, complex symbolic communications seem to have been the springboard that vaulted our species to preeminence. Until about sixty thousand years ago our forebears were marginal hominids barely able to avoid extinction. Small bands wandered through East Africa, living a day-to-day existence. Indifferent predators, they concentrated on lesser game animals and supplemented their diets with fruits, roots, and berries. Most likely saved from extermination by their adaptability, they were a threat to few other species. What made the difference was the sophistication introduced by advanced linguistic skills. These made possible the coordination of elaborate hunting behaviors grounded in technological innovations. People who could talk to each other could also plan well into the future. They could likewise build upon the discoveries of their predecessors by communicating them between generations. Although the archeological record is scanty, dozens of intentionally crafted beads and a treasure trove of beautifully rendered cave paintings testify to an ability to utilize objects to send messages. What makes these especially interesting is that they coincided with quantum leaps in mechanical know-how and population density. It was only when these objects d'art appeared that our ancestors, now equipped with spear-throwers, bows and arrows, and flutes, spread across all the continents, displacing previous hominids such as the Neanderthals and annihilating species as formidable as Mammoths.

As often happens, however, that which is enormously beneficial also has a downside. Symbolic expertise facilitated a cognitive explosion, but also an upsurge in nonsense. Individuals who cannot speak to each other must per force live in a concrete universe. They can understand that which is seen and touched, but not necessarily that which is invisible. Linguistic specialists, in contrast, manipulate things in their heads that are not immediately available. They can think about the past, the future, and the imaginary. They can calculate the simple, the complex, and the impossible. Because symbols are detachable from the world, they are capable of being reorganized without interfacing directly with reality. This permits people to work through what they will do before they do it. It also enables them to work through things that no one will ever do because they are incapable of achievement. Symbols, in short, permit people to create falsehoods and to believe in them. Indeed, they can get so immersed in stories constructed from nothing more than sounds that they cannot distinguish between what is true and what is not.

During the middle ages, people believed that Satan was a genuine being. Their Bibles presented pictures of him, their priests described his deeds, and their cathedrals rendered him in three dimensions. To assume that he could inhabit the bodies of farm animals did not take much imagination. Nor did it seem unreasonable that fire was the best means of driving him out. That this belief in a fictitious life form could also consign people to their deaths would not have occurred to them. In their world, Satan was not fictitious. Although no one had ever seen him, they were exposed to ample testimony that he lay in ambush for the unwary. Then, as now, people lived in cognitive communities. Most of what they believed came from what was symbolically communicated by other members of their society. If the Bishop said Satan existed, and so did Aunt Molly, then, by golly, he must be real. Because everyone believed Satan was factual, few thought to question the matter.

In retrospect we look back and judge this to be foolish, but we are no more immune to such mistakes. We too belong to cognitive communities that influence our understandings. Nor are we any more likely to doubt the conventional wisdom. Television infomercials spread the message that a miraculous machine can shed pounds from the abdomen by delivering a series of electrical impulses, and hundreds of thousands of believers send in their orders. With no evidence other than the unsubstantiated words of a breathless pitchman, they are convinced this is an effortless form of exercise. Even more credulous are the enthusiasts of copper bracelets. Informed through the grapevine that this is a cure-all for arthritis and rheumatism, they swear by a remedy that has no empirical basis. With even less verification, when a chain letter from an anonymous source arrives in the mail promising riches for passing it along, they comply. They trust in the implausible merely because it has been communicated in writing.

Some believe that modern science protects us from such fallacies, but this is itself a fallacy. Although science insists on empirical verification, because it is a human institution, it too is vulnerable to the dynamics of symbolic communities. In early modern times, Galileo Galilei learned this lesson firsthand. After having constructed the most powerful telescope of his day, he turned it toward the heavens. Among the things he saw that no one else had were the moons encircling Jupiter, the lunar-like phases of Venus, and spots on the surface of the sun. Putting two and two together, he realized the sun was neither perfect, nor in orbit around the earth. When he subsequently published these reflections in support of Copernicus's heliocentric hypothesis, he ran into trouble. The inquisition intervened to muzzle his speculations. A large number of influential persons, including popes, cardinals, and lay leaders—one being no less than his own prince, the Grand Duke of Tuscany—concluded that this contradicted biblical accounts and could not be tolerated. Invited by Galileo to see for themselves, they refused to look. Ultimately placed under house arrest, what this great scientist encountered was social pressures more powerful than facts. When a community coalesces around a belief, counterevidence can be irrelevant. If people refuse to see what might discredit their fictions, conscientious individuals, no matter how correct, may not be able to dissuade them.

Things have not changed since Galileo's day. A political consensus can still overrule science. Take the case of school financing. Common sense once decreed that the more money spent on educating children, the better educated they would be. Better-paid teachers would be more effective, better-equipped schools would possess the computers and laboratories to make learning more vivid, and better-designed buildings would provide an atmosphere more conducive to scholarship. It all seemed logical, except that when tested by James Coleman, the results came out otherwise. In a national survey, he found that it was not resources, but parental values that made the greatest difference. When families truly believed in learning, so did their children—hence they fared better. But did this alter the political calculations? It did not. Conventional wisdom refused to be persuaded by discordant facts; hence politicians have continued to pander to what voters want. That billions of dollars have been wasted has had no impact on a community devoted in the conviction that progress was being made.

Nowadays many beliefs are promulgated through the media. In earlier times, gossip was effective in homogenizing public opinion. Societies dominated by small villages were controlled by word of mouth. Mary told Sue, who told John, who told Nathan, and sooner or later everyone "knew" the same things. In large-scale civilizations, a louder megaphone is needed. The invention of printing, and then electronic broadcasting, solved this problem. These made it possible to knead more people together in the same symbolic township. What this did, however, was to concentrate the power to manipulate in fewer hands. Nowadays newspapers and television newscasts are able to set the national agenda. People assume some things are true because they have read them in a prestigious journal or heard them from the lips of a respected anchorperson. Daily chronicles such as the *New York Times* not only reflect that which is, they can create it. When, for instance, *The Times* decided that the admissions policy of the Augusta National Golf Club was the business of all Americans, it became so. Previously unaware that the host of the Master's Golf Tournament only admitted male members, citizens across the country learned of this after local sources picked the story up off the *Time's* wire. Nor would *The Times* let them forget. Despite an absence of developments, it continued to manufacture pieces about what was happening. The result was a nonevent that lingered for months. The same sleight of hand happens repeatedly because in their rush not to be left out, papers from coast to coast rewrite stories from one another.

In illustration of a nonfact that became a national truism is "homelessness." A vast majority of Americans in the 1980s came to believe that millions of their countrymen had suddenly been reduced to living in the streets because there was a shortage of places in which they could dwell. Every day treated to heartrending accounts of families with small children wandering from one overcrowded shelter to another, their compassion was aroused. Something had to be done. In a country as affluent as the United States, it was intolerable that so many had to sleep in cardboard boxes or on heating grates. Capitalism was evidently flawed. If the marketplace could not produce the requisite apartments, the government had to do so. A drumbeat of stories kept this scandal in the national consciousness for years—that is, until a democrat was elected president. Immediately upon Bill Clinton taking office, the decibel level was reduced. No changes in the homeless census occurred; merely one in the level of reportage. But this was sufficient to alter the national perception. Homelessness remained a nonproblem for eight years until George W. Bush was elected, and then out of nowhere the number of homeless stories doubled. Bush the elder might have warned his son of this. His own campaign for reelection had been crippled by media accounts of a recession that would not go away. It was only after he was defeated that journalists discovered that the economy had been moving upward long before the election day.

Cognitive communities are vulnerable to shared mistakes. Large numbers of persons come to believe the same things, and then reinforce these beliefs, whether or not they are true. Sometimes for selfish reasons, but often from the noblest of motives, they promulgate, and defend, egregious falsehoods. Their eyes locked on the symbols they exchange, contradictory evidence never makes it to their psyches. As a consequence, both individually, and as a society, they suffer. When members of a community misunderstand people or events, they can be led astray. In making decisions based on fantasies, they can make bad ones. In such cases, social policies produce consequences diametrically opposed to what is intended. Thus, patients with mental illnesses were released from hospitals in the belief that they could be cured, when they could not.

Were human beings not the captives of their own symbols, a host of fiascos might have been averted. To illustrate, rent control, welfare, and homeless policies might all have been better informed. So might school financing, affirmative action, and the Vietnam War. On a more personal level, many relationships might be salvaged, or never entered upon, were people less prone to misunderstandings. It is even possible that people would make fewer economic errors were they attuned to the realities of the marketplace, rather than to its theatrics. In this case, the dot-com bubble might not have inflated to the point where it bursts. If they did not so much listen to what others said, but paid more heed to market conditions, they might have been more cautious.

Nowadays there is a lot of talk about "critical thinking" in academe. Students are prepared for the real world by teaching them how to appraise it. They are supposed to think things through and reject that which does not pass muster. Above all, they must "think outside the box." What is remarkable about this strategy is that higher education has been infected by "political correctness." A version of reflexive liberalism colors much of what is taught. Professors advocate collectivist interpretations of social problems on the assumption that compassion and tolerance should be the norm. This has given broad currency to efforts at "diversifying" every subject. Not only American history, but calculus courses are supposed to discuss the subject of race. Should it be suggested that this would indoctrinate rather than educate, this is hooted down. Critical thinking, it seems, is reserved for standpoints other than those endorsed by a majority of the faculty. As cynical as it is to say, those who recommend thinking outside the box are notorious for never doing so.

Irrationality

Aristotle told us that man is a rational animal. Unlike the beasts of the field, he can reflect on his situation—even gaining an awareness of his mortality. Able to calculate how to send rockets to the moon or route a book order so that it arrives at an address thousands of miles away, more mundane tasks would seem less demanding. Yet often they are not. Everyone knows how stupid other people can be. Their political opinions don't hold water; their ability to organize complex activities is inept, and their evaluations of one's own merits are way off the mark. It is a wonder they manage to "walk and chew gum at the same time." Ask almost anyone about friends, colleagues, and relatives and stories that would curl a Buddhist monk's hair tumble forth. But change the subject and inquire into their own idiocies, and a bemused silence ensures. The situation seems to be this: other people are irrational, but we personally make a few mistakes. Our faux pas are due to a momentary lapsed of attention, whereas theirs indicate serious mental defects.

The almost incomprehensible reality is that irrationality is as much a function of human nature as rationality. We are so constructed that we routinely make intellectual errors. Amazingly, this propensity flows, in part, from our social natures. That large numbers of people are able to integrate their behaviors in mutually supportive enterprises depends as much on *not* thinking, as on doing so. Were each to verify facts independently or personally deduce valid conclusions from defensible premises, their combined activities would grind to a halt. As a consequence, people routinely accept as fact things they never individually observe and as reasonable that which agrees with what they were groomed to believe. Requested to explain why they think as they do, most haven't the foggiest notion.

Among the mechanisms that keep human beings from thinking is *authority*. People routinely defer to supposed experts. This would not be irrational if these others were truly well informed about the issues in question. Indeed, they frequently are. The irrationality derives from our propensity to abdicate the right to check. Individuals do not investigate to determine if purported experts really are. Both in general, and in particular instances, we figuratively cross our fingers and hope for the best. If authority figures put forward claims in the prescribed manner, for example, with sufficient confidence, these are taken at face value. Displays of credentials, election to public office, or outstanding athletic achievements are all regarded as indicators of knowledge. Why else would advertisers recruit a Michael Jordan to hawk a telephone service? Why else would they pay a former Senate majority leader to promote a cure for impotence?

People are especially vulnerable to influence from groups. The unanimity of a crowd is intimidating. When we appear to be alone in our opinions, most individuals grow cautious and begin to wonder if they are correct. Perhaps others know something we do not. Always more comfortable basking in the radiance of consensual validation, unconfirmed perceptions make isolates nervous. The simplest way to relieve this discomfort is to agree with the majority. It then becomes the ultimate source of authority. Circumstances of this sort persuaded millions of Southerners that blacks were biologically inferior. They were absolutely convinced that African Americans were too dim-witted to vote. Since everyone knew this, no one questioned it.

Even authorities are subject to authority. They too tend to recycle what others have said. Such is the case with college textbooks. These have a way of duplicating materials found in their predecessors. Most use the same concepts and often the same stories. Read almost any primer on race and ethnicity and nearly identical depictions of stereotyping are found. Recent accounts that throw doubt on these theories are not mentioned. Astonishingly, scholars often depend on scholarly reviews for their opinions. Instead of reading what is controversial, they adopt the views of congenial authors. This was the case at Kennesaw State University when Charles Murray came to defend his book *The Bell Curve*. Castigated in the professional journals for a chapter deemed racist, this judgment was not independently assessed by the senior faculty. Of those assembled, only one read Murray's book, the others merely perused unfriendly reviews.

Alluded to earlier during our discussion of rank is the phenomenon of *situational stupidity*. At the time, this was introduced to help understand why people of different social classes make foolish choices. Here it must be reintroduced to clarify why irrationality is both widespread and functional. That some people command simplemindedly and others follow blindly has social advantages. Not just individuals, but societies benefit from irrationality. It fosters a uniformity of belief, and a promptness of action, that can be crucial. Thus, in the midst of World War II, the German people had been exposed to years of propaganda about the mental, and moral, limitations of the Slavic peoples. Professing to act upon the latest scientific advances, their leaders purveyed a blatant racism. After a time, however, ordinary people too came to believe. Thus, when millions marched into the Soviet Union as part of a victorious army, they had no difficulty following orders to murder Russian civilians. Convinced that the enemy was less than human, these soldiers did not brood over their misdeeds. Nor did they hesitate to act. Group dynamics reinforced the tendency of lower status fighters to trust what they were told. As a result, they acted in concert with ruthless efficiency.

Moralism too is productive of reflexive beliefs. People easily confuse prescriptions with descriptions. Ideals are treated like facts and "should" readily substitute for "is." For reasons to be elaborated upon in the next chapter, moral judgments tend to be both emotional and extreme. Rarely thought through, they can be destructive rather than protective. Moreover, because people are committed to particular moral agendas, they accept the cognitive premises upon which these are based. To return to the issue of racial discrimination, those for whom the inferiority of blacks is an article of faith do not pause to examine its truth. Committed to saving the white race from "mongrelization," they do not question the putative mental limitations of African Americans. Even to speculate that blacks are fully human might stay their hands when engaged in cross burning. Radical feminists are as crudely self-righteous. They maintain that all men are inherently rapists. With little or no evidence, they tar every male with the same brush. Determined to defend women from patriarchal exploitation, they discover it whether or not it exists.

Irrationality, or more exactly non-rationality, also flows from the nature of *social negotiations*. So far we have reviewed how ranks, roles, and relationships are negotiated. Now we must also observe that cognitions and moral rules are likewise products of social interactions. What people believe and the regulations they decide upon similarly derive from an interpersonal give and take. Facts are determined as much through social conversations, as firsthand observations. Moral rules are correspondingly forged in polarized exchanges between competing factions. With regard to facts, when authorities and leaders do not possess the clout to impose particular views, people "consult" one another. "Did you see that?" "What do you think about what she said?" These negotiations are not explicit, but after a back and forth, an informal consensus emerges. Conflicting perceptions are evened out and a generalized judgment holds sway.

The Nobel Prize–winning economist Friedrich Hayek characterized people as trapped between reason and instinct. Neither coldly calculating, nor reflexively emotional, much of what they believed derived from interactions in the marketplace. As an economist, he was chiefly concerned with how prices determine what is produced. Comparing this with a Lamarckian cultural evolution, in which acquired improvements gradually mount up, he acknowledged that these developments were not uniformly constructive. Although this progression produced both democracy and unprecedented prosperity, it also gave rise to Nazism and Fascism. Neither Hitler nor Mussolini emerged from of a vacuum. Before either surfaced as paramount leader, they participated in politicized exchanges of ideas. A consensus needed to develop as to why their nations suffered so much during the preceding war prior to either being taken seriously. That these national forums generated such perverted conclusions speaks volumes about the hazards of cognitive negotiations.

Faith

Aristotle notwithstanding, we human beings are more creatures of faith than of reason. Rather than think things through, we cleave to what we already believe with a dangerous tenacity—a tenacity that is loss producing. Actually, faith is a more social phenomenon than might be assumed. It is not so much about individuals maintaining something with a ferocious certitude, as about believing what a particular group believes. Faith is about loyalty. It employs cognitive commitments as a vehicle for demonstrating that one belongs. When a person can establish that he or she accepts as true what others do and is unwilling to be dislodged regardless of contradictory evidence, his or her dependability is confirmed. He or she who has faith can be counted on in a pinch. He or she is worthy of being entrusted with critical assignments.

Religious faith is probably the most obvious form of faith. People join churches with worldviews to which they are expected to subscribe. A Jew is expected to believe that Moses led his people out of Egypt, a Christian that Jesus performed a miracle with the loaves and fishes, and a Muslim that Mohammed rose to heaven from where the Dome of the Rock now stands. Most such beliefs do not have negative consequences, yet some do. First, if the factual commitments of one group contradict those of another, this may provoke warfare. The crusaders were confident that it was their duty to expel the Muslims from Jerusalem. German knights fighting in the Baltic took the same attitude toward heathen Lithuanians. In both cases, the objects of Christian scorn disagreed and resisted. Second, there is a tendency to believe the worst about those who believe something different. Evidently faithless, and therefore incapable of loyalty, there is nothing to which they will not stoop. As a result of these suspicions, Eastern European Jews were subjected to pogroms based on manufactured evidence that they stole Christian children to use their blood for Passover matzos. Third, because professions of faith are taken as tokens of trustworthiness, their lack may be regarded as a sign of duplicity. Shortly after the Germans conquered the Roman Empire, there was a wave of religious conversions. Previously pagan kings became Christian and forced their peoples to do likewise. What they desired were outward signs of conformity. During the Spanish Inquisition, the same was required of the Jews. Those who refused to acknowledge the authority of the New Testament were either killed or deported. Fourth, religious faith trumps other sources of knowledge. Galileo was not alone in having discoveries suppressed. The church earlier brought medical advances to a halt by proscribing autopsies. Because the human body was held sacrosanct, it was not to be violated with the scalpel. There was a similar prohibition against usury. Although essential to economic activity, charging interest was forbidden on the grounds that it was unearned. This sort of attitude slowed the emergence of economics as a science and therefore relegated many people to poverty. More recently fundamentalists have found evolutionary theory anathema. Were they able to enforce their views, medical advances based on genetic knowledge would be stymied. Fifth, some of the beliefs associated with religion have been directly damaging. Credence regarding demonic possession sanctioned capital punishment for witches. Similarly, a belief in the power of curses has turned many lives into hollow shells. In the case of voodoo, some people have expired because they believed in the lethality of incantations.

Many secularists have scoured lists like this and concluded that religion is a threat to personal satisfaction. This, however, is unwarranted. Not all religion is inflexible, but more than this, worldly belief systems can be as ruthless. Indeed, in contemporary society, *ideological faiths* are more ominous. They have become more pervasive and more potent. It has been centuries since the Inquisition had the power to dispatch unbelievers, but only decades since communists and fascists did the same. The breadth of modern ideologies is startling. They range from the innocuous, such as a belief in democracy, to the truly alarming, such as a devotion to anarchism. Some have remained in the realm of theory—the original anarchists were only able to set off a few bombs—but others, such as the communists, took over entire nations. Lastly, some are highly organized, whereas others are ephemeral. Many fads expire before they can do much damage, whereas more long-lasting convictions can obliterate the felicity of generations.

To be more specific about their nature, ideologies consist of sets of orthodox beliefs and prescribed behaviors. They claim to understand why the world is the way it is and how it must be changed in order to be improved. So let us examine an ideology to which most Americans subscribe. "Democracy" tells us that all people are created equal and that they possess the right to govern themselves. It then prescribes specific mechanisms for achieving this God-given parity. "One man, one vote," is an obvious corollary. So too, for those raised in the shadow of English common law, is the jury system. Conceived of as the incarnation of democratic justice that it might be flawed is unthinkable. And yet the United States is experiencing a crisis in tort law. Juries have grown so lavish in their awards for negligence that the premiums physicians pay for malpractice insurance make some forms of practice prohibitive. Many communities have even forgone the services of surgeons and obstetricians because they could not afford them. Nevertheless, trail lawyers continue to cite a constitutional right to "due process" in their defense of a system that directs two-thirds of the proceeds into their pockets.

Radical feminism too has been transformed into an ideological nightmare. Believed by many to be a direct consequence of democracy, it dictates a bloodcurdling interpretation of gender. Consequent to the conviction that all men harbor a barely contained predilection to rape, for a while Take Back the Night rallies sprouted on dozens of college campuses. Despite the fact that stranger rapes rarely transpire within their confines, well-intentioned young women testified to assaults that never occurred. Even when exposed, they defended these falsehoods as emotionally accurate. Feminist true believers have also advocated an embargo on research into gender differences. They are adamant that evidence of disparities will redound against the welfare of women. Instead, committed to insisting that gender distinctions result from socialization, they deny evidence of the actual situation. That this might interfere with people adjusting to reality is not something they contemplate.

Beyond question, the most destructive of contemporary ideologies have been the collectivist variety. Socialism and communism have presided over the deaths of tens of millions. Based upon a belief in the inevitability of universal brotherhood, they have been more successful in promoting "liberte, egalite, et fraternite" than the leading lights of the French Revolution. Robespierre and his ilk introduced the world to the terror, whereas Stalin, Mao, and Pol Pot instituted gulags, cultural revolutions, and killing fields. Oddly, many collectivists are romantics. Like Rousseau, they have faith in the natural goodness of mankind. They believe people have been corrupted by power and property and therefore advocate that these be eliminated. Because they are thought to be an artificial product of selfishness, they are certain these can be purged without any ill effects. Once this is accomplished—initially by ceding all wealth to the government—ordinary people will be mutually supportive. War will be a thing of the past, as will poverty. Love too will reign because everyone will finally realize it makes sense.

That this is a fairy tale should be apparent from the repeated failures to implement it. The collapse of utopian visions into totalitarianism has been so relentless that one would have expected even the ideologues to suspect a causal connection. Lord Acton's caution that absolute power corrupts absolutely is so widely known that its application to the apparatchiks who administer collectivist bureaucracies would seem evident. Eager to promote justice, however, the reformers ignore the facts of human motivation. Indeed, capitalists are not the predatory villains of their mythology, nor workers downtrodden, egalitarian saints. Neither is property an invention of the bourgeoisie. Even small babies clutch their toys when siblings attempt to appropriate them. Their parents do not teach them to scream: Mine! Mine! To the contrary, they are born with this predisposition. Any reorganization of society that disregards such factors condemns itself to irrelevance. Should it succeed in commanding the levers of power, the outcome of compelling people to be what cannot be done must perforce be devastating.

Almost as deadly has been pacifism. Likewise grounded in a faith in the innate goodness of humanity, it bids everyone to refrain from violence. What it does not appreciate is that this opens the field for predators. History demonstrates that there are always rapacious individuals hiding in the closet. The risks of believing universal love will remove their claws were revealed by the career of Neville Chamberlain. When he returned from Munich waving a piece of paper signed by Adolf Hitler and exulting that there would now be "Peace In Our Time," he was hailed as a brilliant statesman. Yet it only took a few years to divulge that he was a naive appeaser.

In today's America, the heralds of peace and love have migrated to college campuses. Faculty members who resisted the Vietnamese War are in the forefront of promulgating political correctness. Prepared to tolerate every shade of opinion—except those of their conservative opponents—they ensure their primacy by monopolizing tenured positions. In many prestigious universities, upward of 90 percent of the humanity and social science faculties identify themselves as liberal or left of liberal. That things will remain this way is assured by their unwillingness to hire adversaries regarded as "uncollegial." This is precisely the sort of tactic Joseph McCarthy employed fifty years earlier against communist fellow travelers. He too required little evidence of menace before consigning individuals to oblivion.

Lies

Many ideologues convey what they take to be the truth. Their beliefs are rigid, and out of touch with reality, but honest. Many other true believers, however, do not shrink from fabrications. In order to promote what they believe, they tell lies. They take advantage of symbols to misrepresent the facts. People are thereby convinced of states of affairs that exist only in the imagination. Then operating on what is not so, they make decisions with dire consequences.

Four thousand Jews never went to The World Trade Center on 9/11 because they knew beforehand that the crashes were imminent. Over one hundred and fifty thousand women die annually of anorexia. Yasser Arafat did not forbid Palestinians suicide from bombing Israeli women and children. The rain forests are disappearing at a rate so great that the balance of atmospheric oxygen is threatened. Uncle Joe (Stalin) discovered a conspiracy among the high-level military officers to overthrow his socialist state. Bill Clinton did not have sex with "that woman." AIDS was introduced into the black community as a surreptitious form of genocide. None of these allegations is true, but each has either frightened or angered the gullible.

People manipulate cognitive environments in a number of ways. One thing they do is distort the facts. They proclaim, for instance, that something they know is true is actually false, or vice versa. When Osama Bin Laden first denied that Al-Qaeda was responsible for 9/11, he knew this was untrue. He himself initiated the operation, gave it the go-ahead, and was alerted when it succeeded. The point of telling the world that this was an Israeli plot was to deflect blame. If he could sidetrack the anger generated, he might save his associates some grief, while simultaneously increasing the discomfort of his enemies. Stalin did the same when he dressed Soviet pilots in mufti so as to deny that he was participating in the Korean War. Hutu government officials did likewise when they refused to admit complicity in the slaughter of thousands Tutsis. Aggressors in general pretend to a touching innocence. They also pretend to a concern for the vulnerable that is perilous if accepted.

Advocates of reform, of whatever stripe, have a nasty habit of being unmindful of the truth. Determined to present their policies in the best possible light, they care not a whit if this is artificial. Feminists happily misrepresent the amount of money spent on female-specific maladies. They know this more than for men, but never admit as much. They also claim that in introducing women into the frontline military, standards will not be diluted. If they did not know, they certainly should, that number of push-ups required of women would be fewer than for men, while the time allowed for the two-mile run would be greater. Comparable lies have been a staple of civil rights and homeless activists. The allegation that Twana Brawley was raped and dishonored by white police officers has long been disproved, but it took the courts to find Al Sharpton guilty of libel. Even so he refused to admit that he perpetrated a fraud. As for homeless advocates, they regularly pretend that additional housing will correct the problem, when they know that street people decline to move into available residences.

People also engage in deception when they resort to storytelling. Myths, legends, and allegories are disseminated to influence opinions. These are exceptionally effective because we human beings understand our world in narrative form. Whereas abstractions leave us cold, concrete histories are easier to track. People enjoy identifying with the characters and following the plot twists. Ever since our ancestors sat around campfires exchanging gossip, we have taken pleasure in thumbnail insights into the motives of others. Tales of friends and enemies, of Gods and devils, and of saints and heroes have served as graphic lessons for young and old alike. They have brought otherwise opaque actions to life and suggested means of coping. Not exactly lies, these are the next best thing. Generally too simple to reflect the way things really are, they are sometimes understood as apocryphal, but others are confused with the truth. Indeed, some stories are believed to reflect higher truths. Even when not about human beings, they are typically anthropomorphized and/or dedicated to Manichean themes. Good battles evil, and listeners are expected to cheer for the good. If this distorts events, it is not considered a drawback.

Jewish grandmothers (mine included) have been charged with teaching their grandchildren the rules of eating kosher. These could simply be stated—eat this, but not that—yet this would be too bloodless. What is needed is something more dramatic. One of the laws requires that meat and milk dishes not be consumed simultaneously. The seriousness of this prohibition is frequently related by telling the young that if they do, when these foods combine in the stomach, they will explode. The fact that children never encounter people with exploded midsections does not seem to render this warning less effective.

Political lessons are regularly imparted by similar means. James Loewen, in his *Lies My Teacher Told Me*, demonstrates how schools simplify lessons about our national past. One of the stories that traditionally surfaces at Thanksgiving time concerns the events that led to the first feast. A favorite tale is of the Indian Squanto. He is described as one day having wandered into the Pilgrim settlement and, in English, explained the best methods for raising local crops such as corn and squash. What is left out of these accounts is how he learned their language or why there were open fields in which to plant these crops. Sometimes it is suggested that he acquired his vocabulary from visiting fishermen. This is only partly true. He was actually kidnapped and taken to England. When he wandered into the Pilgrim settlement, he was, in fact, attempting to return to home. It was not where it had been because his tribe was virtually wiped out by an epidemic spread by Europeans. The empty farmlands that the colonists took over belonged to the former inhabitants. This part of the story is omitted because its implications are embarrassing. The first Americans are portrayed as brave pioneers settling a wild land of unbroken forests. The inference is that they were entitled to do this because the natives were not exploiting the land. In reality, the land had been occupied and farmed before their arrival. It was only a massive die-off that opened a niche for them.

Mythmaking is widespread. The English did it during the halcyon years of their empire. Apologists for their expansion contended that the inhabitants of their island were descended from the lost tribes of Israel. Among God's chosen people, they had a right to dominion over primitive peoples. Stalin did it as well when he commissioned histories that portrayed him as a comrade in arms of Lenin. Eager to legitimize his rise to supremacy, he invented a colleagueship that did not exist. The truth was that he had been a minor player in the Bolshevik Revolution. City-dwelling Americans have done so in inventing urban legends as cautions about living in a world of strangers. Early in the twentieth century, the specter of "white slavers" terrified them. Innocent women were alleged to be vulnerable to prostitution rings that abducted them off the streets and spirited them across state lines. The solution was the Volstead Act that made interstate transportation for immoral purposes a crime. Later in the century, Halloween became a source of anxiety. When children went out trick-or-treating to solicit candy from strangers, they were assumed to risk booby traps. The best known were razor blades hidden in apples. Despite the fact that these were never found, parents made sure to x-ray their children's goodies.

Moral entrepreneurs, such as feminists and civil rights agitators, have been especially fond of propagating fables. Keen to exaggerate the dangers of which they warn, they point to events that supposedly confirm their worst suspicions. Radical feminists, for instance, have sought to demonstrate that men have always been inclined to oppress women. To this end, they assert that colonial men were legally permitted to beat their wives—as long as they used a switch no bigger around than their thumbs. Based on a misreading of history, they publicized a nonexistent "Rule of Thumb." Civil rights advocates did something similar when they exposed white plots to burn down black churches. Depending upon the history of the Ku Klux Klan for credence, they formulated scenarios later disproved by a careful analysis of events. Churches were burned, but as often in the North as the South, and as frequently by blacks as whites. For that matter, there are also professional myths such as the medical one about Pinel liberating the mentally ill from their chains. Like all hagiographies, it does not tell the whole story.

Apparently less capable of distortion, but for that very reason more so, are statistics. Figures, we are told, do not lie, while liars can figure. The exactness of numbers implies a scientific accuracy that is often fictitious. The propagandists that promote them frequently have no scientific credentials and the research to which they allude is either bogus or misrepresented. Nowadays political activists throw figures around with a slapdash confidence born of a desire to embellish their positions. They know that if they make a problem sound sufficiently bad, people will want to help. The result can be fatally inflated data. The militants do not worry about accuracy, however. Thus Al Gore did not care that almost no reputable scientist believed that the oceans would rise two hundred feet to inundate Florida. He knew his audiences were unlikely to verify his allegations; hence he could be offered with impunity.

As usual, radical feminists have been in the vanguard of statistical entrepreneurs. Impatient to build the body count of female victims, they discovered these where they are not to be found. This is why Naomi Wolf, among others, inflated the number of young women dying annually of anorexia. As mentioned above, according to her, this was over one hundred and fifty thousand. Men, in their irrational enthusiasm for slender women, utilized the media to persuade susceptible teenagers to engage in dangerous diets. In fact, the figure broadcast represented the total number of cases, not yearly fatalities. The latter was below one hundred. But that would not have frightened anyone. As a consequence, even when the actual incidence became available, public spokespersons such as Wolf continued to cite the incorrect figures. The same thing happened regarding rapes. These grew to fantastic proportions by including what had previously not counted as rape. Unwanted sexual overtures, for instance, were now considered a species of sexual assault. By this reckoning, most women had been victimized by would-be rapists.

Homeless advocates too have been notoriously lax in vetting their statistics. For years, it was standard practice to claim that three million Americans were on the streets and that most of these were ordinary people who had run out of luck. Anyone who lost a job might find themselves in this predicament. When the census bureau went looking for them, however, all it could find was three hundred thousand. Unsure that its counting techniques were reliable, it doubled this number and estimated the total as six hundred thousand. At this, a hue and cry went up. The government was obviously engaged in a cover-up. Politicians who did not want to be blamed for the catastrophe elected to minimize the damage. Fortunately, an enterprising journalist ferreted out the truth. He went to Mitch Snyder, then the country's foremost spokesman for the homeless, and asked where the three million figure came from. Snyder responded with unprecedented candor. He admitted that he made it up. This did little, however, to change the public perception. It was too firmly established. Nor did investigations such as that of Christopher Jencks. When he discovered that perhaps one-third of the homeless were mentally ill and another third chemically dependent, the image of the innocent victim remained inviolate. Hundreds of millions of dollars continued to be spent on a problem that actually concerned the plight of deinstitutionalized patients who could not cope with life independently.

Another statistical folly inflates the numbers of Americans in poverty. Here the definitions become critical. Most people do not realize that the poverty line is an artificial construct. It was put together by the labor department based upon cost of living assumptions that have since been challenged. One feature, however, is beyond dispute. The figures do not include transfer payments. Food stamps, medical insurance, and housing subsidies are not counted. No matter how generous these provisions are, they are not calculated as income. The result is that however great the additional support poverty warriors extract from the government, the poverty rate will not budge. Poor people given limousines and mansions would still be regarded as poor. Jencks further undermined the poverty figures by discovering that lower-income people spend more than twice their reputed incomes. Measuring consumption, as opposed to earnings, he found that the two do not jibe. Many people apparently have significant undisclosed resources. Perhaps they receive contributions from relatives; more likely they maintain under-the-table sources of income.

Joel Best, in his *Damned Lies and Statistics*, illustrates the kinds of games played. Propagandists, for instance, report raw numbers or the rates for particular events. Thus civil rights activists attempted to play down the differences between blacks and whites by claiming that the numbers of blacks on welfare is lower than for whites. Although this is literally true, it fails to account for the fact that there are fewer blacks. Best uses the figures for white and black arrests to make the same point. As of 1998, 284,523 whites were arrested, whereas only 205,823 blacks were. One might therefore argue that Caucasians are more responsible for violent crime than African Americans. The difficulty with this logic is that blacks constitute only 13 percent of the population. If one calculates the rate of arrests per one thousand people aged ten and above, the rate for whites is 1.5 and that for blacks 7.4. Obviously the incidence of crime within the black community is significantly higher than within the white. To ignore this disparity encourages society to distribute crime-fighting resources in the wrong places.

Another way cognitive distortions operate is through "spin." Facts do not speak for themselves. What is going on must be interpreted. In politics, this has become a truism. Those who want to be elected, or exercise legislative influence, compete to set the tone for the public dialogue. Rather than depend on ordinary citizens to come to their own conclusions, they take advantage of every opportunity to tell them what to believe. Thus Democratic operatives constantly reiterate that their policies help the "little people," whereas Republicans favor the fat cats. Republicans, in their turn, accuse Democrats of being insensitive to the national security, whereas they are hardheaded realists. To this, their adversaries reply that Republicans are hard-hearted, whereas they exhibit compassion. To this, of course, the adherents of the GOP respond by accusing Democrats of being bleeding hearts, whereas they are fiscally responsible. Social security and health care have, in consequence, become electoral footballs. Every four years, Republicans are blamed for attempting to dismantle social supports and Democrats for letting us slide into bankruptcy. Looking at the same facts, the two sides come to different conclusions. With each ready to depict their opponents as brazen opportunists, they are completely at odds about their respective motives. Since neither side is willing to give the other the benefit of any doubt, both peddle errors about the other.

Closely related to this is image control. The words people employ carry connotations. Over and above their factual content, they are larded with moralistic evaluations. Again, politics furnishes a wealth of examples. Think of the reputations of American presidents. Aside from what each accomplished, they have emerged from the political wars with rock-solid public personas. Thus, George W. Bush's verbal flubs consigned him an aura of stupidity that no international victory could overcome. Gerald Ford's occasional clumsiness similarly congealed into the image of an all-American football player who too often took the field without a helmet. Richard Nixon became the eternal used car salesman and Ronald Reagan the everlasting Teflon actor. On the other hand, Jack Kennedy will always be the young hero of Camelot, Harry Truman the give-em-hell Mid-Westerner, and Franklin D. Roosevelt the nation's savior in war and in peace.

Images can be so important in coloring the facts that dictators such as Stalin and Hitler devoted considerable effort to burnishing their own. In the Russia of his day, it was impossible to escape Stalin's smiling portrait looking down like an Orwellian Big Brother. He was the ultimate father figure. Forever showering benefits on his people, he was their indispensable protector. Hitler likewise sought to portray himself as a larger than life benefactor. The leader of his nation, he sought to guide Germany to its rightful place in the world. To this end, his propaganda minister, Joseph Goebbels, always surrounded him with a panoply of dignity and spectacle. Flags fluttered and troops marched, but never was the Fuehrer seen in public wearing a bathing suit. This might have lowered him to the status of a mere mortal.

Even the characteristics of entire peoples have been distorted. American movies used to show the Irish as hard-drinking brawlers and the impression stuck. Italians, however, have had to tolerate a reputation as Mafia henchmen. Jews, of course, have been celebrated as rich connivers and blacks as dim-witted athletes, albeit with a sense of rhythm. The Poles require several people to screw in a light bulb, Southerners are bigots, and Puerto Ricans wear pointy shoes to kill cockroaches in corners. Defamatory as all of these stereotypes are, for many come to represent the essence of those so depicted. One would no more want to make an ally of them than trust Tricky Dick.

Pseudoscience

With cognitive communities as vulnerable to distortion as they are, science would seem to be a haven of relative rationality. The realm of well-educated people dispassionately dedicated to unearthing the truth, it should be immune to the forces that generate falsehoods. But once more appearances are misleading. As a human enterprise, science can be as deceptive as any other. Besides the normal mistakes that can be made by anyone, its virtues are capable of being turned into liabilities. The very believability of science encourages its employment as a tool of persuasion. Given its reputation for incorruptibility, it is frequently accepted at face value. Besides, science is often too complicated to be understood by ordinary folks. They therefore have no choice but to take what scientists say on faith. This has given rise to a cottage industry in advocacy research. Many investigators go to work knowing what they expect to find. Their goal is not to learn something new, but to legitimize what is already believed. If this requires the data to be manipulated, they will. If it demands perverse interpretations of the observations, they too are made. If occasional dishonesty is necessary, even this can be arranged.

Let us begin with the environmentalists. They have flooded the media with testimony to the fragility of the environment. We are repeatedly warned that the ecology is an interlocking whole that can be destroyed by upsetting one small part of the balance. The moral is clear. Unless human beings embrace technological simplicity—unless they renounce their arrogant disregard for other living creatures—they will doom themselves to oblivion. Destined to choke on their own poisons, one day they will rise to find their cities drowning and the air unbreathable. Global warming will turn breadbaskets into arid deserts, and chemical residues will cover bodies with inoperable cancers. Only a decent respect for Mother Nature can reverse these trends. Only it will allow people to close the hole in the ozone layer and save their fellow creatures from extinction.

Sadly, for many people, these conclusions are more like articles of religious faith than scientific deductions. Having heard these hypotheses for decades, they appear to be facts rather than conjectures. This has encouraged a pervasive carelessness with the data. One of the most egregious cases concerns purported mass extinctions. Both on television and in college biology courses, it is asserted that forty thousand species are lost every year. Authoritative sources claim that the Industrial Revolution expanded human sway to such an extent that we are in danger of elbowing out all creatures beyond the domesticated ones. Everything from tigers, to rhinoceroses, to snail darters must fear our encroachment. Tigers get murdered for trophies, rhinos for horns thought to be aphrodisiac, and snail darters by dams not evaluated for their environmental impact. Only stopping in our tracks can prevent these exterminations. If not, the affected species will be like canaries in a coal mine. But rather than alert us, their coresidents of this planet, to impending dangers, we will blithely continue on until we too are snuffed out.

The estimate of forty thousand extinctions is large, but where does it come from? Few ask, because they want to believe. As usual, the most alarming figures come from activists; in this case, Norman Meyers in his 1979 book *The Sinking Ark*. Its broad currency owes to its repetition by an official U.S. environmental report called *Global 2000*. Bjorn Lomborg, a Danish statistician, in his analysis of the claim quotes Myers as writing: "Let us suppose that as a consequence of this mishandling of natural environments ... the final one-quarter of this century witnesses the elimination of one million species—a far from unlikely prospect. This would work out during the course of 25 years to an average extinction rate of 40,000 per year, or rather over 100 species per day" (that is all). As Lomborg notes, "This is Meyers' argument in its entirety. If we assume that 1 million species will become extinct in 25 years, that makes 40,000 a year. A perfectly circular argument. If you assume 40,000, then you get 40,000." Were Meyers' estimate true—and there is no evidence it is—the vast majority of the susceptible creatures would be microorganisms. So far, however, efforts to verify the projected effect on microfauna have come up short. To the contrary, in examining the consequences of eliminating broad swaths of rain forest, it was determined that the adjacent areas continued to provide shelter for the sorts of animals as had been displaced.

Forests too are a favorite object of dire warnings. Ronald Reagan was ridiculed for referring to "tree huggers," but the affection lavished on woody plants often surpasses that reserved for people. One error that flowed from this has been an overestimation of the acres of tropical forest destroyed. Under the Carter administration's *Global 2000*, readers were advised that between 2.3 and 4.8 percent of the world's rainforests were cleared annually. This, however, does not match up with recent estimates that no more than a total of 20 percent disappeared. Were the earlier projection correct, a minimum of 50 percent (and a maximum of 100 percent) should already be gone—just since the 1970s. Statements that we are losing the "lungs of the world" because the eliminated trees no longer produce oxygen via photosynthesis similarly ignore the fact that when plants die, their decomposition uses up precisely the same volume of oxygen. Also ignored is the fact that despite the expansion of the suburbs, the area of forests in the United States has increased. The timber industry notwithstanding, upsurges in agricultural productivity resulted in marginal farms returning to a more pristine state.

Which brings us to the purported depredations of acid rain. It seems like ages ago, but it was only a couple of decades, when projections of the imminent demise of American and European forests flooded the airwaves. Effluents from the smokestacks of advanced industrial nations were supposedly spewing sulfur into the atmosphere where it was converted into sulfuric acid. Rain was then delivering this witch's brew to virgin forests hundreds of miles away. In places like the Adirondack Mountains, lakes were reduced to fish free zones and conifers to standing corpses. In Europe, entire districts of the Black Forest were becoming deserts. Needless to say this did not happen. While part of what did occur can be attributed to controls on sulfur emissions, a larger part is attributable to the fact that sulfuric acid can function as a fertilizer. It does not necessarily kill trees. It may not even kill many fish. Although fish did die, the cause may have been spurt in conifer forestation that increased lake acidification.

There has also been a near panic regarding chemicals released into the environment. Uniformly described as carcinogens, even trace amounts are alleged to be hazardous. Experiments with rats seem to indicate that a wide variety are indeed pathogenic. In many cases, they probably are. The difficulty is that because only small populations of animals can be tested, in order to get statistically valid information huge doses must be administered. As a consequence, it is not always possible to extrapolate laboratory conclusions to the tiny exposures that affect people. This has prompted activists to err on the side of caution and produced stupefying admonitions. Although the risks of drinking coffee or eating lettuce are thousands of times greater than for ingesting some chemicals, billions of dollars have been spent to scrub the latter from the environment. Rachel Carson warned of a *Silent Spring*, but none is in sight. Pesticides and fertilizers have not turned rural communities into disaster areas. Nor did Alar make apples inedible. Despite the Cassandras, life expectancy has not decreased; it has increased. The water is not undrinkable, the air is not unbreathable, and agricultural productivity has not declined. Even the eagles and wolves are making a comeback.

This leaves us with the biggest environmental bugaboo of all: atmospheric warming. Increased levels of carbon dioxide are said to have raised the average global temperature by a degree or two—and threaten to do so by another ten degrees within decades. This should melt the arctic ice caps and flood every major coastal city. It should also shift rainfall patterns to inundate some areas while desiccating others. If so, areas of malaria infestation will drift north and places like Kansas will become too warm to grow wheat. Much of this is accurate. Carbon dioxide levels have gone up, as have average surface temperatures. The problem is that the connection between these two has not been established and neither has the potential extent of the disruptions.

Back in the 1960s, scientists were more worried about an impending ice age. They knew that cycles in solar heating historically altered the earth's climate. Current scientists are also aware of this, but cannot agree on the percentage of observed heating that is due to fossil fuels or fluctuations in solar intensity. As should by now be expected, the activists tilt toward the extreme predictions. Given a choice of estimates, they habitually select the most dire. Some global warming has occurred, and some certainly will, but it is a good bet that this will be substantially less than is projected. Nor will all the effects of warming be dreadful. If some areas become too warm for wheat, others will become warm enough. Indeed, it might be expected that overall herbaceous productivity will increase. Wasn't this the case that during the era of the dinosaurs, when the earth was substantially warmer and the forests lusher? Wasn't it true of medieval Europe where farm production increased dramatically?

Nevertheless, what is most critical to human welfare is the proposed investments in reducing the hothouse effect. Projected restrictions on industrial emissions might gravely decrease manufacturing output. The most advanced economies could go into a tailspin to achieve what are expected to be minor adjustments in global pollution. The activists tell us this is worth it. They applaud the Kyoto Treaty and explain that protecting the environment will save lives. What they do not factor into their equations is that an economic decline implies a reduction in resources. Less money over all, for instance, means less money for health care. It also means that the money to dig wells in impoverished nations will dry up. Even the amount of food available to feed starving peoples could decline. In other words, protections from global warming may be offset by the costs of producing them.

Other losses due to a misuse of science occur in the areas of gender and race. Because these too have been moralized, empiricism has been thrown out the window. Regarding gender, one of the most egregious cases involved research sponsored by the American Association of University Women. Intended to demonstrate that schools were shortchanging girls, it focused on teacher behaviors within classrooms. Direct observations were professed to show that boys, by a factor of seven times, were called upon more often than girls. Their contributions were thus more valued and their self-esteem inflated. Girls, in contrast, could expect to enter their teen years with damaged egos. Diminished in importance by female pedagogues, they learned that they did not count and hence receded into the background. What was needed was eliminate teacher biases. Once they gave girls an equal chance, they too would flourish.

As fair-minded as this sounds, it was completely bogus. Delving into the actual data demonstrated that the researchers misrepresented their findings. While it was true that boys were called on more often than girls, not by a factor of seven, but still substantially more, the reason for this was not because teachers valued them more, but because they were more disruptive. The boys talked more, were more easily distracted, and engaged in greater physical highjinks. They were essentially being disciplined rather than recognized. Why this should result in improved self-esteem is a mystery. Labeling theory would suggest the opposite. In fact, the girls were getting better grades. More than this, they were going to college in greater numbers. This would seem to indicate stronger, not weaker, egos. Ironically, giving them additional attention might shortchange the boys.

With regard to race, reactions to the continued ravages of racism have obscured the realities of contemporary race relations. Whites have been so browbeaten for their assumed biases that many refuse to criticize anything related to the black community. Within sociology this has expressed itself as a condemnation of "blaming the victim." When it is suggested that behavior patterns carried forward from slavery might impede black progress, this is rejected out of hand. Instead of examining the cultural legacy of slavery, the mere thought of doing so is denounced. Wasn't it whites who oppressed blacks? Wasn't it they who introduced slavery and kept it alive throughout the Jim Crow era? Obviously whites need to change, not blacks.

Nevertheless, a closer inspection of the "blaming the victim" argument reveals it is deeply flawed. Purporting to be a scientific observation, it is really a moralistic ploy. Ironically, the intent is to blame those who reject political correctness. Rather than look at the facts, these are disregarded on the grounds that they are irrelevant. But this is nothing less than an ad hominem attack. It questions the integrity of people who believe slave culture might be consequential. Regardless of their motives, they are treated as if they were hurling insults. In fact, to ignore culture is to act exactly as radical feminists do when they lobby against research into gender differences. Moreover, it is those who charge racism who introduce the notion of moral culpability. Far from being scientific, this uses morality to foreclose science. Such was the situation when during the 1960s Daniel Patrick Moynihan argued that the black family was in trouble. In noting the damage done to black children growing up in single-parent homes, he was accused of disrespecting black traditions. Research into his hypotheses quickly dried up, although he was vindicated decades later when number of African American children born out of wedlock more than trebled.

Another piece of moralistic pseudoscience is the adulation heaped on "multiculturalism" and "diversity." These concepts sound democratic. They appear to promote integration and assimilation. The opposite, however, is true. Their advocates are "pluralists." Instead of endorsing a society based on individualism, they favor one based on group identity. People are supposed to celebrate their racial or ethnic origins and receive social benefits based upon their backgrounds. Personal merit is secondary. Such a program rejoices in Balkanization and intergroup suspicions. Rather than encourage the trust essential to a large-scale market economy, people are told that others are essentially different from themselves and they will personally benefit from maintaining these differences. I am Jewish, you are black, and she is a WASP, and that is as it should be. Those who support this arrangement claim to have science on their side, yet once more they indulge in covert moralism. There is zero evidence that diversity per se provides benefits. Assertions they do are merely emotional commitments.

The same can be said of affirmative action. However much it may be decked out in scientific raiments, the policy is fundamentally moralistic. It is said to even out the playing field by promoting an equitable distribution of benefits, but, in fact, promotes quotas. People are selected for positions they would never be asked to occupy if only their abilities were considered. Paradoxically, this devalues the preferences thus obtained. When outsiders suspect someone owes a status to his or her group membership, the tendency is to withhold respect. The beneficiary is thereby provided with cheapened goods. However high the ostensible rank, it is not accorded the deference earned through demonstrable achievement.

To this, those who favor government interventions reply that they have documentary proof that their recommendations pay off. They cite the economic successes of African Americans as confirmation that only vigorous efforts at counteracting bias work. Yet were they genuinely interested in facts, they would discover that this too is not so. It turns out that blacks made greater economic advances before affirmative action than afterwards. What has been responsible for strides in integration was the evolution of the country, not federal programs. A failure to be aware of this is to be defrauded into supporting strategies that make things worse. This is most clear in the case of college admissions. Students admitted to universities for which they do not have the requisite preparation tend to flunk out. In numbers far larger than their better-prepared peers, they prove unable to keep up. Deliberately denied the facts, they make losing choices.

Note

1. Steven Pinker discusses this in his book *The Language Instinct*.

9

Morality

I happened to be visiting New Guinea's Iyau people at a time when a woman anthropologist was interviewing Iyau women about their life histories. Woman after woman, when asked to name her husband, named several sequential husbands, who had died violent deaths. A typical answer went like this: "My first husband was killed by Elopi raiders. My second husband was killed by a man who wanted me, and who became my third husband. That husband was killed by the brother of my second husband, seeking to avenge his murder." (Guns, Germs, and Steel, Jared Diamond)

Moral Communities

The central highlands of New Guinea are quite rugged. Jagged peaks separated by steep valleys make travel difficult. The island's lowlands can also be difficult to traverse. Carpeted in impenetrable jungles, they provide little sustenance for the inexperienced. As a consequence, the region's inhabitants are divided into hundreds of small communities. So diverse is the population, that, within a limited area, scores of mutually unintelligible languages coexist. In his researches, biologist Jared Diamond was startled to discover how hostile these clans could be. Not only did they engage in homicidal raids, but intergroup communications were drastically restricted. Most people rarely traveled more than twenty miles from where they were born. This was partly due to the difficulty of journeying on foot, but more from the hazards of entering unfamiliar territory. The local residents often killed strangers. Indeed, one's next-door neighbors could not always be trusted. Their welcome too might consist of a fusillade of lethal arrows.

New Guinea represents a place where an effective moral community has yet to evolve. Within each diminutive group, there are rules of behavior, but most do not carry very far. With no reliable enforcement agents inside each band, there are none with the power to enforce common standards. In any event, while one's own community might have prohibitions against murder, these scarcely apply to strangers.

To the contrary, they are fair game. As a result conflicts proliferate; an almost Hobbesian war of all against all becomes endemic. People crave peace, but are immersed in a social environment where losing, including the loss of one's life, is the rule.

Centuries earlier, in medieval Europe, very different conditions prevailed. By the thirteenth century, its multitude of feudal hamlets were being knit together into an extended moral community. For the pervious two hundred years, the economy had expanded thanks to a proto-industrial revolution and a Catholic Church then asserting its priority. Among the fruits of this development were the Crusades. Knights from every corner of the continent gathered under the banner of Rome to participate in attacks against the Levant. At the same time, a heresy broke out in southwest France. The Catharists, later referred to as the Albigensians, appeared in Aquitaine in 1012 AD. Ascetic and antisacredotal in their doctrines, they rejected the orthodox principles of the larger community. Convinced that matter was evil, they depicted man as an alien sojourner in a hostile environment. Practices such as a total prohibition on eating meat or engaging in sexual intercourse aroused the suspicions and the active opposition of the Mother Church. Eventually, under the direction of Saint Louis IX, a crusade was inaugurated against them. Put down with incredible ferocity, the movement was literally exterminated. Towns were burned to the ground and its leaders executed. Some members of the sect survived by going underground, but many fled to Italy to preserve their lives.

The Albigensian Crusade epitomizes the polar opposite of the New Guinea situation. Here a well-disciplined moral community exercised its might against a dissenting minority. The Catholic Church knew what it believed and understood that the Cathars threatened its tenets. The upshot was years of brutal repression. Uniformity was enforced by sword and fire, regardless of the losses inflicted on the nonconformists. In inhibiting anarchic tendencies, conflict was thus utilized to suppress conflict. Hobbes' state of nature was not allowed to emerge—but at the price of savage subjugation.

Morality can be immoral. The means utilized to protect a society from losses can themselves inflict losses. Too little effective consensus is an invitation to protracted struggles, whereas too much can viciously extinguish diversity. Either way, people are made unhappy. Nor is morality pure. The product of human interactions, it suffers from the defects inherent in humanity. Moral rules can be wicked. Those who support particular regulations may believe them imperative, but those outside this consensus often disagree. Saint Thomas More provides a surprising illustration. Ultimately to go to the scaffold in defense of his religious convictions, in his early adulthood he was influenced by the intellectual turmoil of the Renaissance. Captivated by ideas about perfecting society, he expressed his thoughts in a book entitled *Utopia*. Indeed, the name he gave his community was to become the prototype of future exercises in romanticism. In the society he envisaged, all of the citizens were equal. No one worried about becoming rich because there was no such thing as money. Indeed, gold was of so little concern that it was used for eating utensils. Nor was authority desired. Citizens rotated these duties as a matter of course, not ambition. It thus comes as a surprise to read More's depiction of their communal meals. Everyone ate together in classless simplicity as an expression of group solidarity. In this, they took turns cooking, but not serving. This was reserved for their slaves. Yes, slaves. This ideal egalitarian community owned slaves. More saw nothing inappropriate in this. Besides, had he sought biblical support, he would have found it, for the ancient Israelites too thought slavery natural. One of the Ten Commandments actually warns against coveting one's neighbor's bondsmen. In other words, More could cite morality to defend what contemporary Americans are agreed is utterly immoral.

Plato is another historical figure customarily regarded as a paragon of virtue. A disciple of Socrates, in *The Republic*, he laid out the parameters of another idyllic community. Largely based upon Sparta, Athens' chief military rival, Plato admired its martial efficiency and its citizens' egalitarian straightforwardness. Even today we use the word "laconic" to indicate an honest, economic use of language. Nevertheless not all Spartans were citizens. A virtual slave class of Helots did most of the work. To keep them in line, Spartan boys, during their military training, traveled around the community to visit death on unruly Helots. Merely demonstrating a spark of initiative could invite a midnight murder. Without notice, and without the semblance of a legal judgment, a death squad, from which there was no appeal, unceremoniously ended an ordinary farmer's life. Plato, himself an aristocrat, was untroubled by this cruelty. Plutarch was similarly in awe of such customs. He tells his fellow Romans the story of a young Spartan boy who stole a fox. As part of their rite of passage into manhood, youths were supposed to demonstrate resourcefulness by engaging in illegal acts. The sin was being caught, not stealing. One youth, however, was caught. To escape detection, he placed the booty under his cloak. There the fox began to eat away at his stomach, yet rather than reveal his culpability, he stood silent as he was eviscerated. For the Spartans, this became a model of courage under pressure. For the youth, of course, it meant death. Nevertheless, for contemporary Americans, his sacrifice does not excite admiration. From our perspective, the Spartans were callous. We are repelled by the standards that rendered them capable of condoning such harshness.

The primary function of morality seems to be to control social conflicts. When it is operating as it evolved to do, the goal is reducing losses. It must be remembered, however, that social functions are abstractions. Since no one literally institutes them, they can only be deduced from observable effects. That which works to preserve society may be assumed to have evolved because it had this consequence. Based upon this supposition, morality seems to provide protection from the excesses of hierarchy, role negotiations, and intimacy. If hierarchy is indeed generated through tests of strength, it clearly inflicts pain. Tyrants murder helpless innocents and plutocrats cheat honest laborers out of the products of their efforts. Christopher Boehm, a primatologist, suggests that this is the principal source of morality. In comparing human beings with chimpanzees, he concludes that both are hierarchical. But he also points out that people hate being subservient. Rather than suffer this indignity, he postulates that lower-ranking individuals band together to resist the alpha animals.[1] Their primary tool in defending themselves against domination is morality. By imposing standards on the more powerful, they reduce their ability to impose arbitrary pain. In forbidding murder, they, in essence, inform potential leaders that if they kill a subordinate, they can expect to answer to for this injury. This gives the alphas pause and reduces random depredations.

Boehm does not consider the matter, but similar considerations apply to role negotiations. Unequal divisions of labor emerge from unequal distributions in power. Those who believe they can get away with getting more are frequently tempted to do so. Not only are they unduly demanding, they sometimes engage in deceptions to achieve their goals. Morality, however, typically forbids such shenanigans. It stipulates standards of justice and compels honest communications. It also insists that promises be kept. People who undertake specific tasks are held to their commitments. This makes for social stability. Predictability becomes the norm and renewed conflicts are often unnecessary.

Relationships too can be fraught with instability and internecine warfare. As has been remarked, intimacy is dangerous. People who are physically and emotionally close can do enormous damage. An unrestricted spontaneity is therefore problematic. If individuals routinely act on impulse, momentary flashes of anger might terminate in murder. Trust would vanish and people have to approach each other with the fabled caution of mating porcupines. As it is, there are even rules to cushion the blows intrinsic to dating. Most people believe that when a partner is found unsuitable, he or she should be let down easily. Rejections being painful, injunctions against gratuitous insults are taken seriously.

The focal paradox in all this is that in order to prevent losing, people impose losses. In the creation and enforcement of moral rules, they regularly mete out pain. The negotiation of moral standards can be ruthless, as can the sanctions for disrespecting them. Individuals who do not honor statutes against murder may themselves be killed. Even societies without capital punishment involuntarily detain them behind bars. This is done to protect others, but also because it is punitive. Murderers are not supposed to profit from their crimes. The difficulty is that in inflicting pain, abuse becomes possible. Those who enforce the rules can go too far. In their enthusiasm, they may create more harm than they avert. Ironically, morality, which is inherently immoderate, is most valuable when executed moderately.

An illustration of the necessary balance is found in how children are disciplined. Parents often claim to punish the young for their own good. As a firm hand comes down on an exposed heiny, they insist, "This is going to hurt me more than it is you." Outsiders snicker at the hypocrisy, but it is grounded in necessity. If children are to internalize moral rules, they must sometimes experience anguish when these are violated. It is the anticipation of this that creates the guilt that later keeps them in line. Yet parents can get carried away. While some are too permissive, others are too coercive. For the latter, this may be an outlet for personal aggressions. Although they claim to be teaching morality, this is a cover for displacing anger that they cannot direct at the source of their frustration. In any event, both extremes cause difficulties. What is best is something in the middle. This, in practice, is difficult to achieve, but it keeps the losses down.

Morality can also be promoted through another outlet. Rule enforcement fundamentally begins with the external imposition of socially fashioned standards. These are then internalized and maintained by emotions such as guilt and shame. But whether internal or external, they prescribe what a person should do. If lying is wrong, one must not lie despite the temptations. A different means of achieving the same end is "character." If an individual possesses an internal disposition to behave in ways consistent with moral imperatives, the latter will not have to be brought to bear. Someone who loves people does not have to be cautioned to avoid hurting them. The impulse is simply not there. Similarly, someone who trusts others is less inclined to lie. Historically, such dispositions have been called virtues. "Honesty," "integrity," and "courage" have all been considered worthy of inculcation. They reduce interpersonal injuries by eliminating the motivation to do harm.

Moral Logic

Before we reflect on the convoluted way moral rules are created, one of the agencies through which they are applied must be reviewed. This will lay bare some of the avenues that facilitate their manipulation and therefore that impose losses. The British philosopher Stephen Toulmin decades ago analyzed what he referred to as moral logic. Using Aristotelian syllogisms as his model, he explained that a moral rule will be coupled with a fact to come to a moral conclusion. The rule is the major premise, the fact the minor premise, and the conclusion that which is deduced. An uncomplicated example would be the following: (A) Lying is wrong. (B) John told a lie. (C) What John said was wrong. In real life, this progression is so straightforward that almost no one consciously proceeds through it. The connections are so obvious that people immediately jump to the bottom line.

The nature of both premises, however, is such as to permit cheating. People play games with them in order to come to endpoints they favor. Having already decided what their judgment will be, what precedes it is stage-managed to achieve this outcome. Let us take the major premise. What a rule means is not always obvious. Lying may be wrong, but what constitutes lying. People disagree. When Bill Clinton was impeached, one of the charges against his was that he lied to a Grand Jury. He insisted that he had not; that lying was not the appropriate description of what he said. What he did was less egregious. Not part of the official indictment, but on most everyone's mind, was the press conference in which he flatly denied having had sex with "that woman." For many people, this was a flat-out falsehood. For others, it was literally correct. The president's defenders maintained that telling an untruth about a sexual infidelity was not really a lie. Since no one could be expected to confess the truth about such matters, a small deception was a "white lie" at worst and a case of "tact" at best.

If we turn to the minor premise, a comparable maneuver is possible. In this instance, the facts can be disputed. John never said what he is alleged to have said and is therefore not guilty. A Clinton defender could have argued that what he said was literally true. There was, in fact, no sexual intercourse and thus his words were accurate. In this case, manipulating the meaning of "sex" finesses the matter. If fellatio is not sex, then he did not engage in it. But it might also have been possible to deny that anything happened. Monica was never present in the Oval Office; hence neither could have participated in the deed. Lying about sex would still be wrong, but since there was none, nothing improper occurred.

If we return to the major premise, we can see that its manipulation is made possible by the nature of moral rules. The ways that these are created and communicated inevitably introduces ambiguities. Moral rules are not absolutes. Exactly what is proscribed when lying is prohibited is not patent. People have different opinions. Some insist that telling a falsehood is always wrong. Others as passionately assert a myriad of exceptions. They may, for example, contend that telling one's wife that a new dress flatters her figure is never a lie, whether or not true. The particular qualifications that are admissible are themselves subject to social negotiations. People engage in mind-numbing disputes to determine what the community should allow. Witness the abortion debates. The disputants are hung up on the definition of murder, that is, on which sorts of killing count as illegitimate. Rules are also open to interpretation. Their very language can be vague. Indeed, it usually is.

First, moral rules are primarily communicated through paradigms. People generally learn them by means of particular cases. They are not so much taught that lying is wrong as that specific lies are wrong. But examples are inherently unclear. This instance may be unambiguous, but its extension might not be. Well then, how similar must other falsehoods be to fall under the same prohibition? Judgments differ. Second, the words employed will usually have elastic referents and broad connotations. Everyone will agree that "genocide" is horrific, but not on what constitutes genocide. Thus, African American social workers have argued that if white parents adopt black children, they are engaging in "cultural genocide." Children ripped away from the customs of their biological relatives are said to have their "negritude" attacked. In this the African American community is diminished and therefore partially exterminated. The term "genocide" was not originally intended to cover cultural matters, but its implication of slaughter is so pronounced that extending it in this direction takes advantage of a preexisting attitude. The intention is to demonstrate that interracial adoption must be wrong because genocide is perceptibly wrong.

With regard to the minor premises of moral syllogisms, the vicissitudes of the cognitive consensus come into play. Because people are vulnerable to social pressures in deciding what is true, they can be persuaded that what is fact is not, and that what is not, is. Millions of Arabs absolved Osama Bin Laden of complicity in the WTC assault because they believed newspaper accounts that attributed this to the Israeli Mossad. Similarly, years before, millions of Germans felt justified in overrunning Poland because they believed Hitler's assertion that the Poles committed a prior act of aggression. Poland may have been smaller and less well armed, but the Fuehrer would not lie. Maneuvered by symbolic means into believing what was not, they concluded that the Poles were guilty of an infraction. Aggression was clearly wrong; hence the true aggressors deserved to be punished.

To add to the confusion, people regularly confound the prescriptive with the descriptive. Statements about what "should" be the case are assumed to have existential validity. They are treated as if they are indisputable because it is imagined that they have been verified by the facts. Ponder the assertion that "blacks are inferior to whites." A bigot might believe that dark skin is second-rate compared with light skin. For him or her, this would appear to be an objective fact. That this is a value judgment derived from the hierarchical superiority of whites is not understood. Nor is it recognized that this verdict would be reversed if the relative statuses were. On the assumption that his or her belief is factual, they never examine the world to see what is out there. Were he or she to do so, they could never perceive inferiority merely in comparing black with white. Skin tones are inherently neutral; it is their social implications that make the difference.

Hardball without an Umpire

Moral negotiations, like the other social negotiations we have examined, have peculiarities. The kinds of things that go wrong are contingent on the manner in which they unfold. Moral rules may seem inviolable; as if carved in stone, but the reality is of standards that vary with the time and contest. During some periods, sexual mores have been lax and during others inordinately strict. In some societies, slavery is accounted a virtue and in others a vice. Depending upon where one sits, what others believe may be deemed correct or erroneous. Hayek suggests that rules tend to evolve in functional directions; that in the long run beneficial standards are carried forward and less useful are jettisoned. This may roughly be true, but it is also true that many painful conventions are adopted along the way. Witches were burned to death, counterrevolutionaries sent to the Gulag, and slavery defended at the cost of hundreds of thousands of lives. Some would say the same of radical feminism. Its efforts to dissuade women from becoming mothers have left many women unfulfilled. Be this as it may, the momentary conclusions of moral negotiations can clearly go awry. Because there exists no safety net to cushion people from their mistakes, many get hurt.

Morality may profitably be compared with hardball played without benefit of an umpire. For the uninitiated, "hardball" is a baseball game that uses the kind of ball employed by the professionals. This is a small, tightly wound, leather-covered sphere. When thrown with velocity or hit with a hardwood bat, it can rocket toward the players at speeds capable of inflicting injury. Most people consider baseball a genteel game, but when it gets out of hand, the consequences can be serious. These rarely are because an umpire normally calls balls and strikes and decides when someone is safe or out. Conflicts are kept to a minimum, and the competition proceeds until a victor is declared. In morality, the potential clashes can be as heated and the calls regarding what is correct as close, but no one is officially designated to settle the issue. There is no umpire in the morality game. Quite the opposite, each of the parties tends to believe themselves the best arbiter. If a third party (e.g., a minister or judge) is called in to resolve disputes, the selection of this intermediary may be determined by the projected decision. In this case, the loser may consider both the choice and the result illegitimate. Unlike baseball where a strike is what the umpire says it is, in morality what is right depends upon what the players (and their respective teams) decide is right. Whatever is momentarily imposed, the final authority resides in their respective hearts—that is, unless a subsequent social consensus forces them to agree to something else.

The absence of definitive umpires makes morality a dangerous proposition. Tempers can flare and the punishments become draconian. Moreover the ambiguities of the game are never fully expunged, therefore the conflicts may proceed interminably. As mentioned above, moral rules are paradigmatic. They are learned and communicated through example. Particular behaviors are consequently regarded as object lessons. People point to them to indicate what they mean. But pointing is inherently vague. If a finger is directed toward a tree, is it obvious whether the referent is its shape, color, or texture? Mistakes are consequently made. With respect to morality, they occur with tedious regularity. People do not agree on exactly what is covered by the term "lie." Nor is there complete accord on what constitutes "murder." Unlike courts of law where disparities in opinion are gradually resolved through an accumulation of precedents, morality is less formal. There are no books with precise formulations of moral rules, nor are there legal decisions with elaborately articulated justifications, nor are law libraries that document the conclusions of generations of preceding moralists. To the contrary, moral rules are indeterminate and elastic. They are what they are at the moment, but they might look very different tomorrow.

Indeed, moral rules are habitually subject to qualification. Lying is wrong—except when someone's feelings might be hurt. Lying is wrong—but not when it is the Nazis one is attempting to deceive. Fascists clearly deserve to be led astray. Lying is wrong—but boasting about a product in advertising copy does not count. This is "puffery" and everyone knows it is allowed. The number of qualifications is not predetermined. They possess an open-endedness that allows for adjustments whenever circumstances change. On the one hand, this introduces a useful flexibility, but on the other hand, it makes definitive covenants impossible.

Given such accommodating standards, individuals are perpetually prepared to massage them in the directions they prefer. This is so general a feature of morality that people organize into factions to promote their perspectives. One group pulls in one direction and the other in an opposite. Each side hopes that its alliance will prevail and thereby set the norms for the entire community. More often than not, these contests last for generations and sometimes centuries. By the time that a majority arrives at a common conclusion, the earlier players have left the stage and the decision agreed upon looks nothing like what was initially proposed. In the meantime, a great deal of energy has been expended and there may even be pools of blood on the floor.

Moral negotiations also tend to be polarized. Whatever the original goals, the parties eventually define themselves in opposition to one another. Each may be for something, but they are definitely against the others. Moreover, each faction believes it is on the side of the angels. They are the good guys and the opposition the bad ones. An example is what has happened with abortion. Some people favor it and others do not, but whatever the view, a jaundiced eye is cast on those who disagree. Illustrative of the typical attitude is what the parties call themselves. Neither advertises itself as for or against "abortion." This term is too negative in its connotations. Thus one side is "pro-choice" and the other "pro-life." Both are eager to advocate something perceived as good, for this is how they perceive themselves. They are similarly eager to defeat manifestly wretched enemies. Bad guys must be forced to lose.

This polarization encourages each side to differentiate itself from the other. The result is that they become progressively more extreme. In reacting to their adversaries, they attempt to move apart as far as possible. In the case of abortion, this means that one side approves of it in almost every case, whereas the other disapproves with as much vigor. Moderate observers think it reasonable to require parental notification for teenagers, but not pro-choice activists. Moderates likewise find it sensible to permit abortions following rape, but pro-life partisans find this an abomination. This tendency is exacerbated by the affinity of moral factions for fanatical leaders. Vocal ax-grinders surge to the fore among moral crusaders. They are commonly the most vehement and/or the most articulate. In designating them the defenders of the faith, less zealous followers thereby find themselves saddled with extremists who enjoy pushing the envelope as far as they can. Not disposed to compromise, these opinion leaders fail to perceive the humanity of their opponents and therefore seek to inflict as much damage as they can.

Polarized factions are also notorious for enforcing orthodoxies. Intent on defeating their opponents, they are equally focused on ensuring that their partisans do not wander far from the reservation. Because effective factions are disciplined, a uniformity in outlook is demanded. Imaginative speculations are discouraged, while blind obedience is rewarded. The result is twofold. First, creative solutions never see the light of day. They are drowned in a sea of hackneyed phrases. Next, even one's friends are exposed to injury. Unless they tow the line, they can be punished as severely as ostensible adversaries.

Another crucial aspect of moral rules is their intense emotionality. Anger, guilt, shame, and disgust are the frontline enforcement agents of the morality game. People are not so much physically compelled to respect injunctions, as intimidated into complying. When someone violates an important principle, the response may be immediate. Anger—clothed as moral indignation—intercedes to demand the required behavior. Individuals committed to upholding a rule are offended when it is contravened and reflexively deliver a reprimand. In the intended circumstance, the person committing the infraction takes this to heart. People actually get angry with themselves for having been so vile. This anger will later arise if he or she is again tempted to break the rule. It is then called guilt and serves as an internal enforcement agent. A comparable objective can be accomplished through shame. It is imposed chiefly through ridicule. An offending person becomes the butt of a joke and is so mortified that he or she wishes to disappear from sight. Never again will they want someone to catch them spitting into the punch bowl. If this impulse should, at a future date, return, they will be restrained by the mere thought of the embarrassment to ensue. Disgust too can achieve this end. To treat a fellow human being as if he or she were ripe excrement is to inflict an excruciating experience. Also called contempt, it makes them feel unworthy of human company. Should they do what they are not supposed to, just as with shame, intimations of rejection stay their hands. Rather than court ostracism, he or she complies with the rule.

Each of these emotions can be characterized as negative. They are designed to hurt, and they do. But love and pride can also be used to enforce moral conformity. Actually, the promise of the loss of love is enormously effective. Children are remarkably sensitive to parental disappointments. The slightest look of displeasure can warn of a withdrawal of support. Rather than sustain this life-threatening outcome, capitulation is preferable. Many parents feel helpless in their efforts to control their offspring, but in this, they miscalculate the power of love. Pride is similarly powerful. People feel good about feeling good about themselves. Their chests swell with satisfaction at the approbation they believe they deserve, and they extend themselves to behave in ways others applaud.

The trouble with these emotional controls is that they can be overdone. In their intensity, they become so extreme that they do more harm than good. As may be recalled, intense emotions can become so strong that they mutate into their primitive doppelgängers. Anger becomes rage, fear becomes terror, and sadness becomes despair. Anger that has become rage, when employed to enforce moral rules remains stupid. So committed is it to dictating a specific endpoint, that it goes overboard and may deal out death. Unable to calculate the response of its target, it instead elicits counter-anger. The upshot is a spiral of mutual recriminations from which no good flows. Not only is compliance forsworn, but additional injuries ensue. Because guilt is an internalized version of anger, it can go too far as well. People enraged with themselves impose unnecessary punishments that elicit internal resistance. Instead of convincing themselves to do the right thing, their guilt is self-defeating.

Shame and disgust are likewise capable of intemperance. A surplus of shame can persuade a person to hide from life itself. Convinced that he or she is too defective to be seen by anyone, he or she may decide to become a recluse. Some anorexics suffer this plight. Ashamed of what they consider untoward weight, they diet to the point of invisibility. Too much disgust can also make a person feel unworthy. Such an individual can feel undeserving of human contact. He or she may prefer to commit suicide rather than endure the continual rejections that crowd out other thoughts. This seems to be part of what occurs in the psyches of those who perpetrate high school violence. Finally, love denied, when it transmutes into feelings of being terminally unlovable, can, in fact, be terminal. Persons who perceive themselves through the reflected disappointments of significant others may come to believe they have no future. The consequence can be arranging matters so there is none. It may mean never seeking love, or never accepting it. Either way, the loneliness can be agonizing.

All in all, paradigmatic rules, polarized negotiations, and emotional sanctions make morality dicey. They enable people to pervert its rules in directions favorable to themselves, to engage in sanguinary clashes with invented foes, and to become excessive in their interpersonal demands. What morality requires, and how it is required, may thus be at odds with human needs. In other words, the rules that get established, the manner in which they are developed, and the means through which they are made compulsory become coercive and unfair. Losses then follow in torrents. Paradoxically, people who feel virtuous commit horrors they never recognize as horrific.

For the Greater Good?

Morality is abused in countless ways. Each of its most salient characteristics lends itself to exploitation. Participants in the game are rarely conscious of it, but moral strictures are employed as a means of achieving power. Although people claim to be invoking them for the greater good, their personal status may be of more concern. Because morality appears to be above criticism, it is ideal for making demands. How could anyone oppose directives intended for universal benefit? How could their provenance be questioned? This would be tantamount to impiety. What is required is automatic deference to that which purports to be pure. Those to whom morality is applied are, in effect, invited to lose voluntarily because this is the appropriate state of affairs; one to which they too should be committed.

One of the ways reflexive obedience is elicited is by taking advantage of the informal nature of moral rules. Concepts, whose meaning is hazy, are brought into play to demand something quite specific. That which they are alleged to cover may not have been part of the original intent, but are asserted as if they were. The extension of the term "genocide" is an example. It elicits assent because to disagree feels malicious. Another recent illustration is the concept of "diversity." Introduced as an alternative to "multiculturalism" when the national objective was "integration," its inherent ambiguity lent itself to promoting pluralism. Originally "multiculturalism"—itself an indistinct term—was used to encourage a familiarity with other cultures. School children were supposed to learn about Africans, Hispanics, and Asians, not just Europeans. In time, this was converted into a celebration of non-Western cultures. It was a small step from this to declaring that preserving distinct cultures was essential. The presence of many such ways of life could then be described as "diverse" and as benefiting those who participated in safeguarding them. Why this was advantageous, however, was never explained. Its advocates did not feel obligated to do so. What they accomplished through their choice of language was to piggyback on contemporary attitudes toward tolerance. Residing in a multiethnic society, most Americans believe a live-and-let-live is best. Diversity in this sense meant acceptance of differences. When applied to endorsing minority representation in almost every social institution, this was hard to oppose. To be against it implied a lack of tolerance. The result was an imperceptible shift in what was considered moral. Now strictly proportional representation became the goal and this produced a raft of political victories.

Two other ambiguous concepts manipulated for moral advantage have been "equality" and "opportunity." Equality may appear to mean only one thing, but in fact differs dramatically in its Jeffersonian and Marxist guises. In America, equality has traditionally referred to an equality of rights. All men (and women) were described as having been born equal in that all were entitled to life, liberty, and the pursuit of happiness. Among Marxists, however, the equality is of property. Only if everyone is equally rich (or poor), does justice prevail. This is to be achieved by redistributing goods. In Bolshevik Russia, the apartments of the wealthy were literally reapportioned among the proletarians. Nowadays neo-Marxists (radical feminists are among them) demand an equivalence in power. They insist that hierarchy smacks of oppression. Only after affirmative action distributes leadership positions more even-handedly can fairness emerge.

"Opportunity" would seem a less likely candidate for moral ambiguity, but it too has been employed to achieve political advantage. In this case, Republicans and Democrats alike interpreted the term so as to derive the benefit of its positive connotations. After Newt Gingrich orchestrated electoral gains by promising greater opportunities, Bill Clinton chimed in to make what seemed the same claim. Gingrich, however, was talking about greater freedom to operate within a market economy, whereas Clinton promised greater availability of government programs. Neither sought to clarify the implications of his pledges, for to do so would have undermined the persuasive power of vagueness.

Another treacherous maneuver follows from the paradigmatic nature of moral rules. Because people generally learn what is required from examples, they may not demand evidence before reaching a moral conclusion. A single case can lead to generalizations with enormous implications. When a young homosexual was brutally murdered by heterosexuals in Wyoming, his death became a *cause célèbre*. Following the lead of gay activists, journalists across the country reported this as a "hate crime" of unprecedented proportions. The victim was a nice-looking young man apparently tortured for no reason beyond his sexuality. This was clearly evidence of extreme prejudice. It was also alleged to be typical of how Americans persecuted gays. Not only was this immoral, but the only way to prevent further occurrences was to employ the law as a shield. Gay-bashers deserved extraordinary punishments. Since their crimes were worse than usual, statutes specifically aimed at them were needed. Not long after this, a heterosexual man was brutally murdered by homosexuals in Arkansas, but this barely made a ripple in the national press. This was not the sort of example that would lead to a moral conclusion favored by the media establishment.

Another instance of this tendency occurred in New York City. An attractive female jogger was apparently raped and nearly murdered by a group of teenage boys in Central Park. The victim was middle class and blameless; the perpetrators poor and inarticulate. Almost immediately reporters latched on to a word that came to exemplify what they had done. The boys were described as having entered the park on a whim. Merely because they were bored, they decided to generate excitement by attacking someone prosperous. They had, it was said, gone "wilding." This term immediately resonated with the public. The image elicited of predatory gangs swooping down on innocent targets spoke to the fears of those dwelling in the midst of millions of strangers. Suddenly wilding became the great urban evil. Its senselessness made it particularly immoral. More than this, ordinary New Yorkers feared that it represented a trend. In fact, the senselessness was overplayed and the typicality never developed. An entire class of wickedness had come into existence based on a single magnified instance; one that later developments indicated never occurred. The effect was to impute blame to guiltless adolescents who fit a fashionable profile.

Polarized negotiations too are productive of consequences that may not promote the greater good. With both sides intent on beating their opponents into the ground, they fail to notice when their objectives become extreme. Implacable in their self-righteousness, they cannot imagine that their choices have negative outcomes. Even mass murder can be excused as defending what is best. Stalin did this without a trace of embarrassment. Nor do partisans hesitate to distort the facts in order to win converts. Even bona fide lies are not out of the question. Told for the best of reasons, they are thought justified. The problem here is that people lose touch with reality. When they come to believe their own propaganda, moralists are oblivious to the mischief they do. They can send people to concentration camps for crimes they never committed, for example, Japanese Americans at the beginning of World War II.

During the nineteenth century, among America's more prominent religious innovators were the Shakers. An offshoot of the Quakers, they never boasted a huge membership, but their spirituality was recognized as special. Living in separate communities in which to conduct communal rituals, their most salient characteristic was celibacy. Persuaded that sex was inherently tainted, they sought to preserve their purity by never indulging in it. Men and women resided in the same large structures, but in discrete wings. The effect, of course, was to prevent them from producing a new generation to inherit their mantle of saintliness. For a time, they were able to compensate by bringing in recruits from the outside. When this source dried up, however, so did they. It might be imagined that the implications of this policy would have been predictable, but in their extremism, the Shakers were blind to the fate awaiting them. Firm in their desire to be perfect, they could not conceive of a need to be anything less.

To modern sensibilities, the Shakers seem fanatical. It is difficult for average Americans to imagine giving up sex for the sake of heaven. But radical feminists do almost the same. Many have denounced sex as equivalent to rape. Men are portrayed as predators who must be resisted. Many have recommended lesbian liaisons in preference to heterosexual entanglements. One of the radical's secrets zealously guarded by a sympathetic media is the prevalence of homosexuality among the activists. Many of their most prominent organizations possess a membership that is 50 percent gay. A large proportion of the leaders also have this orientation. Is it any wonder that male-bashing has become rampant or that the extremists cast aspersions on the family and motherhood? These latter are depicted as forms of slavery that can only be overcome by total emancipation. In essence, a minority that finds heterosexual intimacy disagreeable has recommended a way of life that fits its needs. Women with more conventional aspirations are urged to adopt this perspective on the grounds that they too are exploited. This is advocated as an extension of democracy, but is nothing of the sort. It is much closer to Marxism in its interpretation of equality.

One of the more extreme positions of the gender radicals is embodied in their focal value. They believe in "androgyny." The differences between men and women are supposed to disappear into a sexual neutrality. Arguing that men have manufactured these distinctions in order to solidify their hegemony, they propose to change the way boys and girls are socialized. In this manner, women historically persuaded that they are the weaker sex will come to realize this results from being trained to be "feminine." Once they perceive their abilities as the equivalent of men, they will cease being submissive and step forward to claim their fair share of power. When this occurs, androgyny will triumph. There will be no such thing as men's or women's work and everyone will be "human." Even in sexual matters, though their plumbing will still differ, their behaviors will be virtually identical. Sexual distinctiveness will no longer dominate and the genders will be interchangeable in everything important. Ancient prejudices, such as "vive la diff érence," will be discarded and justice will reign supreme.

Or will it? The radical feminists and Shakers seem to have this in common: neither takes much stock in human nature. The Shakers, to their grief, denied the naturalness of sexual procreation, but were never able to find a substitute. The feminists today deny the distinctiveness of men and women. They claim it is a mirage. Yet despite their idealization of sexlessness, they require people to jettison aspects of their personalities that few are prepared to relinquish. And why should they? Why should men cease being instrumental or women expressive? What benefits are to be derived from males raising young children or females becoming jet pilots? An arbitrary desire for everything to be 50/50 hardly seems sufficient. Pursuing it would indeed deny people satisfactions that in no way harm them or society.

The extremists are as cavalier with the facts as they are with people's needs. When tactical considerations dictate that they should, they cheerfully distort the truth. Thus when a wave of stranger kidnappings horrified the nation, efforts to halt their spread became a crusade. Pictures of children who disappeared from their homes began to appear on milk cartons and television programs dedicated to publicizing the missing. For a while, the public was told two million children were abducted annually. As with other incredible statistics, this one turned out to be exaggerated. The actual number of stranger abductions averages in the low hundreds. The inflated figure was achieved by including runaways and custodial conflicts. Indeed, in order to make the number large enough, multiple runaways were counted as separate events. Only this would excite the revulsion needed to mobilize community opinion.

The same sorts of distortions plague discussions of hate crimes. Activists talk as if these were in the hundreds of thousands, whereas federal reports turn up only dozens. Failing to place incidents in context likewise misrepresents police brutality. When Amadou Diallo was shot forty-one times in front of a New York tenement, the uproar directed against the shooters was deafening. They were portrayed as bloodthirsty bigots who killed an innocent street peddler because he was black. So vicious were they that they riddled him with bullets to make sure he was dead. Worse still, they were representative of a department insensitive to minority needs. Always prepared to trample over the rights of the politically powerless, they showed no regret over the tragedy. What was left out was that Diallo had been acting suspiciously in a neighborhood in which there had been a recent string of rapes. Nor did reporters explain that the shooting was accidental—that the large number of shots was attributable to the rapid discharge of automatic weapons. More significant still, they underplayed the fact that incidents of police brutality were declining and that relative to other cities, New York's finest were guilty of a much smaller number of offences. The image of a constabulary gone wild was simply wrong. It was created in order to support charges of racism and not a reflection of racism on the rise.

One more incident of polarized negotiations generating a high-handed disregard of the truth concerns Jesse Jackson. Well respected in the 1960s as a civil rights activist and a comrade of Martin Luther King, by the 1990s he had become a professional agitator. Always on the lookout for an opportunity to play the race card, a major source of his income came from extorting money from vulnerable corporations. In exchange for promising not to launch a boycott when they appeared to have engaged in a racial impropriety, they made generous contributions to causes he suggested. For Texaco, this amounted to many millions of dollars to quell publicity about a racial slur mistakenly alleged to have been uttered by a board member. Between his excursions into corporate America, Jackson burnished his credentials through periodic ventures to defend the downtrodden. One of these entailed mid-Western high school students. They had been expelled from school in the wake of improprieties during a sporting event. Outraged that minority teenagers could be severely punished for so minor an incident, he organized a series of protests. Ultimately a tape of the underlying episode made its way to the television screen. There the students in question could be seen flagrantly beating up on others. They had not been inoffensive bystanders, but perpetrators of intentional battery. Even after this revelation, Jackson refused to back down. For weeks he stood by his portrayal of this as an instance of white administrators unfairly singling out black victims.

Moral emotionality can also go too far. People fly off the handle. Then they come to conclusions that make no sense or they engage in brutal enforcement activities. Intense emotionality and immaturity are virtually synonymous. Despite claims of altruism, people often act like spoiled children. They demand the total capitulation of opponents regarded as cartoon characters. Entirely unable to recognize the humanity of their adversaries through the veil of their passions, they are insensitive to the anguish they impose. In the end, in order to set things right, they indulge in extremes greater than those of their victims.

Moral panics demonstrate what is possible. Some years ago, both Satanism and sexual abuse entered public awareness. Covens of devil worshipers were purported to engage in bloody sacrifices to their deity. At the same time, sexual perverts were described as preying on defenseless children. These two phenomena were then alleged to have surfaced in nursery schools across the nation. Charges were brought against their operators in locations as diverse as California and North Carolina. Parents, and sometimes teachers, accused them of perpetrating orgiastic rites on preschoolers. The claims made were fantastic. Some entailed murder, some of sending children up in rocket ships. No matter; the public mood demanded revenge. It was time to deliver the message that depravity would not be tolerated. People were frightened; they were angry; they were deeply saddened that such events could take place. Prosecutors, themselves parents, were happy to oblige. So too were social workers who volunteered to interrogate the tiny victims. When the evidence came back, it was overwhelming. Child after child recalled incidents of being disrobed and physically violated. Some professionals doubted the validity of this testimony, but they were shouted down. Across the country, signs sprouted urging people to "Believe the children!"

Initially, many of the suspected offenders were found guilty. Juries too were sympathetic to the plight of vulnerable children. Unfortunately, as more incidents cropped up, they became increasingly bizarre. Eventually they began to strain the credibility of observers. With the initial passion of the movement waning, it became possible to evaluate the data with a balanced eye. This quickly brought many allegations into question. More dispassionate scientists reviewed the videotapes of incriminating interviews and found the questioners had stacked the deck. They asked leading questions and rewarded answers that confirmed their suspicions. The children, being children, wanted to please. They said what was desired and were not required to defend often outlandish reports. Sometimes it even developed that the children lied. Some activist social workers heatedly insisted that "children don't lie," but this was absurd. In the long run, the accusations faded into the mist. They had run their course, and when they no longer possessed emotional fuel, came to a halt. Much as the Salem witch trials were called off when the community reached a point of emotional exhaustion, so were they.

More dangerous emotional episodes have fueled militaristic adventures. In Hitler's Germany, ordinary people came to despise the Slavs. Their long-term neighbors were regarded as subhuman and therefore innately immoral. It was therefore the duty of patriotic citizens to exterminate them. That this sometimes entailed euphoric emotions can be gleaned from the newsreels of the era. Many are replete with crowd scenes in which thousands pressed forward to get a glimpse of their hero. Their eyes glistening with joy, they cheered themselves hoarse. Average people, now part of a throng with goals similar to their own, were transported by an emotional contagion. Strong feelings were communicated from person to person and elicited an orgiastic reaction. As a group, people can become intensely angry, intensely frightened, or intensely happy. Depending upon which of these arise, they can be channeled to the moral purposes of their masters. More powerful than any individual, these passions become the agents of abuse. German Jews, who abruptly became the targets of fellow citizens, could corroborate the effect.

Idealism

The irony of idealism is that it is often the opposite of ideal. One of life's many absurdities is that efforts to seek perfection tend to create imperfection. We human beings are intrinsically flawed. Our knowledge is always incomplete, our skills always limited, and our motives frequently selfish. However luminous the images of an unspoiled future we conjure up in our minds, they cannot come to fruition. Attempts to make them do so regularly end in ruin. They do because they require people to cease being people. Neither Plato, nor More, nor Hitler, nor Stalin, nor Castro, nor Julius Nyerere had the answer. Of these, only Nyerere had the intellectual honesty to admit failure. The first president of Tanzania, he made gallant efforts to institute the democratic socialism he had come to admire through his readings. As the years passed, however, he realized his desperately poor country would not be rescued by the advent of a selflessness not inherent to his people. Plato and More were saved from their naiveté by never having to implement their visions. Hitler's, unfortunately, went on to destroy him and much of Germany. Stalin, luckily for him, died before he could be unmasked, but not before he executed millions of his countrymen rather than concede collective farms were a mistake. Castro made free education universal, but brought a poverty so dismal that the streets of Havana have become a museum for antique American automobiles. All were guilty of confusing fantasy with reality. They were seduced by hope into pursuing phantoms that when converted into flesh produced little save misery.

A homegrown American idealist was Woodrow Wilson. Before he became president, he was a political scientist. The son of a protestant minister, this was for him a moral calling. At first adamantly opposed to bringing the United States into a European war, when German actions made this inevitable, he advocated participation in a war to end war. In anticipation of its favorable conclusion, he put forward Fourteen Points intended to be the blueprint for an honorable settlement. One of the major planks was "self-determination." Instead of the victors greedily scrambling for spoils, previously submerged nationalities would be provided the opportunity to decide their own fates. This proposal was enormously popular. All across the Old World, from the Atlantic to the Pacific, minority groups agitated for recognition in what was to become the Treaty of Versailles.

The problem was that no one knew precisely what self-determination meant. Wilson's Secretary of State, Robert Lansing, was in a quandary. He asked himself, "When the president talks about 'self-determination' what unit has he in mind? Does he mean a race, a territorial area, or a community?" Lansing also wondered about what constituted a nation. Did the American Indians count? How about the Irish, who were then ruled by the British? Or the Ukrainians, then part of Russia? And what of the Kurds, or for that matter, American blacks? Lansing concluded that the concept was a calamity. "It will raise hopes which can never be realized. It will, I fear, cost thousands of lives. In the end it is bound to be discredited, to be called the dream of an idealist who failed to realize the danger until it is too late to check those who attempt to put the principle into force." This, sadly, turned out to be prophetic. As this is being written, nationalism's potential for bloodshed has not been fully worked through in places like Iraq and the former Yugoslavia. Shias are not content to be ruled by Sunnis, nor Kurds by either. Neither to do Croats fancy rule by Serbs, nor Albanians by Slavs.

Speaking primarily to political aspirations, the economist Thomas Sowell refers to *The Quest for Cosmic Justice*. He notes that so enthralled have people become with illusions of total equality and complete freedom that they have sought to balance the scales to a degree possible only in their imaginations. Before discussing what he calls "the tyranny of visions," he quotes the historian Paul Johnson on Lenin. "Lenin surrounded himself with official publications, and works of history and economics. He made no effort to inform himself directly of the views and conditions of the masses... He never visited a factory or set foot on a farm. He had no interest in the way in which wealth was created. He was never to be seen in the working-class quarters of any town in which he resided." Like most prophets, he was transfixed by a dream. Messy facts were beneath his notice. Only in this way could he convince himself of the validity of a panacea that when enacted developed into a cruel dictatorship.

In contemporary America, idealism is supposedly a virtue. It is associated with intelligent young people not yet corrupted by the avarice intrinsic to capitalism. The high point of this attitude occurred during the 1960s. College-age hippies assured one another that it was impossible to trust anyone over the age of thirty. All of their elders had sold out. Another of their cherished beliefs was that if you were not part of the solution, you were part of the problem. Yet they contented themselves in merely protesting the fiascos of their seniors. The only sort of solution they offered was that everyone should love one another. If people just put flowers in their hair, then joined hands to sing Cumbaya, war and poverty would be banished. Even more oblivious of facts than Lenin, they were the victims of "luminosity blindness." With their eyesight obscured by joyful tears in anticipation of the love they would personally receive, they shunned the study of social complexities. The power of their enthusiasm would see them through. It alone would bring out the best in those who had become jaded. At their worst, these vest-pocket revolutionaries metamorphosed into the weathermen. Impatient at the slow pace of progress, these scions of the middle class determined to speed it up with strategically placed bombs. Eventually forced to go underground, they were precursors to later idealistic terrorists.

Religion, unfortunately, has also been productive of excessive romanticism. In Western societies, this penchant has subsided, but in the Islamic world, it is on the ascendant. The Taliban, before they asserted control over Afghanistan, began as earnest scholars of the Koran. Their goal was to impose a fundamentalist faith based on their studies. Men were required to wear beards and women the burka to symbolize a submission to Allah. If they did not, squads of bullies roamed the towns to persuade them otherwise. People were beaten, thrown in jail, or executed for not complying. This was intended to bring heaven on earth, but instilled apprehension instead. Eventually famine and an American invasion were to dislodge them from their perch.

Values

Values are essentially moral goals. They are what ethical rules or personal virtues aim to achieve. More than individual desires, they are a distillation of communal experiences. But this means that what is commended during one era will not be during another. Changing circumstances modify what works to meet the needs of the greatest number and therefore the demands and expectations people exchange. Factored into this process are not just their hopes, but the consequences of their respective actions. During moral negotiations, the participants traffic not merely in ideals, but in their aspirations as amended by feedback from actual events. Hopefully, as time goes by, they learn from their combined mistakes and make better choices.

Hayek's suggestion that social negotiations resemble a Lamarckian cultural evolution is apt. Moral values are analogous to acquired characteristics. They do not spring full-blown from the head of any innovator, but build on the innumerable experiences of multiple contributors. Gradually people start to distinguish what meets their joint needs. These discoveries are then mutually reinforced. This, in turn, helps them become internalized. Once this is achieved, values are automatically sought. Instead of individuals calculating what will meet their needs, they operate according to what appears to be instinctive. This can wind up being in everyone's interest. All benefit from the knowledge and stability incorporated into institutionalized aspirations. Were they instead to careen from one imagined benefit to another, disastrous errors would multiply. On the other hand, were modifications impossible, they might be immobilized in wretched places.

One can cite no better example of what is involved than the evolution of *religious tolerance* in the Western World. The noted criminologist, James Q. Wilson, has commented upon the difference between the United States and Islamic societies. Like many others, he sought an explanation for 9/11. Why were so many Middle Easterners indifferent to the fate of the victims? As human beings, they too should have been appalled by the carnage, but instead concluded that Americans got what they deserved. Wilson believes this is related to religious intolerance. Because they are largely non-Muslims who endorse diversity in beliefs, U.S. citizens have been characterized as "infidels" by followers of Mohammad. Rather than their freedom being respected, it has been derided as dissolute. Failing to support the Sharia (i.e., the Islamic moral code), they are condemned as immoral.

As Wilson observes, a similar intolerance infested Europe at the time of the Protestant Reformation. Adherents of Rome regarded non-Catholics as heretics, whereas Protestants denounced Catholics as devotees of Satan. For hundreds of years thereafter, sanguinary disputes roiled the peace of the continent. In England, Bloody Mary executed over three hundred Protestants in an effort to restore the old faith. In France, over twenty thousand Huguenots were killed and the rest forced to flee for their lives. The Protestants did no better. One of their champions, Oliver Cromwell, is still remembered in Ireland for the devastation he wrought. Indeed, it has been estimated that during the Thirty Years' War, fully one-third of the population of Germany was wiped out, thanks to religious passion. Ultimately, it began to dawn on the participants that no one was going to win these contests. They might not like their opponents, but would have to live with them. In the infant United States, these lessons did not go unheeded. The founding fathers were determined that religion would not be the cause of domestic unrest. To this end, the first amendment to the Constitution forbids "an establishment" of religion. There would be no state-sponsored church imposed on those who did not agree. George Washington was so committed to this proposition that he wrote to assure a congregation of Rhode Island Jews that they too would be permitted to reside in peace under their own "fig trees." More than this, unlike in places such as England, they could run for public office. In due course, the accelerating immigration of assorted minority groups solidified this pledge. A multiethnic nation became a reality, with mutual tolerance its cornerstone.

Wilson goes into greater detail, but his point is that tolerance was an achievement, not an arbitrary decision. Its value has been cemented into the American psyche because its seeds were planted centuries ago. Not a simplistic commitment, but a multifaceted set of objectives, many emotionally saturated clashes were necessary to produce it. The same history, however, has not unfolded in the Middle East. While Christians once cited the Bible to support intolerance, they no longer do. The same cannot be said of Muslims and the Koran. Its instructions "to slay the pagans" are still taken seriously. Democracy has been attempted in the Muslim world, most notably in Turkey, but this remains the exception. Governments based upon accepting a diversity of opinions run afoul of emotional calls to remain faithful to a single deity. Because Islam did not undergo the rigors of a Protestant Reformation, or subsequent efforts to establish a democratic, market-based economy, ordinary people—innately no worse than any others—do not respect diversity. In their heart of hearts, they demand the sort of uniformity that was once fashionable to their northwest.

Another value that evolved in modern America is individualism. Americans have come to treasure a sense of independence and self-worth that is historically atypical. In the past, an obsequious conformity was the norm. Ordinary people were expected to know their place and defer to their betters. Their personal aspirations were of little consequence. Only members of the aristocracy were entitled to feel pride in personal accomplishments. This was to change for a variety of reasons, not the least of which was the emergence of the "frontier." As America came to be occupied, the population surged westward. People took satisfaction in a sturdy self-reliance that enabled them to survive without the amenities of civilization. When eventually the economy began to roar, they transferred this attitude to becoming "successful." The dream was to do something better than anyone else and thereby grow wealthy. Uniqueness was prized both in innovation and self-expression. Everyone aspired to be a Thomas Edison, a Buffalo Bill, or a Theodore Roosevelt.

As the country transformed into a middle-class society, this orientation stood it in good stead. A prosperous market-based society requires the participation of many skilled contributors. Of these, as Melvin Kohn has asserted, a substantial proportion must be self-directed. They must be capable of independent decision-making if complex activities are to be adequately organized. A self-confidence grounded in knowledge and emotional maturity enables individuals to be flexible, risk-taking leaders. Individualism fits in well with this program. In seeking to be the best at what they personally do, people inadvertently groom themselves for tasks that need doing. The effect has been the development of the freest and most affluent society yet to emerge.

Nevertheless, individualism, as a value, has been thrown on the defensive. Collectivist moralists decry it as selfish and dangerous. Since capitalism is regarded as the source of most human misery, anything that supports it is condemned as equally destructive. The alternative is said to be interpersonal cooperation. Rather than endure the travails of competition, people are urged to work together for the common benefit. Radical feminists, radical liberals, and radical civil rights activists agree that a focus on the self results in denigration of the other. The only way in which everyone can gain is if all pursue an egalitarian community. A desire to be special is obviously inimical to this goal. Yet for this collectivist value to be achieved, hierarchical impulses must be squelched. People need to become more like cows and less like people. In fact, many academics have started to train their students in just this attitude. It is not unusual for them to assign group projects, including multiauthored essays. Grades are given in common, and members of committees rise or fall together. This is supposed to foster collaboration, which is indeed useful in contemporary society, but at the expense of personal initiative. Were this value to gain currency, those who buy into it must be prepared to be compliant followers. They must learn to be "good losers."

Little noticed has been the esteem for "integrity" and "trust" that also evolved in conjunction with the market economy. Interpersonal trading, especially large-scale trading between strangers, is contingent upon the parties being able to depend on each other. When they make deals, they must have confidence that they will get what they bargain for. Were this not to occur, they would eventually withdraw from these transactions. But if this transpired, the commerce upon which mass societies rely would collapse. People would literally starve to death because the food currently on their tables would never be transported across county lines. Despite the fact that most Americans are strangers to one another, they can, for the most part, count on each other. They do not expect to be deceived when they go to the supermarket, and generally are not. In addition, the food they order at a restaurant is by and large what they ordered, while their monthly paycheck is what their employer promised. In the wake of the Clinton impeachment scandal, ordinary people began to say that what he had done was not unusual and that everyone lies and cheats. Some of his partisans even praised him for his skills at deception. These were alleged to be a form of political genius. But were this attitude to become deeply entrenched, it would sound the death knell of the nation. A society in which lying is applauded is one in which people must retreat into private enclaves where they depend solely upon those whom they personally know.

Another long-term value in Western society has been sexual fidelity. Interpersonal trust between intimates has been associated with marital vows taken seriously. When a man and woman promised to have sexual relations only with one another, a violation of this pledge was interpreted as a betrayal. With intimacy difficult to manage, a partner who strayed was not trusted. Even so, a value that developed over many generations is once more under siege. With the arrival of dependable birth control, some maintain that sexual loyalty is an anachronism. They advocate "open marriages" in which partner swapping is the norm. Casual sexuality, as opposed to love, has also been extolled in the movies and on television. Successful swingers are routinely portrayed as happier than their humdrum peers. Even the Clinton debacle contributed to this perception. In its wake, cheating on one's wife was described as an exclusively private matter, with some openly admiring the president for his virility. Age-old admonitions against adultery were relegated to the hopelessly stuffy and an open-minded sophistication perceived as progressive. Here too, were this value to gain the upper hand, dependable intimacy would be at risk. Relationship losses would proliferate and both adults and children would suffer. Sex may not be the same as love, but treating it with careless indifference is an invitation to a loveless future.

A final value that protects against losing, but is likewise not automatic, is a belief in democracy. Large societies that do not safeguard the interests of all their members generate massive personal distress. Losing may be endemic to the human condition, but a failure to limit its scope introduces unnecessary misery. Because people know their own interests best, giving them a say in their own fate prevents discounting their needs. While hierarchy is unavoidable, total centralization is not. Decision-making can be dispersed, and, in fact, a techno-commercial community benefits from doing so. As per Hayek, no centralized authority can understand all of the variables that contribute to the successful operation of a large community. Only people on-site can recognize much of what needs to be done.

Consequently, unless their expertise is respected, errors mount up. This would seem to be common sense, but advances in transportation and communication have increased the reach of central authorities. In many quarters, a well-regulated welfare state has become the ideal. More government, not less, is the objective of politicians who promise satisfactions as supplied by a powerful Big Brother. That this is a threat to democracy is not recognized. That it is the value system that produced Stalin's Russia and Hitler's Germany is dismissed as conservative propaganda. Yet conservatives too fail to recognize all that is necessary for democracy to flourish. They do not fully appreciate the importance of internalized norms and values in limiting social conflicts. When people operate according to commitments in harmony with their needs, they don't require external directions. What they decide on their own because of guideposts developed through social negotiations can be broadly advantageous. No central authority needs to intercede—or be resisted. As a result, people are able to reside in peace and mutual support.

Character

No society can exist without moral rules. In their absence, conflict is endemic. But neither can modern societies thrive without personal character. Individual dispositions, as opposed to external sanctions, are essential to promoting altruistic behaviors. The difference between rule-following and private character can be perceived in the way children share toys. Sometimes a brother will allow his sister to play with his football because their mother instructed him to. This is rule-following. But sometimes he will do so because he loves her and wants her to be happy. This is a personal disposition. In the real world, it is useful to have both. Individuals should both be afraid of punishment for hurting others and independently generous.

What counts as personal virtue evolves over many generations. Back in ancient Greece, one of the cardinal virtues was hospitality. When strangers arrived at one's doorstep, one was supposed to take them in and entertain them lavishly. To do less, was churlish. Nowadays this emphasis seems peculiar. This, however, overlooks the context in which it was set. In the Greek world, intercommunity trading was just becoming established. Merchants would set out for parts unknown in hopes of making good deals. When they arrived, the modern infrastructure of hotels and restaurants was nowhere to be found. With travel restricted, the customer-base to support these facilities did not exist. The traveler, therefore, had to depend on the good will of the locals. Unless they were hospitable, there was no point in staying. In essence, hospitality served one of the functions interpersonal trust does today. Moreover, it was associated with the aristocracy. At first it was only they who possessed the accommodations necessary to offer their use, hence the attitude in Ulysses' home after he had gone off to fight at Troy.

Another peculiarity of ancient, and for that matter the medieval, character was the prominence of physical courage. To be cowardly was also churlish, that is, peasant-like. Nobles owed their status largely to their leadership in war. Trained from early childhood to wield weapons, they were expected to do so with panache. Nowadays, while physical courage is still prized, it is of lesser importance. Moral and social courage matter more. Living in a commercial world peopled with millions of unfamiliar faces demands different talents. Our heroes have the audacity to make risky business deals and the foresight to recognize when these will pay off. They get rich, as did Bill Gates of Microsoft fame, because they can make an advantageous bargain with IBM and then protect the proceeds from governmental confiscation. Much of what we have come to value is on display in James Bond movies. Bond, to be sure, is physically brave, but his strongest suit lies elsewhere. As a modern urban hero, he always seems to know the right things to say and do. Unlike most of us, he is never at a loss when surrounded by exotic characters. We become tongue-tied, but he deals with kings and peasants with equal élan. His courage is thus in coping with the socially unpredictable.

In the Bond movies, we do not know from whence his aplomb flows; we merely sit back and enjoy the fantasy. In the actual world, the source of personal character is of enormous import. Most parents would love to understand how to instill courage in their children. And herein lays the crux of the matter. Character is largely acquired, mostly in childhood. For someone to grow up feeling positive about other human beings, it is essential to be raised in a loving manner. Being loved instills a loving feeling about oneself that can later be shared. Similar factors apply to courage. Children who are continuously deluged by criticism have their self-confidence subverted. Regularly threatened, they grow fearful. Persons allowed to take chances at a manageable pace have a different outcome. They experience mastery and come to expect it. Moreover, feeling safe provides the calm to cope with danger. They therefore learn to think things through without panicking.

Whatever their biological equipment, they internalize a confidence in their ability to survive. This, in turn, limits their losses.

The proper socialization is also essential to the development of a sense of personal responsibility. Those who emerge as social leaders must stand up when things go wrong. Not only do they need to make decisions, but must accept the blame for their mistakes. The virtue here is not so much in admitting error, but as in dealing with it when it comes along. Unless a person can face disaster with equanimity, it may be impossible to recover from. Mistakes are bad, but worse still is not correcting them. Persons who are afraid of being blamed tend to deny that anything untoward has happened. Rather than move forward, they become obsessed with maintaining an unblemished self-image. Most likely when they were younger, they experienced torrents of blame. Required to do things right the first time, they became petrified that this was beyond their competence. Since it probably was, the most sensible course was to avoid the new or chancy. In adulthood, this can result in passing the buck. Others are allowed to go first, then should they succeed, they will swoop in to take the credit.

In contemporary America, victimization has become the mode. Many people resent responsibility. They prefer a reputation for being too weak to protect themselves. According to them, others are to blame for whatever goes wrong. It is they who possess the power to be exploitative and must be cut down to size. This is the morality of envy. Its "poor me" mentality seeks power from defenselessness. But as Shelby Steele has argued with respect to African Americans, it also limits the potential for success. Those who are convinced they can only lose do not accurately assess what is needed for victory. Nor do they prepare for it. In orienting themselves to diminish the damage, they diminish their opportunities to do better. This is the case with women fixated on blaming men for their impotence. It is the case with blacks who demand communal hiring policies. In both instances, an insistence that one does not have the ability to make it on one's own translates into a failure to develop the skills needed to win.

Note

1. Frederick Nietzsche comes to a similar conclusion. He, however, is contemptuous of the strategy, dismissing it as a slave morality.

10

Beyond the Utopias

The Eightfold Path: Right view, right aim, right speech, right action, right living, right effort, right mindfulness, right contemplation.
(Some Sayings of the Buddha, F. L. Woodward)

A Distinction with a Difference

The Buddha sat under the Bodhi tree contemplating the secrets of the universe. After years of diligent searching, he found the answer. This pampered son of an Indian prince, having renounced the privileges of his Kshatriya class in order to pursue the existence of an impoverished mendicant, finally understood what life was about. His insight was fourfold. The first of his noble truths was that human existence was suffering. The second was that suffering resulted from desire. The third was that suffering could be banished by renouncing desire. And the fourth, and final truth, was that pursuing an eightfold path could enable a person to overcome desire. The former Siddhartha Gautama thenceforward determined to liberate himself from the cravings of the flesh. In wanting nothing, he would no longer be frustrated. In envying nothing, he could not be enticed into injuring others. Within a relatively short period of time, this philosophy swept through the Indian Subcontinent and ultimately throughout East Asia. Buddhists then and now committed themselves to living simply and ascetically. Intent on achieving nirvana, that is, a cessation of all suffering, they have exercised a spiritual discipline designed to rein in their appetites.

The difficulty with this aspiration is that it is not possible. To be human is to have desires; it is to persistently hunger after goals that are not always capable of accomplishment. This, indeed, is the glory of our species. If we ever reached the point of wanting nothing, we would, in fact, have nothing. Our economic, political, social, not to mention religious, achievements would have come to naught. We would not even have had the impetus to dig for the roots that kept us from starving during our evolutionary apprenticeship. We would, in short, have gone the way of the Shakers. But the downside of desire is that it opens the possibility of loss and losing. Because our wants are not automatically fulfilled, we endure the pangs of disappointment. And because assertions of primacy are not always successful, we anguish over our misfortunes. Just as the Buddha said, suffering is inevitable. There is no such thing as going through life without distress. To make matters worse, as greedy social creatures, we impose defeats upon one another. Nevertheless, this very greed has paved the way for victories. In striving for more and more, in combination with others who also seek more, we do not always fall short. Contemporary Americans have only to look about them to see the fruits of our shared ambitions.

Perfection, however, is not a viable goal. Regardless of how it is conceived, whether in the Buddhist terms of complete equanimity, in Plato's of a republic governed by a philosopher king, in More's of a community in which personal distinction is eschewed, or in Marx's Communist vision of property-free cooperation, it will never arrive as long as people are people. Nor will we ever witness a Johnsonian Great Society from which poverty has been eliminated or an adolescent-style utopia in which everyone is so rich that frustration becomes a historic relic. Utopias, whatever their shape, are fantasies. Human beings are never totally happy. We never obtain everything we want, if for no other reason than when we do, we immediately want something more. To be without a goal is to be intolerably adrift. Nor do we abide complete equality. Almost all of us long to be important. But in our efforts to outdo one another, some invariably get left behind. There is always a better and a worse, and getting stuck with the worse hurts. Nevertheless, what is necessary for personal satisfaction is not perfect tranquility, but getting beyond the notion of utopia. We can improve our situations, but we can never arrive at a state of bliss. If we believe we can, we only exacerbate our frustrations.

The Buddha said suffering must be eradicated. But this is not possible. What is, is learning to cope with loss and losing. People can ascertain how to live with things going wrong and also how to implement improvements. Suffering does not have to be absolute. Indeed, it is, as was claimed millennia ago, a part of life. Dealing with it is one of the existential challenges of being human. To experience the pain of losing, but to persist, and triumph, is one of the finest achievements of the human spirit. It is something in which people can take pride, something that merits admiration. It is not a condition that must be submerged in the ecstasy of the proverbial clam.

Nor should personal distress be dissolved in a medicalized paradise. In fact, it cannot be. Neither pharmacology, nor psychotherapy, can provide an idyllic stasis. Human life is eternally in turmoil. Ongoing negotiations over hierarchies, roles, relationships, knowledge, and morals keep people from attaining a flawless resting place. In our individual imperfections, no matter how benevolent our intentions, we make mistakes. However miraculous the cornucopia of medications, or neurologically informed the therapy, conflicts, heartaches, and errors remain. Besides medicine's own imperfections, it is not equipped to address all forms of individual distress. It certainly does not speak to the consequences of loss and losing. Medicine specializes in biology, not social arrangements. Within its own bailiwick it has been enormously beneficial. Yet in engaging in institutional imperialism, it has overstepped its bounds.

The time has come to correct this historic error. Efforts to rescue us from superstition by interpreting personal discontent as a form of mental illness are misplaced. Unhappiness is not a disease. If someone's misery is caused by sickness, doctors can help, but if it is caused by loss and losing, they can do little. The medical model of personal distress can actually make things worse. In suggesting to a patient that his or her discomforts result from disease, the implication is that they should be cured by medical interventions. But medical ministrations generally require passivity. For the most part, diseases visit one from the outside. All of a sudden, an illness arrives unbidden and ravages the body. Influenza, for instance, may be transmitted from coworkers and one's lungs are wracked with a cough. The muscles ache, the brow burns with a fever, and a person feels horrible. Physicians have learned that a virus attacking cells in the pulmonary system causes these symptoms. Their job is then to assist the body's defenses in expelling the invaders. In this, the patient is a virtually inactive container. An enemy has broken through his or her outer fortifications, but they must wait patiently for the doctor to vanquish the foe. Their job is to swallow the prescribed medicines, lie in bed as ordered, and drink plenty of fluids. Patients are spectators to their own cures. Ignorant of what is going on, they do as they are told. If this is performed conscientiously, one day they will rise up with their familiar vim and vigor. They will have been healed and free to go on their way. Decades ago Talcott Parsons described the "sick role" as a sort of time-out. Unwell persons are excused from ordinary activities in order to allow healing to occur. It is only after they recover that the usual demands of life are reimposed.

When this philosophy is applied to loss and losing, the consequences are regrettable. An unhappy person who appears at the doorstep of a physician seeking treatment may assume that he or she must hand themselves over to the doctor's curative efforts. The physician is regarded the expert and they as a victim in need of assistance. The victim is therefore expected to do as the physician recommends, while eagerly awaiting the promised conclusion. Yet if resocialization is the sovereign remedy for loss and losing, this can delay improvements. Patients who accept the disease model will not understand that they must be active in navigating the process of overcoming their distress. Nor will they realize that the endpoint is not the elimination of a foreign invader, but coping with a natural reaction. For resocialization to work, persons undergoing it can, however, benefit from a zone of safety. If they can count on an absence of distractions, they are better able to mobilize their energies for the emotional turmoil they must endure. But it is they who must apply themselves. If they are essentially given a license to maintain their denials, it will be more difficult to break through. Worse still, if they are promised that a medication can obviate the need to tolerate the rigors of mourning, they are unlikely to escape the defeats hobbling their life.

In addition, what can be accomplished during resocialization depends on an accurate appreciation of what is happening. Going into the process cloaked in ignorance can make it more frightening. Flashes of anger that seem to come from nowhere can feel overwhelming. So can moments of panic that are unconnected with their source. The discomfort can be especially serious when depression arises. Because it seems to imply death, a person may not realize that it will run a predictable course and terminate in their liberation. It is probable that those uninformed about the nature of resocialization will resist it. They may find it preferable to continue experiencing the distress of a suppressed loss than take on the terrors of the unknown. Nor are they handicapped merely by a reluctance to forge ahead. They are also slowed by a lack of knowledge if they inadvertently enter the process. Pinballing from one mystery to another, they are scarcely able to organize an effective campaign to let go of losses.

Still, there is no way around it; resocialization entails suffering. Both loss and losing, and extricating oneself from them, are not fun. The truth is that life can be hard. Happily, for the courageous, it can also be rewarding. Medical explanations of personal distress seek to outflank this reality. Yet the *Brave New World* they promise is no more propitious than the one of which Aldous Huxley wrote. Rather than being scientific or merciful, it buttresses the forces of denial. In this respect, it is like the Buddha's nirvana. The difference is that it offers a medicinal haze as opposed to a spiritual one. The uncomplicated fact is that problems need to be recognized for what they are before they can be corrected. Likewise, the mechanisms of change need to be understood before they can be effectively applied.

Accepting Limits

Politicians, and to a lesser extent physicians, have become experts in making promises. In order to sustain their power, they guarantee results they cannot supply. They realize that unless they provide something special, they may have no takers. As a consequence, they inflate their rhetoric. Public figures engage in a race to outbid one another. Until someone attempts to collect the pot, they keep upping the ante. Then a politician gets elected, their new program is funded, or the latest wonder drug is tested on a battery of patients. Sooner or later, the time comes to show one's hand. One might imagine that this would unveil the charlatans, and sometimes it does, but with a disquieting frequency, it does not. Those who promise to save humanity claim marvelous results, whether or not these are achieved. Just as they initially use language to paint a glowing picture of what they will accomplish, so they employ it to extol what they have achieved. Hyperbole, rather than performance, rules the day, and like the emperor in his new clothes, leaders stride around the community to rave reviews. It is remarkable how many psychotropic drugs were going to cure schizophrenia, and then did cure it, then—oops—they did not. Progress is often made, but it is surprising how regularly the pendulum swings from one answer to its opposite. Mistakes are eventually revealed, but in the meantime they do immense harm.

The point of this mini-excursion into political science is that that which sounds too good to be true frequently is. This is certainly the case with medical promises regarding the elimination of personal distress. However much partisans of the medical model believe they provide cures, they cannot make loss and losing disappear. Life is fraught with limitations. Regardless of how unwelcome it is, sooner or later everyone sustains a defeat. Those who expect endless triumphs are in for a rude awakening. When their turn to fail arrives, they are unprepared to manage the shock, and as a result, it hurts more. For most people, the sensible course is to accept the reality of loss and losing. This helps because with foresight it is possible to restrict the impact of one's limits.

In the last chapter, idealism was given rough treatment. It was portrayed as seducing people into pursuing the impossible. And yet, in small doses, idealism can be useful. The trick is not to be too sanguine. Optimism can provide the confidence to try something new, but if unqualified, can be rash. Calculated risks are generally the most productive. When one hopes for the best, but contemplates what can go wrong, one's prospects are enhanced. One does not want to dive off a cliff only to discover there are rocks below the surface. Idealism coupled with caution tests the waters before jumping in. This strategy does not eschew novel techniques; it merely puts them on trial to determine if they work. If they do not, they may be modified. Then they will need to be tested again. This approach keeps the losses down and prevents hyperbole from overpowering reality. An idealism that both dreams and remains awake enables the dreamer to determine how solid a vision is.

Hierarchy has been one of the areas in which idealism has run riot. Because people hate to lose, they imagine a world in which losing does not occur. A completely egalitarian society is alluring because it promises calm sailing into the indefinite future. With everyone on the same level, there are no embarrassing tests of strength. Nor is there a need to defer to the more successful. If everyone is just as victorious as everyone else, all can lead a comfortable and untroubled existence. In the imagination, at least, everyone is a winner. Even though winning is impossible without the presence of losers, dreams can be edited however one likes. The reality is that hierarchy is part of the human condition and its boundaries need to be acknowledged for what they are. This does not mean that tyranny or oppression must be accepted, just inequality. Individually everyone is free to improve his or her status. Likewise, in a hierarchical society, people can cooperate in their efforts to reduce the injuries done to the most vulnerable members of their community. Suffering cannot be eliminated, but it can be controlled.

Similar factors apply to social roles. They too are inevitable and they too resist an egalitarian distribution. No complex society can exist without a complex division of labor. Just as it is impossible for a mass civilization to survive without ranks, so it is impossible to subsist without a variation in tasks. If everyone does precisely the same thing, no one can specialize in anything that requires lengthy preparation. There was a time when most people did similar work, but that was when the choice was between being a hunter or being a gatherer. The only way to revive a comparable situation is to go back to that way of life, but this would entail eliminating everyone on earth—save for a few million. Nevertheless, if there are different jobs, there are bound to be disparities. As a consequence, some people will get what they want, while others will not. Relatively speaking the losers will be unhappy, yet if this is admitted, it can be managed. Fairness, albeit not absolute fairness, can be pursued. Overreaching ambitions exacerbate problems by exciting conflicts. The realization that one may have to perform tasks one does not relish can free one's energies to make adjustments that improve the distribution. As usual, battling against the inescapable reduces the range of the possible.

The need to allow for limits is probably most obvious with respect to personal relationships. The rise of a divorce culture has disabused many people of their romanticism. They have come to realize that successful intimacy requires effort. In a society in which long-term heterosexual relationships have become voluntary, they have learned that a dual-concern approach is essential. This, of course, implies a give-and-take in which not all desires are fulfilled. Marriage requires sacrifice, and parenthood requires even more. The benefits of each are available only to those who are willing to regulate their demands. To be sure, not everyone has discovered this. An eruption of "reality" TV shows promised to match bachelors and "bachelorettes" with their soul mates for the titillation of juvenile audiences. The ratings for these programs were high enough to suggest that fantasy romance is far from dead.

Knowledge too has been romanticized. The advent of an information age has persuaded many people that whatever they need to know is available at the touch of a computer key. Understanding is supposed to come easily; indeed prospective teachers are told it is their job to make learning fun. Now in competition with an MTV mentality, they cannot afford to allow their students' attention spans to wander. This means that what is difficult gets jettisoned in favor of entertainment. Nor is deception distinguished from truth. Comforting stories are extolled as true, simply because they are what people want to hear. The new mantras are thus: Everyone lies, everyone spins. Keats's words, "That is all Ye know on earth; and that is all ye need to know," have been taken to heart, albeit in a different context. Not conceded is that knowledge is limited. While it must be admitted that modern human beings have learned a great deal, they have not learned everything. True, science has made the formerly incomprehensible simple, and technology has provided instant communications that make it possible for people to track each other's daily routines. But we still do not understand how the brain works or what motivates many of our closest associates. In a word, modesty is in order. To assume that we know everything is to flirt with catastrophe. It is to close our eyes and refuse to investigate facts that may prevent us from stepping in front of a speeding train.

Then there are the limits imposed by morality. The British philosopher G. E. Moore believed the "good" was observable. He compared it to the color yellow and argued that everyone could see it for themselves. Then again, Moore also believed in séances as a means of conversing with the dead. In fact, disputes about morality have been interminable. As a socially constructed mechanism of interpersonal control, its outlines shift to meet changing requirements. No absolute standards protect people from every contingency. Nor is there any way to preclude moral manipulation. The nature of morality is such that it is both tempting and simple to arrange. Far from shielding people from every evil, moral codes can be treacherous. Sometimes self-serving, sometimes idealistic, they dazzle with their pretensions and torture with their punishments. Safety thus lies with vigilance. Morality may be indispensable, but not a blind allegiance to an imperfect instrument.

Finally, it must not be forgotten that we human beings are emotional creatures. Whatever our affectations of rationality, intense feelings often shoulder good sense to the sidelines. Whether we are dealing with hierarchy, social roles, personal relationships, apparently objective knowledge, and certainly morality, we frequently act on impulse. Often more in touch with a sentiment we cannot verbalize than concrete events, we take action based on the former. No wonder we are habitually out of touch with reality. Even under the best of circumstances, we are led astray by our passions. This problem is intensified by a vulnerability to primitive emotions. When circumstances are at their most extreme, our feelings are apt to be most intense. But intense emotions are prone to stupidity. They rush out to stop speeding locomotives with their bare hands. People who are enraged, or in a panic, compound their problems. Unable to think clearly, they act precipitously. The secret to avoiding this is emotional maturity. Those who have learned to control their feelings are able to implement them more effectively. They understand that their biological equipment and social environments are such as to prompt them to react inappropriately. They also understand that this is best addressed by becoming skilled at using the emotions. Socialization in how to get angry, or manage fears, is imperative for those who want to achieve their goals or reduce their losses.

Amelioration

The ancient Greeks knew a thing or two. One piece of wisdom upon which most agreed was the utility of "moderation in all things." Not long ago Barry Goldwater told a Republican convention that extremism in defense of freedom was no vice, but the voting public rejected this logic with a decisiveness that no subsequent mainstream politician has sought to repeat. Whatever their momentary enthusiasms, most contemporary Americans concur with the classical philosophers. They understand that far-out positions are often perched on limbs that are about to break—or be sawed off. When an Air Force general proposed the use of the atomic bomb, they were horrified. When the wife of a president concocted a medical plan that would nationalize the practice of medicine, they sent another message through the polls. They likewise rebelled when a president managed to get one through despite their disapproval. Nevertheless, they are also fascinated with exaggerated claims of instant gratification. Many a con man has been able to retire in luxury because they heeded P. T. Barnum's advice that there is a sucker born every minute.

Sadly, the snake oil has flowed in virtual rivers with regard to the elimination of personal misery. People want to feel good about themselves. Moreover, they want to feel good today, not tomorrow. This desire keeps politicians in business. As long as they can make believable claims, they can depend upon attracting a constituency. Americans have been spoiled by an industrial infrastructure that bridged the broadest rivers and raised towers that scrape the sky. Not unnaturally, they assume that a nation that can put a man on the moon can do almost anything to which it sets its mind. The result has been a faith in social engineering. It is taken for granted that if experts get together, they can cobble together a plan to solve any problem. All that is needed is to set them at the task and fund their recommendations. Far from moderate in conception, this postulates a virtual omnipotence. The implication is that whatever we want, we can achieve—if we try hard enough.

While it is true that many people were chastened by the collapse of the war on poverty, a few were not dissuaded. Poverty is still with us, and many poverty programs have gone the way of all flesh—but not all. Training programs to get people jobs have been cut back, but their lack of success did not convince their sponsors that they will never work. Nor has futilely showering billions of dollars on education, the homeless, and affirmative action resulted in the conclusion that the experts did not know what they were talking about. These objectives are deemed so important that people cannot allow themselves to recognize that a solution is not at hand. They believe the engineers when they say they understand what is wrong, that they know how to fix it, and that all that remains is to do the job. That this faith is a form of extremism is not perceived. That it is idealistic is scorned. Instead of testing proposals to see if they work, they are packaged in legislation that is never read. One batch of politicians give speeches in which they insist their plans cannot fail and then another batch maintains that they will never succeed. The winners then spend years explaining that their promise was not fulfilled because the funding was too stingy. Just a few more dollars and it would have worked. An obvious example is affirmative action. Its advocates claim that only it can bring fairness, but then assert that persistent bigotry requires it remain in effect for decades longer. Somehow, even though such programs are declared to be a success, they are never successful enough to be terminated.

The intractable truth is that we human beings have limited control over our social world. There are many things we would like to change, but do not possess the means to alter. The pop-psychologist Wayne Dyer got rich advising people to pull their own strings. His message was, don't be a puppet for others! Be you own puppeteer! Yet in many ways we are at the mercy of a fate we do not understand, never mind master. Garth Brooks's image of being on journey down a river is apt. Our small vessels do not have the horsepower to fight the current. Try as we may, we cannot muscle our way upstream. But we are not helpless. We can guide our boats from shore to shore, and around treacherous shoals. Because we are limited, we cannot do everything, but we can do some things—that is, if we are careful, honest, and reasonably intelligent. And oh, yes, if we have the courage to admit our weaknesses, but are nevertheless willing to risk the possible.

The best strategy, the one most in accord with moderation, is to *ameliorate*, not to optimize. Small incremental changes in a positive direction have a better chance of achieving progress than huge leaps into the unknown. Modest improvements always leave work to be done, but create genuine accomplishments. Unlike visions of perfection, they are tangible. This sort of progress can occur both on a social and on a personal level. On an individual level, resocialization is frequently necessary and by its very nature ameliorative. An inherently slow process, it only gradually enriches a person's lot. Nonetheless, fashioning a better personal world can reduce individual losses. Social structures and cultural phenomena can also be modified to limit the damage done. As long as miracles are not required, and limitations are respected, advances are possible. The history of humankind proves as much. Whatever the problems we today confront, they pale in comparison to those faced by our ancestors. Most of us do not worry about seasonal starvation or a homicidal raid from a neighboring tribe. Nor will we die prematurely from an infectious disease or are crippled by an occupation that breaks our back. To judge only by life expectancy or height, we are doing fairly well. Throw in our electronic gadgets, our spacious homes, and our democratic institutions, and the image brightens further. A century ago, prominent scientists opined that there was nothing left to be invented. They were wrong. It would be equally incorrect to assume that our social arrangements are incapable of enhancement.

Let us begin with *hierarchy*. Its glaring imbalances are unquestionably productive of suffering. Every day people lose out in the scramble to move up the greasy pole. This cannot be prevented, but it can be regulated. Hierarchies will always have a top and a bottom, and the relative deprivation of those at their lower rungs will always hurt. Nevertheless, the distance between the top and the bottom is not predestined. Historically the gap has sometimes widened and sometimes narrowed. During the heyday of the ancient empires, the emperor was considered a deity. The chasm between himself and his slaves was so great that in places like Persia, the lowest persons were not allowed to look at the highest. By contrast, any contemporary American can shake the hand of the president. The nation's leader may be the most powerful person in the world, but he or she is regarded as a human being like any other and after his (or her) term has concluded will return to a less exalted status. In the future it is possible that this gap will narrow yet more. Individual citizens may then have more power and the president less. Similarly the richest may one day own relatively less compared with the poorest.

Another potential modification is in the distribution within a hierarchy. Karl Marx believed that during any era, there was always a dichotomy between an upper and a lower class, and that, in his lifetime, this was between the capitalists and the proletarians. He further predicted that the abyss between these would grow so deep that only a revolution could correct the injustice. What Marx failed to reckon with was the growth of the middle class. In contemporary America, most people describe themselves as belonging to a segment of society he considered trivial. Their resources are now such that they do not perceive themselves as poor, but neither so great that they are rich. By their own estimation, they are "comfortable." Contrary to Marx, that the wealthy could sustain themselves only by impoverishing the vast majority of their inferiors was not inevitable. As a result, the number of people who feel like losers has been drastically reduced. They know they are not at the top, but neither do they experience a jackboot pressing on their necks.

Related to this development is social mobility. Today many people have improved their situations because they are free to move up the ladder. This then is another dimension in which hierarchies differ. Some are more rigid than others. In the most ossified, the status into which one is born is the one in which one dies. The effect of this is that some arrangements preclude change by restricting efforts to overcome losses, whereas the more flexible provide hope. Opportunities to improve oneself relative to others make it possible to alter past decisions. Dreams become achievable, and people gain a measure of control over their destinies. This has been one of the major benefits in replacing caste and estate systems with social class. Statuses based on marketplace judgments are more supple. They vary as social needs and estimations of merit change. Worth, as determined by anonymous others, rather than birth, becomes the arbiter of who ends up with the greatest power.

For social mobility to operate effectively, a society's rules must be equitable. While opportunity can never be distributed with complete fairness, it can be broadly available. Because some people are born into better-off families, and others are more biologically talented, they have an advantage. Nevertheless, this disparity does not have to be aggravated by stacking the deck. Laws can be written down, they can be put into operation by an impartial judiciary, and legislators can be elected by a broad franchise. A constitutional democracy, in short, can diminish losses by ensuring that people can redress grievances. When others gain an unwarranted advantage, they can be challenged in the courts or at the ballot box. This makes all the difference in who gets ahead.

Also useful in diminishing the disparities inherent in hierarchy is economic prosperity. The more goods and services a society has available, the less painful the bite of an unequal allocation. If the rich man lives in a castle, whereas the workingman resides in a multiroom suburban split-level, the latter has less cause for envy. By the same token, an affluent society can afford to provide health benefits for those at the top and the bottom. While it is true that the more powerful go to the head of the line, the quality of services can be such that everyone enjoys greater life expectancy. Such a society also provides a broader variety of diversions. People have more time for leisure. This too reduces levels of envy, for those who feel good about themselves are less likely to desire what others have.

Hierarchical conflicts can likewise be shrunk by decentralization. The more decisions people are allowed to make regarding their own lives, the less they resent the power of others. When social leaders are prohibited from interfering in private matters, those lower on the social scale do not have to fret about their choices being preempted. They do not lose to the eight hundred–pound gorilla barred from entering their homes. The same considerations apply to work. The more broadly authority is distributed, the less need to dread close supervision. When the boss is in their office, and the worker schedules their own tasks, potential sources of friction are diminished. The secret in this case is subordinates who are known to be capable of making good choices. Individuals with the skills and motivation to perform on their own can be allowed to do so.

This is where self-direction comes in. People who are responsible and prepared to make decisions even in an environment of uncertainty can be delegated more freedom. They require less imperative coordination because they understand what needs doing. One way to ensure competence is to promote professionalism. Professionals are specially trained to care about what they do and be proficient at doing it. Integrated into communities of mutually supportive professionals, they are inspired by cultural, as well as structural, constraints to do their best. Another way to promote competence is to encourage a middle-class mentality. Individuals who grow up understanding that one day they will be social leaders have an incentive to prepare for this. They, and their parents, care about why and how things work. Potentially responsible for group plans, they recognize that an awareness of causality makes it possible to draw up better ones. They are also apt to dedicate more time to learning how social relationships function. Looking forward to someday being called upon to manage others, they have an interest in being able to predict how they respond. Thus, when problems arise, they make better choices and function as better coordinating agents. Independently competent, they are in less need of superiors to guide their performances.

Social roles are similarly capable of amelioration. These too can be constructed to be fairer and less disruptive. Once upon a time, the number of available roles was limited. Small-scale societies had room for only a few specialties. As societies grew, however, the number of positions expanded geometrically. Agrarian empires needed to be coordinated, classical city-states required experienced traders, and commercial nations benefited from skilled financiers. Eventually global industrialization blew the roof off potential areas of expertise. So many different types of work became available that the question became the following: "What shall I be when I grow up?" This developed into such a dilemma that its answer was frequently postponed into adulthood. It was made particularly difficult by the fact that a vast multiplicity of jobs is not visible to their potential occupants. Little boys knew what a cowboy is, but also that they would probably not become one. On the other hand, they did not know what an arbitrageur does and might not find out until after they graduated from business school. The result is that most people are ignorant of their options.

This expansion of the division of labor increased personal confusions. Although people were more interdependent, there was a growing unease about where to fit in. This created not only insecurities but also opportunities. People were no longer destined for the same occupations as their parents. They might even switch jobs several times during their careers. This allowed them to develop a better fit between who they were and what they did. Individuals started to talk about "finding themselves." What was it that they enjoyed doing? What were they good at? Work became something from which satisfaction is derived. Yes, there was a wealth of choices—not all of which were visible—but a diligent search might be rewarded with personal fulfillment. The bad old days of working just to earn a living were replaced by an expectation that one should look forward to going to work.

Such a detailed division of labor brought freedom. If the job one did was unique, how was a boss to supervise its execution? If only the worker understood what needed to be done, he or she had to be self-directive. The proliferation of tasks was therefore accompanied by professionalization, with the result that hierarchy became less important. A complex division of labor, in essence, became a substitute for imperative coordination. This in turn reduced the level of interpersonal conflict, but only when individual expertise was genuine.

As has been repeatedly remarked, not all jobs are equally fulfilling. Some people lose the occupational lottery and get stuck digging ditches. Yet there are fewer bad jobs than there once were. More differentiated tasks tend to be more satisfying. Many are sufficiently complex that people revel in their uniqueness and the attendant in personal control. Besides, having a broader choice, they are more likely to discover a better match. Even if this isn't perfect, the opportunity for change makes a selection more palatable. But more than this, modern jobs are measurably better. They are cleaner, healthier, and less muscle intensive. Technology not only substituted machines for strong backs but also automated less desirable tasks. Because people are motivated to avoid them, entrepreneurs are stimulated to find alternatives. And they have. Even dishwashing has been made less onerous by the advent of dishwashing machines.

Improvements in *personal relationships* are likewise feasible. Advocates of "free love" once assumed that only temporary liaisons could be satisfying. Anything more permanent amounted to an entangling alliance that by definition was unfree. That people might derive benefits from voluntary attachments seemed anomalous in a world where arranged marriages were common. Living alone, unfettered by the demands of a selfish partner, was obviously preferable. Given the affluence of modern societies, single parenthood also became practical. In the 1920s, Bertrand Russell argued that the government should provide the resources for this. Taxes could be levied on the rich to pay welfare benefits to the poor. By the 1970s, millions of people were taking him up on this promise. Welfare rolls and single parenthood increased exponentially. By the 1990s, however, these were found to be barren. People learned that interpersonal intimacy was preferable.

They discovered that individual television sets were neither a substitute for a trustworthy companion, nor an adequate replacement for parents in raising children. They now began to ask how they might stay together, rather than break apart.

Gradually an understanding of voluntary intimacy has begun to replace romanticism and antiromanticism. Forced to examine what it takes to remain bonded, more people are aware that there are limitations to what love can do. Nevertheless, love was determined not to be a myth. It could bring contentment if judiciously sought. What was necessary was a better understanding of how it worked. Gains in material wealth made independence viable, but did not bestow insight into personal relationships. That these thrive on equitable negotiations was not immediately apparent. Nevertheless people have been learning. Some are getting better at collaborating on a shared life space because they devote themselves to the endeavor. So far the improvements have not been spectacular, but domestic violence has declined and levels of divorce have leveled off.

Enhanced relationships also depend on a better knowledge of one's partner. Each has to understand himself or herself and the other. Both must recognize the differences between the genders and be aware of individual peculiarities. Since no one is perfect, they must accept imperfections. Adjustments have to be made if two people are to live comfortably with each other, but these cannot entail wholesale reconstruction projects. Most important of all is emotional maturity. Unless both parties are grown-ups, they cannot have a stable relationship. Intimacy is too dangerous to be entrusted to people who cannot control themselves. If they want to help—not to save one another—they must possess the desire and ability to work together. But if they do, they can improve their situation.

More accurate, *knowledge*, in general, is ameliorative. Remarkably, not everyone agrees with this. Postmodernists argue that there is no such thing as truth. They say that since everyone sees things from an idiosyncratic vantage point, no one can see them for what they are. People have opinions, attitudes, and interpretations, never facts. As a consequence, each one's perspective is as valid as anyone else's. Since no one is totally correct, the best that can be hoped for is to persuade others to agree with one's own outlook. In fact, the postmodernists expend a great deal of energy in convincing others of their views. Skeptics do not amuse them.

What the postmodernists imperfectly expressed is that knowledge is limited. No human being, or groups of humans, can ever know everything. The universe is too massive and our minds too feeble. Individuals cannot even come close to understanding most of what is occurring in their own lives. Too much is hidden from view and too much is beyond comprehension. Moreover, they make mistakes—lots of them. They may believe that they know what is going on only to discover they were wrong. The earth is not flat. The stars do not cause influenza. The Spanish did not use a mine to sink the battleship *Maine*. To extrapolate from this, however, to the impossibility of ever being right is itself wrong. Knowledge is conditional. It is also cumulative. Genuine understandings develop through time and an exposure to disconfirmation. People do not move from absolute ignorance to absolute truth, but gradually develop a closer approximation of that which is so. They are not either right or wrong, but more right than previously. Knowledge is asymptotic, not absolute. People approach it; they never fully embrace it.

This means that while knowledge is limited, it is expandable. In light of the enormous increase in our understanding over the last several millennia, this should be common sense. It should also be conventional wisdom that this information contributed enormously to our well-being. People are much happier and healthier than they once were, thanks to the control this provided. If losses are to be reduced, it makes sense that learning should be encouraged. Falling back on personal tastes risks self-righteous ignorance. Likewise, assuming there is nothing left to discover risks stasis and decline.

But as the postmodernists also warn, people are subjective. What we see is often what we want to see. Contemporary skeptics conclude that this means science is flawed. A search for knowledge it may be, but because it is human, it is replete with personal biases. In their opinion—and remember they have a high regard for their opinions—art is preferable. It is more personal and therefore closer to what exists. Art, of course, does have its place. It can communicate truths science leaves unstudied. But art is not a substitute for science. Nor is science a bastion of absolute truth. It is an enterprise in which people seek knowledge, but cannot claim to monopolize it. Scientists make mistakes. They are not totally objective. Yet when science is done properly, its practitioners compare their results. They are careful and monitor missteps. Several hundred years of empirical experience has demonstrated the method works. Science has helped us learn more than we once did.

The past is said to be prologue to the future, and one surely hopes this is so with respect to science. If the pace of learning approaches what it has been, we will discover many facts that protect us from grief. Medical researchers will undoubtedly make many of these advances. They will find new ways to treat currently incurable diseases. They will also learn more about how the brain functions. Perhaps mental illnesses will be among their conquests. One hopes so. But the social sciences will also make progress. They may be more subjective, yet they too advance learning. Among the things they may study in greater detail are loss and losing. Eventually we may better understand how these are related to hierarchies, social roles, and personal relationships. They may also discover more about resocialization. If so, new doorways to decreasing human misery will swing open.

Lastly, an ameliorative orientation should include *morality*. Its impact on human satisfactions is so profound that it must not be neglected. In some ways, however, to speak of advances in morality is a contradiction in terms. As a negotiated phenomenon, morality is always in flux, while as a tradition-bound enterprise, it also looks to the past. Indeed, its rules are contingent on a balance of flexibility and stability. Too narrow-minded an attachment to the wisdom of our ancestors hazards rigidity in the face of change, whereas too ready a flirtation with novelty gambles with untested standards. Put another way, a thoroughgoing ethical relativism is dangerous. In assuming that moral standards are interchangeable, that all are equally valid, it fails to distinguish between prescriptions that are not uniformly beneficial. Runaway slave laws and color-blind hiring practices must never be placed on a par. Nor is absolute tolerance constructive. Tolerating language differences is one thing; reacting to Cambodian killing fields in the same manner is another. On the other hand, a hidebound orthodoxy is treacherous. To exclude blacks from juries because that is how it was always done deprives society of justice.

What is probably best is a modified fundamentalism. Long-standing moral rules deserve to be respected. They should never be rejected on a whim. Nevertheless, when circumstances dictate new approaches, these should be considered. What is needed is a "realistic relativism." Alternate standards must be compared so that the superior ones are adopted. The same goes for tolerance. Small differences that make no difference should not trigger large conflicts. Nevertheless, depraved practices must be recognized as depraved. Even dysfunctional customs, such as single parenthood, warrant rejection. Idealism, it must be recognized, is not consistently positive. Imagined improvements can prelude actual advances. Romantic idealism is credulous. It flirts with impossible fantasies. A "critical idealism," however, examines innovative proposals with a calculating eye. It weighs the possibilities and considers alternatives. In this case, prospective changes are *carefully* considered. Whereas thoughtless enthusiasms are deadly, a go-slow approach is less likely to be. New possibilities deserve to be tested before they are widely adopted. However beneficial they seem, only experience can reveal the full extent of their effects.

In Mayor Rudy Giuliani's New York, the murder rate declined by over two-thirds in less than eight years. In his book *Leadership*, he attributes this, in large part, to the broken window theory of policing. Impressed by arguments that people obey laws when they perceive that these are taken seriously, he determined to enforce even relatively trivial ones. Where previously graffiti and panhandling were tolerated, they became the objects of a crackdown. The change this produced in the city's ambience was electric. A town the media declared ungovernable responded with unanticipated discipline. Feeling safer than previously, people began to treat each other with greater decency. No longer obliged to avert their eyes from strangers who might take offense, they began to smile at one another. Would-be crooks, moreover, were persuaded to curb their activities. The inherent uncertainties of their occupation induced them to pay attention to law enforcement agents dedicated to implementing their responsibilities. As a consequence, crime declined. The city became safer and its inhabitants more secure.

The moral of this story is that if rules are to be respected, they must be enforced. Standards that are enunciated, but never applied, are not standards. Only if their violation draws sanctions are they rules. If a society is to have morality, there must be a consensus regarding what is proscribed. When excuses are indiscriminately respected, as they were in recent years, rules cease to mean anything. A proliferation of defenses robs them of their power and efficacy. In a society in transition, where moral regulations are being renegotiated, this can be a problem. A lack of agreement provides the space for people to cheat. This does not make cheating acceptable, but it does make an honest effort at developing an accord imperative.

Sometimes, however, there is little choice. When social change is as rapid as it has been in recent decades, people may have to live with uncertainty because it is impossible to determine what is best. This has been the situation with marijuana. Its use in the United States is too new, but its effects too ambiguous for people to agree on whether it should be banned. Only time will allow them to work out their differences. Some day experience should teach us whether pot is a gateway drug or undermines motivation in a technological society. Until then the debates will rage on. What people must avoid is utopianism. Efforts to achieve perfection are, in fact, immoral. Visions of a flawless society are appealing only when the effects of specific proposals are ignored. When people are mesmerized by good intentions, they forget that what is good is so only if it makes things better. To pay no attention to the impact of one's schemes is to have a reckless disregard for human welfare. It is wrong because it substitutes fantasies for genuine satisfactions.

Cyclic Therapy

As has been repeated several times, however much society is reformed, loss and losing will not disappear. Things will continue to go wrong, and some people will do less well than others. Moreover, the relative losers will be unhappy and remain so unless they can emotionally relinquish their losses. Fortunately, because they feel trapped, some will seek relief. Yet if they look to medicine for a cure, most will be making a mistake. Since they are not suffering from a disease, a cure is not the appropriate goal. There is no colony of bacteria that will succumb to an antibiotic, no cancer that can be removed by a scalpel, and no arterial blockage available to be bypassed with a shunt. A "cure" assumes a biological state that can be rectified. When this is achieved, the patient can make a full recovery. The problem will be gone and health restored. Yet this is not the situation with personal losses.

With losing, a definitive outcome is not possible. The alterations interpersonal defeats make in the brain are to some extent permanent. They can be ameliorated, but not expunged. Nor can the circumstances that create losses be definitively removed. The social nature of what goes wrong makes challenges inevitable. The best people can do is cope. If they are able to anticipate the sorts of difficulty that arise, they can limit the damage. From time to time, they may even prevail. Nevertheless, for some the only way out is resocialization. When the damage is extensive, they may have to grieve what occurred. Many will find that this can be achieved on an informal basis, but others will require professional assistance.

Resocialization can be thought of as a species of *liberation*, rather than a cure. In letting go of what went wrong, people free themselves to move on to something better. While they cannot undo the past, they can limit its impact on the present and, as importantly, on the future. The cognitive, emotional, volitional, and social fetters that prevent unfamiliar solutions from emerging can be adjusted so that untoward consequences are reduced. The result is not euphoria, and certainly not superhuman invulnerability, but an opportunity to experiment with new strategies. In the best cases, a person learns how to win. Their future victories will not be complete, and definitely not inevitable, but the probability of success is improved.

People who have been released from the effects of losing can approach hierarchical social role and relationship negotiations with renewed vigor. No longer laboring under the assumption that defeats in previous tests of strength indicate preordained weaknesses, it becomes possible to cultivate the powers that provide successes. Now realizing that previous role partners treated them unfairly, it makes sense to seek more equitable ones. The same clearly applies to relationships. For love to be realized, it is essential to recognize who is able to supply it. All of this alters the nature of the playing field. Having become more level, losing is less likely.

Those who have been released from losses are also able to expand their knowledge and moral flexibility. No longer in need of huddling in an opaque cocoon to protect themselves from imminent threats, they are better able to see things for what they are and evaluate rules in terms of their effectiveness. This makes it possible to plan more intelligently and to collaborate with others on enforcing beneficial standards. Winning is thereby enhanced.

Nevertheless, in order to win, people must play these games well. For opportunities to be converted into victories, they must be grasped. Thus, for freedom to make a difference, it has to inspire efforts at getting stronger. If, in the wake of resocialization, renewed negotiations are carried out as ineptly as previously, these too will conclude unhappily. Social mobility, for instance, is not available to those who fail to develop an expertise that can be converted into winning tests of strength. Getting ahead depends on having power and knowing how to employ it. Emotional maturity is particularly valuable to would-be winners. An ability to control anger, manage fear, and endure sadness lays the foundation for successful interpersonal transactions, not just intimate ones. This prevents lethal conflicts, avoids unnecessary panics, and short-circuits interminable depressions. As importantly, it provides the courage to move forward. Those at the mercy of their own emotions tend to hold back. Unsure of passions they cannot predict, they hesitate to enter unknown waters.

Also of inestimable value is skill at negotiating. Interpersonal contests, in which losing is possible, can pit people against formidable opponents. Rarely do these others automatically agree to cooperate in sharing the spoils. Collaboration, when feasible, is an accomplishment. One must consequently know when to push forward and when to retreat, and when to offer a compromise and when to pummel others with threats. In some cases, one must also understand the utility of dual-concern negotiations. But these abilities take practice. No one is born with them. To be effectively persuasive, for instance, requires one to be articulate in a manner unavailable to young children.

Resocialization can be a precondition for the acquisition of essential competences. Heretofore, this process, when facilitated by a professional, has been called psychotherapy. The dictionary defines therapy as a treatment for disease. "Psychotherapy" is therefore presumably the treatment of a diseased mind. As such, it would seem an inappropriate synonym for resocialization. Nonetheless, language takes unexpected twists. What becomes conventional is not necessarily what makes literal sense. That is the situation here. The term "therapy" has become so closely associated with relinquishing losses that it is retained in what follows. This in no way, however, should be interpreted as endorsing its medical connotations.

The appropriate therapy for loss and losing, unlike most medical cures, is not a discrete event. It is not like going to a physician for a prescription to clear up acne. Because psychotherapy has been connected with the medical profession, there is an implication that a therapist's task is to make everything better. If they do their job, their client's anger should subside, anxieties be relieved, and depression be lifted. What the therapist does to achieve this is beside the point—as long as it works. Over the years, hundreds of therapies have evolved. Sometimes it seems that practitioners are dedicated to inventing unique forms of treatment merely to enhance their reputations and build their practices. In any event, in the best circumstances, these interventions take weeks, in the more intractable, months, and, in the most problematic, years. They are not, however, expected to take a lifetime. The reality can be different. Many therapies remain incomplete at death. In one of his movies, Woody Allen remarks after arising more than a century later that his analysis would almost be done had he not been asleep. This apparent interminability results from the fact that resocialization tends to occur in waves. People do not relinquish losses all at once, but in stages.

When Freud introduced the world to psychoanalysis, it was an intensive procedure. His clients came to his office for one-hour sessions, six times a week, often for years. The objective was to unearth fixations and remove them completely. Actually, Freud spoke of returning his clients to a state of normal neuroticism. He did not expect perfection, but many who sought his services did. Moreover, most of those who made the pilgrimage to his couch were upper middle class or better. They had to be because they needed to be well fixed financially to afford his fees. This was before the days of medical insurance, and treating patients was how he earned a living. It even became the practice among psychoanalysts to charge analysands for missed sessions. The rationale was that the physician made this time available to the patient and deserved to be recompensed for their time.

After Freudianism migrated across the Atlantic Ocean, modifications were instituted. Since its practitioners were still psychiatrists who expected to earn a living comparable to other doctors, psychoanalysis remained expensive. Reducing the number of weekly sessions, however, increased the number of patients seen. This was then compensated for by increasing the number of years in treatment. Eventually nonphysicians began to provide therapy, but were forced to call it "psychotherapy" in deference to Freud's insistence that only doctors be trained in his techniques. The psychologists and social workers that now entered the scene, having lesser credentials, charged less. Perceived as less qualified, they offered bargains to keep busy. Many, in order to boost their incomes, also began seeing patients in groups, ergo the advent of group therapy. They could not demand as much for this less personal treatment, but collecting fees from several individuals offset this disadvantage.

In time, the ground rules for therapy were further modified. Because the remedy was still too costly for most people, efforts were made to have it paid for by medical insurance. This was at first made workable by reducing the average number of sessions to once a week, but eventually a dramatic increase in demand made this a financial burden for the third-party payers. The problem was that where once ordinary people considered psychiatric treatment for the mentally ill, high-profile celebrity clients made seeing a "shrink" seem normal. Eventually the insurance companies rebelled. In fear of going broke, they made certain "brief" therapy came into vogue. Clients were seen for only short periods of time until their immediate complaints were resolved. If they had to come back later to address subsequent problems, that would be dealt with when it arose. For many, covering therapy, that is, strengthening a client's defenses so that she or he could cope with their daily routine, became the goal. This was a far cry from the radical personality reorganization envisioned by the field's pioneers.

Many patients were not even recommended for brief interventions. They were merely provided with medications to control their "symptoms." Some practitioners, to be sure, used psychoactive drugs as an adjunct to psychotherapy. They believed that this reduced the anxieties and depressions that interfered with therapeutic progress. Others, however, were content to relieve distress. The recourse to medications became so common that drug companies began advertising their products to the general public. Ordinary people were urged to go to their physicians to request the medications touted as correcting chemical imbalances.

A radically different way to conceive of what is appropriate in addressing personal problems is "cyclic therapy." Instead of the let's-fix-it-all approach of the early practitioners, or the let's-make-you-feel-better-for-the-moment orientation of contemporary therapists, a long-term view to coping with, and liberating people from, loss and losing is possible. Resocialization does not have to be achieved all at once. Cutting ties with what has been lost can be accomplished intermittently. Because, contrary to the early Freudians, the relevant losses are not always discrete; they cannot be extirpated as one might a wart. In order to be dealt with, they have to be split into successive parts. Individual episodes of resocialization may be relatively brief, but are an element in a larger process that possesses coherence beyond that of the moment. Moreover, the person undergoing this progression can achieve much of what needs to be accomplished. Part of what makes traditional therapy so lengthy and expensive is its dependence on professional assistance. The change process is treated as a mystery that can only be effected with expert help, hence must always be paid for. In fact, when people understand what resocialization entails, they can guide much of their own progress. They can make decisions about what to do, when to do it, and often how it is best done. Rather than be tethered to passive compliance, they can take advantage of the sweat equity of do-it-yourselfers.

This cyclic therapy is not an inferior alternative to more intense interventions. Far from second best, it is often the only way to relinquish serious instances of loss. The emotional single-mindedness of resocialization can be such as to thwart heroic efforts at mourning what cannot be retrieved. If people do not possess the strength to face their terrors all at once, there is no reason they should not be allowed to do so as they develop the potency to move forward. Nor is there a compelling rationale for forcing clients to endure the rigors of resocialization when reality demands their energies be directed elsewhere. If raising a family, or pursuing occupational success, requires postponing introspection and its accompanying emotional turmoil, why not? People can return to the process of letting go of losses when they are ready to do so. Often the best judges of what they are prepared to handle, they can determine when to do so. Even when in therapy, they are frequently best situated to determine which should be addressed. Until the moment arrives when they are voluntarily prepared to confront particular demons, they may engage in what Freud called "resistance." They stonewall their helpers and nothing happens. When they are ready, however, they accelerate the process.

Helping professionals can, of course, assist in this sequence. If they are able to recognize the nature of resocialization, they can better understand where in the process to intervene. They can explain what is happening and provide the emotional security needed to endure its terrors. Therapists, who realize that resocialization is inherently slow, with multiple troughs, can introduce a level of optimism that makes it easier to take risks. Such therapists can also place what is happening. Instead of interpreting each return for help as a separate incident, what is attempted can be linked to the larger enterprise. This makes sense of the client's misery and helps make it endurable. That a person is recognized as being in the midst of an inherently long-term process also reduces feelings of guilt. A failure to achieve immediate results need no longer be interpreted as a personal defect. Nor will an inability to attain perfection be perceived as an indicator of insufficient effort.

To be effective in facilitating resocialization, therapists must be knowledgeable and mature. They must understand how cyclic therapy works—preferably from the inside. Intellectual knowledge is useful, but pales compared with personal experience in coping with loss and losing. Unless a person has endured the pain of defeat and the agony of letting go, these may be difficult to recognize in someone else. Similarly, unless a person has succeeded in liberating himself or herself from ancient losses, it may be difficult to impart optimism. Again, most critical of all is emotional maturity. A helper who cannot manage his or her own feelings can hardly teach someone else to manage theirs. Unsocialized emotions are supersensitive. Anger, fear, or sadness that are barely under control are in danger of escaping when confronted with the intense emotions of another person. The result may be a defensiveness that impels a would-be helper to demand clients suppress what they are feeling. Rather than smooth the progress of resocialization, this stops it in its tracks. It can teach a vulnerable person that what seems dangerous is impossibly so.

In sum, cyclic therapy requires time, patience, and courage. Even then, what it achieves can be limited. Nothing can banish all the hazards of loss; these can only be reduced. Life is a perilous adventure, the dimensions of which gradually come into focus. Cyclic therapy can help a person understand his or her place in the universe, not convert it into a feather bed. Ever since human beings had the wit to travel out of Africa and conquer our planet to its furthest reaches, there have been mysteries we have been required to solve. The dimensions of our own social nature are among of these. If we have the daring to be honest about our situation, we can make it better. Not perfect, but better. If we do not, we have to take what comes.

Bibliography

Adler, A. *Understanding Human Nature.* Greenwich, CT: Fawcett, 1954.
Ainsworth, M., M. Blehar, E. Waters, and S. Wall. *Patterns of Attachment.* Hillsdale, NJ: Erlbaum, 1978.
Alexander, F. *Fundamentals of Psychoanalysis.* New York: W. W. Norton & Co., 1948.
Alexander, F. and S. Selsnick. *The History of Psychiatry.* New York: Harper & Row, 1966.
Allport, G. *The Nature of Prejudice.* Boston: Beacon Press, 1954.
Ambrose, S. E. *Nixon: The Education of a Politician 1913–1962.* New York: Simon & Schuster, 1987.
American Psychiatric Association Committee on Nomenclature and Statistics. *Diagnostic and Statistical Manual of Mental Disorders.* 2nd ed. Washington, DC, 1968.
American Psychiatric Association Task Force on DSM-IV. *Diagnostic and Statistical Manual of Mental Disorders.* 4th ed. Washington, DC, 1994.
American Psychiatric Association Task Force on Nomenclature and Statistics. *Diagnostic and Statistical Manual of Mental Disorders.* 3rd ed. Washington, DC, 1980.
Anderson, E. *Code of the Street: Decency, Violence, and the Moral Life of the Inner City.* New York: W.W. Norton & Co., 1999.
Apt, C. E. and I. R. Stuart. *The Newer Therapies: A Sourcebook.* New York: Van Nostrand Reinhold, 1982.
Aries, P. *Centuries of Childhood: A Social History of Family Life.* New York: Vintage Books, 1962.
Aristotle. *The Basic Works of Aristotle.* Edited by R. McKeon. New York: Random House, 1941.
Arnold, M. *The Nature of Emotion.* Middlesex, England: Penguin Books, 1968.
Aronson, E. *The Social Animal.* 5th ed. New York: W.H. Freeman & Co., 1988.
Augustine, Saint. *Confessions.* Translated by R. S. Pine-Coffin. New York: Dorset Press, 1961.
Ausubel, D. "Personality Disorder is Disease." In *Mental Illness and Social Process*, edited by T. Scheff. New York: Harper & Row, 1967.

Bach, G. R. and P. Wyden. *The Intimate Enemy*. New York: Avon, 1968.
Baker, P. *The Breach: Inside the Impeachment and Trial of William Jefferson Clinton*. New York: Scribner, 2000.
Bales, R. F. *Interaction Process Analysis: A Method for the Study of Small Groups*. Reading, MA: Addison-Wesley, 1950.
Bandura, A. *Social Learning Theory*. Englewood Cliffs, NJ: Prentice-Hall, 1977.
Bannister, R. C. *Social Darwinism: Science and Myth in Anglo-American Social Thought*. Philadelphia: Temple University Press, 1979.
Barlow, D. H. *Anxiety and Its Disorders: The Nature and Treatment of Anxiety and Panic*. New York: Guilford Press, 1988.
Barnard, C. *The Function of the Executive*. Cambridge, MA: Harvard University Press, 1938.
Barnes, B. *The Nature of Power*. Chicago: University of Illinois Press, 1988.
Baron-Cohen, S. *The Essential Difference: The Truth about the Male and Female Brain*. New York: Basic Books, 2003.
Bateson, G. *Steps to an Ecology of Mind*. New York: Ballantine Books, 1972.
Bauer, G. P. and J. C. Kobos. *Brief Therapy: Short-Term Psychodynamic Intervention*. Northvale, NJ: Jason Aronson, 1987.
Baum, L. F. *The Wonderful Wizard of Oz*. Chicago: George M. Hill, Co., 1900.
Beattie, M. *Codependent No More*. San Francisco: Harper & Row, 1987.
Beck, A. *Cognitive Therapy and the Emotional Disorders*. New York: International Universities Press, 1976.
Becker, H. *The Outsiders*. New York: Free Press, 1963.
_____. *The Other Side: Perspectives on Deviance*. New York: Free Press, 1964.
_____. *Sociological Work: Method and Substance*. Chicago: Aldine Publishing Co., 1970.
Belenky, M. F., et al. *Women's Ways of Knowing: The Development of Self, Voice and Mind*. New York: Basic Books, 1988.
Bellah, R. N., R. Madsen, W. M. Sullivan, A. Swindler, and S. M. Tipton. *Habits of the Heart: Individualism and Commitment in American Life*. Berkeley, CA: University of California Press, 1985.
Bennett, A. *The Madness of King George III*. London: Faber and Faber, 1995.
Bennett, W. J., ed. *The Book of Virtues: A Treasury of Great Moral Stories*. New York: Simon & Schuster, 1993.
Berger, D. *Clinical Empathy*. Northvale, NJ: Jason Aronson, 1987.
Berger, M. M., ed. *Beyond the Double Bind*. New York: Brunner/Mazel, 1978.

Best, J. *Damned Lies and Statistics: Untangling Numbers from the Media, Politicians, and Activists.* Berkeley, CA: University of California Press, 2001.
Bettleheim, B. *Love Is Not Enough.* New York: Free Press, 1950.
_____. *A Good Enough Parent.* New York: Alfred A. Knopf, 1987.
Blankenhorn, D. *Fatherless America: Confronting Our Most Urgent Social Problem.* New York: Basic Books, 1995.
Blyth, M. *Spin Sisters: How the Women of the Media Sell Unhappiness and Liberalism to the Women of America.* New York: St. Martin's Press, 2004.
Boas, F. *Anthropology and Modern Life.* New York: Dover Publishers, 1928.
Boehm, C. *Hierarchy in the Forest: The Evolution of Egalitarian Behavior.* Cambridge, MA: Harvard University Press, 1999.
Boone, J. L. "Competition, Conflicts and the Development of Social Hierarchies." In *Evolutionary Ecology and Human Behavior*, edited by E. Smith and B. Winterhalter. New York: Aldine de Gruyter, 1992.
_____. "Status Signaling, Social Power, and Lineage Survival." In *Hierarchies in Action: Cui Bono?*, edited by M. W. Diehl. Carbondale, IL: Center for Archaeological Investigations, 2000.
Boswell, R. B. *The Kindness of Strangers.* New York: Pantheon Books, 1988.
Bowlby, J. *Attachment.* New York: Basic Books, 1969.
_____. *Separation: Anxiety and Anger.* New York: Basic Books, 1973.
_____. *Loss: Sadness and Depression.* New York: Basic Books, 1980.
_____. *Charles Darwin: A New Life.* New York: W.W. Norton & Co., 1990.
Breuer, J. and S. Freud. *Studies on Hysteria.* New York: Basic Books, 1957.
Brim, O. and J. Kagen, eds. *Constancy and Change in Human Development.* Cambridge, MA: Harvard University Press, 1980.
Brooks, D. *Bobos in Paradise: The New Upper Class and How They Got There.* New York: Simon & Schuster, 2000.
Brown, G. and T. Harris. *Social Origins of Depression.* New York: Free Press, 1978.
Brownmiller, S. *Against Our Will: Men, Women and Rape.* New York: Bantam, 1975.
Buckley, K. W. *Mechanical Man: John Broadus Watson and the Beginnings of Behaviorism.* New York: Guilford Press, 1989.
Butterfield, F. *All God's Children: The Bosket Family and the Tradition of Violence.* New York: Alfred A. Knopf, 1995.
Cannon, W. B. *Bodily Changes in Pain, Hunger, Fear and Rage: An Account of Recent Research on the Function of Emotional Excitement.* New York: Appleton-Century-Crofts, 1929.

Cassidy, J. and P. R. Shaver. *Handbook of Attachment: Theory Research and Clinical Applications.* New York: Guilford Press, 1999.

Cavalli-Sforza, L., P. Menozzi, and A. Piazza. *The History and Geography of Human Genes.* Princeton, NJ: Princeton University Press, 1994.

Cherlin, A. J. *Marriage, Divorce, and Remarriage.* Cambridge, MA: Harvard University Press, 1992.

Chess, S. and A. Thomas. *Temperament in Clinical Practice.* New York: Guilford Press, 1986.

Chirot, D. *Social Change in the Modern Era.* New York: Harcourt, Brace, Jovanovich, 1986.

_____. *Modern Tyrants.* Princeton, NJ: Princeton University Press, 1994.

Chong, D. *Rational Lives: Norms and Values in Politics and Society.* Chicago: University of Chicago Press, 2000.

Christensen, H. T., ed. *Handbook of Marriage and the Family.* Chicago: Rand, McNally, 1964.

Claster, D. S. *Good Guys and Bad Guys: Moral Polarization and Crime.* Westport, CT: Greenwood, 1992.

Clausen, J., ed. *Socialization and Society.* Boston: Little, Brown and Co., 1968.

Clausewitz, C. *On War.* New York: Penguin Books, 1908.

Clinard, M. *Sociology of Deviant Behavior.* New York: Holt, Rinehart and Winston, 1968.

Cockerham, William C. *The Sociology of Mental Disorder.* 8th ed. Upper Saddle River, NJ: Prentice-Hall, 2011.

Coleman, J. S., E. Q. Campbell, C. J. Hobson, J. McPartland, A. M. Mood, F. D. Weinfeld, and R. L. York. *Equality of Educational Opportunity.* Washington, DC: U.S. Government Printing Office, 1966.

Collins, R. and M. Makowsky. *The Discovery of Society.* 5th ed. New York: McGraw-Hill, 1993.

Coltrane, S. *Family Man: Fatherhood, Housework, and Gender Equity.* New York: Oxford University Press, 1996.

Conrad, P. *The Medicalization of Society.* Baltimore: Johns Hopkins University Press, 2007.

Cooley, C. H. *Human Nature and the Social Order.* Glencoe, IL: Free Press, 1956.

Coontz, S. *The Way We Never Were: American Families and the Nostalgia Trap.* New York: Basic Books, 1992.

Corsini, R. *Roleplaying in Psychotherapy: A Manual.* Chicago: Aldine Publishing Co., 1966.

Corsini, R. and D. Wedding, eds. *Current Psychotherapies.* 4th ed. Itasca, IL: F.E. Peacock Publishers, 1989.

Coser, R. *Training in Ambiguity: Learning through Doing in a Mental Hospital.* New York: Free Press, 1979.

Cotter, S. and J. Guerra. *Assertion Training.* Chicago: Research Press, 1976.
Critchlow, D. T. and E. W. Hawley, eds. *Poverty and Public Policy in America.* Chicago: Dorsey Press, 1989.
Cronk, L. *That Complex Whole: Culture and the Evolution of Human Behavior.* Boulder, CO: Westview Press, 1999.
Cronk, L., N. Chanon, and W. Irons, eds. *Adaptation and Human Behavior: An Anthropological Perspective.* New York: Aldine de Gruyter, 2000.
Crozier, M. *The Bureaucratic Phenomenon.* Chicago: University of Chicago Press, 1964.
Cumston, C. G. *The History of Medicine.* New York: Dorset Press, 1987.
Dahrendorf, R. *Class and Class Conflict in Industrial Society.* Stanford, CA: Stanford University Press, 1959.
Dalrymple, T. *Life at the Bottom: The Worldview that Makes the Underclass.* Chicago: Ivan R. Dee, 2001.
Dalton, M. *Men Who Manage.* New York: John Wiley & Sons, Inc., 1959.
Darwin, C. *The Expression of Emotions in Man and Animals.* Chicago: University of Chicago Press, 1965.
_____. *The Descent of Man, and Selection in Relation to Sex.* Detroit: Gale Research, 1974.
Dash, L. *Rosa Lee: A Mother and Her Family in Urban America.* New York: Basic Books, 1996.
Davis, K. and W. Moore. "Some Principles of Stratification." *American Sociological Review* 10 (1945): 242–49.
Davis, M. *Intimate Relations.* New York: Free Press, 1973.
Denzin, N. R. *On Understanding Emotion.* San Francisco: Jossey-Bass, 1984.
Desroche, H. *The American Shakers: From Neo-Christianity to Presocialism.* Amherst: University of Massachusetts Press, 1971.
Deutsch, M. and M. E. Collins. *Interracial Housing: A Psychological Evaluation of a Social Experiment.* Minneapolis: University of Minnesota Press, 1951.
Diamond, J. *Guns, Germs, and Steel: The Fates of Human Societies.* New York: W.W. Norton and Co., 1997.
Diehl, M. W. *Hierarchies in Action: Cui Bono?* Carbondale, IL: Center for Archaeological Investigations, 2000.
Dollard, J. R., L. W. Doob, N. E. Miller, and R. R. Sears. *Frustration and Aggression.* New Haven, CT: Yale University Press, 1939.
Donnelly, M. *Managing the Mind: A Study of Medical Psychology in Early Nineteenth Century Britain.* London: Tavistock Publications, 1983.
Dorpat, T. L. *Denial and Defense in the Therapeutic Situation.* New York: Jason Aronson, 1985.

Dreitzel, H. P., ed. *Family, Marriage and the Struggle of the Sexes.* New York: MacMillan, 1972.
Drinka, G. F. *The Birth of Neurosis: Myth, Malady and the Victorians.* New York: Simon & Schuster, 1984.
Dunbar, R., C. Knight, and C. Power, eds. *The Evolution of Culture.* New Brunswick, NJ: Rutgers University Press, 1999.
Dunning, A. J. *Extremes: Reflections on Human Behavior.* New York: Harcourt, Brace, Jovanovich, 1990.
Durkheim, E. *The Elementary Forms of Religious Life.* New York: Free Press, 1915.
_____. *The Division of Labor in Society.* New York: Free Press, 1933.
_____. *Moral Education.* New York: Free Press, 1961.
Dutton, D. G. *The Abusive Personality: Violence and Control in Intimate Relationships.* New York: Guilford Press, 1998.
Dyer, W. *Pulling Your Own Strings.* New York: Crowell Co., 1978.
Eaton, William E. *The Sociology of Mental Disorders.* 2nd ed. New York: Praeger Publishing, 1986.
Elias, N. *On Civilization, Power, and Knowledge.* Edited by Stephen Mennell and Johan Goudsblom. Chicago: University of Chicago Press, 1998.
Ellenbogen, G. C., ed. *Oral Sadism and the Vegetarian Personality.* New York: Brunner/Mazel, 1986.
Ellis, A. *Reason and Emotion in Psychotherapy.* Secaucus, NJ: Lyle Stewart, 1962.
Engels, F. *The Origin of the Family, Private Property, and the State.* New York: International Publishers, 1972.
Entine, J. *Taboo: Why Black Athletes Dominate Sports and Why We're Afraid to Talk About It.* New York: Public Affairs, 2000.
Entwisle, D. R., K. L. Alexander, and L. S. Olson. *Children, Schools and Inequality.* Boulder, CO: Westview Press, 1997.
Epstein, C. F. *Woman's Place: Options and Limits in Professional Careers.* Berkeley, CA: University of California Press, 1970.
Epstein, J. *Snobbery: The American Version.* Boston: Houghton Mifflin Co., 2002.
Erikson, E. *Childhood and Society.* New York: W.W. Norton & Co., 1950.
_____. *Insight and Responsibility.* New York: W.W. Norton & Co., 1964.
_____. *Identity: Youth and Crisis.* New York: W.W. Norton & Co., 1968.
Erikson, K. *Notes on the Sociology of Deviance.* In *The Other Side: Perspectives on Deviance,* edited by H. Becker. New York: Free Press, 1964.
Faludi, S. *Backlash: The Undeclared War against American Women.* New York: Crown Publishers, 1991.

Fein, M. *Role Change: A Resocialization Perspective.* New York: Praeger, 1990.
———. *Analyzing Psychotherapy: A Social Role Perspective.* New York: Praeger, 1992.
———. *I.A.M.: A Common Sense Guide to Coping with Anger.* Westport, CT: Praeger, 1993.
———. *Hardball without an Umpire: The Sociology of Morality.* Westport, CT: Praeger, 1997.
———. *The Limits of Idealism: When Good Intentions Go Bad.* New York: Kluwer/Plenum, 1999.
———. *Race and Morality: How Good Intentions Undermine Social Justice and Perpetuate Inequality.* New York: Kluwer/Plenum, 2001.
———. *Peoplization: An Introduction to Social Life.* Dubuque: Kendall-Hunt, 2007.
Fenster, B. *Duh!: The Stupid History of the Human Race.* Kansas City: Andrew McMeel Publishing, 2000.
Festinger, L. *A Theory of Cognitive Dissonance.* Evanston, IL: Row, Peterson, 1957.
Festinger, L., H. W. Rieken, and S. Schacter. *When Prophesy Fails.* New York: Harper & Row, 1964.
Fisher, H. E. *The Sex Contract: The Evolution of Human Behavior.* New York: William Morrow and Co., 1982.
———. *Anatomy of Love: The Natural History of Monogamy, Adultery and Divorce.* New York: W.W. Norton & Co., 1992
Foucault, Michel. *Discipline and Punish: The Birth of the Prison.* New York: Random House, 1979.
———. *Madness and Civilization: A History of Insanity in the Age of Reason.* New York: Random House, 1982.
Fox-Genovese, E. *Feminism Is Not the Story of My Life: How Today's Feminist Elite Has Lost Touch with the Real Concerns of Women.* New York: Doubleday, 1996.
Frank, J. "The Role of Influence in Psychotherapy." In *Contemporary Psychotherapies*, edited by M. Stein. New York: Free Press of Glencoe, 1961.
———. *Persuasion and Healing; A Comparative Study of Psychotherapy.* Baltimore: Johns Hopkins Press, 1973.
Frank, R. *Passions with Reasons: The Strategic Role of the Emotions.* New York: W.W. Norton & Co., 1988.
Frank, S. A. *Foundations of Social Evolution.* Princeton, NJ: Princeton University Press, 1998.
Franks, D. and D. McCarthy, eds. *Sociology of Emotions.* New York: JAI Press, 1989.
Fraser, A. *King Charles II.* London: Weidenfeld and Nicolson, 1979.
Frattaroli, E. *Healing the Soul in the Age of the Brain: Becoming Conscious in an Unconscious World.* New York: Viking, 2001.

Freeman, L. and H. S. Strean. *Freud and Women*. New York: Frederick Ungar Publishing, 1981.
French, M. *The War against Women*. New York: Summit Books, 1992.
Freud, A. *The Ego and the Mechanisms of Defense*. New York: International Universities Press, 1966.
Freud, S. *The Standard Edition of the Complete Psychological Works of Sigmund Freud*. Edited by J. Strachey. London: Hogarth Press and Institute for Psychoanalysis, 1953–1974.
Friedan, B. *The Feminine Mystique*. New York: W.W. Norton & Co., 1963.
Frijda, N. H. *The Emotions*. Cambridge: Cambridge University Press, 1987.
Fritz, J. *The Clinical Sociology Handbook*. New York: Garland, 1985.
Fukuyama, F. *Trust: The Social Virtues and the Creation of Prosperity*. New York: Free Press, 1995.
_____. *The Great Disruption: Human Nature and the Reconstitution of Social Order*. New York: Free Press, 1999.
Fussell, P. *Class: A Guide through the American Status System*. New York: Simon & Schuster, 1983.
Galileo. *Galileo on the World Systems*. Berkeley, CA: University of California Press, 1997.
Gallant, D. M. *Alcoholism: A Guide to Diagnosis, Intervention, and Treatment*. New York: W.W. Norton & Co., 1987.
Garbarino, J., C. J. Schellenbach, and J. Sebes. *Troubled Youth, Troubled Families*. New York: Aldine de Gruyter, 1986.
Gardner, M. *Fads and Fallacies in the Name of Science*. New York: Dover, 1957.
_____. *Did Adam and Eve Have Navels?: Debunking Pseudoscience*. New York: W.W. Norton & Co., 2000.
_____. *Are Universes Thicker than Blackberries?* New York: W.W. Norton & Co., 2003.
Gay, P. *Freud: A Life for Our Time*. New York: W.W. Norton & Co., 1988.
Gelles, R. J. *Intimate Violence in Families*. 3rd ed. Beverly Hills: Sage Publications, 1997.
Gelles, R. J. and M. A. Straus. *Intimate Violence: The Causes and Consequences of Abuse in the American Family*. New York: Touchstone Books, 1989.
Gerth, H. and C. W. Mills, eds. *From Max Weber: Essays in Sociology*. New York: Oxford University Press, 1946.
Gilligan, C. *In a Different Voice*. Cambridge, MA: Harvard University Press, 1982.
Giuliani, R. W. *Leadership*. New York: Miramax Books, 2002.
Gladwell, M. *The Tipping Point: How Little Things Can Make a Big Difference*. Boston: Little, Brown and Co., 2000.
Glasser, W. *Reality Therapy*. New York: Harper & Row, 1965.

Glendon, M. A. and D. Blankenhorn, eds. *Seedbeds of Virtue: Sources of Competence, Character, and Citizenship in American Society.* Lanham, MD: Madison Books, 1995.
Goffman, Erving. *The Presentation of Self in Everyday Life.* Garden City: Doubleday, 1959.
_____. *Asylums.* New York: Anchor, 1961.
_____. *Stigma.* Englewood Cliffs, NJ: Prentice-Hall, 1963.
Goleman, D. *Emotional Intelligence: Why It Can Matter More Than IQ.* New York: Bantam Books, 1995.
Goode, E. and N. Ben-Yehuda. *Moral Panics: The Social Construction of Deviance.* Cambridge: Blackwell, 1994.
Gottfredson, M. R. and T. Hirschi. *A General Theory of Crime.* Stanford, CA: Stanford University Press, 1990.
Gouldner, A. W. "The Norm of Reciprocity." *American Sociological Review* 25 (1960): 161–78.
Gove, W., ed. *Deviance and Mental Illness.* Beverly Hills: Sage Publications, 1982.
Graglia, F. C. *Domestic Tranquility: A Brief against Feminism.* Dallas, TX: Spence Publishing Co., 1998.
Green, R. *The Sissy Boy Syndrome and the Development of Homosexuality.* New Haven, CT: Yale University Press, 1987.
Greenberg, D. F. *The Construction of Homosexuality.* Chicago: University of Chicago Press, 1988.
Greenberg, L. and J. Safran. *Emotion in Psychotherapy.* New York: Guilford Press, 1987.
Greer, C. and H. Kohl. *A Call to Character.* New York: HarperCollins, 1995.
Griswold, W. *Cultures and Societies in a Changing World.* Thousand Oaks: Pine Forge Press, 1994.
Gut, E. *Productive and Unproductive Depression: Success or Failure of a Vital Process.* New York: Basic Books, 1989.
Guze, S. B. *Why Psychiatry Is a Branch of Medicine.* New York: Oxford University Press, 1992.
Handel, G., ed. *The Psychosocial Interior of the Family: A Sourcebook for the Study of Whole Families.* Chicago: Aldine-Atherton, 1967.
Hanson, V. D. *Carnage and Culture: Landmark Battles in the Rise of Western Power.* New York: Doubleday, 2001.
_____. *Mexifornia: A State of Being.* San Francisco: Encounter Books, 2003.
Harrison, L. E. and S. P. Huntington, eds. *Culture Matters: How Values Shape Human Progress.* New York: Basic Books, 2000.
Haskins, J. *A New Kind of Joy: The Story of the Special Olympics.* Garden City, NY: Doubleday, 1976.
Hawke, D. F. *Benjamin Rush: Revolutionary Gadfly.* Indianapolis: Bobbs-Merrill, 1971.
Hayek, F. A. *The Fatal Conceit: The Errors of Socialism.* Chicago: University of Chicago Press, 1988.

Henry, J. *Culture against Man*. New York: Vintage Books, 1963.
Herink, R. *The Psychotherapy Handbook: The A to Z Guide to More Than 250 Different Therapies in Use Today*. New York: New American Library, 1980.
Herrnstein, R. J. and C. Murray. *The Bell Curve: The Reshaping of American Life by Differences in Intelligence*. New York: Basic Books, 1994.
Herson, M., A. E. Kardin, and A. S. Bellack, eds. *The Clinical Psychology Handbook*. New York: Pergamon Press, 1983.
Hewitt, J. P. *The Myth of Self-Esteem: Finding Happiness and Solving Problems in America*. New York: St. Martin's Press, 1998.
Himmelfarb, G. *The De-Moralization of Society: From Victorian Virtues to Modern Values*. New York: Alfred A. Knopf, 1995.
Hobbes, T. *Leviathan; Part I*. Chicago: Henry Regnery Co., 1956.
Hobson, J. A. *Out of Its Mind: Psychiatry in Crisis*. New York: Perseus Publishing, 2001.
Hochschild, A. R. *The Managed Heart: Commercialization of Human Feeling*. Berkeley, CA: University of California Press, 1983.
Hochschild, J. *Facing Up to the American Dream*. Princeton, NJ: Princeton University Press, 1995.
Hollingshead, A. and F. Redlich. *Social Class and Mental Health*. New York: John Wiley & Sons, Inc., 1958.
Holmes, T. H. and R. H. Rahe. "The Social Readjustment Scale." *Journal of Psychosomatic Research* 11 (1967): 213–18.
Horney, K. *Our Inner Conflicts: A Constructive Theory of Neuroses*. New York: W.W. Norton & Co., 1945.
Horowitz, D. *Betty Friedan and the Making of the Feminine Mystique*. Amherst: University of Massachusetts Press, 1998.
Horwitz, A. V. *The Social Control of Mental Illness*. New York: Academic Press, 1982.
———. *Creating Mental Illness*. Chicago: University of Chicago Press, 2002.
Horwitz, A. V. and T. L. Scheid, eds. *A Handbooks for the Study of Mental Health: Social Contexts, Theories and Systems*. New York: Cambridge University Press, 1999.
Horwitz, A. V. and J. C. Wakefield. *The Loss of Sadness*. New York: Oxford University Press, 2007.
Howard, P. K. *The Lost Art of Drawing the Line: How Fairness Went Too Far*. New York: Random House, 2001.
Hughes, R. *Culture of Complaint: The Fraying of America*. New York: Oxford University Press, 1993.
Hunter, J. D. *The Death of Character: Moral Education in an Age without Good and Evil*. New York: Basic Books, 2000.
Hurst, C. E. *Social Inequality: Forms, Causes, and Consequences*. 2nd ed. Boston: Allyn and Bacon, 1995.
Iuppa, N. *Management by Guilt*. Belmont, CA: Pitman Press, 1985.

Izard, C. *Human Emotions*. New York: Plenum Press, 1977.
Jagger, A. M. *Feminist Politics and Human Nature*. Totowa, NJ: Rowman & Littlefield, 1988.
James, W. *The Principles of Psychology*. New York: Dover, 1950.
Janov, A. *The Primal Scream, Primal Therapy: The Cure for Neurosis*. New York: G.H. Putnam and Sons, 1970.
Jencks, C. *Rethinking Social Policy: Race, Poverty and the Underclass*. Cambridge, MA: Harvard University Press, 1992.
_____. *The Homeless: Rethinking Social Policy*. Cambridge, MA: Harvard University Press, 1994.
Jourard, S. M. *The Transparent Self: Self Disclosure and Well Being*. Princeton, NJ: Van Norstrand, 1964.
Jung, C. G. *Collected Works*. Edited by H. Read, M. Fordham, and G. Adler. Princeton, NJ: Princeton University Press, 1953–1978.
Kagan, J. *The Nature of the Child*. New York: Basic Books, 1984.
Kagan, J. and S. Lamb, eds. *The Emergence of Morality in Young Children*. Chicago: University of Chicago Press, 1987.
Kantor, D. and W. Lehr. *Inside the Family*. San Francisco: Jossey-Bass, 1973.
Katz, L. D., ed. *Evolutionary Origins of Morality: Cross-Disciplinary Perspectives*. Bowling Green, OH: Imprint Academic, 2000.
Kemper, T. D. *A Social Interactionist Theory of Emotions*. New York: John Wiley & Sons, Inc., 1978.
Kendall, P. M. *Louis XI: The Universal Spider*. New York: W.W. Norton & Co., 1971.
Kennedy, D. B. and A. Kerber *Resocialization: An American Experiment*. New York: Behavioral Publications, 1973.
Kirk, S. A. and H. Kutchins. *The Selling of DSM: The Rhetoric of Science in Psychiatry*. New York: Aldine de Gruyter, 1992.
Klama, J. *Aggression: The Myth of the Beast Within*. New York: John Wiley & Sons, Inc., 1988.
Klein, R. G. and B. Elgar. *The Dawn of Human Culture: A Bold New Theory on What Sparked the "Big Bang" of Human Consciousness*. New York: John Wiley & Sons, Inc., 2002.
Kluckhohn, C. and H. A. Murray, eds. *Personality in Nature, Society and Culture*. New York: Alfred A. Knopf, 1948.
Kohlberg, L. *Stage and Sequence: The Cognitive Developmental Approach to Socialization*. In *Handbook of Socialization Theory and Research*, edited by D. Goslin. Chicago: Rand McNally, 1969.
_____. *The Philosophy of Moral Development: Moral Stages and the Idea of Justice*. New York: Harper & Row, 1981.
Kohn, B. *Journalistic Fraud: How the New York Times Distorts the News and Why It Can No Longer Be Trusted*. Nashville: WND Books, 2003.
Kohn, M. L. *Class and Conformity: A Study in Values*. Homewood, IL: Dorsey Press, 1969.

Kohn, M. L. and C. Schooler. *Work and Personality: An Inquiry into the Impact of Social Stratification*. Norwood, NJ: Ablex Publishing, 1983.
Kohut, H. *The Restoration of the Self.* New York: International Universities Press, 1977.
Komarovsky, M. and J. H. Phillips. *Blue Collar Marriage*. New York: Vintage, 1967.
Kramer, P. D. *Listening to Prozac: A Psychiatrist Explores Antidepressant Drugs and the Remaking of the Self.* New York: Viking, 1993.
Kubler-Ross, E. *On Death and Dying*. New York: MacMillan, 1969.
Kuhn, T. S. *The Structure of Scientific Revolutions*. 2nd ed. Chicago: University of Chicago Press, 1970.
Kurtines, W. M. and J. L. Gewirtz, eds. *Moral Development through Social Interaction*. New York: John Wiley & Sons, Inc., 1987.
Kutash, I. and L. Schlesinger, eds. *Handbook on Stress and Anxiety*. San Francisco: Jossey-Bass, 1980.
Laing, R. D. *The Divided Self.* London: Tavistock, 1960.
Lantham, R., ed. *The Illustrated Pepys: Extracts from the Diary*. Berkeley, CA: University of California Press, 1983.
Lazarus, R. A. *Emotion and Adaptation*. New York: Oxford University Press, 1991.
Leaky, R. *The Making of Mankind*. London: Michael Joseph Ltd., 1981.
Leary, M. *Understanding Social Anxiety: Social, Personality and Clinical Perspectives*. Beverly Hills: Sage Publications, 1983.
Leifer, R. *In the Name of Mental Health*. New York: Science, 1969.
Lever, J. "Sex Differences in the Games Children Play." *Social Problems* 23 (1976): 478–87.
Lewin, K. *Field Theory in Social Science: Selected Theoretical Papers*. Edited by D. Cartwright. Chicago: University of Chicago Press, 1951.
Lewis, M. and C. Saarni, eds. *The Socialization of Emotions*. New York: Plenum Press, 1985.
Lewontin, R., S. Rose, and L. Kamin. *Not in Our Genes: Biological Ideologies and Human Nature*. New York: Pantheon Books, 1984.
Lidz, T. *The Person: His and Her Development through the Life Cycle*. New York: Basic Books, 1968.
Lindzey, G. and E. Aronson, eds. *Handbook of Social Psychology*. 3rd ed. New York: Random House, 1985.
Linton, R. *The Study of Man*. New York: Appleton-Century-Crofts, 1936.
Loewen, J. W. *Lies My Teacher Told Me: Everything Your American History Textbook Got Wrong*. New York: The New Press, 1995.
Lofland, L. H. *A World of Strangers*. New York: Basic Books, 1973.
Lomborg, B. *The Skeptical Environmentalist: Measuring the Real State of the World*. New York: Cambridge University Press, 2001.

London, P. *The Modes and Morals of Psychotherapy*. New York: Holt, Rinehart and Winston, 1964.
Lorber, J. *Paradoxes of Gender*. New Haven, CT: Yale University Press, 1994.
Lorenz, K. *On Aggression*. London: Metheun, 1966.
Lowery, R. *Legacy: Paying the Price for the Clinton Years*. Washington, DC: Regnery Publishing, 2003.
Ludwig, A. M. *King of the Mountain: The Nature of Political Leadership*. Lexington: University of Kentucky Press, 2002.
Lundberg, G. D. *Severed Trust: Why American Medicine Hasn't Been Fixed*. New York: Basic Books, 2000.
Lynch, F. R. *The Diversity Machine*. New York: Free Press, 1997.
Lynd, H. M. *On Shame and the Search for Identity*. New York: Harcourt, Brace and World, 1958.
Lynn, D. B. *The Father: His Role in Child Development*. Monterey, CA: Brooks/Cole, 1974.
Maccoby, E. E., ed. *The Development of Sex Differences*. Stanford: Stanford University Press, 1966.
MacDonald, H. *The Burden of Bad Ideas: How Modern Intellectuals Misshape Our Society*. Chicago: Ivan R. Dee, 2000.
_____. *Are Cops Racist?: How the Wear against the Police Harms Black Americans*. Chicago: Ivan R. Dee, 2003.
MacDougall, H. A. *Racial Myth and English History: Trojans, Teutons and Anglo-Saxons*. Hanover, NH: University Press of New England, 1982.
MacKinnon, C. A. *Feminism Unmodified: Discourses on Life and Law*. Cambridge, MA: Harvard University Press, 1987.
MacMillan, M. *Paris 1919: Six Months that Changed the World*. New York: Random House, 2001.
Majors, R. and J. M. Billson. *The Cool Pose: The Dilemma of Black Manhood in America*. New York: Simon & Schuster, 1993.
Mann, W. E. *The Man Who Dreamed of Tomorrow: A Conceptual Biography of Wilhelm Reich*. Los Angeles: J.P. Tarcher, 1980.
Manuel, F. E. and F. P. Manuel. *Utopian Thought in the Western World*. Cambridge, MA: Belknap Press, 1979.
Maslow, A. *Motivation and Personality*. New York: Harper & Row, 1954.
McClelland, D. *Power: The Inner Experience*. New York: Irvington Pub, 1975.
McHugh, P. "Social Disintegration as a Requisite of Resocialization." *Social Forces*, XLIV (March 1966): 355–63.
McNally, R. J. *Remembering Trauma*. Cambridge, MA: Harvard University Press, 2003.
Mead, G. H. *Mind, Self and Society*. Chicago: University of Chicago Press, 1934.
Mead, M. *Coming of Age in Samoa*. New York: William Morrow and Co., 1928.

Mechanic, D. *Mental Health and Social Policy*. Englewood Cliffs, NJ: Prentice-Hall, 1969.
Merton, R. *Social Theory and Social Structure*. New York: Free Press, 1949.
Meyers, N. *The Sinking Ark: A New Look at the Problem of Disappearing Species*. New York: Pergamon Press, 1979.
Michael, R. T., J. H. Gagnon, E. O. Laumann, and G. Kolata. *Sex in America: A Definitive Study*. New York: Warner Books, 1994.
Michels, R. *Political Parties*. Translated by Eden Paul and Cedar Paul. New York: Crowell-Collier, 1962.
Millon, T. and G. L. Klerman. *Contemporary Directions in Psychotherapy: Toward the DSM-IV*. New York: Guilford Press, 1986.
Mirowsky, John and Catherine E. Ross. *Social Causes of Psychological Distress*. New York: Aldine de Gruyter, 1989.
Mischel, W. *Personality and Assessment*. New York: John Wiley & Sons, Inc., 1968.
Moir, A. and D. Jessel. *Brain Sex: The Real Difference between Men and Women*. New York: Delta, 1989.
Money, J. and A. Ehrhardt. *Man and Woman; Boy and Girl*. Baltimore: Johns Hopkins Press, 1972.
Moynihan, D. P. "Defining Deviancy Down." *American Scholar* (1993): 17–30.
Murray, C. *Losing Ground: American Social Policy*. New York: Basic Books, 1986.
Murray, H. A. *Explorations in Personality*. New York: Oxford University Press, 1938.
Nichols, M. P. *The Self in the System: Expanding the Limits of Family Therapy*. New York: Brunner/Mazel, 1987.
Nietzsche, F. *Beyond Good and Evil*. Translated by Helen Zimmern. Amherst, NY: Prometheus Books, 1989.
Norris, C. *Against Relativism: Philosophy of Science, Deconstruction and Critical Theory*. Oxford, UK: Blackwell Publishers, 1997.
Nye, F. I. *Role Structure and the Analysis of the Family*. Beverly Hills: Sage Publications, 1976.
_____, ed. *Family Relationships: Rewards and Costs*. Beverly Hills: Sage Publications, 1982.
Ogbu, J. U. *The Next Generation: An Ethnography of Education in an Urban School*. New York: Academic Press, 1974.
Ogburn, W. *Social Change with Respect to Culture and Original Nature*. New York: Heubsch, [1922] 1966.
Olasky, M. *The Tragedy of American Compassion*. Washington, DC: Regnery Publishing, 1992.
Oliver, W. *The Violent Social World of Black Men*. New York: Lexington Books, 1994.
Olson, S. *Mapping Human History: Discovering the Past through Our Genes*. Boston: Houghton Mifflin Co., 2000.

Olson, W. K. *The Rule of Lawyers: How the New Litigation Elite Threatens America's Rule of Law*. New York: St. Martin's Press, 2002.
Pareto, V. *The Rise and Fall of Elites: An Application of Theoretical Sociology*. New Brunswick, NJ: Transaction Publishers, 1991.
Park, R. *Race and Culture*. Glencoe, IL: Free Press, 1950.
Parsons, T. *Social Structure and Personality*. New York: MacMillan, 1970.
Parsons, T. and R. F. Bales. *Family, Socialization and Interaction Process*. New York: Free Press, 1955.
Pattice, F. A. *Mesmer and Animal Magnetism: A Chapter in the History of Medicine*. Hamilton, NY: Edmonston Pub, 1994.
Payne, R. *The Rise and Fall of Stalin*. New York: Avon Books, 1965.
Perls, F. *Gestalt Therapy Verbatim*. New York: Bantam Books, 1969.
Piaget, J. *The Moral Judgment of the Child*. New York: Free Press, 1969.
_____. *The Construction of Reality in the Child*. New York: Ballantine Books, 1971.
Pinel, P. *A Treatise on Insanity*. Birmingham, AL: Classics in Medicine Library, 1983.
Pinker, S. *The Language Instinct: How the Mind Creates Language*. New York: William Morrow and Co., 1994.
_____. *How the Mind Works*. New York: W.W. Norton & Co., 1997.
_____. *The Blank Slate: The Modern Denial of Human Nature*. New York: Viking, 2002.
Plato *The Works of Plato*. Translated by Jowett. New York: The Modern Library, 1928.
Plato *The Republic*. Translated by Jowett. New York: The Modern Library, 1941.
Popenoe, D. *Life Without Father: Compelling New Evidence that Fatherhood and Marriage Are Indispensable for the Good of Children and Society*. New York: Free Press, 1996.
Popper, K. R. *The Logic of Scientific Discovery*. London: Hutchinson & Co., 1959.
Potter, J. M. "Ritual, Power, and Social Differentiation in Small-Scale Societies." In *Hierarchies in Action: Cui Bono?*, edited by M. W. Diehl. Carbondale, IL: Center for Archaeological Investigations, 2000.
Pruitt, D. G. *Negotiation Behavior*. New York: Academic, 1981.
_____. "Strategic Choice in Negotiation." *American Behavioral Scientist* 27, no. 22 (1983): 167–94.
Ravitch, D. *Left Back: A Century of Failed School Reforms*. New York: Simon & Schuster, 2000.
_____. *The Language Police: How Pressure Groups Restrict What Students Learn*. New York: Alfred A. Knopf, 2003.
Rawls, J. *A Theory of Justice*. Cambridge, MA: Belknap Press, 1971.
Rebach, H. M. and J. G. Bruhn, eds. *Clinical Sociology: An Agenda for Action*. New York: Plenum Publishing, 1991.

Rhode, D. *Speaking of Sex: The Denial of Gender Inequality.* Cambridge, MA: Harvard University Press, 1997.
Rieff, P. *Freud: The Mind of a Moralist.* Garden City, NY: Doubleday Anchor, 1961.
Roach, M. K. *The Salem Witch Trials: A Day-by-Day Chronicle of a Community Under Siege.* New York: Cooper Square Press, 2002.
Rogers, C. *Client Centered Therapy.* Boston: Houghton Mifflin Co., 1951.
_____. *On Becoming a Person.* Boston: Houghton Mifflin Co., 1961.
Roiphe, K. *The Morning After: Sex, Fear, and Feminism on Campus.* Boston: Little, Brown and Co., 1993.
Roscoe, P. "Costs, Benefits, Typologies and Power: The Evolution of Political Hierarchy." In *Hierarchies in Action: Cui Bono?*, edited by M. W. Diehl. Carbondale, IL: Center for Archaeological Investigations, 2000.
Rosenhan, M. "On Being Sane in Insane Places." *Science,* CLXXIX (January 1973): 150–58.
Rossi, A. S., ed. *The Feminist Papers: From Adams to de Beauvoir.* New York: Bantam Books, 1973.
Rousseau, Jean-Jacques. *The Social Contract.* Translated by Maurice Cranston. New York: Penguin Books, 1968 [1762].
_____. *Emile.* Translated by A. Bloom. New York: Basic Books, [1762] 1979.
_____. *The Discourse on the Origins of Inequality.* Edited by Roger D. Masters and Christopher Kelly. Hanover, NH: University Press of New England, 1992.
Scarf, M. *Unfinished Business: Pressure Points in the Lives of Women.* New York: Ballantine Books, 1980.
_____. *Intimate Partners: Patterns in Love and Marriage.* New York: Random House, 1987.
Schaffer, H. *The Growth of Sociability.* Baltimore: Penguin Books, 1971.
Schama, S. *Citizens: A Chronicle of the French Revolution.* New York: Alfred A. Knopf, 1989.
Scheff, T. *Being Mentally Ill: A Sociological Theory.* Chicago: Aldine Publishing Co., 1966.
_____. *Catharsis in Healing, Ritual, and Drama.* Berkeley, CA: University of California Press, 1979.
_____. *Microsociology: Discourse, Emotion, and Social Structure.* Chicago: University of Chicago Press, 1990.
Scott, M. B. and S. Lyman."Accounts." *American Sociological Review* 33, no. 1 (1968): 46–62.
Scull, A. "Museums of Madness: The Social Organization of Insanity in Nineteenth Century England." Ph.D., Princeton University, 1974.
_____. *Madhouses, Mad-Doctors, and Madmen: The Social History of Psychiatry in the Victorian Era.* London: Athlone Press, 1981.

———. *Social Order/Mental Disorder: Anglo-American Psychiatry in Historical Perspective*. Berkeley, CA: University of California Press, 1989.
Selye, H. *The Stress of Life*. New York: McGraw-Hill, 1956.
Sennett, R. and J. Cobb. *The Hidden Injuries of Class*. New York: Free Press, 1966.
Seward, K. *The American Family: A Demographic History*. Beverly Hills: Sage Publications, 1978.
Shapiro, F. and M. S. Forrest. *EMDR: The Breakthrough Therapy for Overcoming Anxiety, Stress, and Trauma*. New York: Basic Books, 1997.
Sheed, W. *Muhammad Ali: A Portrait in Words and Photographs*. New York: Crowell, 1975.
Sherif, M. *The Psychology of Social Norms*. New York: HarperCollins, 1936.
———. *Social Interaction Process and Products: Selected Essays*. Chicago: Aldine Publishing Co., 1967.
Shirer, W. L. *The Rise and Fall of the Third Reich*. New York: Simon & Schuster, 1960.
Sidanius, J. and F. Pratto. *Social Dominance: An Intergroup Theory of Social Hierarchy and Oppression*. Cambridge: Cambridge University Press, 1999.
Sills, J. *A Fine Romance: The Psychology of Successful Courtship*. Los Angles: Jeremy P. Tarcher, Inc., 1987.
Skultans, V. *English Madness: Ideas on Insanity 1580–1890*. London: Routledge and Kegan Paul, 1979.
Smith, A. *An Inquiry into the Nature and Causes of the Wealth of Nations*. London: W. Strahan & T. Cadell, 1776.
Smith, E. and B. Winterhalter, eds. *Evolutionary Ecology and Human Behavior*. New York: Aldine de Gruyter, 1992.
Sniderman, P. M. and T. Piazza. *The Scar of Race*. Cambridge, MA: Belknap Press of Harvard University Press, 1993.
Sobel, D. *Galileo's Daughter: A Historical Memoir of Science, Faith, and Love*. New York: Walker & Co., 1999.
Sober, E. and D. S. Wilson. *Unto Others: The Evolution and Psychology of Unselfish Behavior*. Cambridge, MA: Harvard University Press, 1998.
Sommers, C. H. *Who Stole Feminism: How Women Have Betrayed Women*. New York: Simon & Schuster, 1994.
———. *The War Against Boys: How Misguided Feminism Is Harming Our Young Men*. New York: Simon & Schuster, 2000.
Sowell, T. *Migrations and Cultures: A World View*. New York: Basic Books, 1996.
———. *The Quest for Cosmic Justice*. New York: Free Press, 1999.
———. *A Conflict of Visions: Ideological Origins of Political Struggles*. New York: Basic Books, 2007.

Spencer, H. *The Study of Sociology*. New York: Appleton, 1891.
———. *The Principles of Sociology*. Edited by S. Andreski. 3 vols. New York: MacMillan, [1899] 1969.
Spenger, J. and H. Kraemer. *The Malleus Maleficarum of Heinrich Kraemer and James Spenger*. Translated by Montague Summers. New York: Dover, 1971.
Spitzer, R. L. *Psychopathology: A Case Book*. New York: McGraw-Hill, 1983.
Spitzer, R. L. and J. Williams. "The Definition and Diagnosis of Mental Disorder." In *Deviance and Mental Illness*, edited by W. Gove. Beverly Hills: Sage Publications, 1982.
Stacey, J. *In the Name of the Family: Rethinking Family Values in the Postmodern Age*. Boston, MA: Beacon Press, 1996.
Staddon, J. "On Responsibility and Punishment." *The Atlantic Monthly*, February 1995, 88–94.
Stampp, K. M. *The Era of Reconstruction: 1865–1877*. New York: Vintage Books, 1965.
Stanford, C. B. *The Hunting Apes: Meat Eating and the Origins of Human Behavior*. Princeton, NJ: Princeton University Press, 1999.
Starr, P. *The Social Transformation of American Medicine*. New York: Basic Books, 1982.
Steele, S. *The Content of Our Character: A New Vision of Race in America*. New York: St. Martin's Press, 1990.
Stein, A. *Sex and Sensibility: Stories of a Lesbian Generation*. Berkeley, CA: University of California Press, 1997.
Steinem, G. *Revolution from Within: A Book of Self-Esteem*. Boston: Little, Brown and Co., 1992.
Stengel, R. *You're Too Kind: A Brief History of Flattery*. New York: Simon & Schuster, 2000.
Strauss, A. *Mirrors and Masks: The Search for Identity*. Glencoe, IL: Free Press, 1959.
———. *Negotiations: Varieties, Contexts, Processes and Social Order*. San Francisco: Jossey-Bass, 1978.
Stryker, S. *Symbolic Interactionism*. Menlo Park, CA: Benjamin/Cummings, 1980.
Sullivan, H. S. *Conceptions of Modern Psychiatry*. New York: W.W. Norton & Co., 1940.
———. *The Interpersonal Theory of Psychiatry*. New York: W.W. Norton & Co., 1953.
———. *The Psychiatric Interview*. New York: W.W. Norton & Co., 1954.
Sykes, B. *The Seven Daughter of Eve: The Science That Reveals Our Genetic Ancestry*. New York: W.W. Norton & Co., 2001.
Szasz, T. *The Myth of Mental Illness: Foundations of a Theory of Personal Conduct*. New York: Dell, 1961.
———. *Ideology and Insanity*. New York: Anchor, 1970.

Tannen, D. *You Just Don't Understand: Women and Men in Conversation*. New York: William Morrow and Co., 1990.
Tharpa, R. *A History of India*. Vols. I and II. London: Penguin Books, 1966.
Thernstrom, S. and A. Thernstrom. *No Excuses: Closing the Racial Gap in Learning*. New York: Simon & Schuster, 2003.
Tiger, L. *Men in Groups*. New York: Vintage Books, 1970.
Tiger, L. and H. T. Fowler, eds. *Female Hierarchies*. Chicago: Beresford Book Service.
Timmerman, K. R. *Shakedown: Exposing the Real Jesse Jackson*. Washington, DC: Regnery Publishing, 2002.
Tittle, C. K. *Careers and Family: Sex Roles and Adolescent Life Plans*. Beverly Hills: Sage Publications, 1981.
Toulmin, S. *Reason in Ethics*. Cambridge: Cambridge University Press, 1960.
Tuke, S. *Description of the Retreat: An Institution near York for Insane Persons of the Society of Friends*. Edited by Richard A. Hunter and Ida Macalpine. London: Dawsons, 1964 [1813].
Turner, R. H. "Role Taking: Process vs. Conformity?" In *Human Behavior and Social Processes*, edited by A. M. Rose. Boston: Houghton Mifflin Co., 1962.
_____. *Family Interaction*. New York: Wiley, 1970.
Valenstein, E. S. *Great and Desperate Cures: The Rise and Decline of Psychosurgery and Other Radical Treatments for Mental Illness*. New York: Basic Books, 1986.
Van der Kolk, B., A. C. McFarlane, and L. Weisaeth, eds. *Traumatic Stress: The Effects of Overwhelming Experience on Mind, Body, and Society*. New York: Guilford Press, 1996.
Veith, I. *Hysteria: The History of a Disease*. Chicago: University of Chicago Press, 1965.
Viorst, J. *Necessary Losses*. New York: Fawcett, 1986.
de Waal, F. *Chimpanzee Politics*. New York: Harper & Row, 1982.
_____. *Peacekeeping among Primates*. Cambridge, MA: Harvard University Press, 1989.
_____. *Good Natured: The Origins of Right and Wrong in Humans and Other Animals*. Cambridge, MA: Harvard University Press, 1996.
_____, ed. *Tree of Origin: What Primate Behavior Can Tell Us about Human Social Evolution*. Cambridge, MA: Harvard University Press, 2001.
Waite, C. J. and M. Gallagher. *The Case for Marriage: Why Married People are Happier, Healthier, and Better Off Financially*. New York: Doubleday, 2000.
Walker, L. E. *The Battered Woman*. New York: Harper & Row, 1979.
Wallenstein, J. S., J. M. Lewis, and S. Blakesee. *The Unexpected Legacy of Divorce: A 25 Year Landmark Study*. New York: Hyperion, 2000.

Waller, W. *The Family: A Dynamic Interpretation*. New York: Dryden Press, 1951.

Watson, J. B. *Behavior: An Introduction to Comparative Psychology*. New York: Holt, Rinehart and Winston, 1914.

_____. *Psychological Care of Infant and Child*. New York: W.W. Norton & Co., 1928.

Wead, D. *All The Presidents' Children: Triumph and Tragedy in the Lives of America's First Families*. New York: Atria Books, 2003.

Weis, R. *The Yellow Cross: The Story of the Last Cathers 1290–1329*. New York; Alfred A. Knopf, 2001.

Weiss, R. S. *Marital Separation: Coping with the End of Marriage*. New York: Basic Books, 1975.

_____. *Staying the Course: The Emotional and Social Lives of Men Who Do Well at Work*. New York: Free Press, 1990.

Wells, S. *The Journey of Man: A Genetic Odyssey*. Princeton, NJ: Princeton University Press, 2002.

Wender, P. H. and D. F. Klein. *Mind, Mood, and Medicine: A Guide to the New Biopsychiatry*. New York: Farrar, Straus, Giroux, 1981.

Westermarck, E. *Ethical Relativity*. Paterson, NJ: Littlefield, Adams, and Co., 1960.

Whitehead, B. D. *The Divorce Culture: Rethinking Our Commitments to Marriage and the Family*. New York: Random House, 1998.

Whiting, J. and I. Child. *Child Training and Personality*. New Haven, CT: Yale University Press, 1953.

Whittier, N. *Feminist Generations: The Persistence of the Radical Women's Movement*. Philadelphia: Temple University Press, 1995.

Whyte, W. F. *Street Corner Society*. Chicago: University of Chicago Press, 1943.

Williams, M. *Heaven's Harlots: My Fifteen Years as a Sacred Prostitute in the Children of God Cult*. New York: William Morrow and Co., 1998.

Wills, G. *Nixon Agonistes: The Crisis of the Self-Made Man*. Boston: Houghton Mifflin Co., 1969.

Wilson, D. C. *Stranger and Traveler: The Story of Dorothea Dix, American Reformer*. Boston: Little, Brown and Co., 1975.

Wilson, J. Q. *The Moral Sense*. New York: Free Press, 1993.

_____. *Moral Judgment*. New York: Free Press, 1997.

_____. *The Marriage Problem: How Culture Has Weakened Families*. New York: HarperCollins, 2002.

Windmiller, M., N. Lambert, and E. Turiel, eds. *Moral Development and Socialization*. Boston: Allyn and Bacon, 1980.

Wing, J. K. *Reasoning about Madness*. Oxford: Oxford University Press, 1978.

Wolfe, A. *Marginalized in the Middle*. Chicago: University of Chicago Press, 1996.

_____. *One Nation, After All: What Middle-Class Americans Really Think*. New York: Viking, 1998.

———. *Moral Freedom: The Search for Virtue in a World of Choice.* New York: W.W. Norton & Co., 2001.
Wolff, K. H., ed. *The Sociology of Georg Simmel.* New York: Free Press, 1950.
Wood, P. *Diversity: The Invention of a Concept.* San Francisco: Encounter Books, 2003.
Woodward, F. L. *Some Sayings of the Buddha.* Oxford: Oxford University Press, 1973.
Wrong, D. "The Oversocialized Conception of Man in Modern Sociology." *American Sociological Review* 26, no. 2 (1961).
Yalom, I. D. *Existential Psychotherapy.* New York: Basic Books, 1980.
Zahavi, A. "Mate Selection—A Selection for a Handicap." *Journal of Theoretical Biology* 53 (1975): 205–14.
Zahavi, A. and A. Zahavi. *The Handicap Principle: A Missing Piece of Darwin's Puzzle.* New York: Oxford University Press, 1997.
Zajonc, R. B. "Feeling and Thinking: Preferences Need No Inferences." *American Psychologist* 35 (1980): 153–75.
Zartman, I. W. *The Negotiation Process: Theories and Applications.* Beverly Hills: Sage Publications, 1978.
Zeldin, T. *An Intimate History of Humanity.* New York: HarperCollins, 1994.
Zurcher, L. *Social Roles: Conformity, Conflict and Creativity.* Beverly Hills: Sage Publications, 1983.

Index

abandonment, 121-122
abortion, 286
abuse, 43-44, 89, 288-295
acceptance, 134, 258
accounts, 114-115
Acton, Lord, 259
Adler, Alfred, 54
African Americans, 198, 282
Ainsworth, Mary, 65-66
Albigensians, 276
Alexander, Franz, 103
alcoholism, 92-93
alliances, 125, 179-180; anonymous, 182
ambivalence, 220
amelioration, 315-322
American Association of University Women, 272
American Psychiatric Association. *See*: Diagnostic and Statistical Manuals (APA)
Amin, Idi, 191
amygdala 42, 105, 148 *see also* limbic system
anatomy is destiny, 223
androgyny, 225
animal magnetism, 29
anger, 79, 86, 117-118, 123-128, 237, 286-287
anorexia, 264
anti-social personality disorder, 48, 91-92, 218
anxiety, 86; disorder, 21-22; stranger 64
Aristotle, 253, 280
arrogance, 203
Arsenic and Old Lace, 27
APA, 46
asylums, 33-34

Ataturk, 191
attachment, 54, 64; types, 217
authority, 254

Bales, Robert, 176
bargaining, 237, 241
Barnard, Chester, 177
Bateson, Gregory, 51
Baum, Frank, 178
beauty, 178
Bedlam, 25-26
beliefs. 10, 247-273
Best, Joel, 266
Bettleheim, Bruno, 52
bin Laden, 192, 261, 286
biology, 38, 96
biography swapping, 231
bipolar disorder, 88, 95
Blankenhorn, David, 245
bleeding patients, 28
Boehm, Christopher, 278
bookworms, 167
Boone, James, 186-187
Bowlby, John, 54, 63-67, 86-87, 95, 122, 129, 236
brain doctors, 21; science, 106, 148
brief therapies, 36, 330
Brown, George, 54, 67, 95
Buddha, 307
bureaucracy, 206-210

Cannon, Walter, 40
caregiver, 151, 159
Carson, Rachel, 270
cascade effect, 84, 128, 132
caste, 195-198
castration, 45
Castro, Fidel, 296

355

catatonic, 15-16
Catholic Church, 165, 276
cerebellum, 148-149
character, 303-305
Charles II, 32
chimpanzees, 7; politics, 179
chemical dependency, 92-94
chemical imbalance, 23, 31
Chirot, Daniel, 210
Chomsky, Noam, 180
civil inattention, 114
Civilization and Its Discontents, 54
class, social, 181, 195-196, 198-202
Clinton, William J., 191, 261, 280-281, 289, 302-303
Cobb, Jonathan, 200
codependent, 160-161
cognitive community, 10, 73-74, 247, 253; dissonance, 113
collectivism, 301
commitment, 213-214
community mental health centers, 36-37
competition, 62
Comte, August, 20, 50, 137
conduct disorders, 47-48, 89
conformists, 199
Conrad, Peter, 56
constructivist rationalism, 190
Cooley, Charles Horton, 136
corrective emotional experience, 103
courtship, 230-235
crazy, 13, 16, 52
criminals, 163
critical thinking, 252-253
culture, 73
cure, 29, 326-327, 330-332
cupping, 32
cyclic therapy, 326-332

Dahrendorf, Ralf, 188
dating, 226
Davis & Moore, 186, 200
death and dying, 54, 67-68, 129
defense mechanisms, 111-113, 157
deinstitutionalization, 37, 126
democracy, 302-303
denial, 111, 236, 280
denial phase, 108-117 *see also* resocialization
dependent personality, 219

depression, 56, 64, 129, 131
depressive disorders, 21-22, 88
desires, 307
desensitization, 42, 126
deviance, 52-53
devil, 27, 262 *See also*, Satan
Diagnostic and Statistical Manuals (APA), 1, 30-31, 39, 45-50, 87-88, 91
Diallo, Amadou, 292-293
diagnoses, 39, 47, 49, 96-97, 132, 192
Diamond, Jared, 275
discipline, 279
disease model, 19, 30-31; normal, 38-39
disgust, 287
disorder, functional, 30, 39, 46; mental, 47
diversity, 273, 278
division of labor, 70, 135-141, 185, 320-321
divorce, 235-238; children of, 239-245
Dix, Dorothea, 27, 33
dominance, 4, 9, 177, 189, 208, 222
dopamine, 31
double bind, 220
double standard, 223
drugs, psychoactive, 34
dual concern negotiations. *See* negotiations,
Durkheim, Emile, 19, 70, 137-138
dysfunctional roles *see* roles, dysfunctional
dysthymia, 88, 138

ego, 30
eightfold path, 307
electricity, 34
electro-convulsive therapy, 34-35
emetics, 32-33
emotionality, 286
emotions, communication, 120; goals, 119; motivation, 120; social, 55, 78-80, 105-106, 148-149, 314 *see also* anger, fear, sadness
entertainers, 166
entitlements, 208
environmentalists, 268-269
equality, 289; moral, 215
Erikson, Erik, 131
ethology, 4, 64
excuses, 115-116 *see also* accounts
exhibitionism, 91

Index

expectations, 140
expressive role, 170

facts, social *see* social facts
failure to thrive, 64
failures, 163
faith, 256-260; ideological, 258; religious, 257
family 201; hero, 160; reconstituted, 244
fantasies, 12 *see also* myths
fathers, 244-245
fear, 78-79, 88, 117-118, 121-122, 134 *see also* panic attacks
feminists, 44, 169-171, 244, 259, 261, 263, 292, 301
Festinger, Leon, 113
fight/flight, 40 *see also* Cannon, Walter
Fisher, Helen, 224-225
flattery, 202-203
flirt, 165, 231
fools, 166, 204-205; ship of, 26
Foucault, Michel, 26
Frattaroli, Elio, 22-23
Freeman, Walter, 34
Freud, Anna, 111
Freud, Sigmund, 12, 23, 29-30, 35, 41, 45, 54, 102-104, 107, 111, 128, 147, 223, 329-330
French Revolution, 259
functional, disorder *see* disorder, functional

Galileo, 250
George III, madness of, 32-33
gender, 169-171
glass ceiling, 171
goals, displaced, 207
Goffman, Erving, 231
good, the, 314
gossips, 166
Grafen, Alan, 186
Great Chain of Being, 197
Greece, ancient, 303
grief 66-67, 130-131 *see also* mourning

hallucinations, 14, 95-96
happiness, 1
hardball, 283
hate crime, 298-290
Hayek, Friedrich, 190, 256, 298

Herrnstein, Richard, 198
hierarchical disintegration, 194-195
hierarchy, 9, 11, 62, 69-70, 174-182, 312, 317-319
hippocampus, 105, 148 *see also* limbic system
Hippocratic oath, 31
histrionic personality, 217, 219 *see also* hysteria and hysterics
Hitler, Adolf, 44, 192, 208, 256-267, 295, 303
Hobbes, Thomas, 7-8, 189
Hobson, Allen, 21-22, 36, 86-89, 105, 148
Holmes & Rahe, 40
homelessness, 37-38, 251-252, 265
homogamy, 227
homosexuality, 45-46, 103; ego dystonic, 46; intimacy, 245; latent, 103
hope, 62
Horney, Karen, 54, 217-218
Horwitz, Alan, 55-56
humors, four, 18, 28
Hume, David, 74
Hussein, Saddam, 192
Huxley, Aldous, 31
hysteria, 29
hysterics, 167

Id, 30
ideal types, 175
idealism, 295-298, 312; critical, 325; romantic, 325
identification with aggressor, 112-113 *see also* defense mechanisms
ideology, 204, 209
image, 267
immaturity, emotional, 206 *see also* emotions
imperative coordination 188
impression management *see* Goffman, Erving
incremental tolerance, 126-127 *see also* integrated anger management
India, 196-197
individualism, 300-301
industrial revolution, 170
infatuation, 232-233
institutionalized, 53
instrumental roles *see* roles, instrumental

insulin shock, 34
integrated anger management,
  125-128 *see also* anger
integrity, 301
intimacy, 211-216, 279; voluntary, 322
intolerance, religious, 299 *see also*
  religion
IQ, 178
Iron Law of Oligarchy, 208
irrationality, 253-256

Jackson, Jesse, 293
Jencks, Christopher, 265
job description, 142
jocks, 168
justice, cosmic, 297

karma, 197
killers, social, 6-11
kindergarten, 61-62
king of the mountain, 69, 173
knowledge, 313, 322-324; of other, 214,
  of self, 214
Kohn, Melvin, 198-199, 300
Kubler-Ross, Elizabeth, 54, 68, 236

labeling theory, 53
Laing, R.D., 52
Lansing, Robert, 296
leadership, 190
Lenin, Vladimir, 297
libido, 30
lies, 260-267
limbic system, 31, 105, 148
limits, 311-316
linguistics, 247-248
lobotomy, 34
Loewen, James, 262-263
Lomborg, Bjorn, 269-270
looking glass self, 136
Lorenz, Konrad, 64
losers, 5, 59, 109
losing, 11, 55-56, 59-63, 68-75
loss, 54, 63-68, 96, 105, 129-130; correctives, 84-86; of father, 245
loss/losing nexus, 76-81
losses, types, 77-78; hierarchical, 77-78, 82, 85, 110; relationship, 77-78, 85, 107; roles, 78, 82, 85, 110
love, 10-11, 72-73, 212, 230; dangers of, 212-213; free, 321
Ludwig, Arnold, 173, 190, 192

Malleus Maleficarum, 26
macho, 165
mad doctors, 32-33
manic depression, 13, 16, 31, 81 *see also*
  bipolar disorder
marasmus, 129 *see also* failure to thrive
marriage and family therapy, 54-55
Marx, Karl, 51, 308, 318
Marxists, 50-51, 289
mascot, 160
masturbation, 29
maturity, 214
melancholia, 28-29 *see also* depression
medicalization, 21; of disease, 56
medications, 36-37
mechanical solidarity, 138 *see also* Durkheim, Emile
media, 251
mental disorder, 57; illness, 51, 309 *see also* disease model
Merton, Robert, 218
Mesmer, Friedrich, 29
Michels, Robert, 208-209
Midler, Bette, 211
mobility, social *see* social mobility
moderation, 315
monarchies, 191
monk, 165
Moniz, Egas, 34
Moore, G.E., 314
moral, abuse, 288-295; commitments, 116-117, 275-280; emotionality, 294; entrepreneurs, 263; leadership, 180; logic, 280-282; negotiations, 285; panics, 294; superiority, 179; treatment, 33; values, 162
moral rules, 10-11, 74-75, 280-281, 285, 325
moralism, 255
moralized, 19, 44-45, 48
More, Thomas, 277, 308
mourning, 54, 66, 67, 78-81, 85, 128-130
Moynihan, Daniel Patrick, 273
Murray, Charles, 198, 254
mysterious, 21-23, 87
myths, 116, 262-263

Nader, Ralph, 180
narcissists, 167, 219
Nazis, 10 *see also* Hitler
neglect, 121-122 *see also* abuse

Index

negotiations, coercive, 140, dual concern, 219-220, 222; intimate, 214-15, 234; role, 71-72, 85, 91, 117, 153-154, 278, 328; social 255-256
nerds, 25
neurasthenia, 29
neurons, 22 *see also* brain science
neuroses, 22, 29, 31; types 217
neurotransmitters, 5, 31 *see also* brain science
neurotic wolf, legend of, 1-4
New Guinea, 275-276
Nietzsche, Friedrich, 50, 305
normal, 16
norms, 150, 152
Nyerere, Julius, 295

obsessive-compulsive disorder, 90, 219
Oedipus complex, 42, 45, 62
organic solidarity, 138 *see also* Durkheim, Emile
orgone, 30
Orwell, George, 4, 267
opportunity, 289
opposites attract, 227 *see also* love
oppositional defiant disorder, 57
oppositionalism, 201
over achievers, 163

pain, 41, 43-45, 81-82
panic attacks, 22 *see also* fear, anxiety
paraphilias, 48-49, 89-90, 167
parent trap, 241
parenting, responsive, 65-66 *see also* Ainsworth, Mary
Parsons, Talcott, 309
passive-aggressive, 168, 219, 221
pedophilia, 90 *see also* paraphilias
peeling the onion, 128
Perry, William, 171
personality disorders, 31, 90-91; types 218-219
phrenology, 28, 31
pin factory, 137
Pinel, Philippe, 32-33, 135
Plato, 18, 147, 277, 308
Plutarch, 277-178
polarization, 285-286, 290
politics, 179, 208; of personal destruction, 191
Popenoe, David, 245
post-modernism, 51, 135, 323

post traumatic stress disorder, 41 *see also* trauma, fear
poverty, 200, 265; culture of, 205
primal hordes, 54
primal scene, 41, 111
problems of living, 52
protection, social 189
protest, 86, 125, 241; phase, 117-128 *see also* resocialization, loss
Prozac, 5, 23
Pruitt, Dean, 219
pseudoscience, 267-274 *see also* science
psyched-out, 177
psychoanalysis, 329
psycho-social moratorium, 131 *see also* Erikson, Eric
psychosurgery, 34-35 *see also* lobotomy
psychotherapy, 13, 29-30, 35, 101, 328 *see also* resocialization
punctuated equilibrium, 174-175

quarrel, lovers, 233

race, 197-198
racism, 49
rage, 287 *see also* anger
ranking *see* hierarchy
rating dating, 226
rationalization, 111
rebels, 163
red tape, 207
Reich, Wilhelm, 30
relationships, personal, 9-10, 313, 321-322
religion, 18, 297-298
renegotiation, 132-134 *see also* negotiations
repetition compulsion, 102-105, 229
reputations, 176-177, 184
rescuer, 161-162, 230 *see also* savior
resocialization, 23, 86, 99-102, 108-134, 310, 327-328, 330-332 *see also* psychotherapy
rigidity, 206
rite of passage, 183
role change, 100; complementarity, 139, 228-229; conservatism, 153; coordination, 139-140; partners, 153-157; stability, 138-139; strain, 155-157, taking, 216 *see also* resocialization
role scripts, 146-153; cognitive, 149; emotional, 150; social, 151-152; volitional, 150

359

roles, alcoholic, 55, 160; achieved, 144-145; ascribed, 144; basic, 145-146; dysfunctional, 157-169; expressive, 170; gender, 169-171; instrumental, 170; personal, 142-144, 159-162; position oriented, 142, 169; social, 9, 70-72, 312-313, 320-321; task oriented 142, 158-159
roles and hierarchy, 182-184
romanticism, 297, 313, 322
Rome, ancient, 180, 276, 299
Roscoe, Paul, 210
Rosenhan, David, 52
Rousseau, Jean-Jacques, 7-8, 50, 135, 259
Rush, Benjamin, 33
Russell, Bertram, 321

sadness, 79-80, 87, 128-132, 238, 242 *see also* depression
Saint-Simon, 50
Salem MA, 27
Satan, 249, 294 *see also* devil
savior, 161-162 *see also* rescuer
scapegoat, 149-156, 159, 229
scarce resources, 188
Scheff, Thomas, 53-54
Schizoid personality, 219
schizophrenia, 13, 21, 31, 34, 81, 94-95; catatonic, 15, 95
schizophrenogenic mother, 51
Schmahmann, Jeremy, 148
science, 18, 250, 323-324
selective perception, 113, 157
self-direction, 198-199, 300, 319-320
selfishness, 206
Selye, Hans, 40
Sennett, Richard, 200
separation, 63 *see also* loss
serotonin, 5, 31
sex, 164-165, 216, 222-225
sex contract, 224-225
sexual fidelity, 302; selection, 198-190
Shakers, 291-292, 308
shame, 287
Sherif, Muzafer, 181
sick role, 309-310
situational stupidity, 202-206, 255
Skinner, B.F., 122
slavery, 197-198
Smith, Adam, 137

Snyder, Mitch, 265
social class *see* class
Social Darwinism, 197
social facts, 19
social mobility, 318-319
social psychology, 113
socialism, 254
socialization, 157, 304-305
sociology, 20, 39, 50-54
solutions, invisible, 17; visible, 17
soul, the, 22-23
Sowell, Thomas, 297
Spartans, 277-278
spastic, 25, 168
spectators, 176-177
spectral evidence, 27
Spencer, Herbert, 137
spin, 266
spiritual, 17 *see also* religion
Spitzer, Robert, 45-47
Sprenger, Johann, 26
Stalin, Joseph, 191, 193, 209, 259, 261, 263, 267
Star trek, 16-17
statistics, 264-266
Stengel, Richard, 202-203
strain theory, 218-219
straitjacket, 34
stranger anxiety, 64
stress, 21, 40-42, 57, 87, 89, 94, 156
submission, 4
sublimation, 112
suffering, 81-86, 307-308 *see also* pain
suicide, 19-20
Sullivan, Harry Stack, 54
super-ego, 30
superstition, 309
suppression, 111
symptoms, 330
Szasz, Thomas, 52

talking cure, 29
tardive dyskinesia, 35
testing trustworthiness, 232
tests of strength, 69, 83, 175-182, 184-185, 312; group, 197
therapy, 13; covering, 36; electroconvulsive, 34-35; uncovering, 36
Timber, legend of, 1-5, 11
tolerance, religious, 298-300
toughness, 181

Index

Toulmin, Stephen, 280
traits *see* roles
transference, 107
transitivity, 144
transmigration of souls, 194 *see also* soul, the
trauma hypothesis, 41-43, 131
Trivino, Wilson, 172
trust, 232, 301
Tuke, Samuel, 33
tyrants, 190-193

ugly ones, 168-169
umpires, 383-284
unconscious, 105, 111
uncovering therapy *see* therapy
uterus, 28
Utopia, 277, 308

values, 150, 152, 184, 298-303
vapors, the, 29
Versailles, Treaty of, 296
victimization, 305
visual rape, 44, 225

de Waal, Frans, 179
Wagner-Smith, Karen, 43-44
Wakefield, Jerome, 56
Waller, Willard, 61, 226
Wallerstein, Judith, 239-240
Washington, George, 32, 299
wasteful display, 186-187
Weber, Max, 142, 175
Weiss, Robert, 236
Whyte, William Foote, 175-177
wilding, 290
Wilson, James Q., 299-300
Wilson, Woodrow, 296-297
winning, 11, 60 *see also* losing
witches, 26-27, 31
Wolf, Naomi, 264
working through, 121

York Retreat, 33

Zahavi, Amotz, 186
zero sum game, 61, 69, 174
Zoloft, 24